Learning Java through Alice 3
3rd Edition

- An Introduction to Programming

Tebring Daly and Eileen Wrigley

Table of Contents

---

[*] *Ongoing project*

----

[*] *Ongoing project*

Ongoing project

---

[*] *Ongoing project*

_____

[*] *Ongoing project*

Acknowledgments

First and foremost, the authors would like to convey special thanks to the Alice Software team at Carnegie Mellon University for providing the Alice software to make this text possible. Also, we would like to take this opportunity to thank Electronic Arts, Inc. for providing their rich set of graphics which certainly makes Java and Alice programming more interesting. In addition, we would like to express our gratitude to the National Science Foundation and the Alice ATE grant team members for their continued support. Words cannot express our gratitude to Wanda Dann who was abundantly helpful and offered invaluable assistance, encouragement, and guidance.

A heartfelt thanks to those colleagues that helped with revisions to this book: Bob Benavides (Computer Science Professor at Collin College in Plano, TX), Branden Simbeck (Computer Information Technology Professor at Community College of Allegheny County), and Rod Farkas (Computer Information Technology Professor at Community College of Allegheny County).

About the Authors

This book has been a joint effort by a mother and daughter team.

Eileen Wrigley, full-time Professor of Computer Information Technology courses at the Community College of Allegheny County in Pittsburgh, Pennsylvania brings more than 40 years of teaching experience to her writing. She earned her B.S. and M.S. degrees from the University of Pittsburgh in Mathematics and Computer Science.

Dr. Tebring Daly has been teaching full-time in the Computer Science department at Collin College in Plano, Texas since 2006. She has earned her B.S. and M.S. degrees from the University of Pittsburgh and Ph.D. from the University of North Texas. Professor Daly has been teaching Java courses for 9 years.

Approach

This book is designed for students wanting to learn fundamental programming concepts. No previous programming experience is required. All of the software used in this text are available to download free of charge. The versions of the software may differ slightly from the versions used in this text since the versions are constantly being updated.

This book will teach you how to program by using Java code. We will use a Java editing tool called NetBeans[1] to help write the code. The environment can be used on a Windows® operating system[2], Apple Macintosh® operating system[3] (Mac), or Linux® operating system[4].

---

[1] Supported by Oracle, http://netbeans.org
[2] Microsoft Corporation, http://www.microsoft.com
[3] Apple Macintosh Corporation, http://www.apple.com/osx

We are also using a tool called Alice 3[5], to provide visuals for abstract programming concepts. This environment works on Windows, Mac, and Linux operating systems. Alice 3 is a drag and drop environment that can be transferred into Java code in the NetBeans environment as shown below.

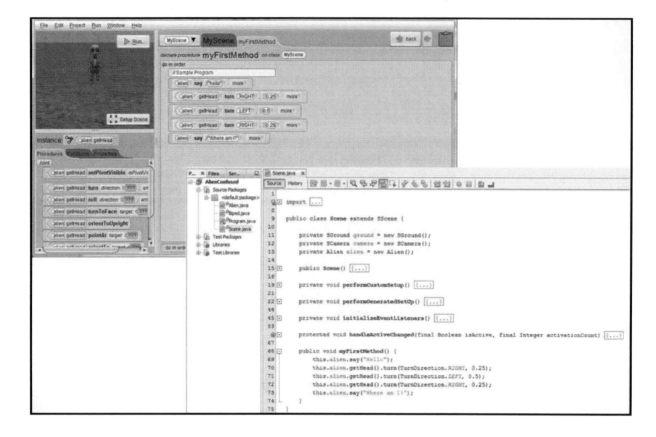

---

[4] Linux Foundation, http://www.linux.org

[5] Developed by Carnegie Mellon University (CMU), Alice, http://www.alice.org

Chapter Breakdown

Preface provides an overview of the text.

Chapter 0 will help you download the required software and introduce you to the Alice 3 environment.

Chapter 1 describes the history of Java, basic programming terminology, and provides hands-on practice coding in the Alice 3 environment, writing Java code from scratch in NetBeans, and transferring Alice 3 projects into the NetBeans environment to look at the Java code.

Chapter 2 covers naming rules, creating and using variables in code, using arithmetic statements, order of operation, shorthand operators, and casting rules.

Chapter 3 explains various ways of formatting output and receiving user inputs. The user is introduced to import statements.

Chapter 4 shows the user how to modularize programs using procedural methods. The user is introduced to the Java documentation and the syntax for writing procedural methods.

Chapter 5 expands upon chapter 4 to include methods that return values which are known as functional methods.

Chapter 6 provides an explanation and practice with relational and logical operators using conditionals.

Chapter 7 talks about object-oriented terms (encapsulation, inheritance, and polymorphism) and their use.

Chapter 8 provides an introduction to GUI and the structure for creating basic drawings.

Chapter 9 shows three types of repetition techniques (while, do while, and for loop).

Chapter 10 explains how to use an array to store multiple values of the same type.

Organization

Each chapter is divided into content segments, hands-on exercises, a summary, and review questions. You should work through the hands-on exercises in each chapter.

The data files needed for the hands-on exercises and assignments can be found at http://iws.collin.edu/tdaly/book3.

You may want to create an organizational method for keeping track of your files. Each chapter has several exercises that will walk you through the programming concepts for that chapter. There is at least one assignment at the end of every chapter. The assignments test your ability to put the concepts from the chapter into action on your own. Please save the chapter exercises to the "Exercises" folder and the assignments at the end of each chapter to the "Assignments" folder so that you don't get confused.

Instructors: Please email tdaly@collin.edu for solutions, sample syllabi, etc.

Chapter 0

Getting Started

Installing the Java and NetBeans

Java is an object-oriented programming language. We will be writing all of our Java code in NetBeans. NetBeans is not the only environment for writing Java code, but it is what we will be using for this text.

You should download the NetBeans and Java SDK (Software Development Kit) bundle. This bundle will include everything that you will need to write and run Java programs. Please follow the install directions located on the following website: http://iws.collin.edu/tdaly/book3

Installing the Alice Environment

Alice 3 provides a 3D environment for manipulating objects using drag and drop code segments. This environment helps to provide visual representations of abstract programming concepts. Please follow the install directions located on the following website: http://iws.collin.edu/tdaly/book3

Setting up NetBeans to Work with Alice

There is an Alice 3 plugin file that you will also need to download and add to the NetBeans environment. Please follow the install directions located at the following website: http://iws.collin.edu/tdaly/book3

What is Alice?

The Alice team at Carnegie Mellon University named the Alice programming software in honor of Lewis Carroll who wrote Alice's Adventures in Wonderland. Lewis Carroll was able to do complex mathematics and logic, but he knew that the most important thing was to make things simple and fascinating to a learner.

Alice makes it easy to create an animation or interactive game. It is designed for beginners who want to learn object-oriented programming. In Alice, 3-D objects (e.g., people, aliens, animals, props) are placed in a scene. Then, students drag and drop tiles to create a program to animate the objects. These tiles correspond closely to statements in Java. Alice allows student to immediately see how their programs run, enabling them to easily understand the relationship between the programming statements and the behavior of objects in their program.

Alice 3 is the newest version of the Alice software. This version of the software allows users to transfer Alice projects into the NetBeans environment to edit the Java code. This text will be using Alice to demonstrate fundamental programming concepts in Java such as objects, methods, looping, etc. by creating animations.

An Alice scene begins with a template for an initial scene. These templates can be grass, water, snow, etc. Then, you add various objects to the scene to create the virtual scene that you desire.

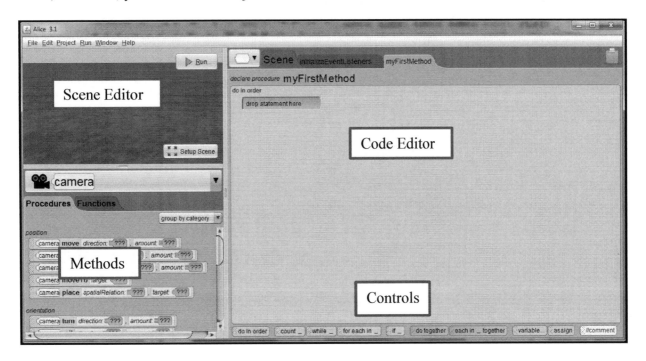

Alice Scene Setup

Objects are added to the scene via the scene editor (Click on Setup Scene button).

There are several choices for selecting objects from the gallery. The **hierarchy** choice is broken down by physical makeup. A biped has 2 legs, a flyer has wings, a prop is something that is inanimate, a quadruped has 4 legs, and a swimmer has fins.

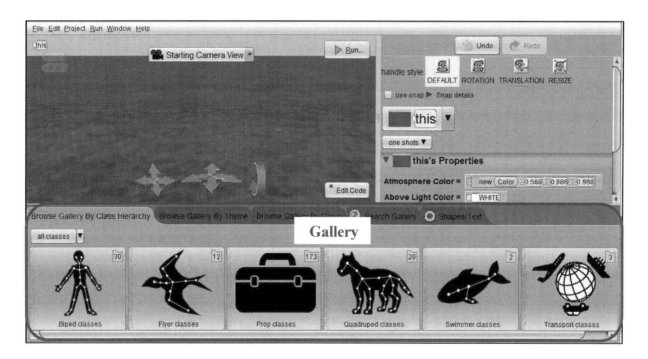

If you want you can also view the objects by **theme** or by **group** as shown below. The **search** feature is nice if you are looking for a particular object. If you want to add a 2D image to your world you could add a billboard object (located in the **shapes/text** tab) and change the image to an image that you have saved (this works nicely for background images).

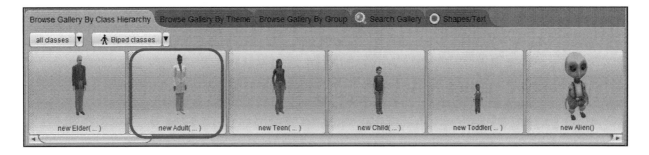

The Alice developers have provided a number of 3D models for you to use in your animations. **An Alice 3D model (class) is a blueprint that tells Alice how to create a new object in the scene.** The 3D model provides instructions on how to draw the object, what color it should be, what parts it should have, its size (height, width, and depth), and many other details. Once you decide what objects, you would like to have, you will need to click on the class to create an object of that type. For example, if I want a girl object in my world, I would select the Biped folder and then the Adult class to create the girl object.

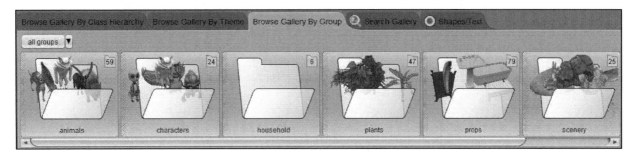

When you create an object, you will need to give it a name. You can leave the default name or give it your own name. You cannot give two objects the same name. Be careful when you are creating objects, if you try and use the name girl more than once, it won't let you create the new object.

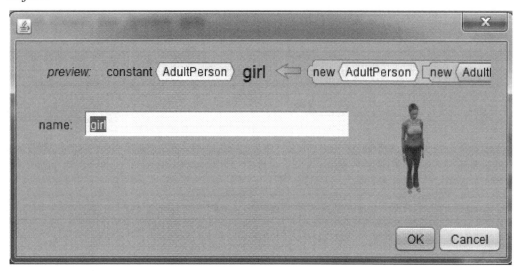

All objects will initially be placed into the middle of the scene and then can be manipulated to any position desired. Alternatively, objects can be dragged to any position in the scene.

Alice objects are represented in a 3 dimensional space. Each object has width, height, and depth as shown below. The height is measured vertically, the width is measured horizontally, and the depth is measured from front to back.

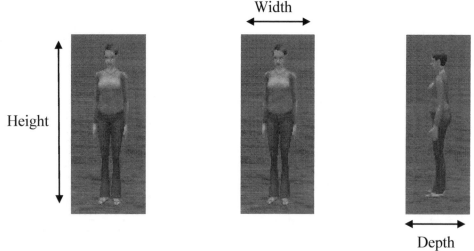

There are six possible directions in which an object may move – **forward, backward, up, down, left and right**. Remember that directions are left and right with respect to the object, not the camera's point of view. For example, this girl object can move forward, backward, up (in air), down (into ground), her left, or her right. The direction an object is facing and where the top of the object is located (relative to the world) is known as the **object's orientation**. In the scene editor, there are 4 buttons that allow you to manipulate the object.

The **DEFAULT** button allows you to move the object and do some rotations. Hold down the left mouse button and drag the circle to rotate the object. To move the object, hold down the left mouse button and drag the object wherever you want.

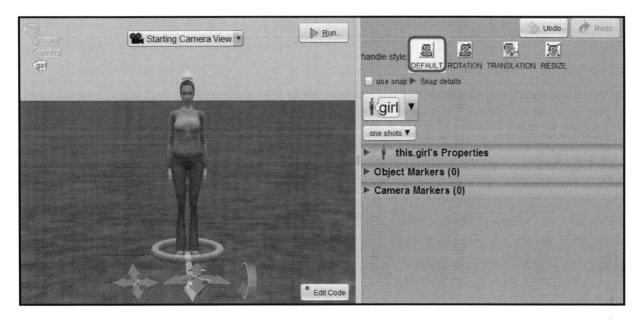

The **ROTATION** button allows you to do rotations in all directions. Hold down the left mouse button and drag the appropriate circle to rotate the object.

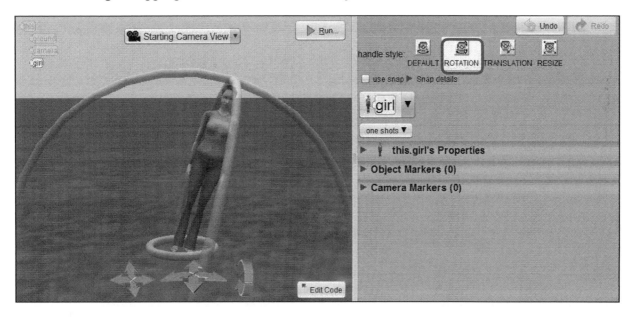

The **TRANSLATION** (move) button allows you to move the object in all directions. Hold down the left mouse button and drag the arrows to move the object. The arrow at the top of the object moves the object up and down, the arrow on the right of the object moves the object left and right, and the arrow in front of the object moves the object forward and backward.

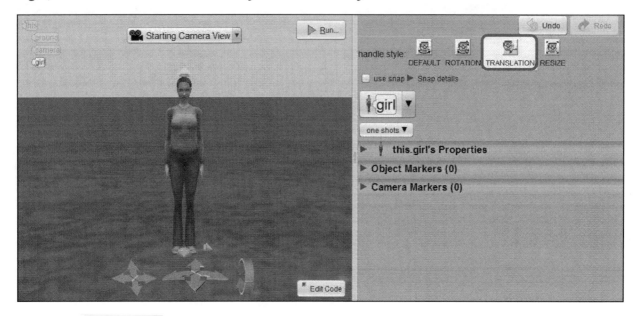

The **RESIZE** button allows you to resize the object. Hold down the left mouse button and drag the arrow at the top of the object. The object will resize proportionately.

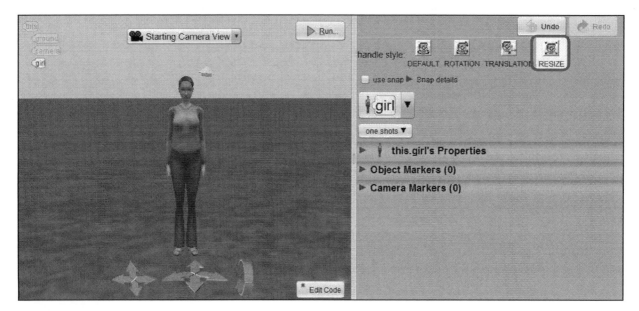

All of the Alice models have body parts that can be manipulated with rolls, turns, etc. You can access the subparts for an object by clicking the part drop down next to the object drop down.

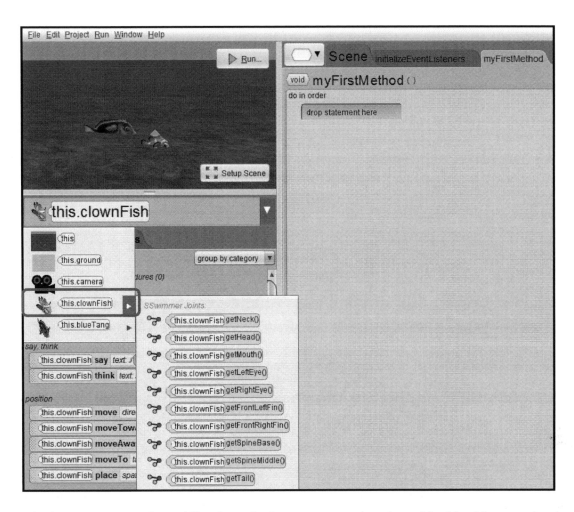

The best way to see how Alice 3 works is to create a virtual world with objects and animate the objects in that world. This will be done in the hands-on exercises.

Hands-on Exercises

Exercise 1: Manipulating the Alice Environment

1. Open up Alice 3. You will need to find the installed Alice 3 folder and double click on the Alice 3 application file.

2. We are going to add a few objects to the Alice environment so that we can manipulate the objects and scene to get a better idea of how Alice works.

3. When you open the Alice program, you will be prompted to select a template. You also have the choice of selecting an old project. We will use this option at the end of this exercise. Make sure that the **Templates** tab is selected. Scroll down and select **Dirt**. Click **OK**.

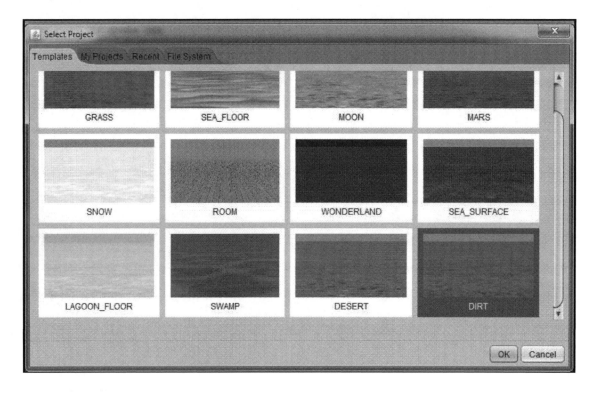

4. Your screen should look similar to the following. Before we can write any code, we need to add some objects to our scene. You will need to click on **Setup Scene** to add objects.

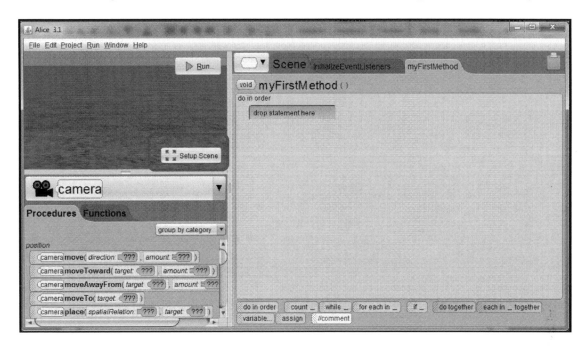

5. The scene setup area will look similar to the following. You currently have 2 objects in this scene: the camera and ground. You can see the objects in your scene by looking at the **object tree**. You can add objects to your scene by using the **gallery** options.

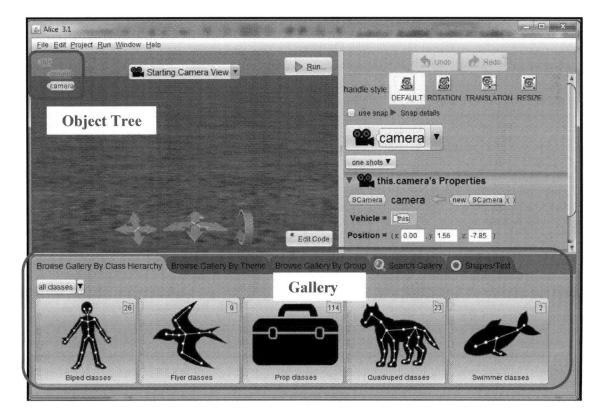

6. There are several choices for selecting objects from the gallery. Please take a moment to explore the possibilities.

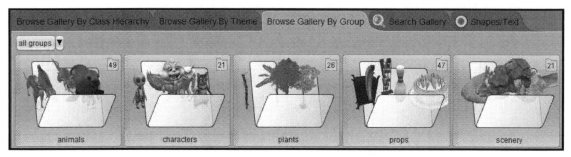

7. Please click back on the **Browse Gallery by Class Hierarchy**. Then select **Prop Classes** and scroll until you find **Cauldron** (they are in alphabetical order). We are going to add this to our scene. Go ahead and click on it. You should be prompted to give this new object a name. We are going to leave the default name **cauldron** and click **OK**. We will talk about naming objects later in this chapter. Please leave the default names for this exercise.

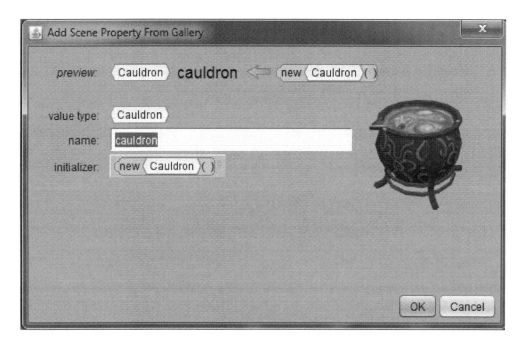

8. You will notice that the cauldron appears in the center of the scene by default. It is also added to your object tree. The properties for the object are listed on the right pane as shown below. You can change the location, orientation, color, opacity, size, etc.

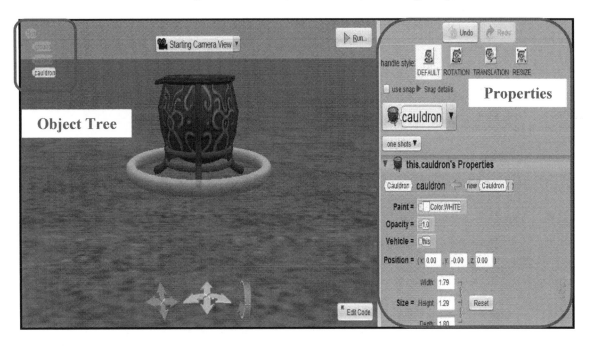

9. Let's change the color of the cauldron to blue. Click the drop down next to **Paint** and select **Color.BLUE**. You cauldron should change color.

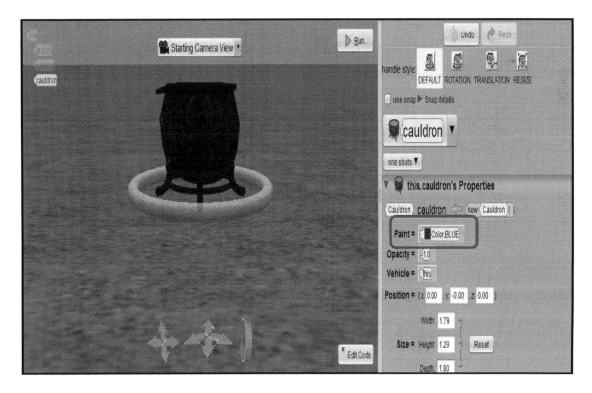

10. Next, we want to move the cauldron to the left side of the scene. The ring around the cauldron indicates that you can rotate the cauldron 360 degrees (this is the default option). I do not want to rotate the cauldron since it would look the same all the way around. I want to move it. To move an object, make sure that the object is selected from the object tree or from the drop down on the properties pane as shown below and select **Translation**.

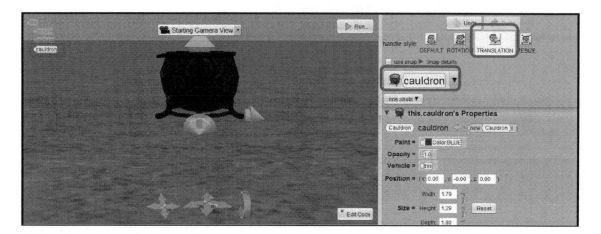

11. You will notice that the handle style changes to arrows. The arrow on top of the cauldron will move the cauldron up and down if you hold down your left mouse button on the arrow and drag up or down. The arrow to the right of the cauldron, will move the cauldron to the right or left. The front arrow will move the cauldron forwards and backwards. Try moving the cauldron to the left and forward.

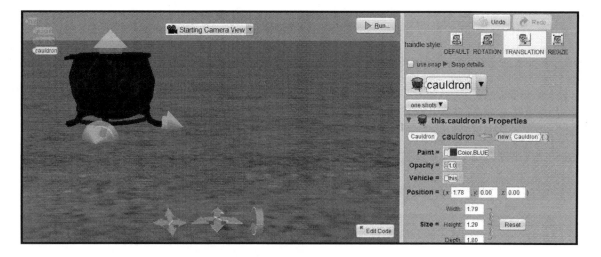

12. If you move the cauldron up or down, it will be off the ground. Go ahead and try it. You don't have to worry about messing up the environment because you can undo. If your cauldron is in the ground or floating in the air, click the **undo** button as shown below.

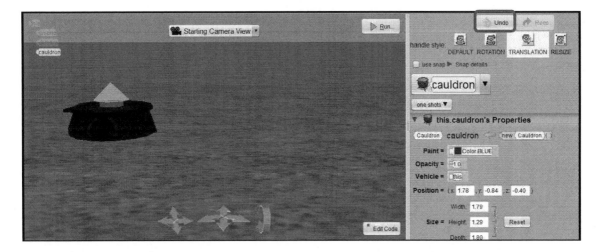

13. Do not resize the cauldron. We are going to add the cauldron lid and if we resize the cauldon, it won't fit and we will have to resize the cauldron lid to fit. We will practice with rotating and resizing in the next exercise.

14. Next, let's add the cauldron lid. See if you can find it. You can try using the search since we know the object that we want to add. Click on the CauldronLid to add a cauldron lid to your scene. Leave the default name for the object.

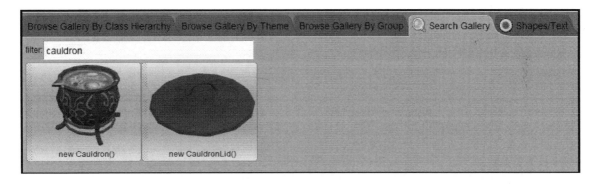

15. The cauldron lid is added to our scene, but it is on the ground. We could move the cauldron up, to the left, and forward to get it on top of the cauldron, but there is an easier way. There is a One Shot drop down that will allow us to move the cauldron lid onto the cauldron without having to move it ourselves. Make sure the cauldron lid is selected and right click on the cauldron lid from the object tree. Choose **procedures**, **place**, **above**, and select **cauldron**. Be careful with the cascading menus when you are selecting options. You can think of procedures as actions.

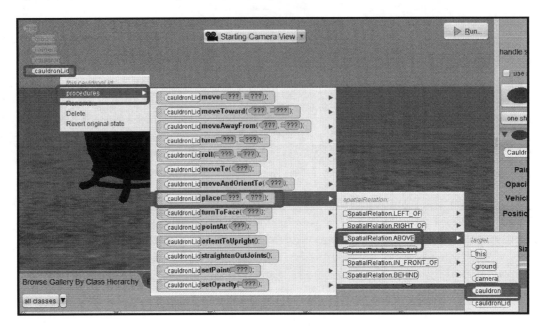

16. The cauldron lid should now be on top of the cauldron, but if we move the cauldron the lid will not move with it. To make the lid move with the cauldron, we need to change the vehicle property of the lid to the cauldron. Make sure that the cauldron lid is selected and change the **vehicle property** (makes one object move in conjunction with the other object) to **cauldron** as shown below. Try moving the cauldron, does the lid move with it?

17. We are going to save our project and continue our work in next exercise. To save the project, you should click on **File**, **Save As**. Name the project **PracticeWithAlice**. Please get in the habit of capitalizing the first letter of every word in your filename and do not use space when naming your files. You should save this file in your **Chapter0Exercises** folder. Exit Alice by clicking **File, Exit.**

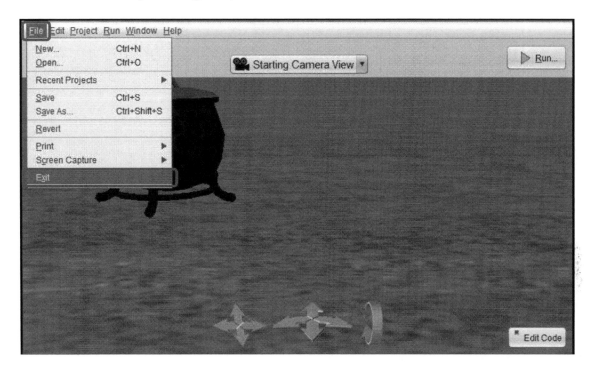

Exercise 2: Manipulating the Alice Environment – Part 2

1. Open up Alice 3. You will need to find the installed Alice 3 folder and double click on the Alice 3 application file.

2. Click on the **File System** tab and choose **browse...** You will need to locate your **PracticeWithAlice** file and click **OK**. *(Note: Alice files have an .a3p file extension. If you double click on this file, it will not open in Alice. Unless you create a file association, you will need to open all of your Alice projects from the Alice software.)*

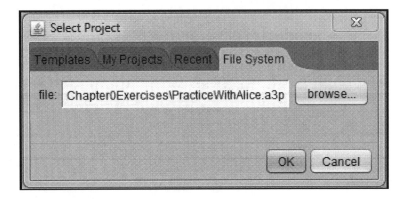

3. You should have a cauldron and a cauldron lid in your scene from exercise 1. Click **Scene Setup** so that we can practice some more with manipulating objects.

4. Let's add a **witch** to the scene. There are multiple ways to find her. You can search for her, click on hierarchy and biped class, click on theme and fantasy, or click on group and characters. Instead of clicking on the witch to add her to the scene, hold down your left mouse button on the **new Witch()** and drag onto the scene and release where you want her. You will notice a yellow bounding box on the screen indicating where she is going to appear. Leave the default name for her. If this method of adding objects does not work for you, then you can add the object by clicking on it and then moving it once it is added to the scene.

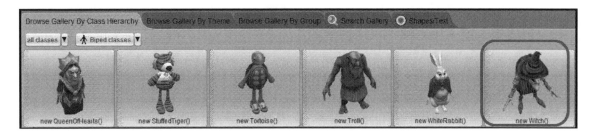

5. Make sure that the **witch** is selected on your scene and then click on **resize**. You should notice an arrow above the witch's head. This will resize the witch proportionally if you hold down your left mouse button and drag up or down. Make her bigger. Whatever you think looks good.

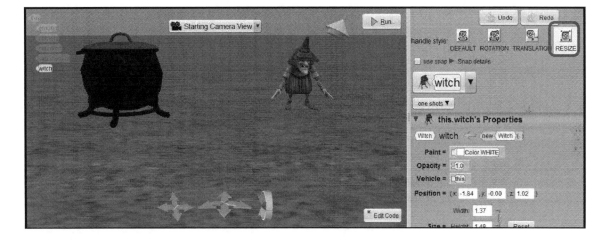

6. Now, let's rotate her. Click on **rotation**. The up and down yellow lines will rotate the witch forwards and backwards if you hold down your left mouse button and drag. The yellow circle on the bottom of the witch will rotate the witch 360 degrees. Hold down your left mouse button on the bottom circle and drag to the left. Rotate the witch so that she is facing the cauldron.

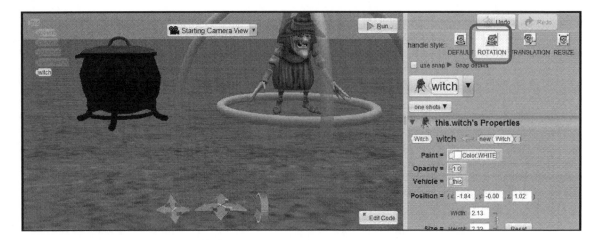

7. Now, we are going to practice with the camera movements. The first set of arrows on the left will move the scene up, down, left, and right. The second set of arrows will move the witch forwards and backwards. The last set of arrows will adjust the scene up and down (more or less sky). Please try out each of the camera arrows.

8. Please take some time to add more objects and manipulate those objects. Practicing with the environemnt is the best way to get acquainted with it. Save your work.

Exercise 3: Alice in Wonderland Mad Tea Party Scene Setup (ongoing exercise)

1. Open up Alice 3. You will need to find the installed Alice 3 folder and double click on the **Alice 3** application file. The first step in programming is understanding the problem. We would like to create a trimmed version of the Alice in Wonderland unbirthday tea party. Once you understand the problem, you setup the scene and create a storyboard for animating the scene.

2. Our goal for the scene setup is to have the following characters: Alice, Mad Hatter, and the March Hare. We will also add some objects to make the scene more interesting: a table, chairs, a tea pot, tea cups, and a birthday cake. When we are finished it should look similar to the following:

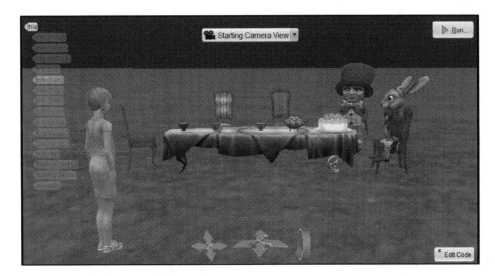

3. Select the **wonderland** template:

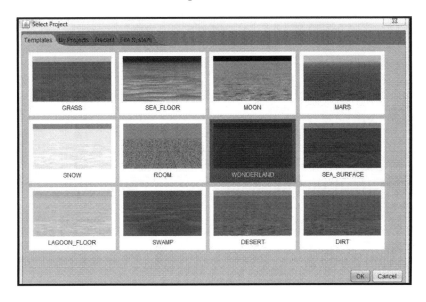

4. Select **File** from the menu, then **Save As**. Save this file as **TeaParty**. Please get in the habit of capitalizing the first letter of every word in your filename and do not use spaces when naming your files. You should save your work often. You can click Save from the File menu from this point on. You should save this file in your **Chapter0Exercises** folder.

5. Click on **Setup Scene button.**

6. We are going to add a table to the scene for the characters to gather around. There is a tea table specifically designed for Alice in Wonderland. Click on the tab called **Browse Gallery By Class Hierarchy**. Click on the **Prop classes** category.

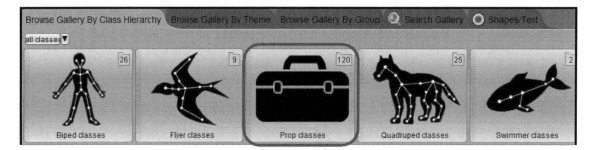

7. Scroll to the end (they are in alphabetical order) until you see the **TeaTable** class. You could have used the *Search Gallery* tab to find the table as well.

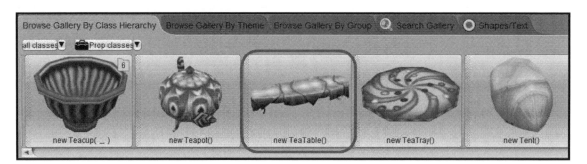

8. Click on the **TeaTable** class to add a tea table to your world or hold down your left mouse button and drag this object to wherever you would like to place it in your scene. If you choose to click on the TeaTable class, the new object will be placed automatically in the center of the scene.

9. When you click on the class it will ask you for a name for the object. You can leave the name teaTable or rename if you want. Do not put spaces in your object name and the first letter of your object name should begin with a lowercase letter and the first letter of the second word should be a capital letter. Object names begin with a lowercase letter; we will talk more about this in the next chapter.

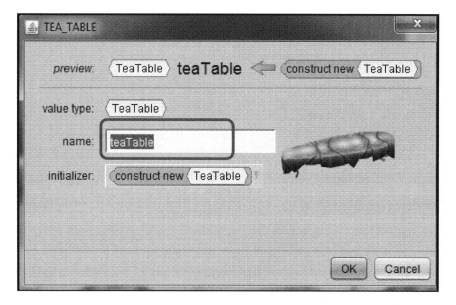

10. Next, we are going to **add a chair**. Now we can test out the search feature in Alice by typing chair into the search box. You will have a list of all the chair models. Please choose the chair that you like.

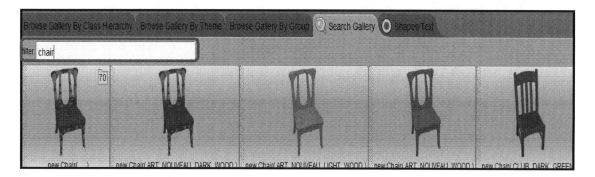

11. Drag the chair that you want onto the scene where you want it by holding down the left mouse button and dragging from the class that you are choosing to add. You will see a yellow bounding box that shows you were your new object will be placed. When you get the object where you want it, release and it will ask you for a name for the object.

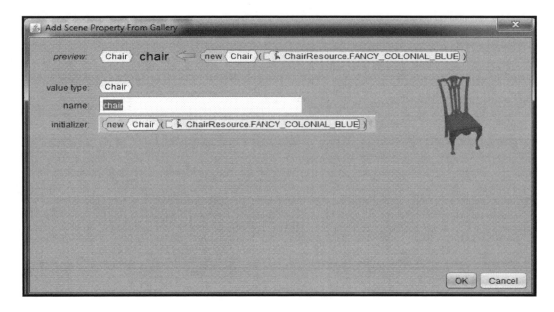

You should name this object something simple. Let's name it **chair**.

12. We should resize the chair so that it matches the size of the table. To do this, you will need to select the chair and then click on the **resize** button from the handle style choices. When you click on the button, an arrow will appear above the chair. Holding down your left mouse button on the arrow and move your mouse up and down to resize the chair.

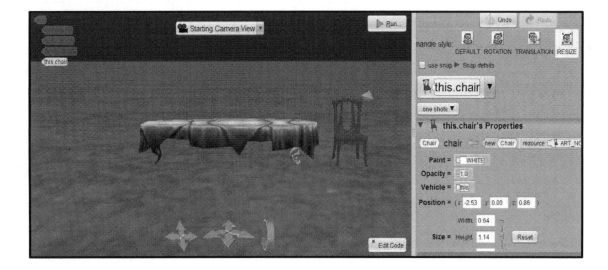

13. To rotate the chair, click on the **rotation** button from the handle style choices. If you hold down the left mouse button on the bottom ring and drag to the right and left, it will spin the chair around so that you can have it face the table.

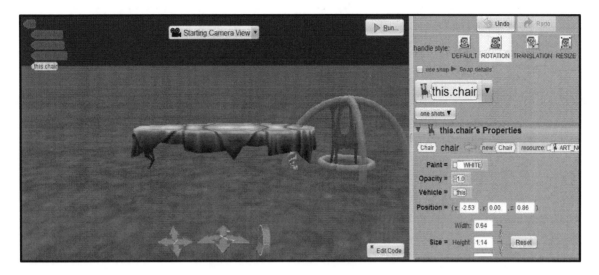

14. To move the chair, click on the **translation** button from the handle style choices. If you hold down your left mouse button on the arrow on top of the chair and drag up and down, the chair will move up and down. The arrow in the front will move the chair forward and backward. The arrow to the right will move the chair left and right.

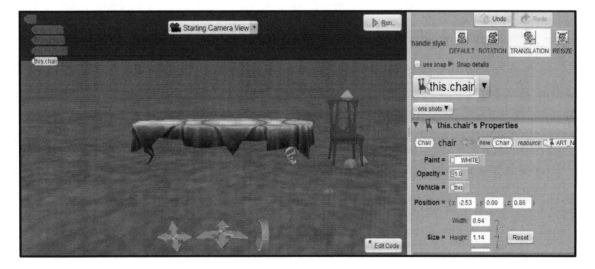

15. **Add 3 more chairs** to the scene around the table. Be careful not to give the chairs the same name. You will see the following error if you try to name your objects the same name. You can call the other chairs: chair2, chair3, and chair4. Do not put spaces in your names. The Alice software will not allow you to name your objects with spaces and this is because the Java language does not allow you to have spaces when naming.

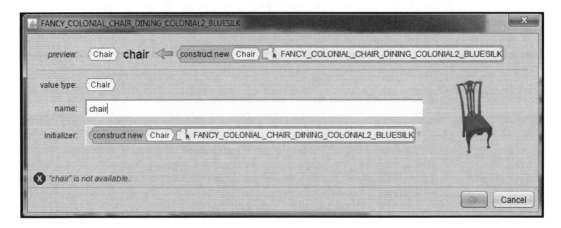

16. It should look similar to the following:

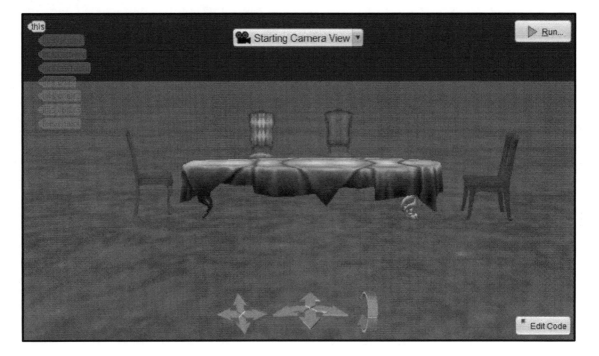

17. Next, we need to **add some teacups and a teapot onto the table**. If you search for tea in the gallery, you will be given the teapot, teacups, saucers, etc. I would like to start with the teapot. When you create the teapot, you can use the default name. We can play with trying to get this teapot onto the table, but this would take a while and there is an easier way. If you **right click on the teapot**, select **procedures**, **teapot place…**, **above**, and **teaTable**, it will place the teapot on top of the table for you.

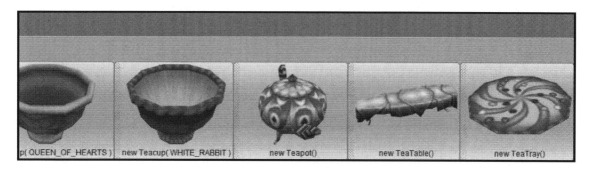

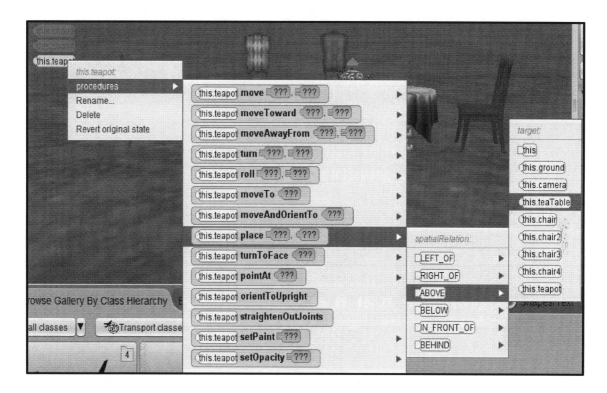

18. **Add a few teacups onto the table** and adjust them how you want them. *Be careful not to give 2 teacups the same name.*

19. **Add a birthday cake onto the table** and readjust the items on the table. It should look similar to the following.

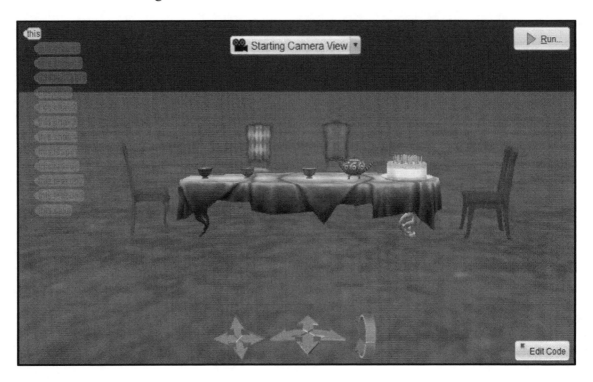

20. Next, we are going to add the characters. The characters can be found in the biped folder in the gallery. Let's add the March Hare first. Place him directly in front of one of the chairs. It doesn't matter which chair you choose. You will need to rotate him so that he lined up with the chair. We are going to make him sit in the chair.

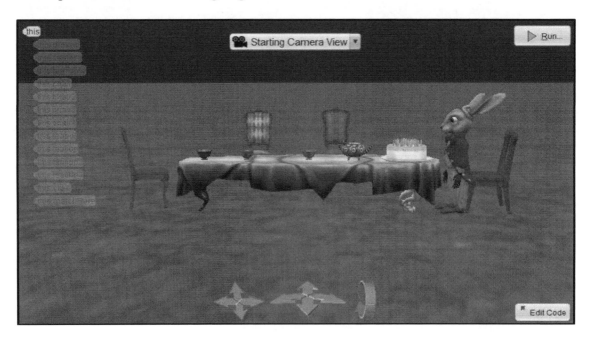

21. To move the marchHare's joints, we will need to select the marchHare and drop down his subparts as shown below. Choose the hare's right hip.

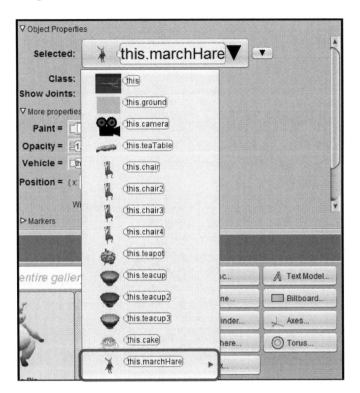

Now, we need to select **ONE SHOT, procedures, marchHare.getRightHip.turn…, BACKWARD**, and **0.25**

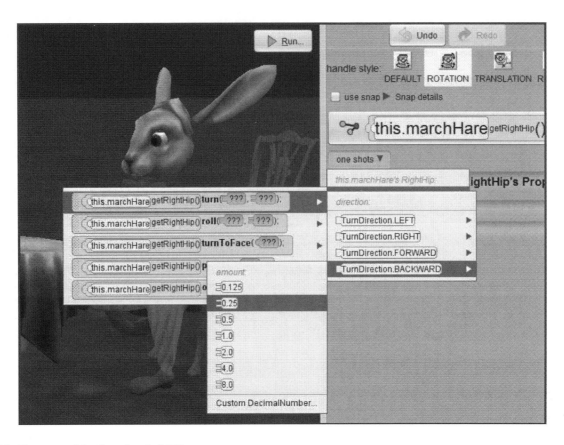

22. **Repeat this for the leftHip**.

23. Select the **marchHare's rightKnee**, then select **one shots**, **procedures**, **turn**, **forward**, and **0.25**.

24. **Repeat this for the leftKnee**. You may need to move the entire marchHare back and up to get him onto the chair.

25. Now, let's **add the madHatter** to the scene. Place him next to the marchHare. It doesn't matter which side he is on. You may need to resize, rotate, and move him to get the scene to look the way you want.

26. Finally, we are going to add Alice to the scene. We will need to create Alice using the Child class in the biped classes. The Child class allows you to select male or female, the skin tone, the attire, the hair color, eye color, and shape of the person. **Create a girl** that looks like Alice and name her **alice**. Normally you would capitalize a name, but when we name objects, we don't capitalize the object names.

27. Place alice off to the side of the animation window looking at the tea party as shown below.

28. We are finished with the scene setup. If you want to add some wonderland trees or other objects to your scene, feel free.

29. We have not added any code to our projects. This chapter was all about working with scene setup. We will be adding code in chapter 1.

30. Save this program and exit Alice.

Exercise 4: Alice Card Game Scene Setup (ongoing exercise)

1. Open up Alice 3. You will need to find the installed Alice 3 folder and double click on the Alice 3 application file.

2. The first step in programming is understanding the problem. We would like to create a trimmed version of a card game. We will have 2 players that each get dealt a playing card. The player with the highest card wins. We will be gradually adding to this project throughout the text. In this project, we are going to set up the scene for the card game. We will need to add the playing cards to the scene and we will need cones to set the locations for our playing cards so that it looks as if the cards are being dealt. We will want to add text to the screen that displays each player, who won, and the score for each player. The castle wall will just act as a background for our game (it is not necessary).

3. Our goal for the scene setup is to have a castle background with the following characters: 10 Alice Playing Cards, **Player 1** text sign, **Player 2** text sign, 2 **WIN** signs (one for each player), 2 scores (one for each player). When we are finished it should look similar to the following:

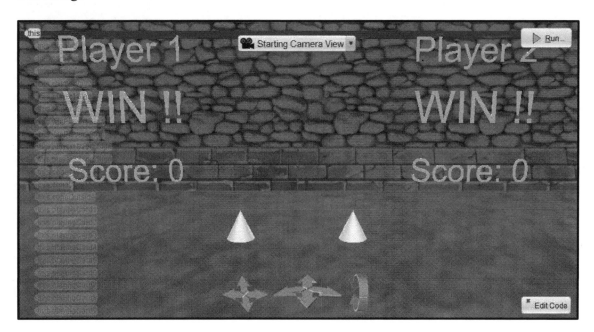

4. Select the **grass** template:

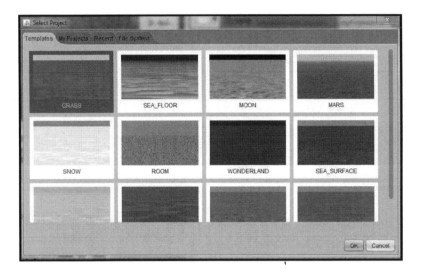

5. Select **File** from the menu, then **Save As**. Save this file as **CardGame**. Please get in the habit of capitalizing the first letter of every word in your filename and do not use spaces when naming your files. You should save your work often. You can click Save from the File menu from this point on. You should save this file in your **Chapter0Exercises** folder.

6. Click on **Setup Scene button.**

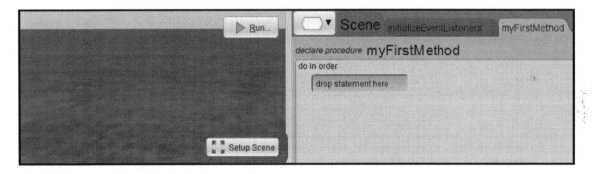

7. To add a castle wall to the background, click on the tab called **Browse Gallery By Theme.** Then click on **fantasy**.

8. Next, choose **castle.**

9. Then choose **new CastleWall** (last choice).

10. Then, choose the first choice for the castle walls.

11. You can use the default name given as **castleWall** and click on OK. Your screen should look similar to the following:

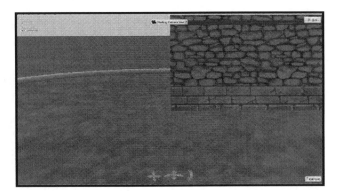

12. Click on the castle wall choice at bottom of screen again so that you will have 2 castle walls. It will name this piece as **castleWall2** and that is fine. Click on OK. It will put this piece of the wall right over top of the last piece that was already on the screen.

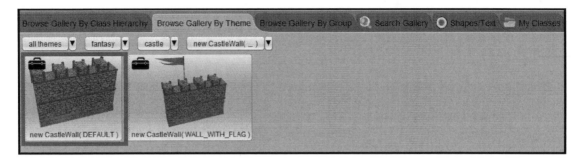

13. You can use the handles to pick this piece up and move it to the left until it looks like one continuous wall. Another way is to move it using the X Y Z axis positions listed on the far right of your scene setup screen. Change the **x** location to be **5.20** and press ENTER key and it will move it to the left.

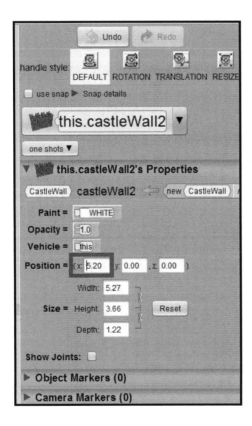

14. The screen should look similar to the following:

15. The background for the Card Game is now set up. Now, player signs are needed in the upper corners. These are text boxes. Choose the **Shapes/Text** tab and select **new TextModel** and **drag it onto the grass**.

16. Name the text model as **player1Sign**. By default, the color is white and the opacity is 1 (visible). Change the value by clicking in value and choosing custom textString and then typing in **Player 1** (with a space). Your screen should look as follows and then click **OK**.

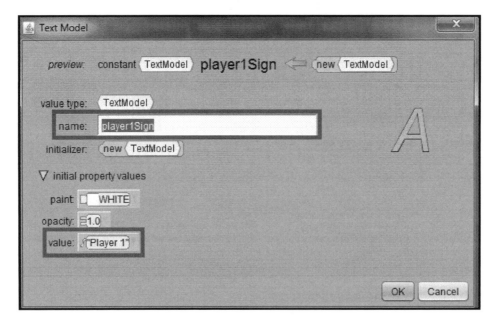

17. A text box will appear quite large in the grass as follows *(if you cannot see the text, do not worry it will be fixed in the next step)*:

18. To place this sign in upper left corner it will need to be resized and moved. One way is to move and resize the object by using arrows, etc. Another way is to use the right side of the screen to place it at a specific location by using the x, y, and z etc. Change the **width** to be **1** and press ENTER key. Change the **x, y, and z** to be as follows (make sure to press ENTER key after making each entry):

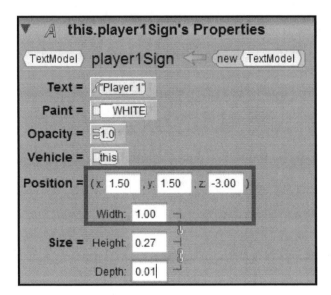

19. The screen should appear as follows:

20. The Player 2 sign will be done the same way. Drag the **new TextModel** into the grass. Name it **player2Sign** and change the custom testString to be **Player 2**.

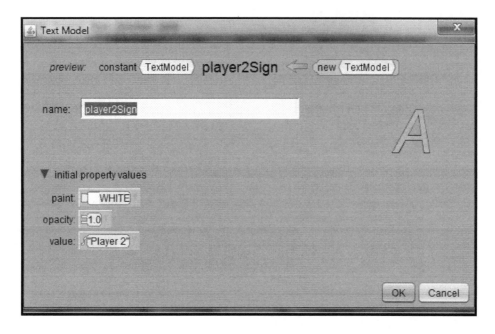

21. The player2Sign comes in large. The width and location will need to be adjusted. Change the width and the x, y, and z to be as follows (make sure to press ENTER key after making each entry):

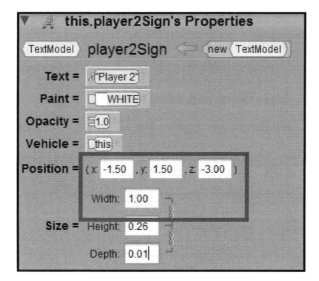

22. Your screen should look as follows:

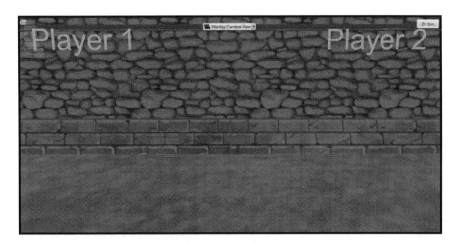

23. The player 1 and 2 signs are headings. The WIN signs and scores will be displayed underneath of these. They will also be Text Models. The first WIN sign will appear directly under the Player 1 sign. Choose the **TextModel** again and drag it to the grass area. Fill in the box with a name of **winPlayer1Sign** and custom textString value as **WIN !!** Change the width and the positions as follows:

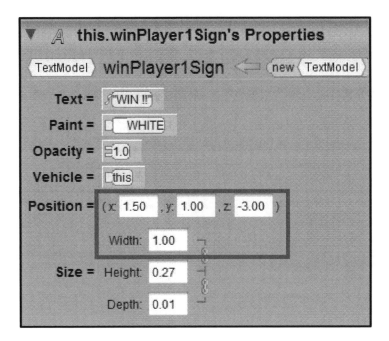

24. You will do the same thing for **winPlayer2Sign**. It will be named winPlayer2Sign and the textString value will be **WIN!!** Its width will be **1.0**. Its position will be x of **-1.5**, y of **1.0**, and z of **-3.0**. Make sure you press ENTER after each entry. If you have done everything correctly, your screen will look as follows:

25. Below these signs will be the SCORE signs. To set these up, drag another **TextModel** to the grass. Name it **player1ScoreSign**. The custom textString value will be **Score: 0**. The width is **1.0**. The x position is **1.5**, y position is **0.5**, and z position is **-3.0**. Your screen should look as follows:

26. To do the second SCORE sign on right side, you will drag a **TextModel** to the grass again. Name the object as **player2ScoreSign** and make the custom textString as **Score: 0**. Change the width to be **1.0** and press ENTER key. Change the x position to be **-1.5**, y position to be **0.5**, and z position to be **-3.0**. Your screen should look as follows:

27. Two placement markers will be needed as markers for the playing cards. Cones will be used for these markers. Two small cones will be placed towards the middle of the scene and the cards will be dealt to these cone markers. From the Shape area, drag the cone to the grass. Give it the name of **cone1**. Change the width to be **0.25**. Change the x position to be **0.5**. Change the y position to be **0.0**. Change the z position to be **-3.0**. This could have also been done by using the arrows and lining up the positions by trial and error.

28. Now, place the second cone with a name of **cone2**, width of **0.25**, x position of **-0.5**, y position of **0.0**, and z position of **-3.0**. The screen should look as follows:

29. Another marker needs to be placed far off the scene. Since camera movement will be involved, a marker will be placed to remember this camera position so we can return to this camera angle later. On the right side of screen by the sizes and locations is a section called **Camera Markers**.

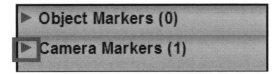

Click on the triangle (expand) to open the Camera Markers part of the screen. Choose the **Add Camera Marker...** button. Name this camera marker as **originalCamera** and make it RED. Now, we will be able to return to this view any time we want. (It is good idea to have an original camera marker for any scene you develop.)

30. Click on the first camera arrow at bottom of scene.

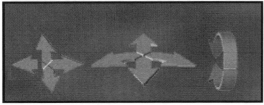

Choose the LEFT arrow. Your screen should scroll to the left. The goal is to scroll far enough to the left to place a marker to the left of the wall. Create a cone named **coneOutside**. Make the length of it **0.25**. Make the x position as **8.0**, y position as **0.0**, and z position as **-3.0**. Each of the playing cards will be placed at this same position. This way each of the cards will be at the exact same location and they will be off the original scene.

31. **To place the first card, we will click on the tab that is Browse** Gallery by Class Hierarchy and choose the **Biped Classes**

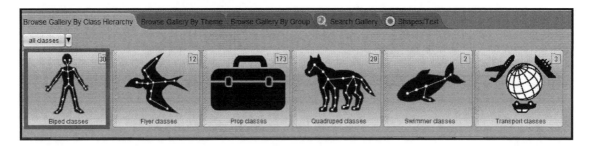

32. Find **new PlayingCard**.

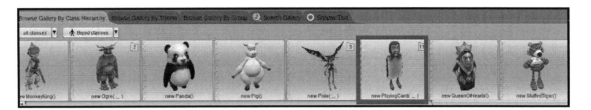

33. Scroll right and choose new **PlayingCard (ONE 1)** and drag it to the screen. Name this card **playingCard1**. Change the width to be 0.5. Click on the **one shots** drop down (or right click on the object). Choose **procedures**, then **moveTo**, and then choose **coneOutside**.

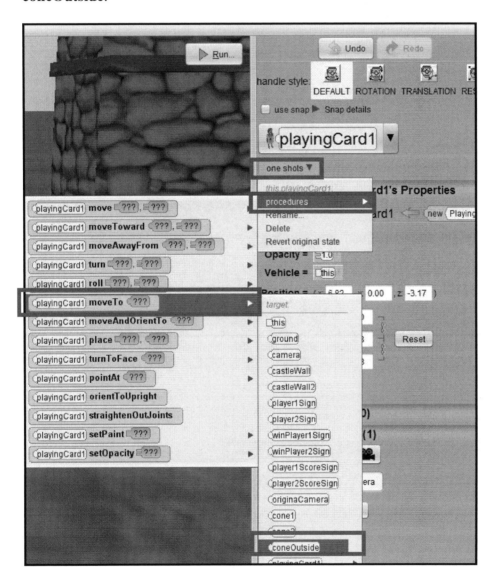

34. The first playing card should now be placed exactly on the coneOutside. Now, nine more playing cards will be placed in this exact same location and the exact same size. To place the second card, scroll to the right of the playing cards and find **newPlayingCard (TWO2)**. Drag it to the grass. It will automatically name it **playingCard2**. Change the width to be **0.5** and press ENTER key. Use the one shots to place playingCard2 on the coneOutside as you did in the previous step. You will continue to place all ten cards on the screen in the grass, size each one as a width of **0.5** and the use one shots to **move each one to the coneOutside**. When all are done, your screen should look as follows:

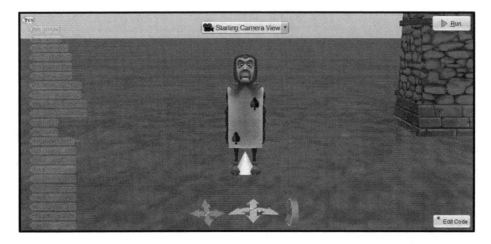

If done correctly, the object tree on left should have playingCard1 to playingCard10 and all of the cards should be sitting on top of each other and on top of our coneOutside.

35. To return to the original camera view, change object to **camera** and then choose **one shots**, **procedures**, **moveTo**, and **orignalCamera**.

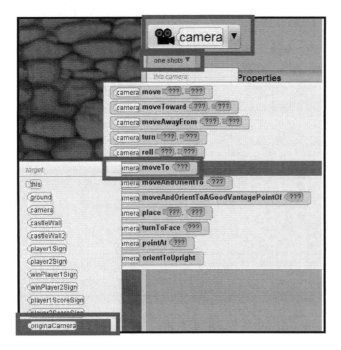

36. In later chapters, you will have these cards come on to the screen, determine which player is the winner, have the WIN sign flash, have the score updated, etc. The scene is now complete and should look as follows:

37. Make sure to save this final version as **CardGame** in the Chapter0Exercises folder.

Summary

- Alice is an innovative 3D programming environment that makes it easy to create an animation or interactive game. The team named the system "Alice" in honor of Lewis Carroll who wrote Alice's Adventures in Wonderland.
- An Alice virtual world begins with a template for an initial scene. These templates can be grass, water, snow, etc.
- An Alice 3D model is like a blueprint that tells Alice how to create a new object in the scene. The 3D model provides instructions on how to draw the object, what color it should be, what parts it should have, its size (height, width, and depth), and many other details.
- When you choose to place an Alice object into your world, Alice will create an object (instance) of that class in your world and ask you to name that object.
- When naming an object (instance) of a class, you should begin the name with a lowercase letter. If the name will have multiple words in it, each successive word with then begin with a capital letter. An example would be *myLittleSnowman*.
- Objects from the galleries are added to the scene via the SCENE EDITOR (a click on Setup Scene button).
- Objects in an Alice world are three dimensional. Each object has width, height, and depth.
- There are six possible directions in which an object may move – forward, backward, up, down, left and right.
- Each object in Alice has a unique "center." An object's center is used for measuring distance to another object and for determining its position in the world.

Review Questions

1. Alice was named in honor of Lewis Carroll.
    a. True
    b. False

2. An Alice 3D model is like a blueprint that tells Alice how to create a new object in the scene.
    a. True
    b. False

3. Once an object is placed into a scene, it can't be manipulated by moving, rotating, etc.
    a. True
    b. False

4. If you were to name an object (instance) of an Airplane class, which of the following names would be proper?
    a. MyAirplane
    b. my airplane
    c. myairplane
    d. myAirplane

5. You can have more than one object of the same class in the same world?
    a. True
    b. False

Solutions: 1) a   2) a   3) b   4) d   5) a

Assignments

0-1   **Cola Commercial:** Create a scene in Alice that could be used for a cola commercial. You must have at least 7 appropriately placed objects in your scene. Name this project ColaCommercial.

0-2   **Greeting Card**: Create a scene in Alice that could be used for a greeting card. You must have at least 7 appropriately placed objects in your scene. Name this project GreetingCard.

0-3   **Animation**: Create a scene in Alice that could be used for a short animation. You must have at least 7 appropriately placed objects in your scene. Name this project as Animation.

0-4   **Card Game Adjusted**: Adjust exercise 4 in this chapter to have at least 7 more appropriate scenery items. Name the project as MyCardGame.

Chapter 1

Coding Introduction

Objectives

- ☑ Explain the difference between high and low level programming languages
- ☑ Describe the history of how the Java programming language was started
- ☑ Briefly describe the following:
  - o Object Oriented Programming
  - o Platform-Independence
  - o Garbage Collection
  - o Java Development Kit
- ☑ Explain the difference between applets, applications, and servlets
- ☑ Explain the difference between Java and JavaScript
- ☑ Compile and execute a Java program
- ☑ Debug errors
- ☑ Identify and fix compiler errors

Introduction to Programming

A computer program is a way to tell a computer what to do. When you want a computer to perform a task, you must give it line-by-line instructions on how to accomplish that task. These line-by-line instructions are called a **computer program**.

The computer stores information based on electronic signals, referred to as **binary**. A **bit** (binary digit), the smallest unit of information storage, is represented by either an on (1) or off (0) signal inside the computer. One **byte** (a character such as the letter "A" on the keyboard) uses eight bits.

There are many different computer programming languages available and the choice of what programming language to use will depend upon the task for the computer to accomplish. A programming language that is written at the very low technical circuitry level of the computer is called a **low-level programming language**. Some examples of low-level programming languages are machine language and assembler language. Machine language is composed of binary 1's and 0's and is not intended for humans to read. Machine language varies from computer to computer. The machine language for a PC is entirely different from machine language for Mac. A computer only understands programs (without any conversion) written in its machine language (binary).

High-level programming languages allow programmers to write programs using English terms. Computers do not understand high-level languages directly so this means that computer programs written in a high-level language must be converted to machine language by an interpreter or compiler. Some high-level computer programming languages available are: C++, Visual Basic.NET, C#, and Java. Each of these programming languages is best-suited to a certain type of computer or problem such as mainframes, business, games and/or science.

Computer languages each have their own **syntax**, or rules of the language. For instance, in a high-level programming language the verb to display information might be "write", "print", "show", etc. In a low-level programming language the verb to display information might be a code of "101011" in binary. *Java is a high-level programming language with a specific vocabulary and specific rules for using that vocabulary.*

What is Java?

History of Java

In 1990, **James Gosling** was given the task of creating programs to control consumer electronics (TVs, VCRs, toasters, etc.). Gosling and his team at **Sun Microsystems** started designing their software using C++. The team found that C++ was not suitable for the projects they had in mind. They ran into trouble with complicated aspects of C++ such as multiple inheritances of classes and with program bugs such as memory leaks. So, Gosling created a simplified computer language that would avoid all the problems he had with C++. Thus, **a new programming language named Oak** (after a tree outside his window) was born.

Oak was first used in something called the Green project, which was a control system for use in the home using a hand-held computer called Star Seven. Oak was then used in another project which involved video-on-demand. Neither project ever made it to the public eye, but Oak gained some recognition. Sun discovered that the name Oak was already copyrighted. After going out for coffee one day, they named their new powerful language **Java**.

In 1993, the Java team realized that the Java language they had developed would be perfect for web page programming. The team came up with the concept of web applets, small programs that could be included in web pages, and created a complete web browser called HotJava (originally called Webrunner) that demonstrated the language's power.

In the second quarter of 1995, Sun Microsystems officially announced Java. The "new" language was quickly embraced as a powerful tool for developing Internet applications. Netscape Communications added support for Java to its Netscape Navigator 2.0. Java became an instant "hit" and also made the Netscape browser very popular. Other Internet software developers such as Microsoft eventually followed suit and reluctantly included Java in their browsers. These browsers were called "Java-enabled". Java-enabled meant that the browser could download and play Java classes (applets) on the user's system. (Applets appear in a web page much the same way as images do, but unlike images, applets can be dynamic and interactive.)

Java Capabilities

- **Java is easier than C++.** Although Java looks similar to C and C++, most of the complex parts such as pointers, multiple inheritance, and memory management have been excluded from Java.

- **Java is an Object Oriented Programming (OOP) language,** which allows you to create flexible, modular programs and reuse code. OOP is based on the theory that everything in the world can be modeled as an object. An object has attributes (data) and behavior (methods).

- **Java is platform-independent.** Platform-independence is a program's capability of moving easily from one computer system to another. **Java slogan is "You can write once and run anywhere."** If you write a game using the Java programming language, theoretically, you should be able to run that game on a PC, Linux, or Mac.

- **Java supports the Internet** by enabling people to write interactive programs for the Internet. Java applets can easily be invoked from web browsers to provide valuable and spectacular web pages.

- **Java is general purpose.** Although used mainly for writing internet applications, Java is a truly general-purpose language. Almost anything that most other computer programming languages such as C++ or Visual Basic can do, Java can also do. Java programs can be applets for the Internet or standalone applications for local PCs.

    o **Applets** appear in a web page much in the same way as images do, but unlike images, applets are dynamic and interactive. Applets can be used to create animations, games, ecommerce, etc.

    o **Applications** are more general programs written in the Java language. Applications don't need a browser. The Java language can be used to create programs, like those made in other computer languages.

    o **Servlets** are programs that respond to requests from clients.

- **Java is secure**. Since the Java program is isolated from the native operating system of a computer, the Java program is insulated from the particular hardware on which it is run. Because of this insulation, the Java Virtual Machine provides security against intruders getting at your computer's hardware through the operating system.

- **Java programs can contain multiple threads** of execution, which enables programs to handle several tasks simultaneously. For example, a multi-threaded program can render an animation on the screen in one thread while continuing to accept keyboard input from the user in the main thread. All applications have at least one thread.

- **Java has multimedia capabilities** of graphics, images, animations, audio and videos. It also runs on networks.

- **Java programs do their own garbage collection**, which means that programs are not required to delete objects that they allocate to memory. This relieves programmers of virtually all memory-management problems.

- **Java programs are reliable and robust**. When a serious error is discovered, Java programs create an **exception**. This exception can be captured and managed by the program and then terminated gracefully.

- **Java vs. JavaScript**. The Java language was developed by Sun MicroSystems and is full programming language that can be used in applications or as applets on the Internet. JavaScript was developed by Netscape as a scripting language to be used only in HTML web pages.

Programming Process

Develop an algorithm: Think about the problem before coding. Create a flowchart, storyboard, or pseudo code to represent a solution to the problem.

Create Project: Create a new project in NetBeans. The NetBeans environment is known as our **IDE** (Integrated Development Environment). There are many IDEs that can be downloaded free of charge, but NetBeans provides many features that will be helpful to us for this course. In NetBeans, when you create a project, it creates a folder structure. The following is an example of a folder structure for a HelloWorld project created in NetBeans.

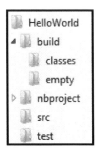

Code: Type the Java code. As you type, NetBeans checks your program for syntax errors. Red lines indicate errors in your code. The Java code (HelloWorld.java) for the HelloWorld project will be in the **src** folder in the folder structure above.

Compile: When you are finished typing the program, you will need to do a final compile of the program (also known as building). The Java compiler checks your code for errors. If it compiles with no syntax errors, it creates a **class file** (bytecode) that will be capable of running on different operating systems. Bytecode are a set of instructions that look a lot like machine code, but are not specific to any one processor. Compiling the HelloWorld.java creates the HelloWorld.class file located in the **build** folder inside the **classes** subfolder in the folder structure above.

Run: These bytecode are then fed to a **JVM** (Java Virtual Machine) where they are interpreted and executed.

The **JDK** (Java Development Kit) includes the Java library (code), JVM, as well as the Java compiler. The version of NetBeans that you installed included the JDK. Oracle owns Java and it is constantly releasing new versions of the JDK. It is good to know what JDK you are using so that you know what Java code is available to you. We will talk more about the Java library and JDK in a later chapter. You can check to see what version of the JDK that you have by clicking **Help** from the menu and then **About** in the NetBeans environment. The JDK version shown below is 1.8. You do not need to put the update number which is the number after the underscore.

Product Version: NetBeans IDE 8.0 (Build 201403101706)
Updates: NetBeans IDE is updated to version NetBeans 8.0 Patch 1.1
Java: 1.8.0_05; Java HotSpot(TM) Client VM 25.5-b02
Runtime: Java(TM) SE Runtime Environment 1.8.0_05-b13
System: Windows 7 version 6.1 running on x86; Cp1252; en_US (nb)
User directory: C:\Users\Administrator\AppData\Roaming\NetBeans\8.0

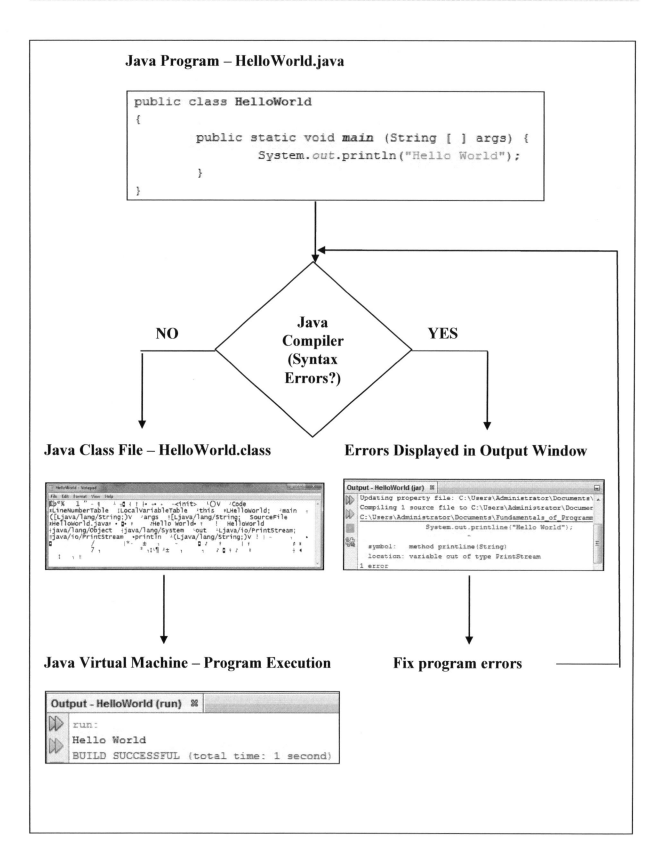

Documentation

Comments are used to document code so that other people reading our code can understand our logic. Comments are useful for adding extra information to our programs that we don't necessarily want to show up in the output of our program such as: author, date, JDK used, program description, etc. Also, it is a good idea to comment your programs extensively when you are just starting out so that you have well-documented examples.

A **single line comment** is represented by two forward slashes. This comment will continue until the end of the line. This type of comment can be placed on a line by itself or it can be placed on the end of a line of code to describe the code. The following are examples of a single line comments.

//Single Line Comment

System.out.println("Hello World");   **//Prints "Hello World" to the output window**

A **multi-line comment** is represented by a forward slash followed by an asterisk and an asterisk followed by a forward slash to end the multi-line comment. The following is an example of a multi-line comment.

/* Multi-Line
  Comment */

You can even be creative and separate your multi-line comments from your code by adding asterisks after the first forward slash and before the last forward slash.

/**
* Multi-Line Comment
* Typical Java Documentation
*/

Note: Java documentation will be explained in a later chapter.

Alice Comments

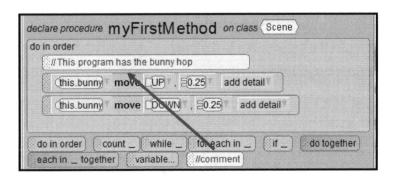

Program Errors

There are 3 different types of programming errors: compiler, run-time, and logic errors.

- **Syntax errors** are caused when the user writes code that is not understood by the compiler. A syntax error can be caused by incorrect capitalization or spelling mistakes. The compiler informs the user of a syntax error by displaying an error message. Typing "Public Class" instead of "public class" would result in a syntax error. NetBeans checks for errors as you type. If you see a red exclamation point before a line of code, you can hover over it with your mouse to see the error.

  This line of code should have been: **System.out.println("Hello World");**

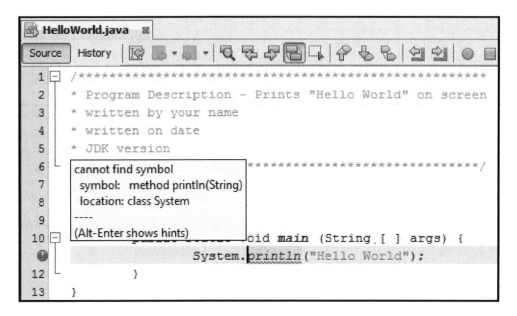

- **Run-time errors** are caused by invalid data. Run-time errors do not affect the compilation of your program thus the program will compile and execute, but it may crash or hang after execution. If you try to divide 12 by 0 you would get a run-time error because you cannot divide by 0.

- **Logic errors** (also known as human error) are caused by mistakes that do not defy the rules of the language and do not crash or hang the program, but instead yield incorrect results. The user may not understand the problem that the program is trying to solve and therefore uses the wrong equation, wrong strategy, etc. An example of a logic error would be moving left instead of right.

Hands-on Exercises

Exercise 1: Alice in Wonderland Tea Party Coding (ongoing exercise)

1. Open up Alice 3.

2. Open the **TeaParty** file that was created in the **Chapter0Exercises** folder. Click on the **File System** tab, then choose **browse…** and locate your file. Select the file and click the **Open** button and then the **OK** button.

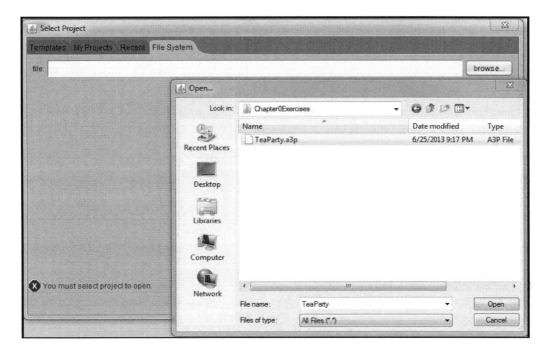

3. Before writing the code for our animation, we should first create a storyboard of what we wish to accomplish.

> - Scene opens with the Mad Hatter and the March Hare gathered around a table with tea and a birthday cake
> - The unbirthday song plays
> - Alice approaches the table
> - Alice tells the characters that she enjoyed their singing
> - They tell her that nobody ever compliments their singing and insist that she has a cup of tea
> - She apologizes for interrupting their birthday party
> - They explain that it isn't their birthday; it is their "unbirthday"
> - Alice then asks them to explain an "unbirthday"
> - They then tell her that everyone has 364 "unbirthdays" each year
> - Alice realizes that it is her "unbirthday" too

4. We need to save the new version of this file in the **Chapter1Exercises** folder instead of the Chapter0Exercises folder. Click on **File** from the menu, then **Save As**, locate the **Chapter1Exercises** folder, and save this file as **TeaParty**.

5. Drag the **//comment** block to the editor and enter your comments. You need to put your name, the date, and a description of the program in comments at the top of all of your programs.

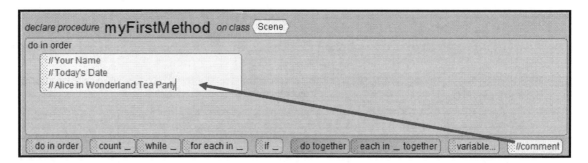

6. Click on the **this**, make sure that the **Procedures** tab is selected, drag the **playAudio** method to the editor, select **Import Audio**, use the **Unbirthday Song** file *(located in your Data_Files folder: http://iws.collin.edu/tdaly/book2/).* Procedural methods are actions that objects can do. The word "this" refers to the scene and we are telling the scene to play the audio.

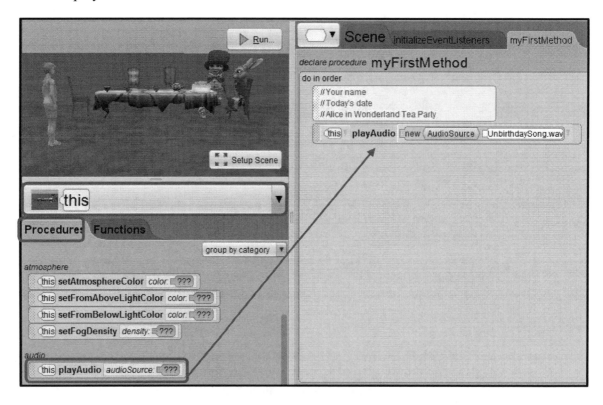

7. We need to test the program by clicking the **Run** button to play the animation. You should hear the song play but nothing else happens yet.

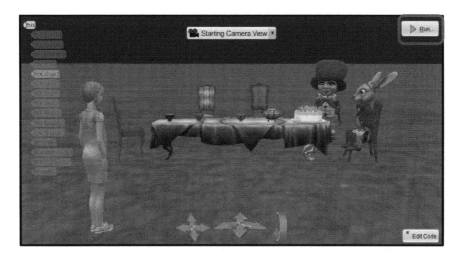

8. Next, we will select alice, make sure that the procedures tab is selected, and drag the **moveToward method** onto the editor underneath the playAudio method. When you release the mouse, you will be prompted to select the target that you want alice to move toward and the amount that you want her to move. Select **marchHare** as the target and **2.0** as the amount. If you wanted a number that isn't on the list, you would select Custom DecimalNumber and type in your own number. These choices (target and amount) are known as arguments in programming. Run the animation to see if alice moves toward the marchHare; you will have to wait until the song finishes to see her move. The program happens in order. The next line doesn't execute until the previous line is finished.

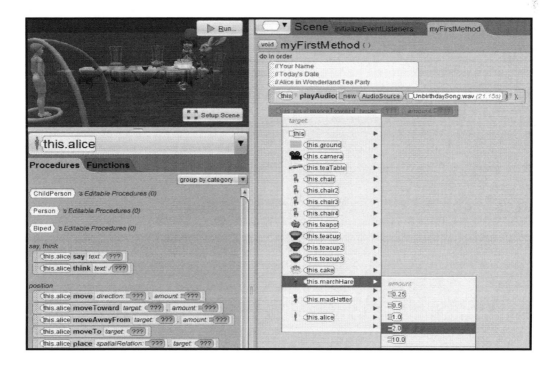

9. If you don't want to wait for the song to finish every time you want to test out your animation, you can disable lines of code and enable them later. To do this, you would need to right click on the **playAudio** line and **uncheck Is Enabled**. You will see the line will now have gray lines over it.

10. Now, we want alice to praise their singing. You will need to select alice and then drag the **say** method onto the editor underneath the moveToward method. When you do this, you will be prompted (argument) to enter the text of what you want alice to say. You should select **Custom TextString…** and then enter **I enjoyed your singing**. You can select **add detail** if you want to make adjustments such as text color, speech bubble color, outline color, or the duration that the bubble stays on the screen. You can leave the default settings if you want. The duration is defaulted to 1 second.

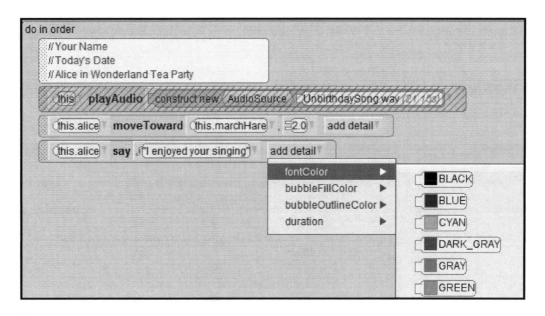

11. Create the following dialog between the characters:

> **madHatter** – We never get compliments, you must have a cup of tea.
> **alice** – Sorry for interrupting your birthday party.
> **marchHare** – This is an unbirthday party.
> **alice** – Unbirthday?
> **madHatter** - Statistics prove, prove that you've got one birthday. One birthday every year, but there are 364 unbirthdays. That's exactly why we are gathered here to cheer.
> **alice** – Well I guess it's my unbirthday too!

12. Have Alice joyously jump up and down at the end. If you want her to jump at a faster pace, you can change the duration to be 0.5 seconds instead of 1 second (Click the *add detail* drop down to change the duration.

13. To test the full program with the song, you will need to **enable** the **playAudio** method. Right click on the **playAudio** line and **check Is Enabled**. The grey lines through the playAudio method should disappear.

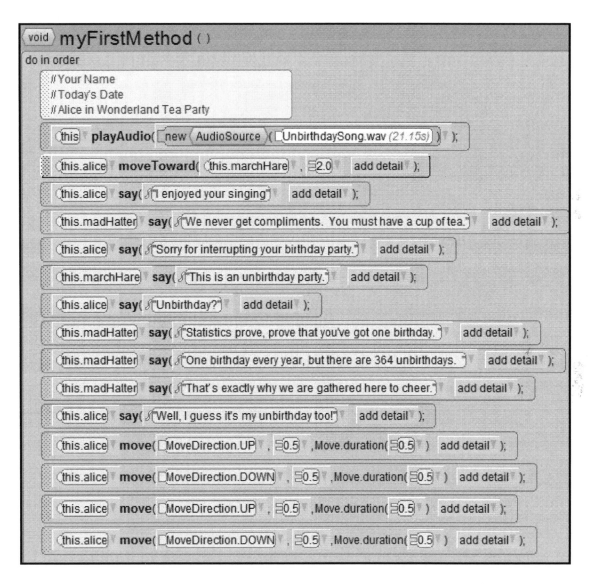

14. Challenge: Make this your own by adjusting it how you want. For example, you may want to challenge yourself and make the Mad Hatter and the March Hare dance to the unbirthday song. This would require that you use the **Do Together** block to make the dancing happen while the song is playing.

15. Save your work and exit Alice.

Exercise 2: Compiling and Executing a Java Program

1. Open up the NetBeans environment.

2. You can close the Start Page. The tutorials provided in the Start Page can be confusing for a first timer.

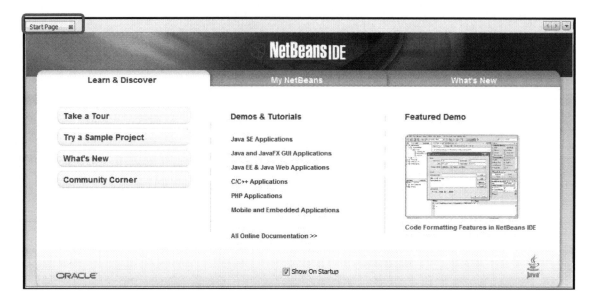

3. Select the **File** menu and then choose **New Project**. Then choose **Java Application** as shown below.

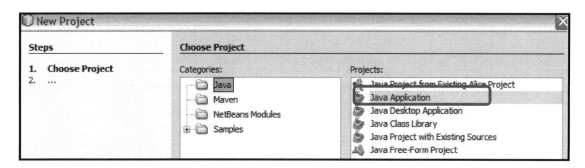

4. Click **Next**. Name your NetBeans project, select the **location** of where you would like to save your file, give your file *(Main Class)* a name *(make this name the same as your project name)*, and click **finish**. Although it is not necessary, we are going to name our projects and Java files *(main class)* have the same name. Therefore, make sure that the top and bottom boxes have the same name. NetBeans automatically will try to name your file (main class) helloworld.HelloWorld. **Erase the helloworld.** that NetBeans inserts before your file name. Make sure it looks like the following screenshot. Capitalization is important.

> *Project the name **HelloWorld**. (no spaces)*
> *Main class name of **HelloWorld** (no spaces)*
> *Select the **Location** of where you would like to save your NetBeans project*

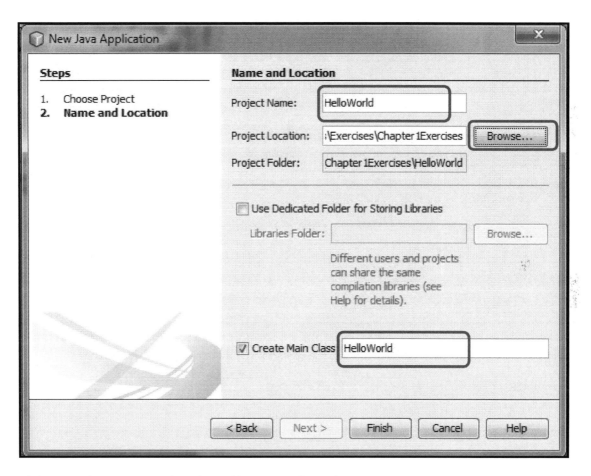

5. If line numbers are not showing, click **View** from the menu, then **Show Line Numbers.**

6. Your project should look as follows. HelloWorld.java is the file that we will be working with. *(Note: If your code has a package statement on line 5, then exit NetBeans and delete the project folder and do step 4 again. Make sure it looks like the screen shot provided. Look carefully at the textbox next to the Create Main Class label in the New Java Application dialog. For your information a package in Java is a folder. The package line indicates that you put your file in a folder when you created the project. We will not be using package statements in this text.)*

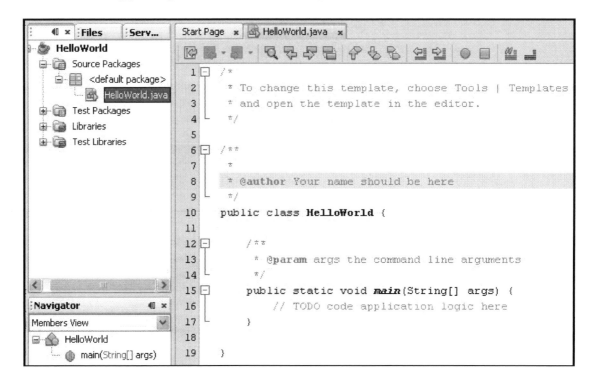

7. Type in the following Java program. You will need to delete some comment lines and add some lines. Be careful to make your program look exactly as shown below. Try to keep your statements on the same lines as those shown below and also try to use the same approximate indentation to make your program more understandable. Change line 3 to be your name, line 4 to be today's date, and line 5 to be the JDK version that you are using *(You can check to see what version of the JDK that you have by clicking* ***Help*** *from the menu and then* ***About*** *in the NetBeans environment. It will have* ***Java:*** *and then a number, this is your JDK version. You do not need the number after the underscore).*

HelloWorld.java

```
1  /*
2   * Program Description - Prints "Hello World" on screen
3   * written by your name
4   * written on date
5   * JDK version
6   */
7
8  public class HelloWorld {
9
10     public static void main(String[] args) {
11         System.out.println("Hello World");
12     }
13 }
```

What does the above program do? You will not understand everything about this program YET. However, here is a brief explanation line by line:

1-6)	Lines 1-6 are known as comments. Comments are used to document code so that other people reading our code can understand our logic. Comments are useful for adding extra information to our programs that we don't necessarily want to show up in the output of our program such as: author, date, JDK used, program description, etc. Also, it is a good idea to comment your programs extensively when you are just starting out so that you have well-documented examples. This is a multi-line comment which is represented by a /* at beginning of comment and */ to end the multi-line comment.
7)	Blank line for readability purposes. Does nothing. (not necessary)
8)	States this will be a public program called HelloWorld. Class names should begin with a capital letter. Be careful of capitalization in Java programs.
9)	Blank line for readability purposes. Does nothing. (not necessary)
10)	This is the main method declaration in this Java application. Every Java application must contain a main method and it must always be public static. The arguments for a method always appear in parentheses. In this case, the argument is a String array called args. The variable name of args can be whatever the programmer wants it to be, but most programmers use the variable name of args. The square brackets appearing after the word String are found to the right of the "P" key on keyboard.
11)	The statement of **System.out.println("Hello World");** prints Hello World to the screen and positions the insertion point on the next line. *System* is a Java class in the library and the *out* object is the screen. Java is case sensitive so be careful of capitalization. Java uses a punctuation method of class-dot-object-dot-method syntax. All methods have arguments in parenthesis which is a way of telling a method from a variable. This println method has an argument of a literal string of "Hello World". All Java statement lines will end with a semicolon. *Note: The next to last character in "println" is a lowercase L, not the number 1.*
12)	A right curly brace ends the main method. It is important to balance all your left and right curly braces and left and right parentheses in all Java programs. The right curly brace is found 2 keys to the right of the P key on keyboard.
13)	A right curly brace to end the program.

8. This Java program needs compiled. Compiling a program will have the computer look at each line of your program for syntax errors such as typos, mispunctuation, etc. To compile your program, click on **Run** from the File menu, then **Build Project**. The compiler will check this file for syntax errors and let you know on what lines you made errors. Errors (along with line numbers of errors) will list in bottom panel of the screen. If you have errors, correct your typos on the top of the screen and compile again. Make sure you adjust the bottom output panel large enough to see your errors and your output.

9. If there are no compilation errors (denoted by the words BUILD SUCCESSFUL), the compiler will convert this Java program into a bytecode file called ***HelloWorld.class.*** This bytecode file is a generic file that may be used on any operating system. This file is located under the **project** folder, under the **build** folder, and in the **classes** folder.

```
Output - HelloWorld (jar)
To run this application from the command line without Ant, try:
java -jar "D:\HelloWorld\dist\HelloWorld.jar"
jar:
BUILD SUCCESSFUL (total time: 2 seconds)
```

10. Once compiled and you have a bytecode file (.*class* file extension), you are ready to have the Java interpreter execute your Java program. To execute your first Java program, you will click on **Run** from the NetBeans menu, then **Run Project**. "Hello World" should be displayed in the output window as shown below:

```
Output - HelloWorld (run)
run:
Hello World
BUILD SUCCESSFUL (total time: 1 second)
```

11. The process you have seen so far is typing a Java program into NetBeans, compiling a Java program, and executing the Java program. This is the process that you will be going through over and over as you progress through Java. The output that you have at bottom of screen is simply the computer displaying the words "Hello World".

12. Now, let's adjust the Java program. Add the following line as shown in the diagram below. *(Note: if you type **sout** and hit the **tab key**, it will type the **System.out.println("");** line for you.)*

System.out.println("Your name");

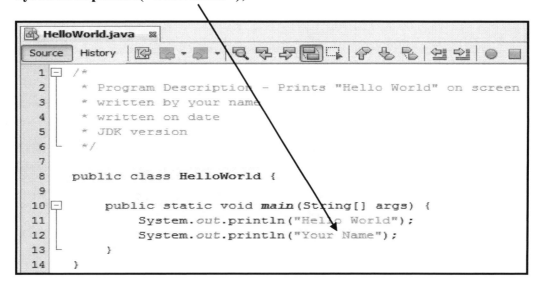

13. Now, save the new version of the program by clicking on **Save** from the File menu. (**DO NOT** click "Save As" and save this outside the project folder. NetBeans has a file structure and you cannot pull your files out of this structure or else NetBeans will not open them in the future. Compile the program (**Run** menu and then **Build Project**).

14. Execute the program (**Run** menu and then **Run Project**). Your display window should look similar to the following:

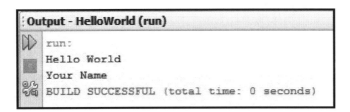

Note: If you are getting compiler errors at bottom of screen, please double check the capitalization, spelling, and punctuation.

15. To ensure that your code indentation is correct, you should always choose **Source** from the menu, then **Format**. Make sure that you compile your program (Run menu, Build Project) and run it (Run menu, Run Project).

16. Close the project by right clicking on the project on the left pane and choosing **Close**.

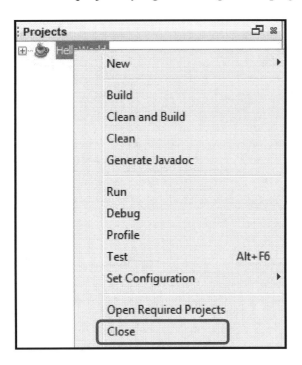

Exercise 3: Simple Java Debugging

1. Open up the NetBeans environment if you have exited.

2. Choose **File**, **Open Project...**, select the **HelloWorld** NetBeans project (should have a coffee cup next to your project), and click **Open Project**.

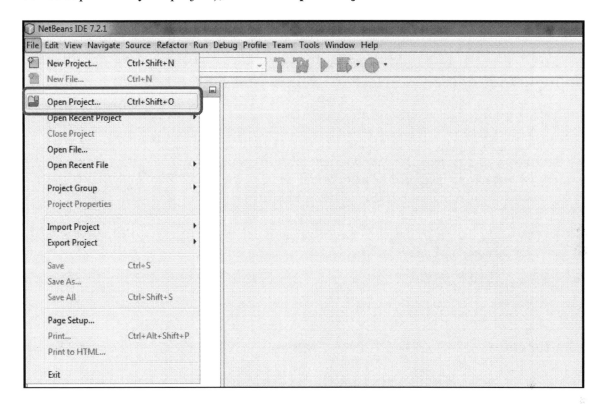

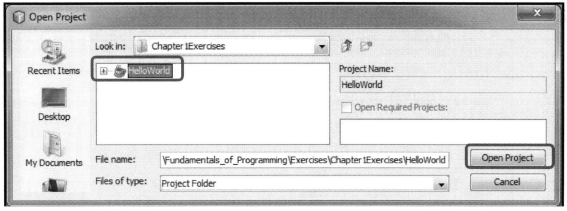

3. Open your code, by expanding the **HelloWorld project folder**, then expanding the **Source Package folder**, then expanding the **default package folder** *(this is default since we did not name this folder when we created the project)* as shown below. You will need to double click on the **HelloWorld.java** file to open the code.

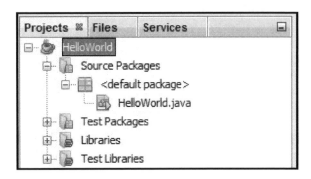

4. You will now purposely make some errors in your program. Change the spelling of **println** to be **printline** as follows:
    System.out.printline("Hello World");

5. Compile the program by clicking on **Run** menu and choosing **Build Project**. You should get an error at the bottom of your screen as follows:

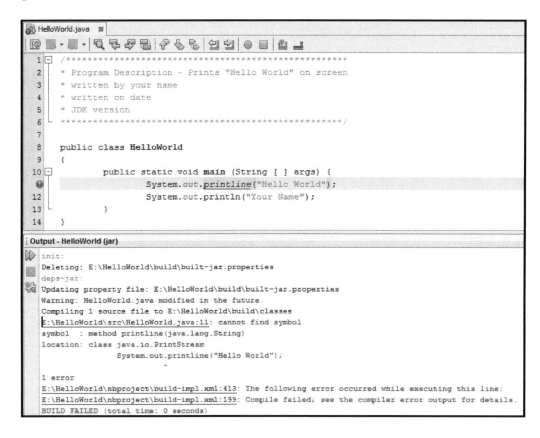

6. It is telling you that there is an error on line 11. It could not find a method spelled as **printline**. Some errors will be obvious and those are the nice ones to solve. Change the word **printline** to be **println** so that this error is corrected.

7. Compile the program. You should be rid of all errors and it should say BUILD SUCCESSFUL. Lesson learned: Names must be spelled exactly as Java expects.

8. Change line 11 by deleting the opening set of double quotes around Hello World as follows: **System.out.println(Hello World");**

9. Compile the program. You should get 3 errors at the bottom of your screen:

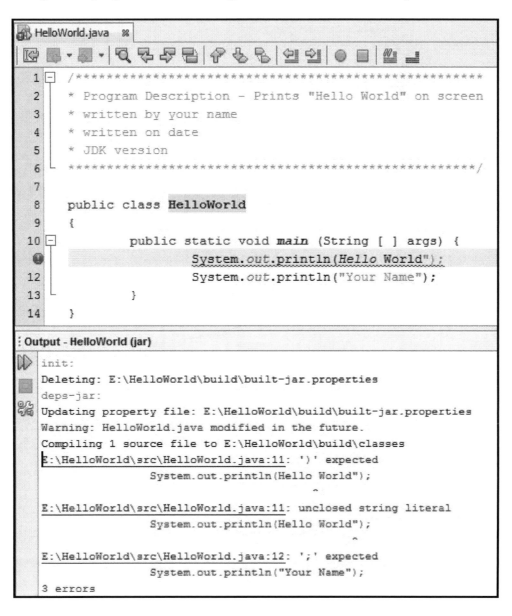

10. So, why would you get multiple error messages when you just made one mistake? This can happen. You may even get 15 errors for just one mistake. It really depends upon what mistake you make. In this case, it is saying it doesn't understand the Hello World and is saying it thinks it needs a parenthesis. This is not really the case. What it needs is a string enclosed in double quotes, but the error it shows is not real helpful. Now, insert the double quote back in front of the word *Hello*.

11. Compile the program. You should be rid of all errors. Lesson learned: The Java compiler doesn't always pinpoint the exact error. You must learn to look for errors anywhere on that line or previous line.

12. Not all errors are compilation errors. We now have a bug-free (no errors) Java program.

13. A programmer sometimes makes logic errors. Change line 11 to say:
System.out.println("Helo Warld");
Note: Hello and World are incorrectly spelled.

14. Compile the program. The program should get a compile with BUILD SUCCESSFUL. However, when this program is executed (RUN menu, then RUN MAIN PROJECT), you will not get the words displayed that you wanted. The reason that you get no errors in the compilation is because the words inside of double quotes can be anything. The computer has no idea what you are trying to accomplish. It will display anything that is in double quotes and doesn't check that part for incorrect spellings.

15. Please fix all of your errors and recompile. NetBeans automatically saves files when your project is compiled.

16. Close the HelloWorld project by right clicking on the project in the left pane as shown below:

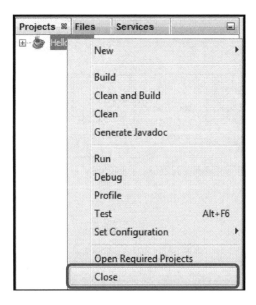

Exercise 4: Transitioning Alice to Java (ongoing exercise)

1. We already wrote the Alice code for the tea party in a previous exercise. Now let's see the Java code for this exercise using NetBeans. Open NetBeans if you have closed it.

2. Select **File** from the menu and then choose **New Project**. Then choose **Java Project from Existing Alice Project** as shown below. *(If this is not an option under the Java folder, then you need to install the Alice plugin for NetBeans from the install directions).*

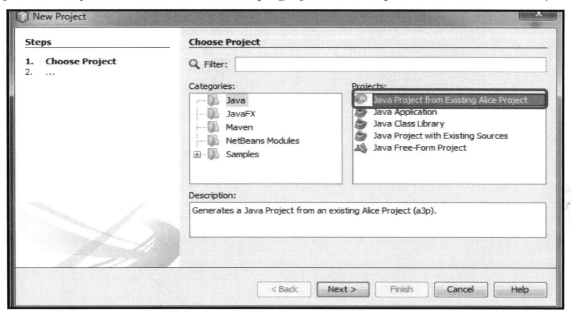

3. Select **Next**, Click the **Browse** button next to the Alice world and find where you saved your Alice TeaParty file; it should be in the Chapter1Exercises folder. Click **Browse** to change the location of where it is going to save the new project. You should save this in the same place as your Alice project under the **Chapter1Exercises** folder. Click **Finish**. It may take a few minutes to pull up the Java files.

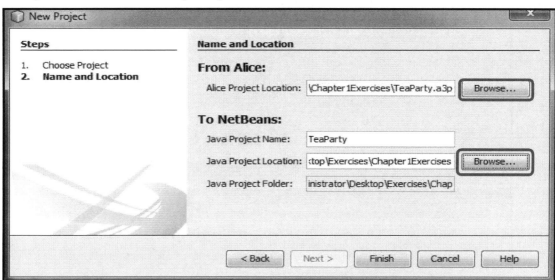

4. You should see the TeaParty project on the left hand side of the window. If you click the plus sign next to the TeaParty project, it will **expand** the **TeaParty folder** and you will see the folders inside of the project that are used to make the NetBeans project work. If you **expand** the **Source Packages folder** and the **default package folder**, you will see all of the Java files for your project. This may be overwhelming at first, but eventually it will make sense.

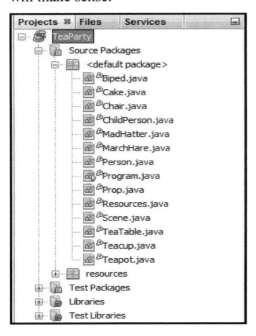

5. You should double click on the **Scene.java** file to open it up. This is where the code that we wrote in Alice will be. We wrote our Alice code in the myFirstMethod of the Scene tab. We are going to compare this Alice code with the NetBeans Java code.

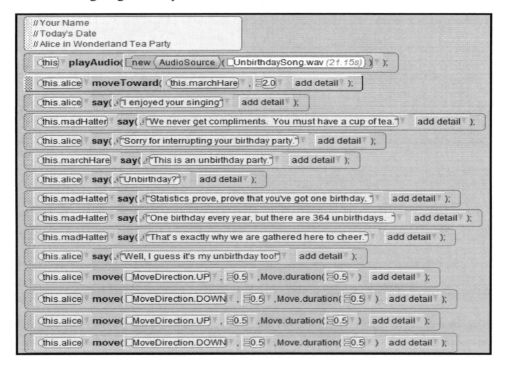

6. We are going to take a look at a few sections of this **Scene** file. The following code creates the objects for your scene.

```
private SGround ground = new SGround();
private SCamera camera = new SCamera();
private TeaTable teaTable = new TeaTable();
private Chair chair = new Chair(ChairResource.FANCY_COLONIAL_CHAIR_DINING_COLONIAL2_BLUESILK);
private Chair chair2 = new Chair(ChairResource.FANCY_COLONIAL_CHAIR_DINING_COLONIAL2_BLUESILK);
private Chair chair3 = new Chair(ChairResource.FANCY_COLONIAL_CHAIR_DINING_COLONIAL2_BLUESILK);
private Chair chair4 = new Chair(ChairResource.FANCY_COLONIAL_CHAIR_DINING_COLONIAL2_BLUESILK);
private Teapot teapot = new Teapot();
private Teacup teacup = new Teacup(TeacupResource.TEACUP_WHITE_RABBIT);
private Teacup teacup2 = new Teacup(TeacupResource.TEACUP_PLAYING_CARD);
private Teacup teacup3 = new Teacup(TeacupResource.TEACUP_MARCH_HARE);
private Cake cake = new Cake();
private MarchHare marchHare = new MarchHare();
private MadHatter madHatter = new MadHatter();
private ChildPerson alice = new ChildPerson(new ChildPersonResource(Gender.FEMALE, BaseSkinTone.LIGHTER,
        BaseEyeColor.LIGHT_BLUE, FemaleChildHairBraids.BLOND, 0.0, FemaleChildFullBodyOutfitDressAboveKne
```

7. The **myFirstMethod** is where the code that we added to Alice will be. The word **this** refers to the scene. The first statement is saying to use the playAudio method on the scene. The second statement is telling Java to use the moveToward method on alice from the scene. The marchHare from this scene is the first argument (what you want alice to move towards) and the 2.0 is the second argument (the distance that you want her to move towards the marchHare).

Note: If you are using a JDK earlier than 1.8, the Alice comments will not transfer into NetBeans.

```
public void myFirstMethod() {
    //Your name
    //Today's date
    //Alice in Wonderland Tea Party
    this.alice.playAudio(new AudioSource(Resources.UnbirthdaySong_wav));
    this.alice.moveToward(this.marchHare, 2.0);
    this.alice.say("I enjoyed your singing.");
    this.madHatter.say("We never get compliments. You must have a cup of tea.");
    this.alice.say("Sorry for interrupting your birthday party.");
    this.marchHare.say("This is an unbirthday party.");
    this.alice.say("Unbirthday?");
    this.madHatter.say("Statistics prove, prove that you've got one birthday. ");
    this.madHatter.say("One birthday every year, but there are 364 unbirthdays.");
    this.madHatter.say(" That's exactly why we are gathered here to cheer.");
    this.alice.say("Well I guess it's my unbirthday too!");
    this.alice.move(MoveDirection.UP, 0.5, Move.duration(0.5));
    this.alice.move(MoveDirection.DOWN, 0.5, Move.duration(0.5));
    this.alice.move(MoveDirection.UP, 0.5, Move.duration(0.5));
    this.alice.move(MoveDirection.DOWN, 0.5, Move.duration(0.5));
}
```

8. Add the following line of code to the end of myFirstMethod. You can see below that the end of the myFirstMethod is after the last move statement and before the ending curly brace for the method.

this.marchHare.say("The End!");

```
public void myFirstMethod() {
    //Your name
    //Today's date
    //Alice in Wonderland Tea Party
    this.alice.playAudio(new AudioSource(Resources.UnbirthdaySong_vav));
    this.alice.moveToward(this.marchHare, 2.0);
    this.alice.say("I enjoyed your singing.");
    this.madHatter.say("We never get compliments. You must have a cup of tea.");
    this.alice.say("Sorry for interrupting your birthday party.");
    this.marchHare.say("This is an unbirthday party.");
    this.alice.say("Unbirthday?");
    this.madHatter.say("Statistics prove, prove that you've got one birthday. ");
    this.madHatter.say("One birthday every year, but there are 364 unbirthdays.");
    this.madHatter.say(" That's exactly why we are gathered here to cheer.");
    this.alice.say("Well I guess it's my unbirthday too!");
    this.alice.move(MoveDirection.UP, 0.5, Move.duration(0.5));
    this.alice.move(MoveDirection.DOWN, 0.5, Move.duration(0.5));
    this.alice.move(MoveDirection.UP, 0.5, Move.duration(0.5));
    this.alice.move(MoveDirection.DOWN, 0.5, Move.duration(0.5));
    this.marchHare.say("The end.");
}
```

9. To test this animation, we will click on the **run** button on the menu in NetBeans. The run button is a shortcut way to save, compile, and run.

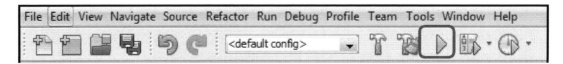

10. In this example the word **this** is optional (it refers to the scene). You can remove it if you find it confusing. Please see the code below. It is up to you if you want to leave it alone or remove it.

```
public void myFirstMethod() {
    //Your name
    //Today's date
    //Alice in Wonderland Tea Party
    alice.playAudio(new AudioSource(Resources.UnbirthdaySong_wav));
    alice.moveToward(marchHare, 2.0);
    alice.say("I enjoyed your singing.");
    madHatter.say("We never get compliments. You must have a cup of tea.");
    alice.say("Sorry for interrupting your birthday party.");
    marchHare.say("This is an unbirthday party.");
    alice.say("Unbirthday?");
    madHatter.say("Statistics prove, prove that you've got one birthday. ");
    madHatter.say("One birthday every year, but there are 364 unbirthdays.");
    madHatter.say(" That's exactly why we are gathered here to cheer.");
    alice.say("Well I guess it's my unbirthday too!");
    alice.move(MoveDirection.UP, 0.5, Move.duration(0.5));
    alice.move(MoveDirection.DOWN, 0.5, Move.duration(0.5));
    alice.move(MoveDirection.UP, 0.5, Move.duration(0.5));
    alice.move(MoveDirection.DOWN, 0.5, Move.duration(0.5));
    marchHare.say("The end.");
}
```

All of this code may seem overwhelming at first, but by the end of this class you will understand most of this code.

11. Run your program before exiting to save and test your changes.

Exercise 5: Alice Card Game Coding (ongoing exercise)

1. Open up Alice 3. Open the file named **CardGame** from the Chapter0Exercises or **MyCardGame** from the Chapter 0 Assignments. In Chapter 0, you set up a Card Game scene as follows:

2. Go to Setup Scene. Some items will need to be adjusted before beginning the playing of the game. The two win signs and the cones need to be made invisible. Choose the **winPlayer1Sign** object on the right side of panel by choosing TextModel and then winPlayer1Sign as follows:

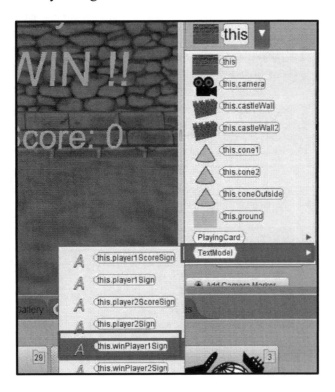

3. The WIN sign on left side of screen should be showing as selected. Change the **opacity** to be **0.0**

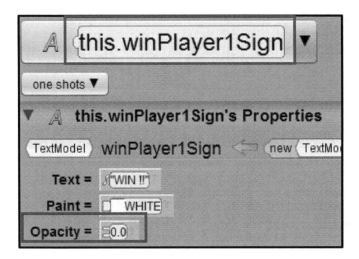

   This will cause the WIN sign to disappear on left side.

4. Select the **winPlayer2Sign** and set its **opacity** to **0.0**. Both WIN signs should now be invisible. Select the **cone1** object and set its **opacity** to **0.0** so that the left cone disappears. It is still there but invisible. Select the **cone2** object and set its opacity to **0.0** so that the right cone disappears. Our game is now ready for code. Click on EDIT CODE button to take you back to main screen.

5. Save the new version of this file in the **Chapter1Exercises** folder instead of the Chapter0Exercises folder. Click on **File** from the menu, then **Save As**, locate the **Chapter1Exercises** folder, and save this file as **CardGame**.

6. Before writing the code for card game, we should first create a storyboard of what we wish to accomplish.

   - Scene opens with the CardGame
   - Player cards are dealt out onto screen
   - Display winner
   - Have these cards disappear
   - New Player cards are dealt out on screen
   - Deteremine and display winner
   - Have these cards disappear

7. Every program you write should begin with comments for documentation. Drag the **//comment** block to the editor and enter your comments. You need to put your name, the date, and a description of the program at the top of all of your programs.

```
do in order
    // Card Game created by
    // on date here
    // This program will deal out cards, display winner, and then cards disappear
```

8. Our scene is complete, so we will move to the next task: "Player cards are dealt out onto screen." This will involve several steps so we will break this down into more detailed steps. This process is called stepwise refinement.

> Player Cards are dealt out onto screen
> - Make an announcement that cards will now be dealt out
> - Playing card for player 1 moves from off screen to cone1 marker
> - Playing card for player 2 moves from off screen to cone 2 marker

9. Grouping sections of program together will make the program more understandable. Therefore, we will begin a new section of code by dragging a DO IN ORDER to our program and then adding a comment to this section stating that this is the deal out cards section.

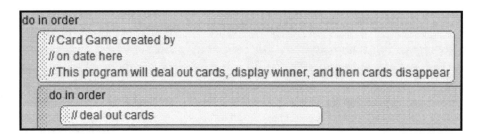

```
do in order
    // Card Game created by
    // on date here
    // This program will deal out cards, display winner, and then cards disappear
    do in order
        // deal out cards
```

10. To make the announcement that cards will now be dealt out, we will choose any object on the scene and choose the **say** procedure. The custom **TextString** should be **DEAL OUT THE CARDS PLEASE!**

The following statement has the castleWall2 displaying the words. It also has the added detail of duration of 3 seconds.

```
do in order
    // deal out cards
    this.castleWall2  say  DEAL OUT THE CARDS PLEASE !  , duration  3.0   add detail
```

11. Click on **Run** button in upper left corner to see the animation so far.

12. A playing card needs to be dealt out onto the screen. We have 10 cards so we will just arbitrarily pick to deal out card 8 to player1. It should move out to our invisible marker of cone1. To choose playingCard8, you will need to click on the down arrow of the object list, choose PlayingCard, and then choose **this.playingCard8** as follows:

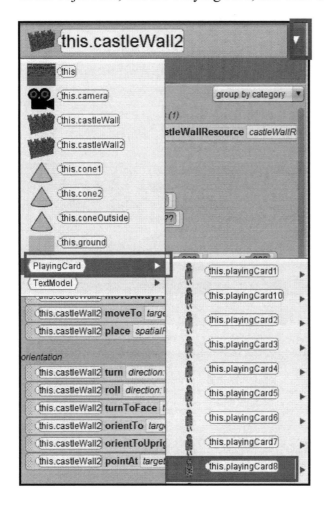

13. Once the **playingCard8** is selected. Choose the **procedure** of **moveTo** and drag it to the coding area. It will ask you what you are moving to and you should choose **cone1**. The statement should be placed in the inner DO IN ORDER block and look as follows:

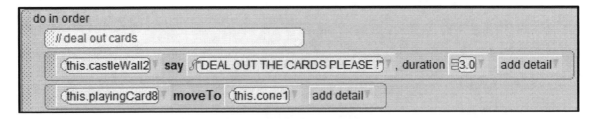

14. A second card should be dealt out for player2. Arbitrarily, we will choose **playingCard3**. Select playingCard3 as your object and then choose the **moveTo** procedure. Choose to move to **cone2**. The program should look as follows:

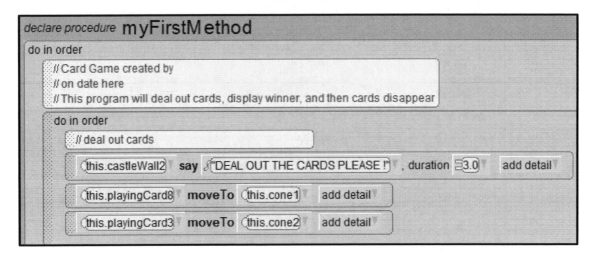

15. Click on the RUN button to see the animation play. If done correctly, an object should say "DEAL OUT THE CARDS PLEASE!", then playingCard8 will appear on screen, and then playingCard3 will appear on screen. Make adjustments to your program if it isn't working correctly.

16. In the storyboard, the next task is "display winner" as seen below:

- Scene opens with the CardGame
- Player cards are dealt out onto screen
- Display winner
- Have these cards disappear
- New Player cards are dealt out on screen
- Deteremine and display winner
- Have these cards disappear

17. Let's break that down into the several steps it will take to display winner.

> Display winner
> * Flash the WIN sign for player 1
> * Change the score for player 1

18. To flash the WIN sign for player 1 (named as winPlayer1Sign), we will have it show on screen (opacity of 1) and then disappear (opacity of 0) and do this process three times. Set the object to be the TextModel of **winPlayer1Sign** as follows:

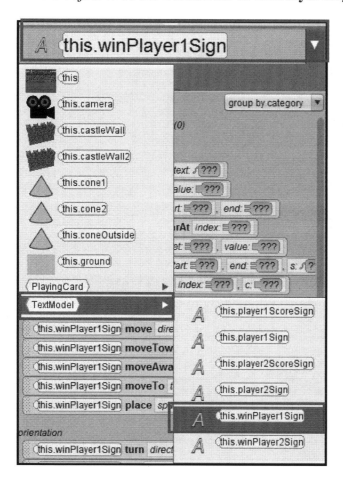

19. Drag a DO IN ORDER block to the program. Drag up a comment line and state that this section of program is to determine and display winner.

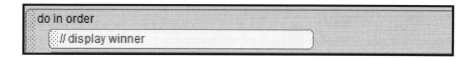

20. In the procedures, drag the **setOpacity** method to the editor. Set the **opacity** to be **1.0**. This makes the WIN sign display on the screen. To make it then disappear, you would drag the setOpacity method to the editor and set it to 0.0. (You can also copy these tiles by holding down the CTRL key and dragging the tile down to empty area). You should continue to have the opacity of this sign change between 1.0 and 0.0. This will cause a flashing effect. You may also change the duration of each to less than 2 seconds to make it flash quicker. In addition, you can add more copies of the statements to make it flash more often. The following shows this section of the code with a one second duration for each statement and flashing 3 times:

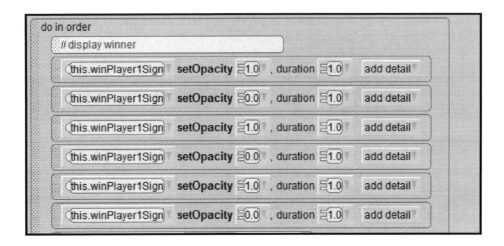

21. In this section, the score also needs to be changed. The player 1 score sign was named player1ScoreSign and is a TextModel. Set the object to be:

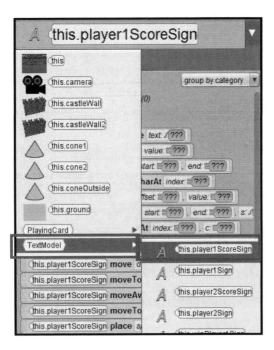

22. Once the player1ScoreSign is the selected object. Drag the **setValue** procedure to the program. It will ask what the value should be and choose **Custom TextString** and then type in **Score: 1** in the window as follows:

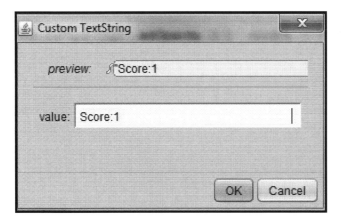

23. The above will produce an Alice statement that will make the score appear to be 1. The entire program should look as follows:

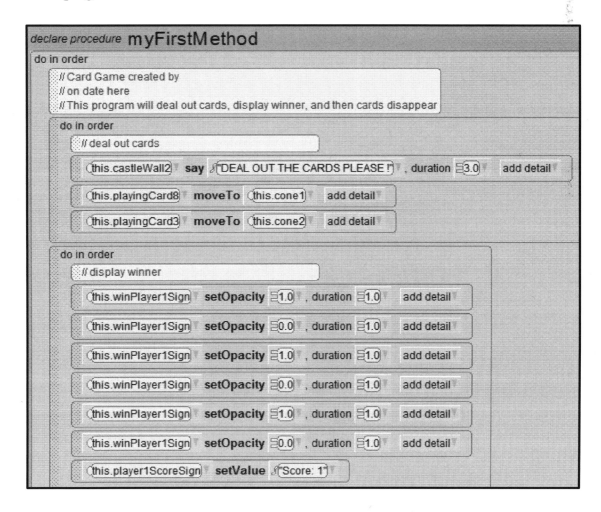

24. Run the animation to see how well the program is working. The program should deal out the cards, the WIN sign should flash for player 1 and then the score for player 1 should change to 1. If your program is not working, you will need to review the above statements and make adjustments to make it work.

25. Reviewing the storyboard, we move on to the next task, which is "Have these cards disappear."

> - Scene opens with the CardGame
> - Player cards are dealt out onto screen
> - Display winner
> - Have these cards disappear
> - New Player cards are dealt out on screen.
> - Deteremine and display winner
> - Have these cards disappear

26. We have to think which steps are involved in making the cards disappear. We would like the cards to spin and then move off the screen to their original location. Let's break this section down as:

> Have the cards disappear.
> - Make the player1's card spin
> - Make the player1's card return to stack of cards
> - Make the player2's card spin
> - Have the player2's card return to stack of cards

27. Let's start a new DO IN ORDER block and drag a comment tile up to the block that states that this section makes the cards disappear:

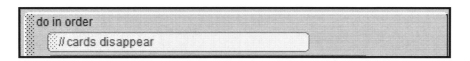

28. Set the object to be **playingCard8** since that is player1's card. Drag the **turn** procedure to the editor and choose for a **LEFT** with a rotation of **8.0**. Also, for this same object, drag the **moveTo** procedure to the editor and choose to have it move to **coneOutside**. These 2 statements will make the left card on screen spin around 8 times then move back to original stack of cards on left side. The statements should be:

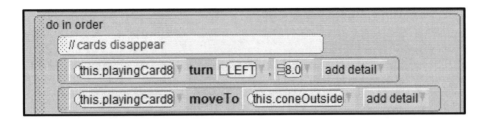

29. Run the program to see that everything is working. Change to **playerCard3** and drag the **turn** procedure to the program and make it turn 8 revolutions to the LEFT. Drag the **moveTo** procedure to the program and tell it to move to the coneOutside. You should now have the following:

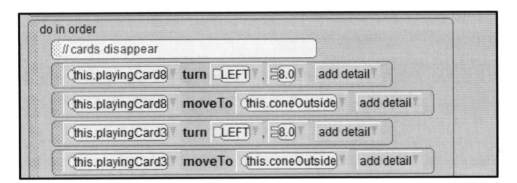

30. Run the program and make sure it is working correctly. Both cards that were dealt out, should now disappear. They are returning to the stack of cards, but you won't be able to see that.

31. Since we will be adding more sections to continue this game, we would like to have a 4 second pause here in this section before it begins the game again. This is done with a delay. Change the object to the ground. You will see that there are very few procedures for the ground. One of them is a delay. Drag the **delay** procedure to the bottom of the DO IN ORDER for this section. When asked for a number, choose **Custom Decimal Number** and then choose **4** on the calculator and press OK. This means there will be a 4 second delay before we begin the game again.

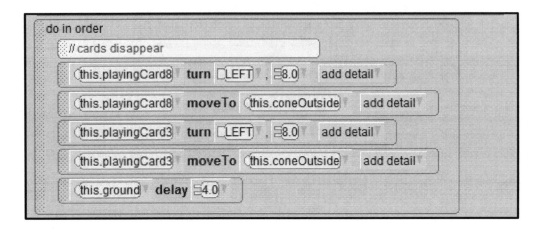

32. We would like to play the game again with player 2 winning. We will arbitrarily choose for playingCard1 to be dealt to player1 and playingCard10 to be dealt to player2 so that player2 has the higher card and will win. Let's review the original storyboard and see where we are:

    - Scene opens with the CardGame
    - Player cards are dealt out onto screen
    - Display winner
    - Have these cards disappear
    - New Player cards are dealt out on screen
    - Deteremine and display winner
    - Have these cards disappear

33. We will duplicate previous sections of this program by copying/pasting them. In later chapters you will learn better ways of doing this, but for now the copy/paste will work fine. The first section to be duplicated will be the "deal out cards" section. Hold down the CTRL key *(alt/option key on the Mac)* and drag the entire "deal out cards" DO IN

    ORDER BLOCK to the Clipboard in upper right corner. ▮ If you don't hold down the CTRL key, it will cut the block of code instead of copying it. If you hover over the clipboard, it will turn green when the copy/cut is successful. Then drag the clipboard to the bottom of the programming area. If everything is done correctly, you should have a deal out cards block at the beginning of the program and a copy of it at the bottom of the program.

34. The lines in the new block at bottom of program, need to be adjusted. Why? We no longer want to use playingCards 8 and 3. We want player 2 to win with playingCard10 and we want player 1 to have playingCard1. Adjust the lines in bottom section so that you click on arrow next to playingCard8 and change it to playingCard1. Adjust the line referring to playingCard3 to refer to playingCard10.

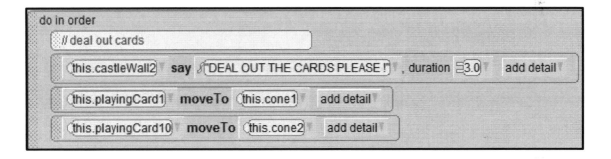

35. Run the program to see if the 2 cards in the second game are dealt out correctly.

36. According to the storyboard, our next step is to "Display winner". We have this already programmed into a block of code that we can copy and adjust. CTRL and drag the entire "display winner" DO IN ORDER BLOCK to the Clipboard. Then drag the copy of this section to the bottom of the editor.

37. This section will need adjusted. Look at the statements and try to decide what should change. Player1 has a 1 and Player2 has a 10. Player2 should win this time. You will need to adjust the setOpacity statements to refer to winPlayer2Sign. This is done by clicking the down arrow next to winPlayer1Sign and choosing winPlayer2Sign from the dropdown list.

38. The last statement of this section changes the score but without adjustment, it changes the score for Player1. We need to change the score for Player 2. Thus, in the last statement, adjust the player1ScoreSign, by clicking on the down arrow next to it, and choosing player2ScoreSign from the dropdown list. The entire new section should now appear as follows:

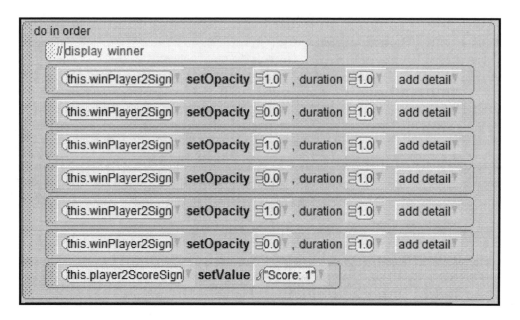

39. Run the program to see if the WIN sign flashes for player 2 in the second game. Did the score change for player 2 also?

40. The last task of the storyboard is to have these last 2 cards disappear. Again, we have that code in an earlier section commented as "cards disappear". Copy that section to the clipboard by using the CTRL key. Drag the copy to the bottom of the editor.

41. What needs adjusted? THINK! These statements are referring to playingCard8 and playingCard3 because that is what they were in the first game. However, in this second game, the playing cards used were playingCard1 and playingCard10. Adjust those lines respectively so that you have the following:

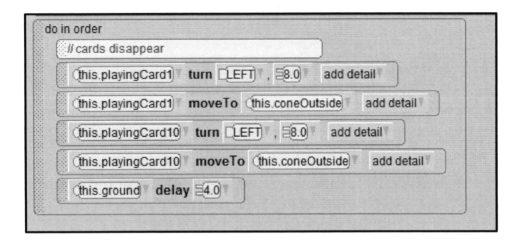

42. The complete program is as follows:

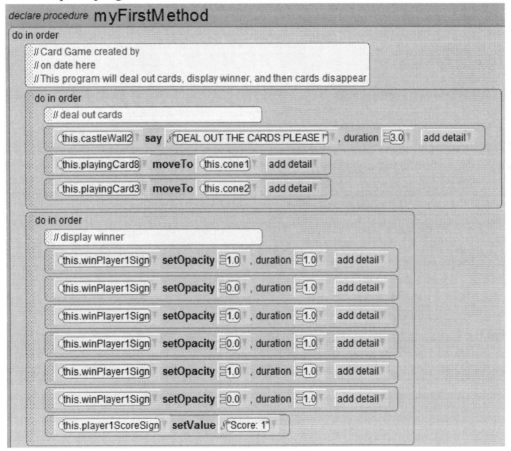

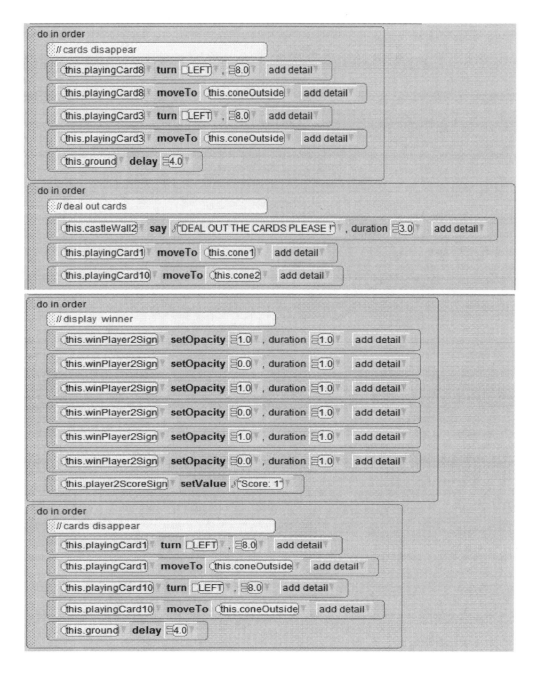

43. This exercise allowed you to set up an animated card game with the 2 players. The player dealt the higher card wins. We executed the first game with player1 winning and second game with player2 winning. You should run this program and make sure everything is working.

44. Make sure to save this file as **CardGame** in **Chapter1Exercises** folder. You can practice coding by adding other elements to this program but make sure you save your practice with a different filename so that you have the completed version for future projects.

Summary

- Line by line instructions that tell a computer how to perform a task is called a **computer program**.
- A programming language that is written at the very low technical circuitry level of the computer is called a **low-level programming language**.
- **High-level programming languages** allow programmers to write programs using English terms.
- James Gosling at Sun Microsystems is credited with creating Java programming language. It was brought to public in 1995.
- Java is an object-oriented programming language that is platform-independent. The Java slogan is "You can write once and run anywhere." The compiler creates a bytecode file (with class extension) that can be used on all types of computer systems (MAC, Linux, Windows, etc.) Bytecode is then fed to a Java Virtual Machine (JVM) where they are interpreted and executed.
- Computer languages each have their own **syntax**, or rules of the language.
- When you write a program, indenting is important so that you and other humans can understand your program.
- In every program that you write, there should be comment lines at beginning of program. There should be a description of the program, author (you), date, and the JDK used for the program.
- Compilation error messages try to pinpoint the problem in your program but they are not always helpful. You may have to look around for the error or correct just the errors that you do understand and then compile again. You will get better at doing this and understanding this with additional experience.
- If your program is compiling fine, there still is no guarantee that it will work. An error-free compilation program only means that the Java compiler understands your commands, but the commands may not do what you want.
- The curly braces in Java are crucial. The symbols { } are generally found to the right of the "P" key.
- Programming can be very frustrating but it also can be rewarding when you succeed.

Review Questions

1. JDK stands for:
    a. Java Details Kit
    b. Java Development Kit
    c. Java Decoder Kit
    d. Java Debugger Kit

2. All programming languages work on the Internet.
    a. True
    b. False

3. Java and JavaScript are the same programming language.
    a. True
    b. False

4. There are many high-level programming languages for computers.
    a. True
    b. False

5. The rules of a programming language are its _____.
    a. Vocabulary
    b. Syntax
    c. Logic
    d. Flowchart

6. Arguments to methods appear within
    a. Parentheses
    b. Semicolons
    c. Curly braces
    d. Quotation marks

7. All Java application programs must have a method called _____.
    a. hello
    b. system
    c. main
    d. Java

8. Non-executing program statements that provide documentation to humans are called _____.
    a. Notes
    b. Classes
    c. Commands
    d. Comments

9. Once a program has compiled without errors, it will always execute perfectly.
    a. True
    b. False

10. A computer _____ tells a computer how to perform a task.
    a. Switch
    b. Program
    c. Interface
    d. Guide

11. Look at the Java program at the top of the following illustration. This Java program was compiled and the compilation errors appear at bottom of screen. What needs to be corrected to make this program compile correctly?

```
Start Page  x    Error1.java  x

1    public class Error1 {
2
3        public static void main(String[] args) {
             system.out.println("First Java Program");
5        }
6    }
```

    a. Change line 1 to say *FirstJavaProgram* instead of *Error1*
    b. Change line 3 to say *first* instead of *main*
    c. Change line 4 to say **System** instead of **system**
    d. Change line 4 to say "*Hello World*" instead of "*First Java Program*"

12. Look at the Java program at the top of the following illustration. This Java program was compiled and the Compilation errors appear at bottom of screen. What needs to be corrected to make this program compile correctly.

```
Start Page  x    Error1.java  x

1    public class Error1 {
2
3        public static void main(String[] args) {
             System.out.println("First Java Program")
5        }
6    }
```

    a. Change line 1 to have semicolon at end of it.
    b. Change line 3 to have semicolon at end of it.
    c. Change line 4 to have semicolon at end of it.
    d. Change line 5 to have semicolon at end of it.

Solutions: *1) b   2) b   3) b   4) a   5) b   6) a   7) c   8) d   9) b   10) b   11) c   12) c*

Assignments

1-1   **Cola Commercial**: Your goal is to create a cola commercial using Alice and NetBeans.

- *Analyze and understand the problem to be solved.* We would like to create a cola commercial animation that is at least 5 seconds long. We need to take a look at the gallery to see what objects we have that could be used in our commercial. Then we need to set up the scene. You may have created the scene in chapter 0.

- *Develop the logic to solve the program.* We should develop a storyboard for our animation. The storyboard is a short description of what you want to happen in your animation.

- *Code the solution in a programming language.* Write the code in Alice. Give the file an appropriate name. Add your name, date, and a description of the program to the top of the program as comments.

- *Test the program.* Test the code in Alice.

1-2   **Greeting Card**: Your goal is to create an animated greeting card using Alice and NetBeans.

- *Analyze and understand the problem to be solved.* We would like to create a greeting card animation that is at least 5 seconds long. We need to take a look at the gallery to see what objects we have that could be used in our commercial. Then we need to set up the scene. You may have created the scene in chapter 0.

- *Develop the logic to solve the program.* We should develop a storyboard for our animation. The storyboard is a short description of what you want to happen in your animation.

- *Code the solution in a programming language.* Write the code in Alice. Give the file an appropriate name. Add your name, date, and a description of the program to the top of the program as comments.

- *Test the program.* Test the code in Alice.

1-3   Animation: Your goal is to create a short animation using Alice and NetBeans.

- ***Analyze and understand the problem to be solved.*** We would like to create a short animation of our choosing that is at least 5 seconds long. We need to take a look at the gallery to see what objects we have that could be used in our commercial. Then we need to set up the scene. You may have created the scene in chapter 0.

- ***Develop the logic to solve the program.*** We should develop a storyboard for our animation. The storyboard is a short description of what you want to happen in your animation.

- ***Code the solution in a programming language.*** Write the code in Alice. Give the file an appropriate name. Add your name, date, and a description of the program to the top of the program as comments.

- ***Test the program.*** Test the code in Alice.

1-4   Card Game adjusted: Your goal is to change the CardGame created in exercise 5 of this chapter to have the playing cards dance out onto the screen by using some hand movements or some leg movements.

- ***Analyze and understand the problem to be solved.*** We would like to create a short animation to have the playing cards dance out onto the screen by using some hand movements or some leg movements. We already have the playing card objects in the scene. Only the "deal Out Cards" code section should be changed.

- ***Develop the logic to solve the program.*** We should develop a storyboard for our animation. The storyboard is a short description of what you want to happen in your animation.

- ***Code the solution in a programming language.*** Write the code in Alice. Save this file as **MyCardGame**. Add your name, date, and a description of the program to the top of the program as comments.

- ***Test the program.*** Test the code in Alice.

1-5 **Printing Initials:** Your goal is to print your initials in block letters. In this exercise, instead of just keying in a program, we will learn the entire programming process to solve a problem. Programming is more than just keying in computer programs and testing them. Most programmers must go through a process to logically solve a problem or obtain a goal. The steps involved in computer programming are:

- *Analyze and understand the problem to be solved.* In this case, we would like the computer to display your initials in block letters. For example, if your initials were "YN" it would look as follows:

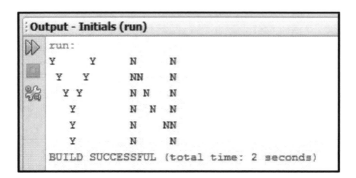

- *Develop the logic to solve the program.* We know how to print characters on a line and the above looks like to could consist of several print statements. We can graph the block letters on graph paper, so we can see the spacing. The letters should be about 7 by 7 characters wide and have 5 spaces in between letters.

Below is a blank grid so that you can draw your initials.

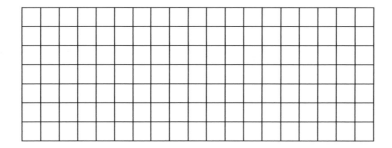

Sample solution for initials YN (your name). You should not use YN unless your initials are YN.

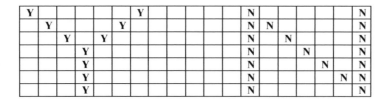

- *Code the solution in a programming language.* We will need to code 7 print statements to accomplish the above graphic of the "YN" block letters. The spacing in these *System.out.println* statements must be perfect. Here is the Java code.

```java
/*****************************************************
 * This is a simple Java program to print block letters
 * written by your name
 * written on date
 * JDK version
 *****************************************************/

public class Initials
{
        public static void main (String [ ] args)
        {

                System.out.println("Y     Y     N     N");
                System.out.println(" Y   Y      NN    N");
                System.out.println("  Y Y       N N   N");
                System.out.println("   Y        N  N  N");
                System.out.println("   Y        N   NN");
                System.out.println("   Y        N     N");

        } //ends the main method
} // ends program
```

Enter the coded solution into a new project in NetBeans. Name this project **Initials**.

- *Test the program.* Translate the program into the language understood by the computer. The Java compiler will do this. When you run your program, it is compiled and a bytecode class file is created if there aren't any syntax errors. This bytecode file may be used on any operating system. Once you have a bytecode file, you will see the results of your program. If you have syntax errors, you will need to fix these errors before running your program (red underlines throughout your code).

```
Output - Initials (run)
run:
Y     Y     N     N
 Y   Y      NN    N
  Y Y       N N   N
   Y        N  N  N
   Y        N   NN
   Y        N     N
BUILD SUCCESSFUL (total time: 2 seconds)
```

Now, it is your turn to go through the programming process above and create block letters of YOUR initials.

Chapter 2

Variables

Java Variables

Data can be categorized as constant or variable. Data is **constant** when it can't be changed after the program compiles. Data is **variable** when it might change after the program compiles. In Algebra, we assign the letters x, n, and y to represent unknowns. In programming, we call these variables and assign these variables longer and more meaningful names. **Variables** are locations in memory in which values can be stored.

Computer programs are generic instructions written to tell the computers how to accomplish a task such as make change for a customer or make paychecks for employees. The same computer instructions must be flexible to make change for various customers or print paychecks for a variety of employees. Since you will be using the same computer instructions to calculate everyone's paycheck, you would not refer to a person's gross pay as 400.57 because that would only be correct for one employee. Therefore, we must use variable names to describe the data instead of exact numbers. For instance, in a payroll program, you might refer to a person's gross pay as *grossPay* or *gp* or *gross_pay*. **Variables have a type, name, and a value.**

Naming Variables

When selecting a name for a Java variable, you must follow the following syntactical and stylistic rules:

- Variable names **consists of letters, digits, underscores (_) or $** (no spaces allowed).
- The **first character** can't be a digit. (First character is generally lowercase letter.)
- Variable names **can be any length, but extremely short or long names are awkward.**
- **A stylistic rule is to begin all variable names with a lowercase letter and following words have an initial uppercase letter** such as *theButton*, *grossPay*, or *myAge* (This is a style standard. Java will accept variable names with any capitalization, but teachers won't!)
- Another stylistic rule is that **variable names should be meaningful**. The variable name of *h* means very little while the variable name of *regularHours* says quite a bit. Teachers will demand that you do this!
- Java is **case sensitive** so that *number* and *Number* and *NUMBER* are different variables to the computer.
- NOTE: **class names** follow same rules as variable names except they **must begin with capital letter.**
- You **cannot use keywords** as variables. Please see list below:

abstract	catch	do	final	implements	long	private	static	throw	while
Boolean	char	double	finally	import	native	protected	super	throws	
break	class	else	float	instanceof	new	public	switch	true	
byte	continue	extends	for	int	null	return	synchronized	try	
case	default	false	if	interface	package	short	this	void	

Variable Name	Valid or Invalid and Why?
grossPay	Valid
Hourly wages	Invalid - Shouldn't begin with capital and spaces aren't allowed
card-game	Invalid - Hyphen (-) is not allowed
total2	Valid
totalscore	Invalid - Java will accept it but it should be totalScore
grand_Total	Valid
java	Valid - Yes, java is not a keyword and is perfectly fine
dollars$	Valid

Using Primitive Data Types

Every variable that you want to use in a Java computer program must be declared with a type so that the computer knows what kind of data to expect. Primitives are your basic type of data. **There are 4 integer primitives (byte, short, int and long), 2 decimal number primitives (float and double), Boolean (true and false), and char (single characters).** The two most common primitives that you should get to know are int for integers and double for decimal numbers. The following is a list of all 8 primitive types, their sizes, and samples of how to declare those types of variables.

Type	Size	Range	Sample
byte (integer)	8 bits	-128 to 127	byte numberOfChildren;
short (integer)	16 bits	-32768 to 32767	short age;
int (integer)	32 bits	-2,147,483,648 to 2,147,483,647	int counter;
long (integer)	64 bits	-9223372036854775808 to 9223372036854775807	long debt;
float (floating point)	32 bits single precision	-3.4028235E+38 to +3.4028235E+38 (7 digits precision)	float rate;
double (floating point)	64 bits double precision	-1.7976931348623157E+308 to +1.7976931348623157E+308 (16 digits precision)	double tax;
char	16 bits unsigned	one character using Unicode system	char answer='Y';
boolean	8 bits	true or false	boolean reply=false;

Declaring Variables

Before you can use a variable, you have to declare it with a type. A primitive variable should only be declared once in a program. Therefore, variables are usually declared at the beginning of a class. For example: **int number;**

The above example sets up a variable to be called *number*. This number will be a primitive of type int. This means that *number* can only be whole numbers between: -2,147,483,648 and 2,147,483,647. The above sample declares the variable called *number* but does not start it with any specific value.

Assigning Values to Variables

You can declare a variable and initialize it (give it a value) at the same time. For example:

int number = 15;

The above example sets up a variable to be called *number* and it will be a primitive of type int. This means that *number* can only be whole numbers between -2,147,483,648 and 2,147,483,647. However, the above statement goes one step further and sets the value of the variable to be 15.

You can declare multiple variable names of same type by separating with commas such as:

int x, y, z;

The above example sets up 3 variables to be called x, y and z. All 3 variables are to be primitives of type int. None of the variables have been set to any values.

You can also declare multiple variable names of same type and initialize the variables in the same statement as follows:

int age = 30, hours = 45, sum =0;

The above example sets up 3 variables called age, hours, and sum to all be primitive ints. It also declares each one to have a different value with age being set to 30, hours being set to 45 and sum being set to 0. The preferred method of declaring variables is to declare them on separate lines so that they may easily be commented as follows:

int age = 30;   // age is the employee age
int hours = 45;   // hours is the employee weekly hours worked
int sum = 0;   // sum is the total of all hours worked

Values may be assigned to variables when they are declared or they may be assigned to variables as needed later in program. **Numeric variables** can be assigned values by setting them equal to a number. Most Java programmers make numeric variables either int (whole numbers without decimal point) or double (numbers with decimal points). These two primitive types are easily assigned values simply by setting them equal to an appropriate number such as:

```
int   x = 12;        // sets x to integer of 12.
double   z = 14.5;   // sets z to 14.5 which is a double
```

An error will show if you try to assign a number with a decimal point to an integer type variable such as:

```
int y = 18.5;   // ERROR!!
```

Besides the int and double variable primitive types, there are other numeric types. They are rarely used but should be explained. In Java, the computer automatically makes any whole number without a decimal point have the type of *int*. It will automatically make any number with a decimal point have the type of *double*. If you declare a variable with a type other than int or double, you will need to attach a letter to the numeric constant or you will get an error. For instance, if you declare the variable called "a" to be a float and want to assign it the value of 100.98 you would need to write it as:

```
float a = 100.98F;  // assigns 100.98 to the float variable of a
float a = 100.98f;  // same as above except you can use f or F
```

If you try to assign 100.98 to the variable "a" without the "f" on the end of the number, you will get a compiler error. This is because 100.98 is a double constant by default and the Java compiler will not let you assign a double constant to a float variable. Because of the hassle of assigning values to primitives other than ints and doubles, the other numeric primitives are rarely used.

A **Boolean** variable can be assigned the values of true or false such as:

```
Boolean x = true;   // assigns the value true to the variable called x
```

A **char** variable can be assigned a value expressed by a single character surrounded by single quotes such as:

```
char myLetter = 'A';  //assigns the character A to variable called myLetter
```

String Variables

If you need to represent a series of characters instead of just one character, we represent a series of characters with a **String.** Strings of characters are very useful in programming languages so that we may display messages, input text, etc. A string may include letters, digits and various special characters. **A String is not a primitive variable but is considered to be an object variable in Java.** Java string literals are written as a sequence of characters in double quotes. Some examples of strings are as follows:

>   "John Doe"
>   "219 Grant Street"

Strings are declared and assigned values as follows:

>   **String message;**   // declare a string called message here
>   **String message = "Go Cougars!!!!";**   // declared and assigned value

String Concatenation: The + operator, when used with strings and other objects, creates a single string that contains the concatenation (combining) of all its operands. The "+" symbol when used with Strings does NOT mean to do arithmetic.

You would guess that the following statement prints: *The total is 35*
It really prints: *The total is 2510 because it concatenates the 25+10*

>   **System.out.println("The total is " + 25 + 10);**

 If you wanted to do arithmetic, you would need to use parenthesis around your equation.

>   **System.out.println("The total is " + (25+10));**

The following Java statement automatically converts the number that is in the variable called total to be part of the entire String because of concatenation (+).

>   **double total = 50.95;**
>   **System.out.println ("The total is " + total) ;**

The above statements will cause the computer to display:

>   **The total is 50.95**

You must be careful to include a space before the ending double quote mark so that a space will display after the word "is" and before the actual number.

Java Basics

Statements

A statement is the simplest thing you can do in Java. A Java statement forms a single Java operation. Each statement generally ends with a semicolon. A block of statements are surrounded by curly braces { }. Some samples of statements are as follows:

int i; //declares variable i to be integer
i = a + 1; // this is an arithmetic statement
System.out.println("Hello World"); // this is a print statement

Escape Codes

Printing of strings in a Java application is done with *System.out.println*. A *System.out.println* statement goes to a new line before printing whatever String is inside parenthesis. A *System.out.print* remains on the same line and prints the next information on same line. With these two Java statements you can use escape codes to make the computer tab over spaces, form feed, etc. Some of the escape codes are as follows:

\n   Newline
\t   Tab
\b   Backspace
\f   Form feed
\\   Displays a Backslash
\'   Displays a single quote
\"   Displays a double quote

Strings can contain character escape codes such as the " (double quote) or ' (single quote) by including a backslash in front of it as:

System.out.println("I am going to earn an \"A\" in this course");

The above sample will print:

I am going to earn an "A" in this course.

The **\"** tells it to print the special character of a double quotes.

Precedence Rules

The five standard arithmetic operators are + for addition, - for subtraction, * for multiplication, / for division and % for modulus. When these operators are combined to make a formula, Java follows a set of rules called precedence to determine which operations get done first. The order of operations of arithmetic is as follows:

1. Innermost parentheses are done first. If the parentheses are on same level, the formula inside of the leftmost parenthesis is done first. If the parenthesis are nested (one inside another), the formula inside of the innermost parenthesis is done first.
2. Multiplication (*), division (/), and modulus (%) are done from left to right. These three operators are all on same level so they are done in the order that they are encountered from left to right.
3. Addition (+) and subtraction (-) are all on same level and done from left to right in order that they are encountered.
4. Assignment operator (=). Places result in variable on left side of = sign.

Note: Modulus (%) is the remainder of the division.

Examples

Let's look at some examples to see how the rules of precedence work. The first example is:

Example 1:	y = 3 + 4* 2;	4* 2 because * is done before any +
	y = 3 + 8	3 + 8 because all * / % are done
	y = 11	result is placed into y
Example 2:	x = 15 / 3 + (1 + 2) * 4	1+2 because of parenthesis
	x = 15 / 3 + 3 * 4	15/3 because of division & leftmost in equation
	x = 5 + 3 * 4	3*4 because multiplication is before +
	x = 5 + 12	5+12 because all * / % are done
	x = 17	17 is placed into x

The rules of order of precedence are the same in all programming languages since the rule of hierarchy of order or precedence is a rule of Mathematics. However, there is one tricky rule that is somewhat unique to Java. When you are working with integer numbers in Java, the result of the intermediate operation will always be an integer. This doesn't have an impact on addition, subtraction, or multiplication. However, it does have an impact on division. When you divide two integers, whether they are integer constants or integer variables, the result is an integer. Thus, any fractional part of the result is lost. It doesn't matter if there are doubles, floats, etc in the remaining part of the formula, if Java encounters two integers in an intermediate division operation, it will truncate the intermediate result to be an integer. For example, the intermediate result of 13 /2 in Java is 6, even though the mathematical result should be 6.5.

Modulus Explained

Modulus is the remainder of a division operation. Therefore, 7 % 3 really means to divide 7 by 3 but don't keep the quotient as your answer ... instead keep the remainder as your answer. So, 7 / 3 really divides 2 times with a remainder of 1. The result of 7 % 3 is 1. The result of 6 % 3 is 0 because 6 divided by 3 gives a remainder of 0. Here are some extra examples:

Equation	Explanation	Answer
13 % 4	13 divided by 4 gives you a quotient of 3 and a remainder of 1	1
6 % 2	6 divided by 2 gives you a quotient of 3 and a remainder of 0	0
int y = 45 % 6 * 5 % 2;	45 divided by 6 gives you a quotient of 7 and remainder of 3. The intermediate result of 45 % 6 is 3 and so now you multiply the 3 by 5 which gives you 15. Now you are left with 15 % 2 which means to divide 15 by 2 giving you a quotient of 7 and remainder of 1.	1

How might modulus be used? If you were making a coin-changing machine and programming it in Java, you would probably need to use modulus. How? If you want to give a customer 63 cents in change... how would you mathematically figure out the number of quarters, dimes, nickels, and pennies? One way is as follows:

```
int centsLeft = 63;           // 63 is number of cents
quarters = centsLeft   / 25;  //  63/25 gives you 2 quarters
centsLeft = centsLeft % 25;   // 63%25 gives you 13 cents remainder
dimes = centsLeft / 10;       // 13/10 gives you 1 dime
centsLeft = centsLeft%10;     //  13 % 10  gives you 3 cents remaining
nickels = centsLeft / 5;      //  3/5  gives you 0 nickels
centsLeft = centsLeft % 5;    // 3%5 gives you 3 cents remainder
pennies = centsLeft;
```

At this point you have the number of quarters at 2, dimes at 1, nickels at 0, and pennies at 3 for a starting number of cents as 63. Now, start at top and make centsLeft be equal to 93 cents and see what you get.

Modulus is also used in card games to determine suits of cards, etc. For now, you should just understand how to calculate a modulus problem.

Shorthand Assignment Operators

The C programming language uses a shorthand notation of ++ which means to add 1.This is why the newer version of C is called C++ (There is no C+ version). Since Java was created from the C programming language, the Java programming language has some shorthand assignment statements, too. For instance, if we want to keep a running tally, we could tell it to add 1 to tally with the Java statement of:

tally = tally + 1;

Assuming that the variable tally was set equal to 5 earlier in program, the above statement will take the tally and add 1 to it making it 6. The next time it comes to this statement it would take a tally of 6 and add 1 to it making it 7. The Java shorthand assignment statement to do the same thing is:

tally ++;

These two statements do the same thing. Any time you see the ++ in Java it means to add 1 to the variable. This is referred to as **incrementing** in programming. To adjust this same concept to do subtraction (decrementing) of 1 you would have:

tally --;

Some other shorthand assignment operators are:

Shorthand Assignment Operator	Longhand Notation
x + = y;	x = x + y;
x - = y;	x = x - y;
x * = y;	x = x * y;
x / = y;	x = x / y;
x % =y;	x = x % y;

Casting Rules

Java supports implicit casts from smaller types such as int to larger types such as long. This is called promoting (putting a smaller result into a larger variable). The order of allowable promoting casts is:

byte $\Rightarrow$ **short** $\Rightarrow$ **int** $\Rightarrow$ **long** $\Rightarrow$ **float** $\Rightarrow$ **double**

If you try to put a result of a calculation into a variable which is of a smaller type than the result (such as a double result being put into an integer variable), you will get a compilation error. You would need to use casting to do this. You can cast to any primitive except Boolean. The syntax for casting is as follows:

(typename) value

Some examples of casting are as follows:

z = (int) 31.56; // puts the integer part which is 31 into z
z = (int) (x / y); // divides x by y and then puts integer part of answer in z

In summary, an int can be promoted to a float with no casting. However, a float can't be placed into an int without doing casting. When casting to an integer, the result is **chopped**, not rounded. As can be seen in chart above, any type can be automatically promoted to any type to the right of it without casting. Thus, double is the rightmost type so it can't be automatically promoted to any other type. The primitive int is considered to be smaller than floats in the casting chain so ints can automatically be made into floats but not vice versa. When doing Java arithmetic, you will get a compiler error or warning "POSSIBLE LOSS OF PRECISION" if any variable or constant in your equation is of larger type than the variable which will receive the answer.

Walk-Through

There are many, many rules to understand when doing a complex arithmetic statement. We have rules of math hierarchy, rules of integers, rules of casting, etc. Let's put this altogether so that you understand the rules and the operations.

double y = 25 % 4 + 3 * 5 / 2.0 + (6 / 5);

1. The first part done in this formula according to math hierarchy would be parenthesis. **6 / 5** has 2 integer operands so integer arithmetic will give you an answer of 1 and not 1.2. Even though y is declared as a double, it has no impact on Java handling integer division inside the formula. Integer division in any formula also gives an intermediate result of an integer. What do we have so far?

double y = 25 % 4 + 3 * 5 / 2.0 + 1;

2. After parenthesis, the math hierarchy will next do multiplication, division and modulus from left to right. None of these 3 operations rank higher than the other. Moving from left to right, the first of these to be encountered is modulus of **25%4.** Both operands are integers so it does integer arithmetic. 25 % 4 means to divide 25 by 4 giving a quotient of 6 and remainder of 1. Modulus only uses the remainder of 1. What do we have so far?

    double y = 1 + 3 * 5 / 2.0 + 1;

3. Moving further to the right, multiplication of **3 * 5** gets done next. Both operands are integer so it does integer arithmetic and gets an answer of 15. We have the following:

    double y = 1 + 15 / 2.0 + 1;

4. Moving further to the right, division of **15 / 2.0** gets done next. One operand is integer (15) and one operand is double (2.0). This is because all constant numbers without decimal points are ints and all constant numbers with decimal points are doubles. When Java has mixed operands, it does the arithmetic using the higher-level which in this case is double. It will do double arithmetic. 15/2.0 gives a result of 7.5 in double arithmetic. (NOTE: If the operand had simply been 2 instead of 2.0 ... both operands would have been integer, thus doing integer arithmetic and getting result of just 7) We place the 7.5 in the formula as:

    double y = 1 + 7.5 + 1;

5. All the modulus, division and multiplication has been done. Math hierarchy now dictates to do addition and subtraction from left to right. Thus, **1 + 7.5** will be done next. One operand (1) is int and one operand is double (7.5) which will make the computer do double arithmetic and get answer of 8.5. We now have the following:

    double y = 8.5 + 1;

6. The last operation is addition of **8.5 + 1** which has a double (8.5) and an int (1) and thus does double arithmetic. The result is 9.5 which is a double. We now have the following:

    double y = 9.5;

7. The 9.5 will then be placed into the variable y.

    Note: If the variable y had been declared as anything less than a double such as int, float, etc., you would have a casting problem and would get a compilation error. The computer cannot take a double and place it into an int. If you want to do that you must cast it and the formula should have been written as follows:

    int y = **(int)** (25 % 4 + 3 * 5 / 2.0 + (6 / 5)) ;

Hands-on Exercises

Exercise 1: Making an Alien Walk in Alice

We are going to using a variable to make an alien walk in Alice.

1. Get into Alice. Choose the **mars** template.

2. Choose Setup Scene. **Add** an **alien** object from the Biped folder. You may want to rotate the alien to the side so that you can see the leg movements easier.

3. Save this program as **AlienWalk**. You save it to the **Chapter2Exercises** folder.

4. Click on **Edit Code**. Select the alien and drag the **move** method to the editor. Choose forward and 1 meter *(these choices are known as arguments)* to fullfill the direction and amount questions. Click the **run** button to test your program.

5. Now select the alien's right hip, by clicking on the object drop down, selecting the arrow to the right of the alien object, and then choosing **getRightHip()**

6. Next, drag the **turn** method for the right hip onto the editor under the move method. Choose **backward** and **0.25** as your arguments. Think of the directions for turning a subpart of an object as clockwise for forward motion and counterclockwise for backward motion. The 0.25 represents the amount that the subpart will turn *(1 would be 1 full revolution, therefore 0.25 would ¼th of the way around)*. Click the **run** button to test your program.

7. Now let's have the right knee turn forward 0.25. Remember to think closewise for forward motions and counterclockwise for backwards motions.

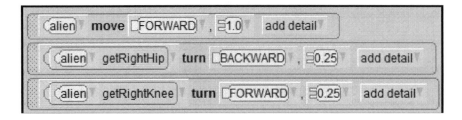

8. Click the **run** button to test your program. This walk looks awkward. We need to fix the timing of these movements. Drag the **do together** block underneath the move method and then drag the right hip and right knee turn methods in the do together block so that it happens simultaneously. Run your animation again. This should look smoother.

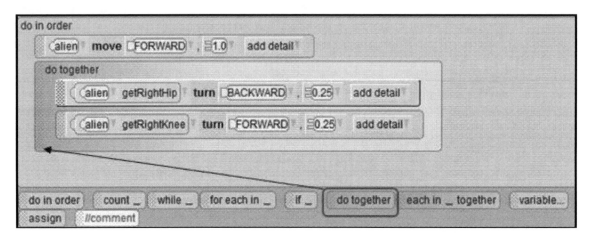

9. Since this leg is raised up, we need to put it back down to create a walking motion. We are going to practice copying the do together block that we already have written to the clipboard. Hold down the **ctrl button** *(alt/option key on the Mac)* and **drag** the **do together block** to the **clipboard** in the right hand corner and release. You should now see a white piece of paper on the clipboard *(this indicates that you copied code to the clipboard)*. If you hover your mouse over the clipboard, you can see the code. *(Note: if you do not hold the ctrl button down when you added code to the clipboard, it will cut instead of copying. Click Edit > Undo from the menu if you did a cut.)*

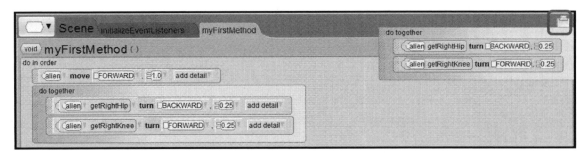

10. Hold down the **Control key** *(alt/option key on the Mac)* and **drag** the piece of paper from the clipboard to underneath your first do together block to create a second do together block. Make sure that the second do together block is not inside of the other block. Change the second do together block **right hip turn to forward** and the **right knee turn to backward** *(click the drop down next to the direction)* as shown below:

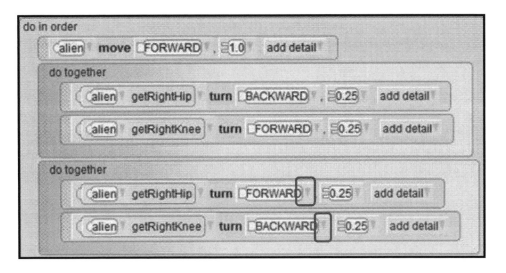

11. It looks silly that the alien moves forward before his right leg bends. We need him to move forward at the same time that he moves his legs. This is a bit challenging because if we add the move to the first do together, then he will be done moving forward before he puts his leg back down. If we combine the 2 do togethers, then he won't bend his leg at all because the forward and backwards motions will cancel each other out. We need to **move the 2 do together blocks** into a **do in order block** and then have the do in order block happening at the same time as the move method. This may take some practice. If you make a mistake click **Edit** on the menu bar and then **Undo**.

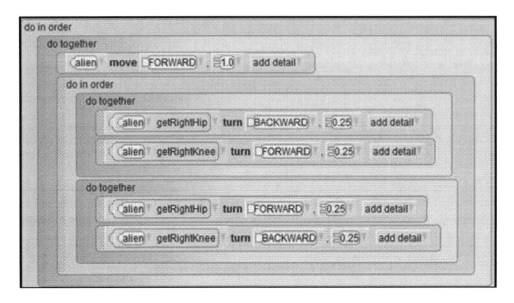

12. You may want to change the duration of the move to be 2 seconds instead of 1 second *(default)*. Since the first do together block will take 1 second and the second do together block will take 1 second, it would be nice if the move took the same amount of time as both do together blocks added together *(which would be 2 seconds)*.

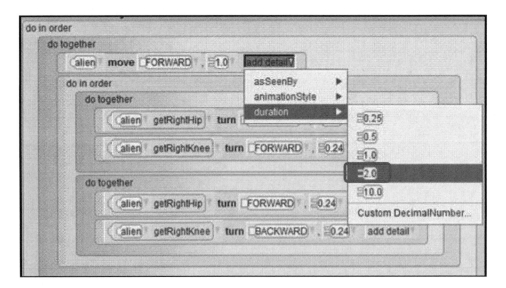

13. Repeat the code for the left hip and left knee to create a walking motion. *Hint: use the clipboard to copy the code that you already have and then change the body part to be left hip and left knee.* The code is shown below if you need some help.

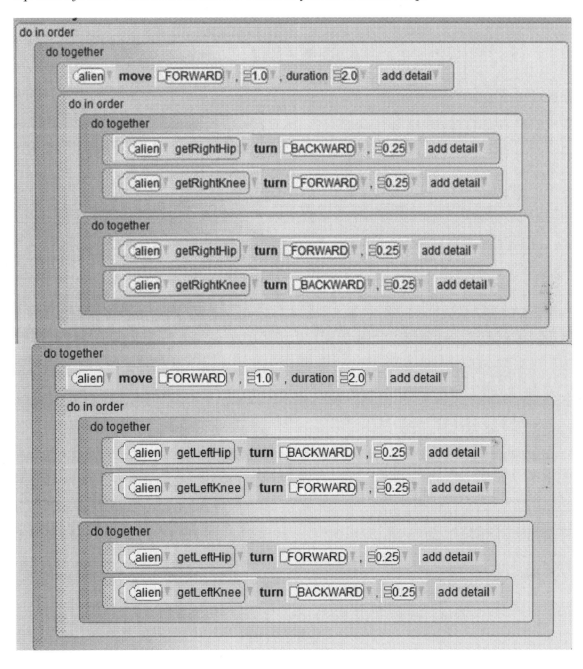

14. Run your animation. It looks good for now, but what if we decided that we wanted to adjust the amount that the alien bends his hip and knees? Let's try changing the amount to be 0.24 instead of 0.25. Select **Custom DecimalNumber...** and type **0.24**. You will need to do this for all 8 movements.

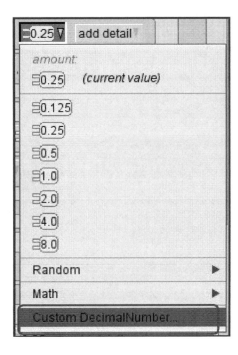

15. Hmmm....now let's say we want 0.23. It is such a pain to keep changing all 8 movements to test what looks good. It would be nice if there was an easier way to change this. Well you are in luck. If we create a variable to replace the 0.24, then we can just change the value of the variable instead of changing all the values every time. Drag the **variable block** to the top of your code editor.

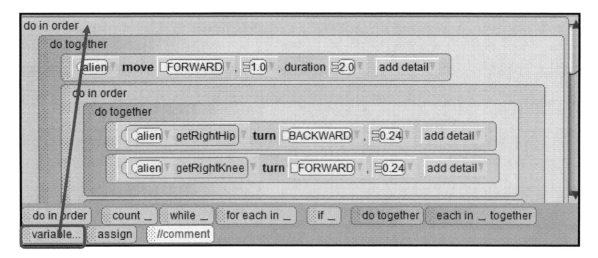

16. Let's choose **DecimalNumber** as the type, **amount** as the variable name, and **0.23** as the intializer *(value)*. Click **OK**. The DecimalNumber is an Alice variable type, if you switch your preferences to Java mode it will show as a Double variable type instead. To change your preferences, you would need to select **Window** from the menu, **Preferences**, **Programming Language**, **Java** *(Note: using Java view in Alice will make Do Together blocks of code look more challenging)*.

17. Now we will need to change the 0.24 to the **amount variable** for all 8 turn movements.

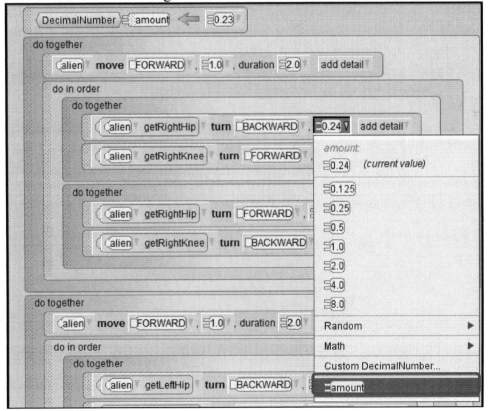

18. From this point on, we can change the value in the amount variable and it will update the value everywhere we used the amount variable. Save and close this program.

Exercise 2: Converting Fahrenheit to Celsius with Java (ongoing exercise)

This program will use variables, primitives, and arithmetic. The program should take a Fahrenheit temperature of 52 and calculate the corresponding Celsius temperature.

1. Get into NetBeans.

2. From the **File** menu, choose **New Project...**

3. Choose the **Java folder** on the left hand side of the window, then choose **Java Application.**

4. Click **Next**. Give your project the name **Celsius**, select the **location** of where you would like to save your file (Chapter2Exercises folder), make sure that the **Create Main Class** box is checked and change the name to **Celsius** instead of *celsius.Celius*, and click **Finish**.

5. The first thing to do in all of our Java programs is to put some comments about the program at the beginning of the program. There should be a comment line for name of program, author, date, and the JDK used. You should eliminate some of the other comment lines. You should have something similar to the following:

```
Celsius.java

Source   History

1    /*
2     * This is a program to change Fahrenheit to Celsius
3     * your name here
4     * the date here
5     * JDK version
6     */
7
8    public class Celsius {
9
10       public static void main(String[] args) {
11           //TODO code application logic here
12       }
13   }
```

6. **Inside of the main method**, should be the statements that you want the computer to do. In this program, we will have two variables. If we want them to contain numbers with decimal points, we could declare them as doubles. If we want them to contain whole numbers, we could declare them as ints. We will declare them as doubles as follows:

double fahrenheit=52.0;
double celsius;

Note: We know the value of fahrenheit but we don't know what the corresponding value of celsius is yet.

7. Next, the computer should calculate the value of celsius based upon the fahrenheit temperature being 52. However, we might want to calculate celsius for a different fahrenheit temperature in the future, so we will refer to the temperature of 52 as the variable of fahrenheit instead of the number 52. What is the formula to do the conversion? The formula in algebra is as follows:

celsius = 5 / 9 (fahrenheit - 32)

8. Converting this algebraic equation into Java, it becomes:

celsius = 5 / 9 * (fahrenheit -32);

9. Next, the computer should display the values for fahrenheit and celsius so the user can see the results. It would be nice to display these values on two separate lines. Therefore, the statements to display this would be:

System.out.println("Fahrenheit: "+ fahrenheit);
System.out.println("Celsius: " + celsius);

10. Once you have added these statements to the main method, your program should look as follows:

```
Celsius.java

Source  History

 1    /*
 2     * This is a program to convert Fahrenheit to Celsius
 3     * your name here
 4     * the date here
 5     * JDK version here
 6     */
 7
 8    public class Celsius {
 9
10        public static void main(String[] args) {
11            double fahrenheit = 52.0;
12            double celsius;
13            celsius = 5/9 * (fahrenheit-32);
14            System.out.println("Fahrenheit:  " + fahrenheit);
15            System.out.println("Celsius:  " + celsius);
16        }
17    }
```

11. Compile this program  and correct any errors you have in syntax.

12. Execute your Java program. Your screen should display:

```
Output - Celsius (run)

run:
Fahrenheit:  52.0
Celsius:  0.0
BUILD SUCCESSFUL (total time: 0 seconds)
```

13. Does this program work? The Celsius temperature should be 11.111111111. It didn't work. Why? **AH OH!!!!** First, the arithmetic takes 52.0 - 32 and gets 20.0. It does this first since it is in parenthesis. Next, it takes 5 / 9 which are 2 integers so the answer is 0 (just the integer part). Then it multiplies 0 times the 20.0 calculated earlier. Thus, the answer becomes 0. The problem is the integer division. It doesn't matter that you are working with doubles in the subtraction or even that the answer will be a double. If the computer sees integer division anywhere, you will get an intermediate result of an integer (decimal part chopped off). How can this be corrected?

14. If the 5 is changed to 5.0 or the 9 to 9.0, it will no longer do integer division. Try it. Compile new version. If there are no errors, then execute it. It should now display:

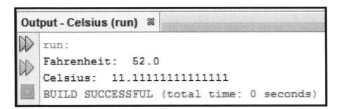

```
Output - Celsius (run)

run:
Fahrenheit:  52.0
Celsius:  11.11111111111111
BUILD SUCCESSFUL (total time: 0 seconds)
```

The program should now be:

```java
/*
 * This is a program to convert Fahrenheit to Celsius
 * your name here
 * the date here
 * JDK version here
 */

public class Celsius {

    public static void main(String[] args) {
        double fahrenheit = 52.0;
        double celsius;
        celsius = 5.0/9 * (fahrenheit-32);
        System.out.println("Fahrenheit:  " + fahrenheit);
        System.out.println("Celsius:  " + celsius);
    }
}
```

15. Try changing the value in the fahrenheit variable to a number of your choice. Run the program. Do you get the right output?

16. Right click on this project and close it. Exit NetBeans.

Exercise 3: Alice Character Movement using Arithmetic

We are going to move a witch to her brew in this project.

1. Get into Alice. Choose the **grass** template.

2. Choose Scene Setup. **Add** a **witch** object from the Biped folder and a **cauldron** object from the Prop folder. Move the witch away from the cauldron.

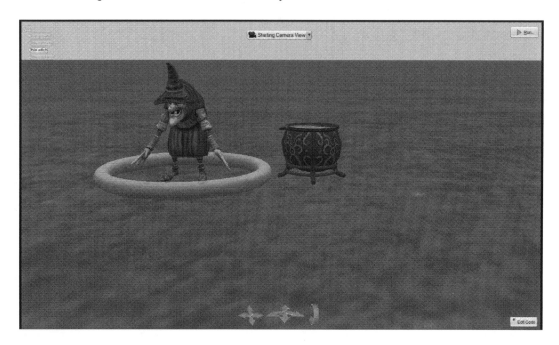

3. Save this program as **WitchBrew**. You should be saving it in the Chapter2Exercises folder.

4. Click on **Edit Code**. Put your comments at the top of the program.

5. Select the witch and drag the **say method** to the editor. Click on **Custom TextString...** to add your message. Make the witch say **I need to check on my brew.**

6. Next, have the **witch turn to face the cauldron**.

7.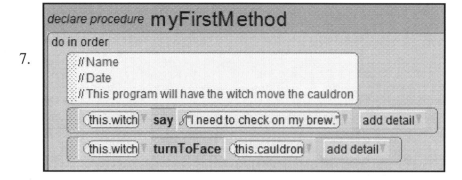

7. Now, use the **moveToward** method on the witch. When you drag this method onto the editor, it will prompt the user for a target to move towards (argument) and a distance of how far to move to that object (argument). Select **cauldron** for the target and **10.0** for the distance.

8. Click the **Run** button to see the animation. You should notice that the witch goes right past the cauldron since 10 meters is too far. We really don't know how far to move the witch and so it becomes a guessing game. If you keep guessing a distance, you will eventually get it to work. As you can probably imagine, trial and error is not very efficient. We are going to create an arithmetical problem that will cause the witch to move to the cauldron; it doesn't matter how far the cauldron is from the witch.

9. Measuring the distance between the witch and the cauldron tells us how far the witch should move. When we want to ask questions about the world (such as measuring distance between 2 objects), we click on the Functions tab. Make sure the **witch** is selected and click the **Functions** tab. If you scroll down towards the bottom of the choices on the Functions tab, you will find a **getDistanceTo** function. Drag this function to the editor and place it on the **10.0** (the 10.0 will be highlighted in a bold black box when it is selected). When you release the mouse button, you should be prompted to make a selection of the other object. We are measuring the distance from the witch to the caulron so you should select **cauldron** as the other object.

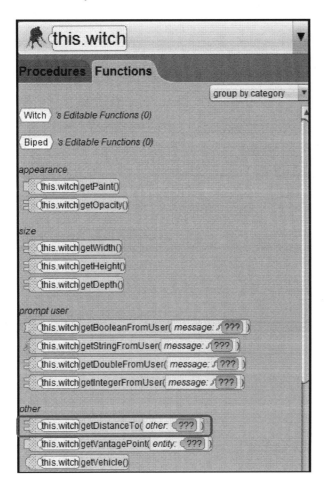

10. Your code should look as follows:

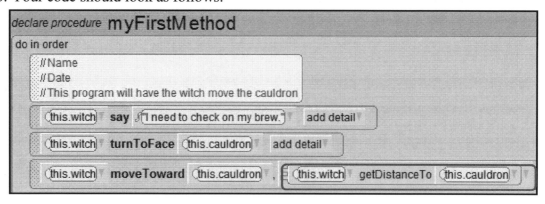

11. Run the animation. You will now notice that the witch is inside of her pot. The **getDistanceTo** method measues the distance from one object to another based upon the centerpoints of the objects. Let's fix this issue. Save and close Alice.

12. Let's take this project into NetBeans to correct it. Open **NetBeans**.

13. Select **File**, **New Project**, then **Java Project from Existing Alice Project** and then the **Next** button.

14.

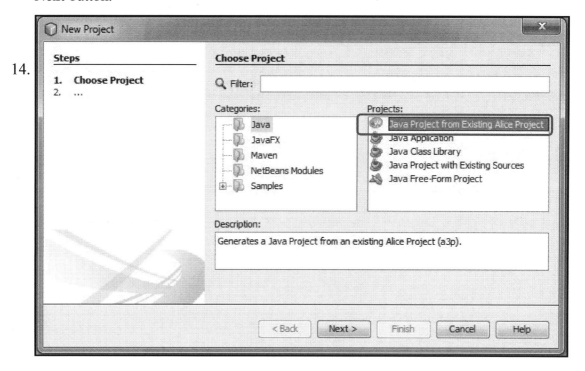

14. **Browse** for the Alice world (it should be in your Chapter2Exercises folder) and then **select the location** of where you would like to save the NetBeans project (you should save this in your Chapter2Exercises folder as well). Click **Finish**.

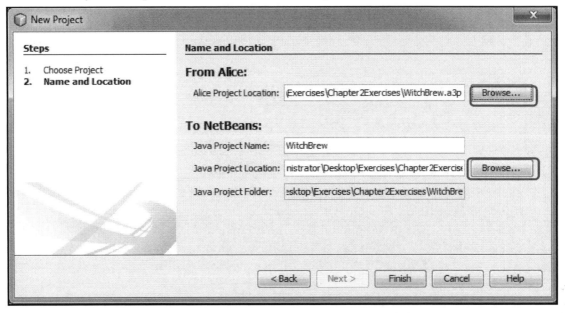

15. **Expand** (click the plus sign) the **WitchBrew project**, expand the **Source Packages**, and expand the **default package**. This is where you will find the Java files. The code that we added to the Alice world will be in the **Scene.java** file. Please double click on this file to view the code.

16. The objects are created by the following code.

```
private SGround ground = new SGround();
private SCamera camera = new SCamera();
private Witch witch = new Witch();
private Cauldron cauldron = new Cauldron();
```

17. The code that you added in Alice, will be in **myFirstMethod**. We are going to add to the Java code in NetBeans to make this program more efficient.

18.
```
public void myFirstMethod() {
    //Name
    //Date
    //This program will have the witch move to the cauldron
    this.witch.say("I need to check on my brew.");
    this.witch.turnToFace(this.cauldron);
    this.witch.moveToward(this.cauldron, this.witch.getDistanceTo(this.cauldron));
}
```

18. There are quite a few references in the scene to the word "this" that are not necessary. You can delete these as shown below if you want. It may make it easier to understand since it won't be as overwhelming.

```
public void myFirstMethod() {
    //Name
    //Date
    //This program will have the witch move to the cauldron
    witch.say("I need to check on my brew.");
    witch.turnToFace(cauldron);
    witch.moveToward(cauldron, witch.getDistanceTo(cauldron));
}
```

19. We will now need to find the depth of the witch and the depth of the cauldron. To do this we will need to create **2 new variables**. We will name them **witchDepth** and **cauldronDepth**. We will make these variables double, since the depth of the objects will most likely be a decimal number. You will notice that NetBeans highlights variables with a gray underline when they are not being used. Don't worry about the gray underlines since we aren't finished yet and we will use these variables.

```
double witchDepth;
double cauldronDepth;
witch.say("I need to check on my brew.");
witch.turnToFace(cauldron);
witch.moveToward(cauldron, witch.getDistanceTo(cauldron));
```

20. Next, we need to find the witches depth and save it in the witchDepth variable and repeat this for the cauldron. There is a function in Alice called **getDepth**. You would type the name of the object.getDepth() to find its depth.

```
double witchDepth = witch.getDepth();
double cauldronDepth;
witch.say("I need to check on my brew.");
witch.turnToFace(cauldron);
witch.moveToward(cauldron, witch.getDistanceTo(cauldron));
```

We are going to the same thing for the cauldronDepth variable. It should look as follows when you are finished. The variables are still underlined in gray because we haven't applied them yet. We have declared 2 variables (witchDepth and cauldronDepth), but we haven't used them. I choose to declare these variables at the top of myFirstMethod, but you don't have to. You just have to make sure that you declare your variable before you try to use them.

```
double witchDepth = witch.getDepth();
double cauldronDepth = cauldron.getDepth();
witch.say("I need to check on my brew.");
witch.turnToFace(cauldron);
witch.moveToward(cauldron, witch.getDistanceTo(cauldron));
```

21. Now, We need to take half of the depth of the witch and half of the depth of the cauldron and add them together. To do this, we will create a new variable called personalSpace. The variable personalSpace will have our equation that be subtracted from the total distance from the witch to the cauldron. This equation and declaration should look as follows.

```
double witchDepth = witch.getDepth();
double cauldronDepth = cauldron.getDepth();
double personalSpace = (witchDepth * 0.5) + (cauldronDepth * 0.5);
witch.say("I need to check on my brew.");
witch.turnToFace(cauldron);
witch.moveToward(cauldron, witch.getDistanceTo(cauldron));
```

Notice that the witchDepth and cauldronDepth no longer have a gray underline since they were used in our equation. The personalSpace variable has a gray underline since it has not been used yet.

22. If you were to run the program right now, the witch would still go into the pot. This is because we did not use the personalSpace variable to subtract half of the depth of the witch and the cauldron. We need to subtract the personalSpace from the getDistanceTo result as shown below. When you use the getDistanceTo function, you are asking for the result when it measures the distance from one object to another. The result that it returns to you is then altered by subtracting the calculated personalSpace from it. Note: Be careful to place this before the last parenthesis)

```
double witchDepth = witch.getDepth();
double cauldronDepth = cauldron.getDepth();
double personalSpace = (witchDepth * 0.5) + (cauldronDepth * 0.5);
witch.say("I need to check on my brew.");
witch.turnToFace(cauldron);
witch.moveToward(cauldron, witch.getDistanceTo(cauldron)-personalSpace);
```

23. Run the animation. Presto! The witch is in front of her brew without being in it.

    Note: When you run your program in NetBeans, it should save the files automatically, but if you are unsure you can save. **DO NOT use the "Save as" option** in NetBeans. You can go to **File** and choose **Save** or you can use the shortcut command to save (Windows: ctrl + s, Mac: command + s). You can tell if the file is saved by looking at the tabs. If the filename is bold, then it has not been saved recently. If it is not bold, then it is saved. When you close NetBeans, it should warn you if you haven't saved. Please do not right click and rename Java files. Renaming Java files, will mess up the structure of your NetBeans projects and they won't work correctly. This is why I recommend you stay away from the "Save As" option; if you change the name or the location of your Java files, they won't work properly next time you open them.

24. Close this project.

Exercise 4: Using Modulus in a Money Changer Java Program (ongoing exercise)

One of the hardest concepts for students to understand when first learning Java programming is MODULUS. Thus, we will do an exercise that will show you how to write a program that will take a total number of cents and decide how many dollars, quarters, dimes, nickels, and pennies should be given out. We will use modulus to accomplish this. This program could be adapted to give change in a vending machine, etc. Our program will just print the answers instead of disbursing coins.

1. From the **File** menu, choose **New Project...**

2. Choose the **Java folder** on the left hand side of the window, then choose **Java Application.**

3. Click **Next**. Give your project the name **MoneyChanger**, select the **location** of where you would like to save your project (Chapter2Exercises folder). Make sure that the **Create Main Class** box is checked and in the textbox change the name to **MoneyChanger** instead of moneychanger.MoneyChanger. Click the **Finish** button.

4. The first thing to do in all Java programs is to put some comments about the program at the beginning of the program. There should be a comment line for name of program, author, date, and the JDK used. These lines should look something like this:
   ```
   /*
    * Your Name and Date
    * This program will break change into corrects coins
    * JDK Version
    */
   ```

5. Inside of the main method, the variables to be used should be declared first. In this program, we will have several variables. All of the variables will be whole numbers so they will all be int. We will declare the following variables as integers:

   ```
   int cents=393;
   int centsLeft;  //temporary variable for storing remaining cents
   int dollars;
   int quarters;
   int dimes;
   int nickels;
   int pennies;
   ```

6. The formula for figuring out the number of coins associated with the cents is a complex series of statements. The general logic of it is to begin with the largest denomination which is dollars. Once we know how many dollars are needed, then it must be determined how much money is left to still figure out. The variable that will contain the cents remaining to still have coins dispensed will be called *centsLeft*. The Java statements that will successively figure out dollars, then quarters, then dimes, etc. is given below:

   ```
   dollars = cents/100;
   centsLeft = cents %100;
   quarters = centsLeft/25;
   centsLeft = centsLeft %25;
   dimes = centsLeft/10;
   centsLeft = centsLeft %10;
   nickels = centsLeft/5;
   centsLeft = centsLeft %5;
   pennies = centsLeft;
   ```

7. **What do the above calculations do?** We begin with 393 cents which is $3.93 is contained in the variable called *cents*. So **cents** contains the total number of cents we have to work with. To figure the dollars we divide by 100 first because there are 100 cents in a dollar. 393/100 will do integer arithmetic because both *cents* and 100 are ints. Integer arithmetic gives us just the integer part as an answer and thus we will get an answer of 3. So the variable dollars will contain the integer 3 which is exactly right!! We now need to know how much money we still need to figure out. We know to give the person 3 dollars in change... but how many quarters, nickels, etc. should they get? To figure out how much money is left, we take cents which is 393 and do a modulus 100. Modulus means to divide but keep the remainder instead of the answer. Dividing 393 by 100 gives you a quotient of 3 (which we don't want at this time) and a remainder of 93 so we put the remainder of 93 (393-300) into *centsLeft*. We are using the variable *centsLeft* to tell us how much change we still need to figure out. In the next formula, we calculate quarters by taking the *centsLeft* of 93 and dividing by 25. This will give us 3 quarters because of integer arithmetic. We are not done so we will figure out *centsLeft* again by doing a modulus of 25 and it gives us a remainder (93-75) of 18 cents. To figure out dimes, we divide the *centsLeft* of 18 by 10 and get 1 dime. The next line calculates *centsLeft* with modulus and gets a remainder (18-10) of 8 cents. Nickels are determined by dividing by 5 and getting 1 nickel. Using modulus again, the *centsLeft* is calculated (8-5) as 3 cents. At this point, all that remains is pennies so the centsLeft is placed into the variable called pennies.

8. The computer has calculated the various denominations of change, but the results are stored in memory and not shown on screen. Each denomination will be placed on a separate line. Instead of using the println method for each line, we can use the "\n" to print a new line after each denomination as follows:

    System.out.println("Total Cents: " + cents
    + "\nDollars: " + dollars
    + "\nQuarters: " + quarters
    + "\nDimes: " + dimes
    + "\nNickels: " + nickels
    + "\nPennies: " + pennies);

9. The above lines print the total cents, dollars, etc. on separate lines. Each line consists of words to print such as "Total cents " and the actual number which is in the corresponding variable such as *cents*. The + symbol used here does not mean arithmetic but means to concatenate or "join" the words and the numbers.

10. Compile this program and then correct any errors you have in syntax. Execute your Java program. Your screen should display:

    Total Cents: 393
    Dollars: 3
    Quarters: 3
    Dimes: 1
    Nickels: 1
    Pennies: 3

11. The program should now be:

```java
/*
 * Your Name and Date
 * This program will break change into corrects coins
 * JDK Version
 */

public class MoneyChanger {

    public static void main(String[] args) {
        //declaring variables
        int cents = 393;
        int centsLeft; //temporary variable for storing remaining cents
        int dollars;
        int quarters;
        int dimes;
        int nickels;
        int pennies;

        //begin calculations
        dollars = cents / 100;
        centsLeft = cents % 100;
        quarters = centsLeft / 25;
        centsLeft = centsLeft % 25;
        dimes = centsLeft / 10;
        centsLeft = centsLeft % 10;
        nickels = centsLeft / 5;
        centsLeft = centsLeft % 5;
        pennies = centsLeft;

        //printing results
        System.out.println("Total Cents: " + cents
                + "\nDollars: " + dollars
                + "\nQuarters: " + quarters
                + "\nDimes: " + dimes
                + "\nNickels: " + nickels
                + "\nPennies: " + pennies);
    }
}
```

12. If you want the computer to calculate what change to give for 549 cents, what would you change in your program?   YES, you would change the line that says 393 to be 549

    int cents = 549;

13. Recompile the program with cents being initialized to 549. Execute the program. The formulas for calculating the change are generic formulas and will work no matter what cents you give it. You just need to change that one line. In later chapters, you will see how you can allow the user to enter the information in without changing the actual Java program

14. Try your own initialization of cents to some number not tried so far and see if it calculates each of the money denominations correctly.

15. Close this project.

Summary

- **Comments** make programs more understandable to other programmers. They do not cause the computer to perform any task.
- **Keywords** have predefined meanings and must be used in a predetermined manner.
- Data can be categorized as constant or variable. Data is constant when it can't be changed after the program compiles. Data is variable when it might change.
- **Variable names** have a type, name, and a value.
- There are 4 integer **primitives** (byte, short, int and long), 2 decimal number primitives (float and double), Boolean (true and false), and char (single characters). The two most common primitives that you should get to know are int for integers and double for decimal numbers.
- **Variable names rules:**
  - Should begin with a letter, $ or underscore(_) and the rest of the name can consist of letters, digits, underscores (_) or $
  - No spaces allowed
  - Can NOT use keywords but should be meaningful name
  - Stylistically should begin with lowercase letter with following words beginning with capital letter
- Before you can use a variable, you have to declare it. A primitive variable should only be declared once in a program. You may also give the variable a value when it is declared. Multiple variables of same type may be declared all in one statement.
- A Java statement forms a single Java operation and ends with a semicolon (;).
- Java represents a series of characters as a String. A String may include letters, digits and various special characters. A String is not a primitive but is considered to be an <u>object in Java.</u> Java String literals are written as a sequence of characters in double quotes.
- The "+" symbol when used with Strings does not mean to do arithmetic but instead means to combine the string with some other data (concatenation).
- Special **escape codes** can be combined in System.out.println statements to tab data, make data go to newline, or to use special characters in strings such as single/double quotes.
- The math rules of hierarchy are: (1) parenthesis; (2) multiplication, division and modulus left to right; (3) addition and subtraction from left to right; (4) place result in variable on left side of = sign.
- Modulus is the remainder of integer division. It is represented with a % sign. Thus, 13%5 means to divide 13 by 5 giving 2 as a quotient and remainder as 3. So, 13%5 is 3.
- There are Java shorthand operators to add 1 to a variable by saying x++; or to subtract 1 from a variable by saying x--;
- Integer division gives integer results (chops off decimal part of answer).
- Java will automatically promote a smaller primitive to a larger primitive. However, larger primitives cannot be demoted to a smaller primitive without casting.
- If you try to put a result of a calculation into a variable which is of a smaller type than the result (such as a double result being put into an integer variable), you will get a compilation error. You would need to use casting to do this. You can cast to any primitive except Boolean. The syntax for casting is as follows: **(typename) value**

Review Questions

1. A Boolean variable can hold
   a. any whole number
   b. any character
   c. the values true or false
   d. any decimal numbers

2. The value of 159.65 can be held by a variable of type _____.
   a. long
   b. int
   c. double
   d. char

3. Names for symbolic memory locations are called _____
   a. interpreters
   b. bugs
   c. variables
   d. slots

4. The variable name of *weeklySales* is a legal Java variable name.
   a. true
   b. false

5. When data can't be changed after a program is compiled, the data is _____.
   a. constant
   b. variable
   c. volatile
   d. flexible

6. Which of the following is not a primitive type in Java?
   a. Boolean
   b. int
   c. decimal
   d. double

7. Which of the following values can you assign to a variable of type int?
   a. 11.5
   b. 's'
   c. 12
   d. 3,333,333,333,333

8. Which of the following is the smallest integer primitive?
    a. short
    b. byte
    c. int
    d. long

9. The variable name of *class* is a legal Java variable name.
    a. true
    b. false

10. If you were setting up a variable to hold the number of dollars that William Gates is worth, you should choose a primitive type of
    a. short
    b. byte
    c. int
    d. long

11. What is the result in y after the following Java statement is executed?
    double y = 15.0/ 2 + 8 * 10 / 3;
    a. 33.5
    b. 51.666666
    c. 33
    d. does not compile

12. What is the result in y after the following Java statement is executed?
    double y = 29 % 4 + 3 / 5 * 5 / 2.0;
    a. 5.0
    b. 1.0
    c. 7.0
    d. does not compile

13. What is the result in y after the following Java statement is executed?
    double y = 7 * 8 % 5 / 5.0 * 2;
    a. 4.2
    b. 0.4
    c. 0.0
    d. does not compile

14. What is the result in y after the following Java statement is executed?
    double y = 8 - 4 / 3 + 10;
    a. 11.3
    b. 16.7
    c. 17.0
    d. does not compile

15. What is the result in y after the following Java statement is executed?
    int y = 45 / 5 * 5 / (45 % 5);
    a. 0
    b. 5
    c. 1
    d. exception

16. What is the result in y after the following Java statement is executed?
    int y = 55 / (5 * 5) + 36 % 6;

    a. 15.66666
    b. 5
    c. 2
    d. 8

17. What is the result in y after the following Java statement is executed?
    int y = 8 - 4 / 3 + 10;

    a. 11
    b. 17
    c. 16.7
    d. 11.3

18. What is the result in y after the following Java statement is executed?
    int y = 7 * 8 % 5 / 5.0 * 2;
    a. 4.2
    b. 0.4
    c. 0.0
    d. will not compile

19. What is the result in y after the following Java statement is executed?
    int y = (int) (5.3 + 6.6);
    a. 9
    b. 10
    c. 11
    d. 12

20. What is the value of x once the following statements are executed?
    int x = 45;
    x++;
    a. 44
    b. 45
    c. 46
    d. does not compile

21. How can the following computer program be changed to fix the error?

```
Inventory.java  ✖

 1   /**
 2    This is a simple program to print the lines of inventory
 3    Name
 4    Date
 5    JDK version
 6    */
 7
 8   public class Inventory {
 9
10       public static void main(String[] args) {
11           int productNumber = 100;
12           String productDesc = "Pens and Pencils";
13           double price = 25.95;
14
15           System.out.println(Prod. Number:\t" + productNumber);
16           System.out.println("Description: \t" + productDesc);
17           System.out.println("Price:\t\t" + price);
18       }
19   }
```

22. How can the following computer program be changed to fix the error?

```
Celsius.java *  x

 8   public class Celsius {
 9
10       public static void main(String[] args) {
         fahrenheit = 52.0;
12           double celsius;
         celsius = 5.0/9 * (fahrenheit -32);
         System.out.println("Fahrenheit: " + fahrenheit);
15           System.out.println("Corresponding celsius temperature: " + celsius);
16       }
17   }
```

Solutions: *1) c   2) c   3) c   4) a   5) a   6) c   7) c   8) b   9) b   10) d   11) a   12) b   13) b   14) c*
15) d   16) c   17) b   18) d   19) c   20) c
21) Missing double quotes around the "Prod. Number:\t" string
22) The fahrenheit variable was not declared as a double.

Problem 11-19 explanations on the next page

Solution Explanations:

11. *Steps:*   double y = 15.0/2 + 8*10 /3;
   7.5 + 8*10/3
   7.5 + 80/3
   7.5 + 26   note: 80/3 is integer arithmetic
   33.5

12. *Steps:*   double y = 29%4+3/5*5/2.0;
   1 + 3/5*5/2.0
   1 + 0*5/2.0   note: 3/5 is integer arithmetic
   1 + 0/2.0
   1 + 0
   1.0

13. *Steps:*   double y = 7 *8 % 5 / 5.0 *2;
   56 %5 / 5.0 * 2
   1 / 5.0*2
   .2 *2   note: 1/5.0 is double arithmetic
   .4

14. *Steps:*   double y = 8 – 4 / 3 + 10;
   8 - 1 + 10   note 4/3 is integer arithmetic
   7 + 10
   17.0   note: add .0 to end of 17 because its double

15. *Steps:*   int y = 45 / 5 * 5 / (45 % 5)
   45 / 5 * 5 / 0
   9 * 5 / 0
   45 /0
   exception   note: can't divide by 0 in math

16. *Steps:*   int y = 55 / (5 * 5) + 36 % 6;
   55 / 25 + 36%6
   2 + 36 % 6   note: 55/25 was integer arithmetic
   2 + 0   note: 36 divided by 6 gives 0 remainder
   2

17. *Steps:*   int y = 8 – 4 / 3 +10;
   8 - 1 + 10   note: 4/3 is done with integer arithmetic
   7 + 10
   17   note: no .0 added since it is an int

18. *Steps:*   int y = 7 * 8 % 5 / 5.0 * 2;
   No math is done because you have a double of 5.0 on right side and that causes answer to be a double. But a double can't be placed into an int so it will throw a compiler error.

19. *Steps:*   int y = (int) (5.3 + 6.6);
   (int) 11.9
   11   note the (int) says to cast result to int

Assignments

2-1 **Calculating Interest**: Your goal is to calculate the interest given the loan amount, rate, and years to be taken out.

Your program should have the following:

- Make the name of the project **Interest**
- 4 comment lines that state the purpose of the program, author, date and JDK used.
- Include 4 variables for the amount of loan, rate, years, and interest. The amount of loan and interest variables are decimal numbers. **The years and rate variables should be integers.** Make up your own meaningful correctly-formed variable names for these 4 items and declare them appropriately as an int or double.
- Set the loan amount to be 5000. Set interest rate to be 6. Set years to be 15.
- With an assignment statement, have the computer calculate the interest using the following formula:

  interest = amount * (rate/100) * years

  Note: Please use your own variable names in above formula.
- Have the computer display the amount of loan, rate, years and the interest that you calculated. You should print this on several lines. It should looks as follows thus far:

```
Years: 15
Rate: 6
Loan: 5000.0
Interest: 4500.0
```

Note: DO NOT type the numbers 15, 6, and 5000.0, and 4500.0 into your output code. These values should be displayed via your variables.

- Compile your program until you have no compilation errors. When you run this application, you should get an answer for interest as 4500.0 If you are getting an answer of 0, THINK!! Don't change the variable types. Don't worry about it appearing with dollars and cents since formatting has not been covered yet.

2-2 **Converting Inches to Feet**: Your goal is to convert a given number of inches to feet with remaining inches.

Your program should have the following:

- Make the name of the project **InchesToFeet**
- 4 comment lines that state the purpose of the program, author, date and JDK used.
- Include 3 variables for the total number of given inches, feet, and the remaining inches after the division.
- Initialize the inches variable to 35.
- Have the computer calculate the number of feet (12 inches in a foot) and the number of remaining inches left after the conversion of inches to feet. For example: 35 inches would give the result of 2 feet with 11 inches remaining.
- Have the computer display the total number of inches, converted number of feet, and the remaining inches left from the feet conversion. You should print this on several lines. It should looks as follows thus far:

```
Total Inches: 35
----------------------------
Feet: 2
Remaining Inches: 11
```

Note: DO NOT type the numbers 35, 2, and 11 into your output code. These values should be displayed via your variables.

- Compile your program until you have no compilation errors. Try changing the number of total inches to a number other than 35. Does the number of feet and remaining inches change as well? Make sure that your calculations are giving you the correct output. Do not worry about the wording of foot versus feet and inch versus inches for this assignment.

Chapter 3

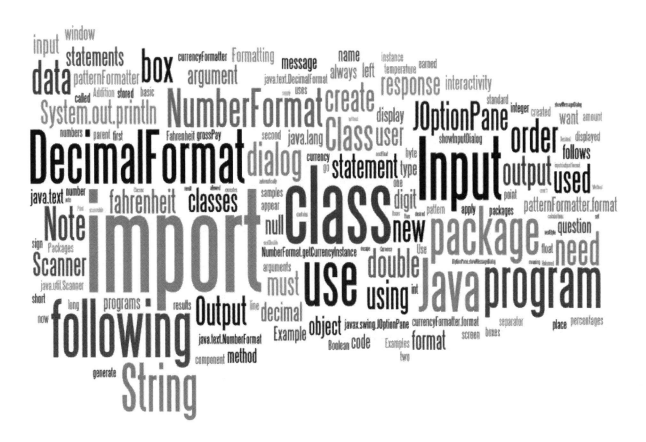

Input/Output

Data Input

All of the programs that have been created thus far have not allowed any interactivity of the user with the program. Variables are set to values, calculations are done, and results are displayed. The user "executes" the program and just watches it display various data. If different results are desired, then the program must be adjusted, compiled, and re-executed. It would be nice if the user could interact with the program and supply the data they choose.

Scanner Class

The Scanner Class provides methods to input data from the Java console.

Value Returned	Method	Returns...
byte	nextByte()	Input as a byte.
short	nextShort()	Input as a short.
int	nextInt()	Input as an integer.
long	nextLong()	Input as a long.
float	nextFloat()	Input as a float.
double	nextDouble()	Input as a double.
Boolean	nextBoolean()	Input as a Boolean.
String	next()	Next word as a String.
String	nextLine()	Input line as a String.

Note: In order to use this class, you must use the following import statement:
import java.util.Scanner;

Age Input Example using the Scanner Class:

```
/*  This program will prompt the user for their age and then display their age
    Written by your name
    Date
    JDK Version  */

import java.util.Scanner;  //import needed for using the Scanner class

public class Age
{
    public static void main(String[] args)
    {
        Scanner keyboard = new Scanner (System.in); //declaring Scanner object
        System.out.print("Enter your age: ");
        int age = keyboard.nextInt(); //take in their age & save in age variable
        System.out.println("You are " + age + " years old."); //output
    }
}
```

```
Output - Age (run)
run:
Enter your age: 21
You are 21 years old.
BUILD SUCCESSFUL (total time: 5 seconds)
```

Addition Input Example using the Scanner Class:

```java
/* This program will prompt the user for 2 numbers, add those 2 numbers
   together, and display the output.
   Written by your name
   Date
   JDK Version  */

import java.util.Scanner;  //import needed for using the Scanner class

public class Adding
{
    public static void main(String[] args)
    {
        Scanner keyboard = new Scanner (System.in); //declaring Scanner object
        System.out.print("Enter a number > ");
        //take in the first number from user & save in number1 variable
        int number1 = keyboard.nextInt();
        System.out.print("Enter another number > ");
        //take in the second number from user & save in number2 variable
        int number2 = keyboard.nextInt();
        int answer = number1 + number2;
        System.out.println(number1 + "+" + number2 + "=" + answer); //output
    }
}
```

```
Output - Adding (run)
run:
Enter a number > 3
Enter another number > 4
3+4=7
BUILD SUCCESSFUL (total time: 5 seconds)
```

JOptionPane Class

The JOptionPane in the Java Library is a class that is used to create standard dialog boxes. These dialog boxes are small windows that ask a question or provide user messages.

Note: In order to use this class, you must use the following import statement:
import javax.swing.JOptionPane;

An input dialog box asks a question and uses a box for entering a response. You can create an input dialog box using the showInputDialog method which is in the JOptionPane class. There are two arguments in the showInputDialog method. The first argument is the parent component that we will simply be null for now. The second argument is a String which should be the question that will appear in the Input window. For instance, the following statements:

String response = JOptionPane.showInputDialog(null, "Enter Fahrenheit");

…will generate the following window on the screen:

The user's answer that they type in the box will be stored in a String called response. If this data is to be used in a calculation, it will need to be converted from String data to double data or integer data with one of the following statements:

> **double fahrenheit = Double.parseDouble(response);**

> or

> **int fahrenheit = Integer.parseInt(response);**

The message dialog box uses a simple window to display (output) information. A message dialog box is created with the showMessageDialog method which is in the JOptionPane class. There are two arguments. The first argument is the parent component that will be null for now. The second argument is a String that will be displayed to the user. For instance, the following statement:

> **JOptionPane.showMessageDialog(null, "Fahrenheit: "**
> **+ fahrenheit + "\nCelsius: " + celsius);**

…will generate the following message on the screen:

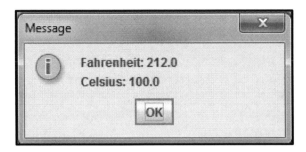

Note: You can have multiple lines by using the escape code of \n to go to new line in the String.

Addition Input Example using JOptionPane Boxes:

```java
/*  This program will prompt the user for 2 numbers, add those 2 numbers
    together, and display the output.
    Written by your name
    Date
    JDK Version  */

import javax.swing.JOptionPane;  //import needed for using JOptionPane Boxes

public class Adding2
{
    public static void main(String[] args)
    {
        String response;
        response = JOptionPane.showInputDialog(null, "Enter a number:");
        double number1 = Double.parseDouble(response);
        response = JOptionPane.showInputDialog(null, "Enter another number:");
        double number2 = Double.parseDouble(response);
        double answer = number1 + number2;
        JOptionPane.showMessageDialog(null, number1 + "+" + number2 + "=" + answer);
    }
}
```

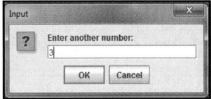

Formatting Output

NumberFormat Class

The class NumberFormat can be used to format output as currency or as percentages. The following code samples create an object of type NumberFormat, name the object, and apply the new format to the output:

Formatting Examples (Currency):

NumberFormat **currencyFormatter** = NumberFormat.getCurrencyInstance( );
System.out.println(**currencyFormatter**.format(20.5));

Output: **$20.50**

---

double grossPay =1250.00;
NumberFormat **currencyFormatter** = NumberFormat.getCurrencyInstance( );
System.out.println("The amount earned is " + **currencyFormatter**.format(grossPay));

Output: The amount earned is $1,250.00

Note: In order to use this NumberFormat class, you must use the following import statement:
import java.text.NumberFormat;

DecimalFormat Class

The class DecimalFormat can be used to format output with a specific number of digits before and after the decimal point.

Character	Meaning
0	Required digit. Print 0 if there isn't a digit in this place.
#	Optional digit. Leave blank if there isn't a digit in this place.
.	Decimal point separator.
,	Comma separator.
%	Multiplies the result by 100 and displays a percent sign.

The following code samples create an object of type DecimalFormat, name the object, and apply the new format to the output.

Formatting Examples:

DecimalFormat **patternFormatter** = new DecimalFormat ("$0.00");
System.out.println(**patternFormatter**.format(.5));

Output: **$0.50**

Note: Java will always display numbers to the left of the decimal if there are any, but if you want a 0 before the decimal if there aren't any numbers, then you need to add this.

DecimalFormat **patternFormatter** = new DecimalFormat (",###.##");
System.out.println(**patternFormatter**.format(11000));

Output: **11,000**

Note: If you want commas, then you will need to carry the pattern out to the left of the decimal three places and put your comma. There is no need to go beyond this, since the pattern will continue to the left.

---

double fahrenheit = 212.5;
DecimalFormat **patternFormatter** = new DecimalFormat ("###.00");
System.out.println("The temperature is " + **patternFormatter**.format(fahrenheit));

Output: **The temperature is 212.50**

Note: In order to use this class, you must use the following import statement:
import java.text.DecimalFormat;

Importing Packages and Classes

Libraries in Java are called **packages**. A package is a collection of classes (files) that are somewhat related, given a name, and stored in such a way to make the package accessible to your Java program. Packages are organized into folders. Java has a large number of standard packages that automatically come with Java. The package **java.lang** contains classes that are basic to Java programming. The java.lang package is so basic that it is always imported into every Java program. Since all of the classes used in previous programs have only needed the java.lang package, it was unnecessary to import any other package in our programs.

In order to use the **Scanner** class, you need to import the java.util package as follows:

import java.util.Scanner;

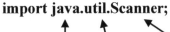

| folder | folder | Class/File |

In order to use the **JOptionPane** class, you need to import the swing class package as follows:

import javax.swing.JOptionPane;

In order to use the **NumberFormat** and **DecimalFormat** class, you need to import the java.text package as follows:

import java.text.DecimalFormat;

import java.text.NumberFormat;

If you want to use both the **NumberFormat** class and the **DecimalFormat** class in the same program, you can import both of these classes by using the following import. The * sign acts as a wildcard symbol meaning that any of the classes in the **java.text** package can be used in the program without doing separate imports for each one.

import java.text.*;

Your import statements always appear at the very beginning of the program before you declare your class.

Hands-on Exercises

Exercise 1: Changing an Alice Clock's Time

1. Get into Alice 3.

2. Choose any ground as for your template (we are going to delete it anyway).

3. Add the pocket watch to your scene and name it **clock**. Delete the ground template by right clicking on it and choosing delete as shown below.

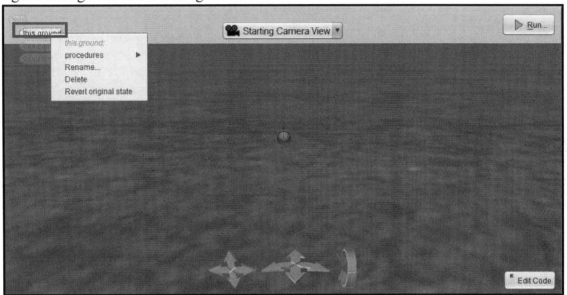

4. Make the clock big so that you can see the hour and minute hands on it.

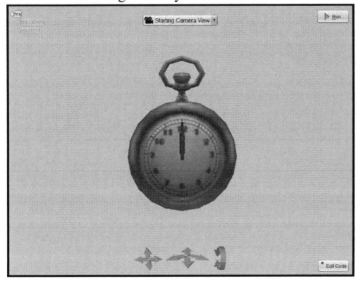

5. Save this program as **Clock** to the appropriate folder.

6. Click **Edit Code** button.

7. Add your comments to the top of the program.

> // Name
> // Date
> // This program will prompt the user for a time and change the clock based on that time

8. Select the **clock** hour hand by clicking the clock arrow and selecting the **getHour()** function as shown below.

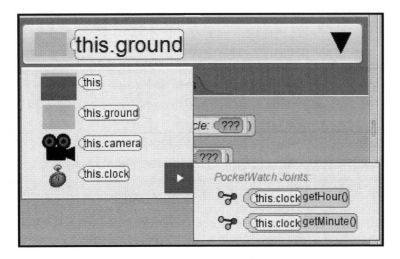

9. Drag the **roll** method onto the editor and choose **LEFT** as the direction and **0.5** as the amount. Save the Alice program file as Clock and exit Alice.

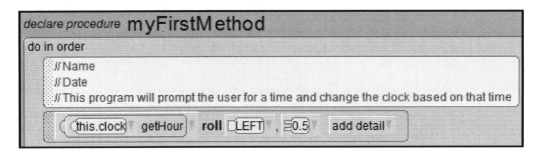

10. Get into **NetBeans**. Choose **File** and **New Project**. Choose the **Java folder** and then **Java Project from Existing Alice Project** on right side (If you don't see this as a choice, then you need to get the nbm plug-in file listed on the installation instructions).

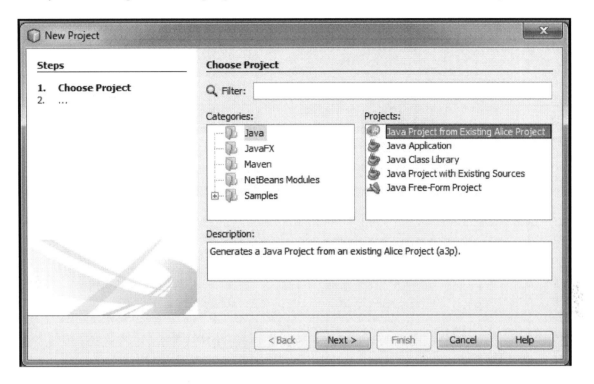

11. Click Next. Browse to find the location of your **Clock.a3p** file Alice project that you just saved. Click **Finish**.

12. Open up the **Scene.java** file. Since we will be prompting the user for a time via JOptionPane message box, we will need to add an import at the top of the program. You will need to expand the imports section to add the JOptionPane import.

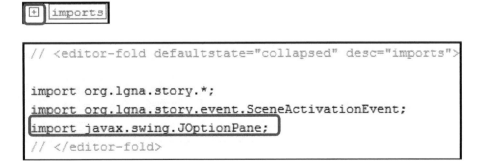

13. Next, we will scroll down to the myFirstMethod and add an input dialog to take in a time from the user. You will notice that the roll method is already there from Alice.

```
public void myFirstMethod() {
    //Name
    //Date
    //This program will prompt the user for a time
    //and change the clock based on that time
    String response = JOptionPane.showInputDialog(null,
            "Enter hours as an integer");
    this.clock.getHour().roll(RollDirection.LEFT, 0.5);
}
```

14. Now we need to convert the String into an integer so that we can use it in an equation to move the hour clock hand.

```
public void myFirstMethod() {
    //Name
    //Date
    //This program will prompt the user for a time
    //and change the clock based on that time
    String response = JOptionPane.showInputDialog(null,
            "Enter hours as an integer");
    int time = Integer.parseInt(response);
    this.clock.getHour().roll(RollDirection.LEFT, 0.5);
}
```

15. Finally, we need to divide the time by 12 since there are 12 hours represented on the clock face. We can create a new variable to save this result and call this variable hour. It is important that we divide the time by 12.0 to avoid the integer division result of 0. We will then need to replace the 0.5 argument with our new hour variable.

```
public void myFirstMethod() {
    //Name
    //Date
    //This program will prompt the user for a time
    //and change the clock based on that time
    String response = JOptionPane.showInputDialog(null,
            "Enter hours as an integer");
    int time = Integer.parseInt(response);
    double hour = time/12.0;
    this.clock.getHour().roll(RollDirection.LEFT, hour);
}
```

16. Click the Run button to view the animation. Type in an hour of day and watch the clock hour hand move to that hour.

17. **Challenge**: program the minute hand to move based on user input. Save and close your program.

Exercise 2: Computing Celsius with Input and Output (ongoing exercise)

1. Get into NetBeans.

2. From the **File** menu, choose **Open Project...**

3. Choose the **Celsius** project that you created in chapter 2. *(If you did not create this project please create a new project with the name Celsius)* Your program should look similar to the following:

```java
/*
 * This is a program to convert Fahrenheit to Celsius
 * your name here
 * the date here
 * JDK version here
 */

public class Celsius {

    public static void main(String[] args) {
        double fahrenheit = 52.0;
        double celsius;
        celsius = 5.0/9 * (fahrenheit-32);
        System.out.println("Fahrenheit:  " + fahrenheit);
        System.out.println("Celsius:  " + celsius);
    }
}
```

4. Since this project was saved in the Chapter2Exercises folder, we should save it in the Chapter3Exercises folder with a new name. To do this we will need to copy the project to a new location with a new name. DO NOT use Save As. **Right click on the project** in the Project Panel and choose **Copy…** as shown below:

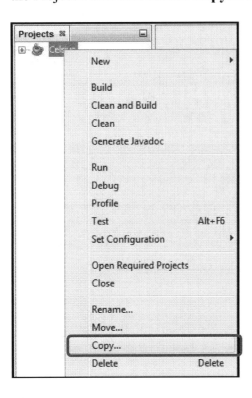

5. Name the new project **CelsiusMessageBox** and save it in the **Chapter3Exercises** folder. Do this by clicking the Copy button.

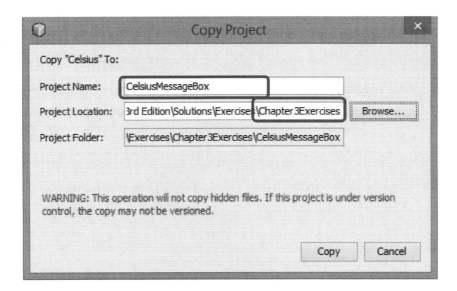

Note: Changing the project name will not change the file and class name. It is okay to have a different project name.

6. It would be ideal for the user to be able to type in any Fahrenheit temperature and see the corresponding Celsius temperature. To accomplish this, the Scanner class will be used to input the Fahrenheit temperature.

7. Line 11, the line that declares the Fahrenheit temperature to be a double and set to 52.0, will be changed to 3 lines as follows:

   Scanner keyboard = new Scanner (System.in);
   System.out.print("Enter the Fahrenheit: ");
   double fahrenheit = keyboard.nextDouble( );

8. Compile the program. You should get an error message stating that it doesn't understand Scanner class. This is because the Scanner class is not part of the basic java.lang package. The Scanner class is in the java.util package so that package must be imported. Place the following line on line 7 of your program (right after your beginning comments):

   import java.util.Scanner;

9. Compile the program. It should compile cleanly. Execute the program. It will ask for a Fahrenheit temperature. Type in 212.0 and press the Enter key. What did it give for the corresponding Celsius temperature?

10. This program is now interactive and you can type in any Fahrenheit temperature and get the corresponding Celsius temperature. However, this is only one way of making the program interactive. The JOptionPane class can also be used to input and show the results via dialog boxes. You will need to add the JOptionPane import after the Scanner import. Try to keep your imports in alphabetical order *(NetBeans will display a warning, denoted by a yellow light bulb, when the imports are out of order).*

    import javax.swing.JOptionPane;

11. First, a String variable is needed to hold the inputted entry on the dialog box. Second, the dialog box should appear asking the user to enter the Fahrenheit number. Last, the string information in the variable called response needs converted to a double so it can be used in a calculation. The *3 Scanner lines* entered in previous steps should be changed to:

    String input = JOptionPane.showInputDialog(null, "Enter Fahrenheit");
    double fahrenheit = Double.parseDouble(input);

12. Compile the program. It should compile cleanly. Execute the program. It will ask for a Fahrenheit temperature in a dialog box. Enter 212.0 and click on the OK button.

13. To adjust the Celsius temperature to also appear in a dialog box, adjust the System.out lines to be:

JOptionPane.showMessageDialog(null, "Fahrenheit: "+ fahrenheit
    + "\nCelsius: " + celsius);

14. Compile and execute the program. It should now be completely interactive and use dialog boxes for input and output. The output dialog box should resemble the following:

15. To format the Celsius temperature, what could you use? The NumberFormat class won't work because this isn't dollars or percentages. The DecimalFormat class will need to be used. To use this class, you need to insert another import at beginning of program as follows:

import java.text.DecimalFormat;

16. Delete the import statement for the Scanner class because it is not needed.

17. The last JOptionPane dialog box needs adjusted to use the DecimalFormat as follows:

DecimalFormat pattern = new DecimalFormat("##0.00");

JOptionPane.showMessageDialog(null, "Fahrenheit: " + fahrenheit
    + "\nCelsius: " + **pattern.format(celsius));**

18. Compile and execute the new version of the program. The program should appear as follows:

```
 * This is a program to convert Fahrenheit to Celsius
 * your name here
 * the date here
 * JDK version here
 */

import java.text.DecimalFormat;
import javax.swing.JOptionPane;

public class Celsius {

    public static void main(String[] args) {
        String input = JOptionPane.showInputDialog(null, "Enter Fahrenheit");
        double fahrenheit = Double.parseDouble(input);
        double celsius;
        celsius = 5.0 / 9.0 * (fahrenheit - 32);
        DecimalFormat pattern = new DecimalFormat("##0.00");
        JOptionPane.showMessageDialog(null, "Fahrenheit: " + fahrenheit
            + "\nCelsius: " + pattern.format(celsius));
    }
}
```

19. Challenge: Format the fahrenheit variable to also have 2 decimal places. You can use the same pattern that was used to format the celsius variable.

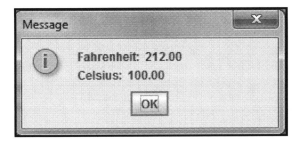

Exercise 3: Money Changer with Input and Output (ongoing exercise)

1. Get into NetBeans.

2. From the **File** menu, choose **Open Project…**

3. Choose the **MoneyChanger** project that you created in chapter 2. *(If you did not create this project please create a new project with the name MoneyChanger.)* Your program should look similar to the following:

```java
/*
 * Your Name and Date
 * This program will break change into corrects coins
 * JDK Version
 */

public class MoneyChanger {

    public static void main(String[] args) {
        //declaring variables
        int cents = 393;
        int centsLeft; //temporary variable for storing remaining cents
        int dollars;
        int quarters;
        int dimes;
        int nickels;
        int pennies;

        //begin calculations
        dollars = cents / 100;
        centsLeft = cents % 100;
        quarters = centsLeft / 25;
        centsLeft = centsLeft % 25;
        dimes = centsLeft / 10;
        centsLeft = centsLeft % 10;
        nickels = centsLeft / 5;
        centsLeft = centsLeft % 5;
        pennies = centsLeft;

        //printing results
        System.out.println("Total Cents: " + cents
                + "\nDollars: " + dollars
                + "\nQuarters: " + quarters
                + "\nDimes: " + dimes
                + "\nNickels: " + nickels
                + "\nPennies: " + pennies);
    }
}
```

4. Since this project was saved in the Chapter2Exercises folder, we should save it in the Chapter3Exercises folder with a new name. To do this we will need to copy the project to a new location with a new name. DO NOT use Save As. **Right click on the project** in the Project Panel and choose **Copy...** as shown below:

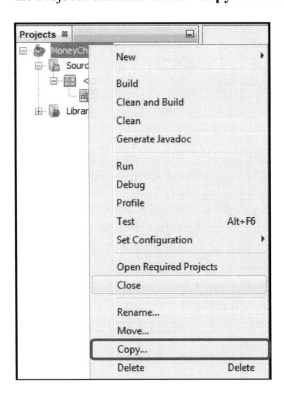

5. Name the new project **MoneyChangerMessageBox** and save it in the **Chapter3Exercises** folder.

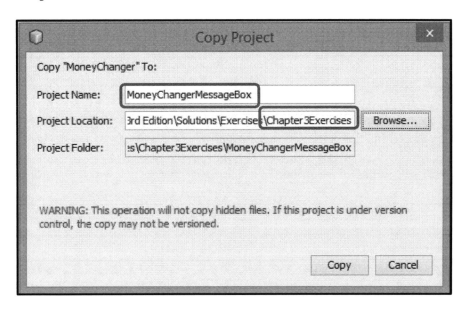

Note: Changing the project name will not change the file and class name. It is okay to have a different project name.

6. To adjust this program to allow the user to input the cents via a dialog box, you would add the JOptionPane input dialog as the first line of your main method and change the cents variable to parse the answer variable.

   String answer = JOptionPane.showInputDialog(null, "Enter total cents");
   int cents = Integer.parseInt(answer);

7. Because you are using the JOptionPane class in this program, you will need an import statement after your beginning comments as follows:

   import javax.swing.JOptionPane;

8. Compile and execute this program. When the dialog box appears requesting cents, enter 393 and click on OK button. The output should look the same as it did in chapter 2 because the System.out.println statements have not been adjusted.

9. To combine all the System.out.println statements into one dialog box that appears with all the money change, one very long continuous JOptionPane.showMessageDialog line will be developed with the usage of the escape code \n to display multiple lines as follows:

   JOptionPane.showMessageDialog(null, "Total Cents: " + cents
   + "\nDollars: " + dollars
   + "\nQuarters: " + quarters
   + "\nDimes: " + dimes
   + "\nNickels: " + nickels
   + "\nPennies: " + pennies);

10. Notice that not only the *System.out.println* lines are eliminated; they are replaced by one JoptionPane statement. The above says to display one dialog box on multiple lines (caused by the \n). Everything is concatenated with + signs so that it really represents one very long String.

11. Compile and execute the program. Enter 393 in the dialog box when it asks for the total cents. Make sure that the output is correct.

12. It seems a bit awkward to ask a user to enter in "total cents". It would make more sense for the user to be asked enter in a decimal amount representing change. Therefore, adjust those two lines early in the program to be:

    String answer = JOptionPane.showInputDialog(null, "Enter amount of change");
    int cents = (int) (Double.parseDouble(answer)   * 100);

13. The above line takes the decimal number that the user enters and saves it as a string in the String variable called answer. It then converts that string to a double, then multiplies by 100, and then takes the integer of that and places that final result into the integer variable called cents.

14. Compile and execute the program. Enter 3.93 when asked to enter the amount of change. It should work fine. Execute the program again entering 4.58 to see if it works for that amount.

15. The final program should look as follows:

```java
/*
 * Your name and date
 * This program will break change into correct coins
 * JDK version
 */
import javax.swing.JOptionPane;

public class MoneyChanger {

    public static void main(String[] args) {
        //declaring variables
        String answer =JOptionPane.showInputDialog(null,
                "Enter amount of change");
        int  cents = (int)(Double.parseDouble(answer) * 100);
        int centsLeft; //temporary variable
        int dollars;
        int quarters;
        int dimes;
        int nickels;
        int pennies;

        //begins calculations
        dollars = cents / 100;
        centsLeft = cents % 100;
        quarters = centsLeft / 25;
        centsLeft = centsLeft % 25;
        dimes = centsLeft / 10;
        centsLeft = centsLeft % 10;
        nickels = centsLeft / 5;
        centsLeft = centsLeft % 5;
        pennies = centsLeft;

        //printing results
        JOptionPane.showMessageDialog(null,
                "Total Cents: " + cents
                + "\nDollars: " + dollars
                + "\nQuarters: " + quarters
                + "\nDimes: " + dimes
                + "\nNickels: " + nickels
                + "\nPennies: " + pennies);

    }
}
```

Exercise 4: Computing Tip Using Input and Dialog

1. Start NetBeans if you have exited and close any open projects. From the **File** menu, choose **New Project…**

2. Choose the **Java folder** on the left hand side of the window, then choose **Java Application.** Click **Next**.

3. In the New Java Application dialog, give your project the name **TipCalculator**, select the **location** of where you would like to save your file (Chapter3Exercises folder), make sure that the **Create Main Class** box is checked and change the Main Class name to **TipCalculator** instead of tipcalculator.TipCalculator. Click **Finish**.

4. The first thing to do in all Java programs is to put some comments about the program at the beginning of the program. There should be a comment line for name of program, author, date, and the JDK used. These lines should look something like this:

   ```
   /*  Computing tip amount
       written by your name on date and JDK version  */
   ```

5. Since we are going to use the JOptionPane dialog boxes to gather input from the user and to show output, we will need to add the import for the JOptionPane class:

   ```
   import javax.swing.JOptionPane;
   ```

6. Next, we are going to display the input dialog for the user to type the total bill that they would like to compute the tax. We will bring up the input dialog for entering the total bill and save in a String variable named input. Remember that the showInputDialog will give you a String even if you type a number into the box. After we have the information from the user saved in our input variable, we need to convert this value to a double and save as a new variable named bill.

   ```
   String input = JOptionPane.showInputDialog(null, "Enter the total bill");
   double bill = Double.parseDouble(input);
   ```

7. Now, we need to add the code to display an input dialog for the user to enter the tip percentage and to convert that percentage into a double. We will use the input variable that we previously declared to save the input from the user *(Note: we do not declare the input variable again since we already declared it as a String)*. We will then convert that input variable which was declared as a String into a double and save in a new double variable which we will name percentage.

   ```
   input=JOptionPane.showInputDialog(null,"Enter the tip percentage as a decimal "
        + "(Example: 10% would be 0.1)");
   double percentage = Double.parseDouble(input);
   ```

8. We now have the total bill amount in a variable called bill and we have the tip percentage in a variable called percentage. Let's compute the tip amount by multiplying the bill variable times the percentage variable.

    double tipAmount = bill * percentage;

9. Add a JOptionPane to print the tip result.

    JOptionPane.showMessageDialog(null, "Bill amount: " + bill
    **   + "\nTip Percentage: " + percentage**
    **   + "\nTip: " + tipAmount);**

10. This works fine for some numbers, but if you were to enter 53 dollars as the total bill and 0.15 as the percentage, you would get the following output:

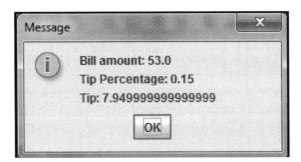

11. Since there is no way to give a tip of 7.9499999999999999, we should format this output as currency. We could use the DecimalFormat and set up our own pattern with 2 decimal places, commas, and a dollar sign, but the NumberFormat class already has a pattern for currency. Let's add the import for the NumberFormat class. Place this import before the JOptionPane import so that the imports are in alphabetical order.

    import java.text.NumberFormat;

12. Now let's set up the NumberFormat object with currency.

    NumberFormat dollars = NumberFormat.getCurrencyInstance();

13. Next, we need to apply the formatting to the values that we want to format. To do this you will use the name of the formatting object with the format method. The value that you want to format will go in parenthesis. The value that we want to format is in our tipAmount variable.

    JOptionPane.showMessageDialog(null, "Bill amount: " + bill
            + "\nTip Percentage: " + percentage
            + "\nTip: " + **dollars.format(tipAmount));**

14.   We could also format the bill to have the currency format. To do this you could use the currency format object that you already created. The code should look as follows:

JOptionPane.showMessageDialog(null, "Bill amount: " + **dollars.format(bill)**
        + "\nTip Percentage: " + percentage
        + "\nTip: " + dollars.format(tipAmount));

15. Compile and execute your program. You should get the following result:

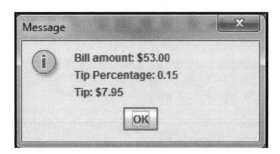

16. The final version of the program should appear as follows:

```
/* Computing tip amount
 * written by your name on date and JDK version  */

import java.text.NumberFormat;
import javax.swing.JOptionPane;

public class TipCalculator {

    public static void main(String[] args) {
        String input = JOptionPane.showInputDialog(null,
                "Enter the total bill");
        double bill = Double.parseDouble(input);
        input = JOptionPane.showInputDialog(null,
                "Enter the tip percentage as a decimal "
                + "(Example: 10% would be 0.1)");
        double percentage = Double.parseDouble(input);
        double tipAmount = bill * percentage;
        NumberFormat dollars = NumberFormat.getCurrencyInstance();
        JOptionPane.showMessageDialog(null, "Bill amount: "
                + dollars.format(bill)
                + "\nTip Percentage: " + percentage
                + "\nTip: " + dollars.format(tipAmount));
    }
}
```

17. Close the project.

Summary

- The class **NumberFormat** can be used to format output as currency.
  NumberFormat currencyFormatter = NumberFormat.getCurrencyInstance( );
  System.out.println(currencyFormatter.format(20.5));
  Output: $20.50
- The class **DecimalFormat** can be used to format output with a specific number of digits before and after the decimal point.
  DecimalFormat patternFormatter = new DecimalFormat ("$##0.00");
  System.out.println(patternFormatter.format(.5));
  Output: $0.50
- The Scanner Class provides methods to input data from the Java console. Example:
  Scanner keyboard = new Scanner (System.in);
  System.out.print("Enter your age > ");
  int age = keyboard.nextInt();
- The **JOptionPane** in the Java Library is a class that is used to create standard dialog boxes for input or output. These dialog boxes are small windows that ask a question or provide user messages.
  String response;
  response = JOptionPane.showInputDialog(null, "Enter Fahrenheit: ");
- A package is a collection of classes that are somewhat related, given a name, and stored in such a way to make the package accessible to your Java program. Java has a large number of standard packages that automatically come with Java. The package **java.lang** contains classes that are basic to Java programming. The java.lang package is so basic that it is always imported into every Java program.
- To use the **NumberFormat** and **DecimalFormat** class, you need to import the java.text package. To use the **Scanner** class, you need to import the java.util package. To use the **JOptionPane** class, you need to import the javax.swing package.

Review Questions

1. The NumberFormat class is used to format currency.
   a. true
   b. false

2. The showInputDialog( ) method shows the results on screen but does not request input from user.
   a. true
   b. false

3. The showMessageDialog() method shows the results on the screen but does not request input from the user.
   a. true
   b. false

4. In order to use the **JOptionPane** class, you need to import what package?
   a. import java.util.JOptionPane;
   b. import java.text.JOptionPane;
   c. import javax.swing.JOptionPane;
   d. import java.swing.JOptionPane;

Solutions: 1) a   2) b   3) a   4) c

Assignments

3-1 Calculating Interest Using JOptionPane Boxes: Your goal is to ask the user 3 different questions with 3 different dialog boxes concerning dollars borrowed, interest rate, and number of years borrowed. The computer should then calculate *simple* interest and display all 4 pieces of information in sentence form on a dialog box.

Your program should have the following:

- Make the name of the project **InterestMessageBox**
- Have a dialog box appear on screen that requests the user to type in amount of dollars borrowed. Place the response that a user types in into a String variable. Convert that string using the *parseDouble* method in *Double* class and place this double into a double variable named *dollars*.

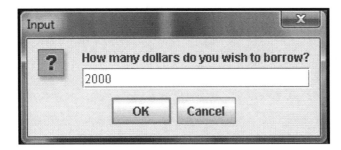

- Have a dialog box appear on screen that requests the interest rate from user. Place the response that a user types in into a new String variable. Convert that string using the *parseDouble* method in *Double* class and place this double into a double variable named *rate*.

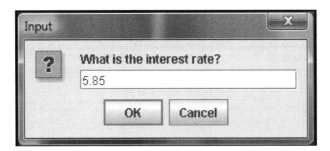

- Have a dialog box appear on screen that requests the number of years of the loan from user. Place the response that a user types in into a new String variable. Convert that string using the *parseInt* method in the *Integer* class and place the result into a variable named *years*.

- Have the computer calculate the total interest by using the following equation:
  dollars * years * rate/100
  Make sure that you are using the variables instead of typing the numbers in your equation.
- Have the computer display the amount borrowed, the interest rate, the number of years, and the calculated interest in a message similar to the following:

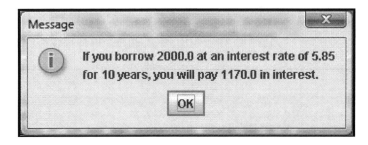

Note: This will require using concatenation of + signs and escape code of \n etc. This is a very long statement that should be broken up at + signs and span over several lines of code. Make sure to have spaces between words and numbers.

- If everything compiles and executes correctly, you should get the above answer of 1170.0 when you type in 2000, 5.85 and 10. Make sure that you are using variables in your output instead of typing in the numbers.
- Format the interest of 1170.0 so that it shows dollars and cents with 2 decimals.

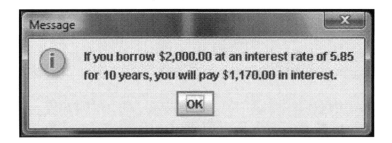

3-2   **Converting Ounces Using JOptionPane Boxes**: Your goal is to ask the user for a total number of ounces and convert this to cups, pints, quarts, and gallons.

Your program should have the following:

- Make the name of the project **OuncesConversion**
- Have a dialog box appear on screen that requests the user to type in the total number of ounces. For this example, I used 92, but you could use any number that you choose.

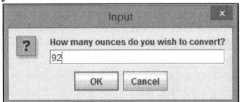

- Place the response that a user types in into a String variable. Then convert that string using the *parseDouble* method in Double class and place this double into a variable (make sure that you follow the Java variable naming rules).
- Have the computer convert the number of ounces entered by the user into cups, pints, quarts, and gallons. You will need to create a variable for each of the conversions. Make sure that you calculations are using the variable that you created for ounces.
  1 cup = 8 oz
  1 pint = 16 oz
  1 quart = 32 oz
  1 gallon = 128 oz
- Have the computer display the number of ounces entered by the user and the converted number of cups, pints, quarts, and gallons. Make sure that you are using variables for your output and not typing the answers into this box. This should look similar to the following message box:

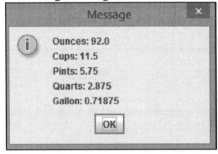

- Format the variables to have 2 decimals places, but only if there is a number to display (Hint: use the "#" for your formatting pattern instead of "0").

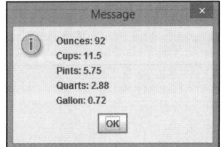

Chapter 4

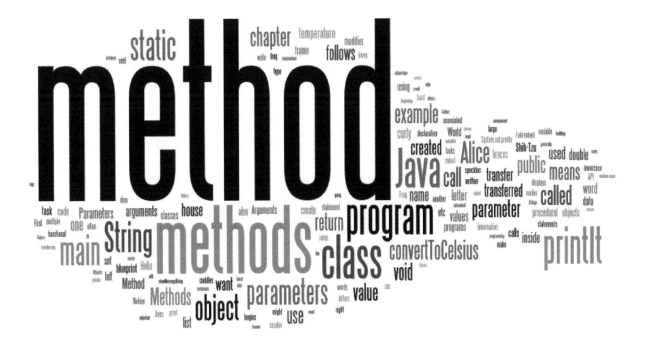

Procedural Methods

Objectives

- ☑ Properly construct and use methods when programming.
- ☑ Build methods with:
  - o No Arguments and No Return Values
  - o Some Arguments and No Return Values
- ☑ Use arguments and return values properly.
- ☑ Create a library and call methods from the library from another class.
- ☑ Explain the purpose of the Java API.

Introduction to Methods

If we were to keep writing all of our code in the main method of our program, we would notice that our programs would quickly become cumbersome and hard to read. When we are given a large task, we often times break this large task into smaller tasks that are easier to carry out. For example: cleaning a house can be a large task, but if broken up into smaller tasks, it is not so overwhelming. We can think about cleaning the house as a series of tasks instead of one giant task. This is true for programming as well. It is easier to read and debug smaller segments of code.

Overview

Classes

A **class** is a blueprint for creating an object. When we create an object from a class, we refer to the object as an instance of the class. For example: when you are building a house, you choose a blueprint before you build the house. The blueprint for building the house would be known as the class and the house that is built would be known as the object or instance of the class.

In Alice, there are predefined 3D models which will act as our classes. The name of a class begins with a capital letter.

Objects

Objects are created from classes. For example, we could create 3 Shih-Tzu objects: speckles, cuddles, and dino from a Shih-Tzu class (blueprint). Notice that the name of an object begins with a lowercase letter. This naming helps us to differentiate the name of a class from the name of an object. Shih-Tzu objects could have properties such as: weight, color, etc. Even though speckles, cuddles, and dino were created from the Shih-Tzu class, they are still going to be different from one another. For example: speckles is white and loves to play, cuddles is brown and white and loves attention, and dino is brown, overweight, and loves to eat.

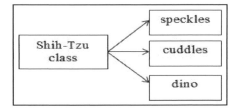

Methods

A **method** is a set of instructions that can be used upon request. You have already used methods such as *move* and *turn* in Alice animations. You have also used the Java JOptionPane methods of *showInputDialog* and *showMessageDialog* in your Java programs.

The main method is generally a starting point of all Java application programs. When you run your program, the main method is called by default. Instead of putting everything in the main method, we are going to start breaking our code up into multiple methods.

Methods are used for a variety of reasons. They are useful for organizing your program into more manageable pieces. Once methods are written they can be reused in other programs. For example: if you write a swim method for a fish, you can reuse that swim method in the future. This modularity allows us to work together to achieve a much larger goal.

The Java language and the Alice environment include built-in libraries of methods for you to use. You can build methods for others to use.

There are 2 types of procedural methods: object methods and static methods.

Object methods are written for the class from which the object was created. Example: if you create a frog from the Frog class in Alice and you want to write a jump method for the frog, this jump method should be written in the Frog class. Any frog that you add to your Alice environment from this Frog class will have this jump method.

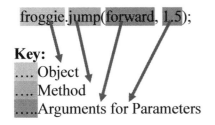

froggie.jump(forward, 1.5);

Key:
.... Object
.... Method
..... Arguments for Parameters

Methods that are not associated with an object are called **static methods**. The JOptionPane methods that we have been using (showInputDialog and showMessageDialog) are static methods. When you want to use a static method, you need to specify the name of the class that the method belongs to.

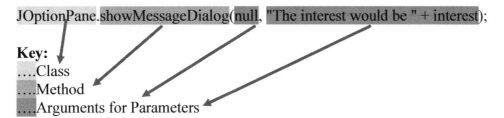

JOptionPane.showMessageDialog(null, "The interest would be " + interest);

Key:
....Class
....Method
....Arguments for Parameters

A **parameter** is a special variable that receives information that we send to a method. Parameters give programmers choices when using a method. For example: most of the built in Alice methods have parameters set up. This means that when you use an Alice method such as *move*, you will have parameters such as *direction* and *distance*. A parameter is what the programmer writing the method sets up to allow arguments to be passed into the method. An argument is what the programmer using the method selects when they call the method. When you use a method we refer to it as **calling or invoking a method**.

The methods in this chapter are all **procedural methods** meaning that they carry out an action, but don't return any values. The word **void** in the method declaration tells you that this is a procedural method. This will be explained in more detail throughout this chapter and in the next chapter. We will call all of the methods that return a value **functional methods**. The next chapter will focus on functional methods.

Procedural Methods in Alice

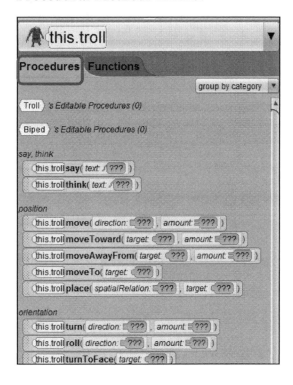

Functional Methods in Alice

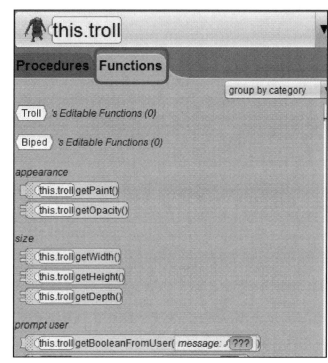

Java Application Programming Interface (API)

The Java API (libraries) has all the classes/methods that Oracle has provided to programmers. To see the Java 2 Platform Standard Edition 8.0 go to the following site:

http://docs.oracle.com/javase/8/docs/api/

On the left side of the screen in its own frame is an alphabetical list of all classes in the JDK. On the right side is a list of all the packages.

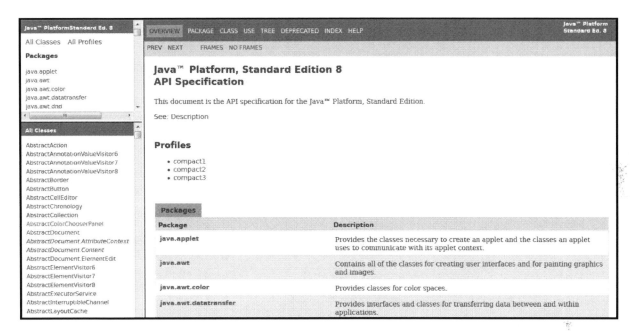

You can also select a package (folder) from the upper left frame, then select a class (file) from the bottom left frame. Once you select a specific class, you will see a list of methods that belong to that class in the right frame.

Java Method Declaration

The syntax for a method is:

modifier static return-type method-name(list of parameters) {
        .... statements to do inside of method
}

- The first thing in a method is the **modifier**. Modifiers determine the scope of a method. The two most common modifiers are public and private. The modifier **public** means that the method is available in this class (program) and other classes. The modifier **private** means that you intend to use the variable or method only in this program.

- The word "**static**" means that the method is not associated with an object. Most of the Alice methods that we create will not be static since they will be created for objects. If a method is not static, then leave the word static off of the declaration.

- The **return-type** can be any of the primitives that you have seen such as int, double, float, etc. If you don't plan on returning any value back from the method then you use the word "*void*". All of the methods in this chapter are void. We will be using methods that return a value in the next chapter. We will call all of the methods that do not return a value "procedural methods" and the methods that return a value "functional methods".

- A **method-name** uses the same guidelines as described for variables as follows:
  - Consists of letters, digits, underscores (_) or $ (no spaces allowed).
  - First character can't be a digit. (First character is generally lowercase letter.)
  - Cannot be keywords (see Keywords section).
  - Stylistic rule: all method names begin with a lowercase letter with all other words beginning with uppercase letter such as displayIt, sumNumbers, etc.
  - Method names should be meaningful.

- List of parameters is a list of all the data that you will be transferring into the method. You might want to transfer nothing to the method, or you might want to transfer several items. These parameters can be integers, doubles, Strings, other objects, etc. The information transferred to a method is often referred to as arguments while the actual placeholders for the information in the method are often called parameters.

- A set of left and right curly braces that surround the statements that you want to accomplish inside of the method.

Note: To make the program more understandable, place the curly braces on separate lines so it can be easily seen where a method begins and ends. You can also place a comment on ending curly brace lines to say what method is ending. Java does not require the curly braces to be on separate lines or to have comments, but it can be very helpful.

Java Method Examples

Methods with No Parameters

The simplest of all methods is the one with NO parameters and NO return values. An example of this would be a method that printed the words "Hello World" whenever we called it. It would not be able to print anything else and it wouldn't need any data transferred to it. The method might be used by others so we could make it public as follows:

public static void **printIt ( )** {
      System.out.println("Hello World");
}

The above method is a public method called printIt. It is static because it is not associated with an object. The word void means it returns no values. The empty set of parentheses means that it receives no transfer of arguments (has no parameters). The statement inside of the curly braces simply prints the String of "Hello World". Now, how do we get the computer to actually call this method? That will be done from the main method of a program as follows:

public static void main (String [ ] args) {
     printIt ( );
}

Now, if we add our traditional comments and the class declaration statement to the beginning of the program, the entire program would be:

```
/*
 * This program will print Hello World using a printIt method
 */

public class SampleMethods1 {
    public static void main(String[] args) {
        printIt();
    }

    public static void printIt(){
        System.out.println("Hello World");
    }
}
```

This program still accomplishes the same thing as the very first program that you did in Chapter 1 except it does it with printIt method that you created. The above main method has only one statement inside of it and that is the call to the printIt method. Notice that there are no arguments in the call to the printIt method because the printIt method has no parameters.

Let's look at another example of a method with no parameters and no return values. We created a program that drew the block letters of "YN". We can write the drawing of the block letters in a method called initials and call it from the main method.

```java
/*
 * This program will print intials using a printInitials method
 */

public class SampleMethods2 {
    public static void main(String[] args) {
        printInitials();
    }

    public static void printInitials(){
        System.out.println("Y     Y    N     N");
        System.out.println(" Y   Y     NN    N");
        System.out.println("  Y Y      N N   N");
        System.out.println("   Y       N  N  N");
        System.out.println("   Y       N   NN");
        System.out.println("   Y       N    N");
    }
}
```

The output display that will result when you execute the above program is as follows:

```
Output - SampleMethods2 (run)
run:
Y     Y    N     N
 Y   Y     NN    N
  Y Y      N N   N
   Y       N  N  N
   Y       N    NN
   Y       N     N
BUILD SUCCESSFUL (total time: 0 seconds)
```

Methods with Some Parameters

A method with a parameter means that some data will be transferred into the method. When declaring the method, the parameters will be declared inside of the parentheses. Each parameter will be listed with a type and a name. The type should be an object or primitive type such as int, Boolean, double, float or String. As an example, let's adjust the *printIt* method that we did earlier in chapter to have a String parameter. This means that instead of always printing the words "Hello World", we would like the method to be more generic and print any String that we want. First, we adjust the *printIt* method to be able to have a String parameter as follows:

```
public static void printIt ( String x ) {
        System.out.println( x );
}
```

Notice, that the above method is more generic than it was earlier in chapter. It says take the String called x that is transferred to this method and simply displays it with a *println* command.

The main method would then be adjusted to make multiple calls to the method so multiple Strings would print as follows:

```
public static void main ( String [ ] args) {
        printIt ("Java can be fun" );
        printIt ("Java can be hard");
        printIt ("Bye bye");
}
```

The above code calls the printIt method with the String of "Java can be fun". Once into the printIt method, the computer displays this transferred String. Next, the main method calls the printIt method with the String of "Java can be hard". It then calls the printIt method with the String of "Bye bye". The result of this is:

```
Output - SampleMethods3 (run)

run:
Java can be fun
Java can be hard
Bye bye
BUILD SUCCESSFUL (total time: 0 seconds)
```

The parameters to a method can also be numbers such as ints and doubles. You can transfer any mix of data to a method. You could transfer an integer, a double, and/or a String. In an earlier chapter, a fahrenheit program was created that took a double value for fahrenheit and calculated what the corresponding celsius value would be and displayed it. This program could be adjusted to have a *convertToCelsius* method as follows:

```java
/*
 * This program will print convert Fahrenheit to Celsius
 * using a convertToCelsius method
 */

public class SampleMethods3 {
    public static void main(String[] args) {
        double fahrenheit = 212;
        convertToCelsius(fahrenheit);
        convertToCelsius(50.5);
        convertToCelsius(83.9 + 14.5);
    }

    public static void convertToCelsius(double f){
        double c = 5/9.0 * (f - 32);
        System.out.println("Fahrenheit: " + f);
        System.out.println("Celsius: " + c);
    }
}
```

The above Java program has a *convertToCelsius* method that has one parameter. That parameter is a double called *f* that is used in a formula to calculate a celsius temperature. Then the two *System.out.println* statements display the Fahreneheit and Celsius temperatures.

The main method in the above Java program makes a call to the *convertToCelsius* with a Fahrenheit temperature of 212.0. This Fahrenheit temperature is transferred to the variable called *f* in the convertToCelsius method. The convertToCelsius method then displays the Fahrenheit temperature of 212.0 and corresponding Celsius temperature of 100.0. The main method then invokes the *convertToCelsius* method again, but this time transfers 50.5 into *f* in the *convertToCelsius* method. The main method invokes the convertToCelsius one last time, but before transferring a value to the method, Java will calculate 83.9 + 14.5 and get 98.4, then transfer the 98.4 to *f* in the convertToCelsius method. The results of the above program would be:

```
Fahrenheit: 212.0
Celsius: 100.0
Fahrenheit: 50.5
Celsius: 10.277777777777779
Fahrenheit: 98.4
Celsius: 36.88888888888889
```

Hands-on Exercises

Exercise 1: Creating a Stomp Method in Alice

Let's say that we want to create a stomp method for a troll. We would be creating a new procedure method called **stomp** for the troll object.

1. Get into Alice 3.

2. Choose the **Grass** template.

3. Save the file as **TrollStomp** to the appropriate exercises folder.

4. Click on **Setup Scene** button.

5. Add a troll to your scene. He is located in the biped folder. Name him **troll.**

6. Click the **Edit Code** button so that we can program the troll to stomp.

7. Normally we would write the code in myFirstMethod, but this time we are going to create a new procedural method called stomp. To do this, you will need to select the class from which you created your object from the drop down menu as shown below. Since we created the troll from the class Troll, you will need to select **Troll** from the list (next to Scene tab).

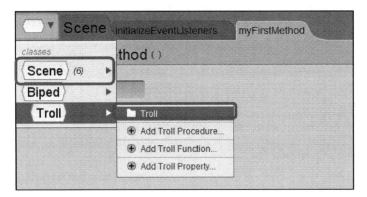

8. Click on **Add Troll Procedure...**

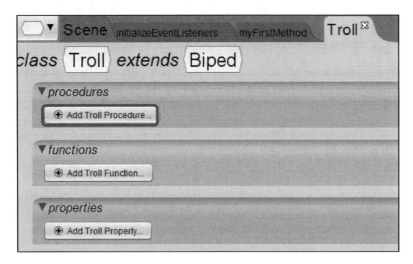

9. Then we have to give our new procedure method a name. Let's call the new procedural method **stomp**. Make sure that your name starts with a lowercase letter. Click **OK** button to create the procedure.

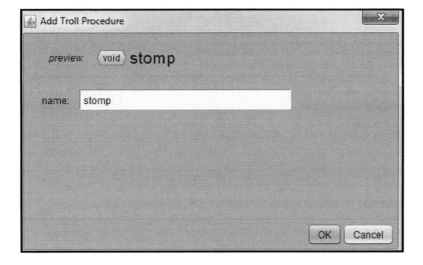

10. In the stomp procedure method that we just created for the troll, we need to move the trolls right hip and knee and left hip and knee to create the stomping motion. To move a body part, you would need to select the arrow next to the object and then select the body part.

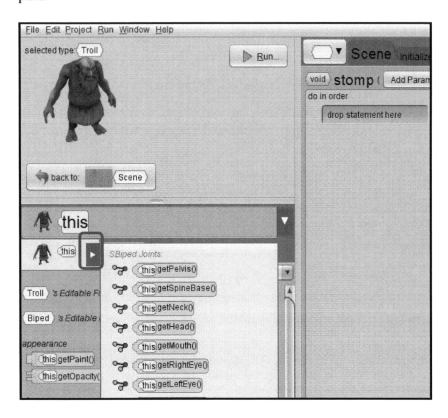

11. Select the **getRightHip.** Make sure you have selected the Procedures tab and then drag the turn method onto the editor. Select **BACKWARD** as the direction argument and **0.25** as the amount argument.

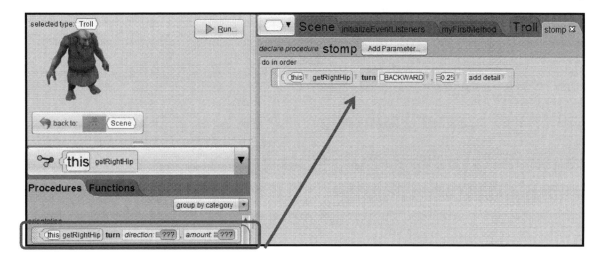

12. Let's add the rest of the movements for the stomp as shown below. *(Note: the preferences for this screenshot are in Alice view. To change your view, select Window>Preferences>Programming Language>Alice)*

13. If you click the **Run** button, you will notice that nothing happens. This is because we created this new stomp method, but we never told our animation to run it. The myFirstMethod code in Alice is run automatically. If you want to use this new method that we created, you must call (invoke) it from some other method such as myFirstMethod. To get back to the **myFirstMethod**, you will need to click on the myFirstMethod tab.

14. The myFirstMethod should now be showing. Make sure the troll is selected and you are on the Procedures tab. You will notice that you have a new method for the troll called stomp.

15. Drag this new method over into the editor and then click the run button. Your troll should now stomp.

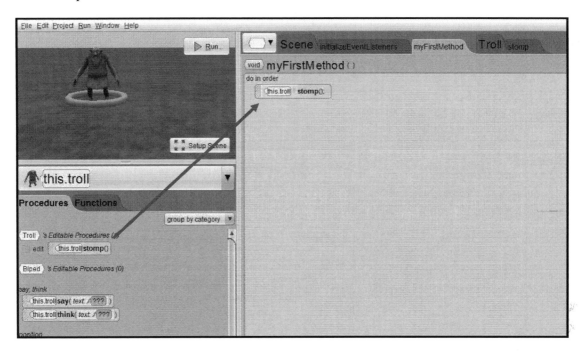

16. Click the **Run** button to see the animation. This isn't quite what we wanted. We really need the troll to move his right hip backwards and his right knee forward at the same time. Then, we need him to move his right hip forward and his right knee backwards at the same time.

17. To adjust this movement to happen at the same time, we will need to go back to the stomp method for the troll. You can right click on the stomp method and choose edit or you can select the Troll class then the stomp method as we did before. The short cut way is shown below:

18. To make the first 2 statements happen at the same time we will need to drag the DoTogether block to the editor and place the first 2 statements inside of this block. Then, we will do the same thing for the next 2 statements. The final code should look as follows.

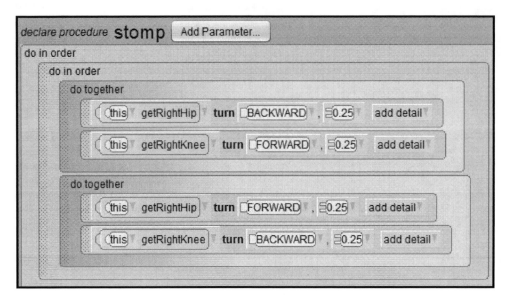

19. Please click the **Run** button to test this code. The troll should have a more fluid stomp. Save and exit Alice.

Exercise 2: Making a Dog's Tail Wag in Alice

1. Get into Alice 3.

2. Choose the **Grass** template.

3. Save the file as **DogWag** to the appropriate exercises folder.

4. Click on **Setup Scene** button.

5. Add a Dalmatian to the scene. Name the dog **spot**. Then click on the **Edit Code** button.

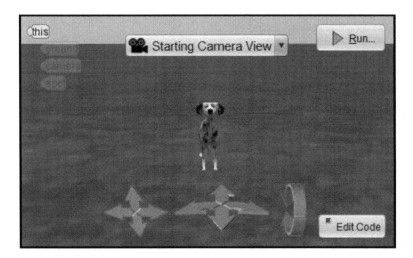

6. We would like to make the dog's tail wag, but instead of writing the code in myFirstMethod, we should add the code to the class that the dog belongs to. Since our dog object was created from the Dalmatian class, we would need to add our wag procedural method to the Dalmatian class. Click on the drop down arrow as shown below. Select the **Dalmatian** class and then select **Add Dalmatian Procedure...**

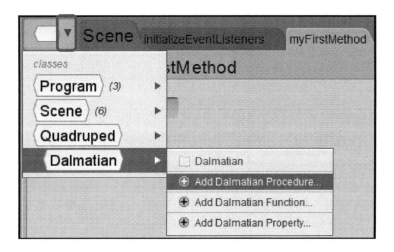

7. Name this new procedure **wag**.

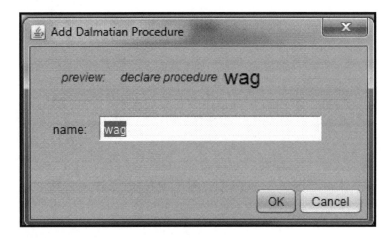

8. Select the subpart tail for the Dalmatian object. Click the drop down next to **this** in your object tree. Then click on the arrow to the right of the word **this** and select **this.getTail**. The word "this" represents the current class which is Dalmatian.

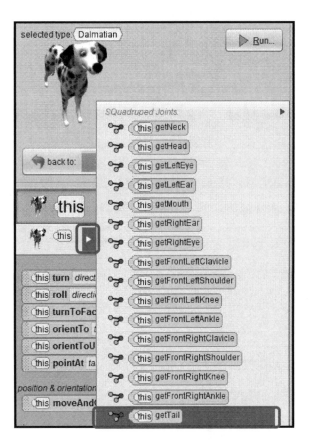

9. Now that the tail subpart for the Dalmatian class selected, let's drag the **turn** method onto the editor for the wag method. Select **LEFT** as the direction argument and **0.125** as the amount argument.

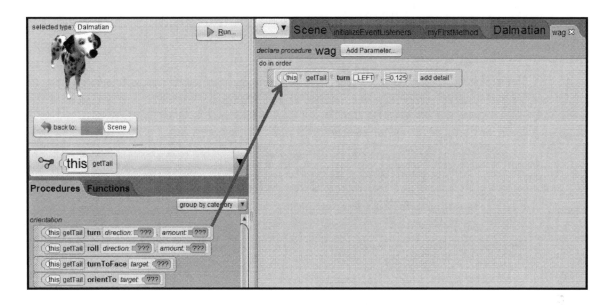

10. Next, let's make the tail wag to the RIGHT. Instead of choosing 0.125 again as our amount, we would need to choose 0.25. The tail has to move double the amount that it moved to the left; otherwise it would end up back at the original starting position. Drag the **turn** method onto the editor choosing a direction argument of **RIGHT** and an amount argument of **0.25**.

11. Finally, let's add the **turn** method with **LEFT** as the direction argument and **0.125** as the amount argument.

12. Click the **Run** button to play the animation. You should notice that nothing happens. Although we create a new wag procedural method for all Dalmatian objects, we did not call (invoke) this method.

13. Click on the **myFirstMethod** tab. Select **spot** from the object tree. Drag the **wag** method into the editor.

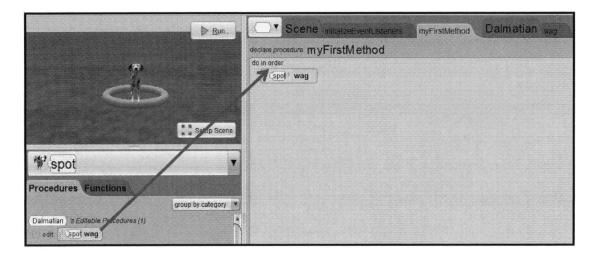

14. Click the **Run** button to play the animation. The dog should wag its tail.

15. What if we want to have the dog wag its tail at different speeds? Let's click back on the wag method to take a look at our code. Click on **add detail**, then **duration**, select **0.5**.

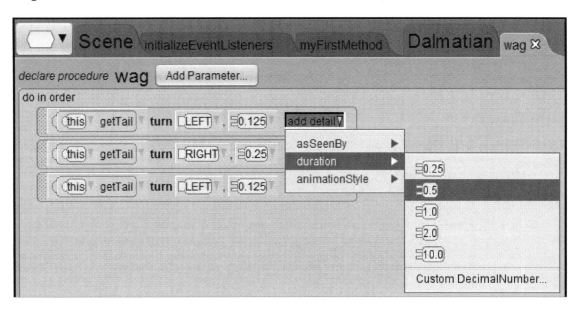

16. Adjust the two turn methods to be 0.5.

17. Click **Setup Scene** button and add another Dalmatian object to your scene. Name this object **spike**.

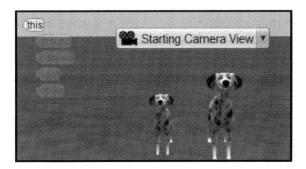

18. Click back on the myFirstMethod tab, select the Dalmatian object **spike**, and drag the **wag** method for spike to the editor. Run your animation. Spot should wag its tail and then spike should wag its tail.

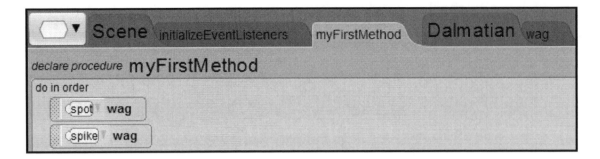

19. If you accidently close the wag method, or closed down the Alice environment and restarted, you will need to reopen the wag method. You can do this by selecting an object from the Dalmatian class (spot or spike) and clicking edit next to the method name as shown below:

20. What if we wanted to have spot wag his tail at a different speed than spike? The way we have the program currently written, this would not be possible. Click back on the **wag** method and click on the **Add Parameter...** button to add a parameter to our wag method.

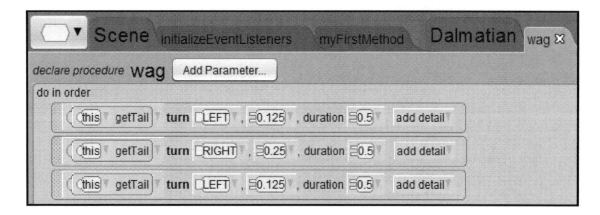

21. Select **DecimalNumber** as the type *(this is an Alice type, but would be a double in Java)*, name the variable **speed**, and **check the box** for understanding the need for updating invocations to this procedure.

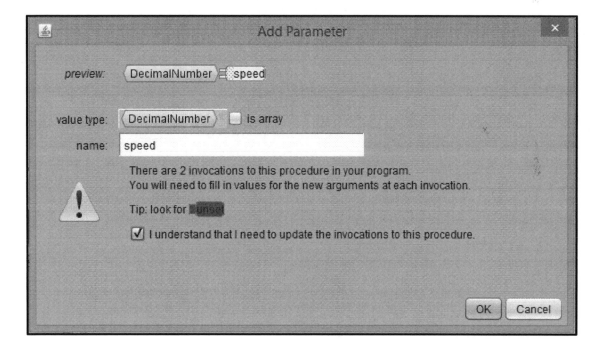

22. We will need to put the parameter that we just created into our turn statements. Put the new **speed** parameter as an argument for the duration for each statement.

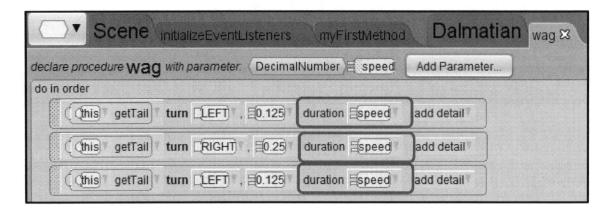

23. Now, we need to change the invocations to the wag procedure. Click back on **myFirstMethod** tab and pick a different speed for the wag for each dog.

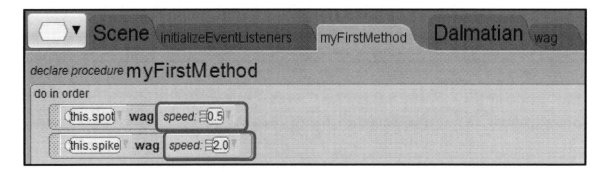

24. Run the animation. Spot and Spike are both able to do the wag method since they are both Dalmatians and the wag method was written for the Dalmatian class. Any Dalmatian object that you add to your scene will be able to wag their tail.

25. Save and exit Alice.

26. Now, let's transfer our Alice project into NetBeans and see what the Java code looks like. Open NetBeans. Click **File**, **New Project**, and select **Java Project from Existing Alice Project** and click the **Next** button.

27. Browse for the **DogWag.a3p** Alice file and then be sure to change the location of where you are saving the new NetBeans project. Click **Finish**.

28. If you look at the Java code for this Alice project, you will notice that **myFirstMethod** in the **Scene.java** file calls the wag method for both dogs.

```
public void myFirstMethod() {
    this.spot.wag(0.5);
    this.spike.wag(2.0);
}
```

29. Double click on the **Dalmatian.java** file in the Projects tab. The wag procedural method is located in the Dalmatian class since the wag method belongs with the Dalmatian. *Note: the some of the methods in this file are collapsed in the screenshot below. You can click the plus and minus sign to the left of the method to collapse or expand the code.*

```
1  [+]  imports
6
7       class Dalmatian extends Quadruped {
8
9  [-]      public Dalmatian() {
10               super(DalmatianResource.DEFAULT);
11           }
12
13 [-]      public void wag(Double speed) {
14               this.getTail().turn(TurnDirection.LEFT, 0.125, Turn.duration(speed));
15               this.getTail().turn(TurnDirection.RIGHT, 0.25, Turn.duration(speed));
16               this.getTail().turn(TurnDirection.LEFT, 0.125, Turn.duration(speed));
17           }
18
19 [-]      public SJoint getLeftEarMiddle() {
20               return this.getJoint(DalmatianResource.LEFT_EAR_MIDDLE);
21           }
22
23 [-]      public SJoint getRightEarMiddle() {
24               return this.getJoint(DalmatianResource.RIGHT_EAR_MIDDLE);
25           }
26
27 [-]      public SJoint getTail5() {
28               return this.getJoint(DalmatianResource.TAIL_4);
29           }
30       }
```

30. Run your project and then close it.

Exercise 3: Creating a Hokey Pokey Method in Alice (ongoing exercise)

1. Get into **Alice 3**.

2. Choose the **Grass Template and then click on the Setup Scene button**.

3. Add a tortoise to your world from the biped folder. Name the object **tortoise**.

4. Resize the tortoise so that you can clearly see him. Go back to the code editor.

5. Name your project **HokeyPokey** and save to the appropriate exercises folder.

6. We are going to have this tortoise do the hokey pokey. Let's add the Hockey Pokey song so that our tortoise could have some music. Please download the HokeyPokey.wav file and place in same folder where you are placing your Alice projects.

7. Choose the Scene by clicking on **.this**. Scroll down to the **playAudio** procedure (method). Drag this method to myFirstMethod and then choose **Import Audio**. Then find the **HokeyPokey.wav** file *(located in your **Data_Files** from iws.collin.edu/tdaly/book2)*. Your statement should look as follows:

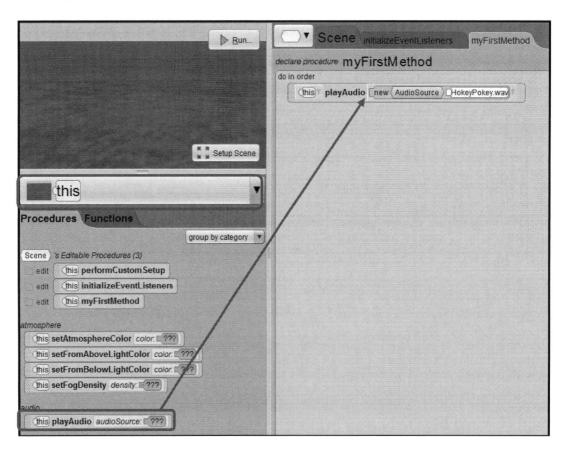

8. Instead of putting all of our code in our run method as we have been doing in previous chapters, we are going to break the code down into separate methods. The first method that we are going to create is going to be the hokeyPokeyVerse. Method names always start with a lowercase letter. Method naming follows the same rules as variable naming. To create this new procedure method for the tortoise, we will click on the **Tortoise** class and then **Add Tortoise Procedure...**

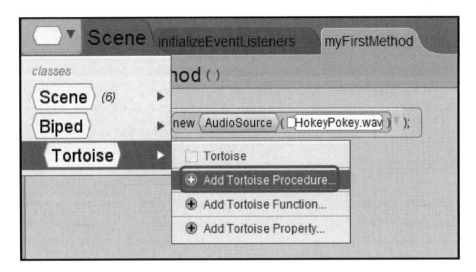

9. Name the new procedure method **hokeyPokeyVerse**.

10. We will add the statements to have the tortoise put his right hip in and right hip out. Select the **RightHip** body part. Choose the **turn** method and then fill in the **BACKWARD** and **0.25** as arguments. Add a turn with **FORWARD** and **0.25** as arguments. *(Note: you can copy the first turn method and make adjustments by holding down the control key, alt/option key on the Mac, dragging it down and releasing or by using the clipboard.)*

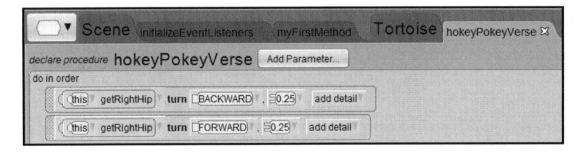

11. If you click on the Run button, you will notice that nothing happens. We need to call the hokeyPokeyVerse procedure method from myFirstMethod. Click on the **myFirstMethod** tab.

12. Click the tortoise from drop down list. Drag the hokeyPokeyVerse onto myFirstMethod.

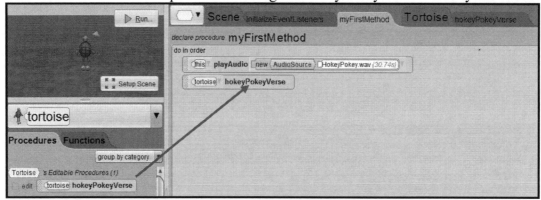

13. Click the **Run** button. What happens? The song is playing to the end and then the tortoise turns his leg. This is a problem. The song and the tortoise hokeyPokeyVerse should be playing at the same time. You can use the **DoTogether** to have the song play at the same time as the leg movements:

14. The shake is going to be 6 lines of code. We will have the tortoise turn his right leg to the right, then left, then right, and then left. Instead of adding these 6 lines to our hokeyPokeyVerse method, we want to separate this code into a new procedure method called **shake** that we call from the **hokeyPokeyVerse** method.

15. To create this new procedure method for the tortoise, we will click on the **Tortoise** class, then **Add Tortoise Procedure…**

16. Name the new procedure method **shake**.

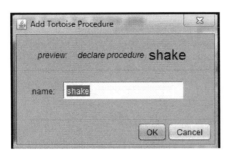

17. We need to add the following lines of code to have the tortoise shake his right hip. We need to turn his right hip backward to get the hip ready for the shake. Then, the right hip should turn 0.125 to the right to begin the shake. To turn his right hip to the left, the tortoise will need to turn his hip 0.25 to right to make up for the 0.125 that his hip has already turned to the right. Then, we repeat this again for the right and left motions except that the left turn should only be 0.125 so that it ends up back at its original position. After, the shaking, we will put the hip back to standing position by turning it forward. Please see the code below.

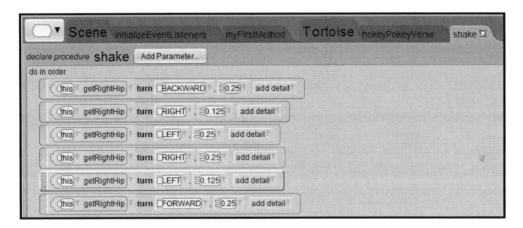

18. Before playing your animation, you need to call the new shake method from the hokeyPokeyVerse method. To get to the hokeyPokey verse method, click on the **hokeyPokeyVerse** tab.

19. Then, click on **this** *(this refers to the current object which is the tortoise)*. Drag the **shake** method into the hokeyPokeyVerse method as shown below:

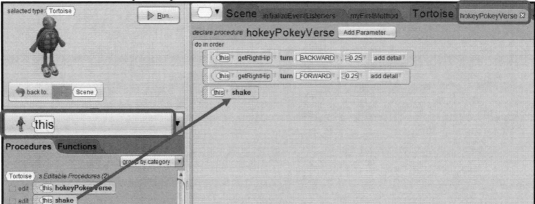

20. Now we are going to have the tortoise put his arms up in the air and turn around. We will create a new method named **turnAround**. Click on the **Tortoise** class, then **Add Tortoise Procedure…**Give the new procedure method the name **turnAround**. Add the following code for the new turnAround method.

21. Now, we need to call the turnAround method from the hokeyPokeyVerse method in order for it to play.

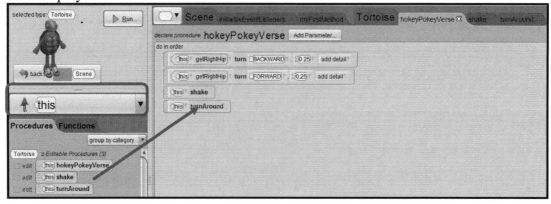

22. Play your animation. This looks pretty good so far, but wouldn't it be nice if this worked for the left leg, right arm, etc.? You are half way done with this exercise. This is a good stopping point if you want to take a break. Please save and exit Alice.

23. **Continue:** If you took a break, please open Alice, open your HokeyPokey program, and open all your method tabs for the Hokey Pokey *(click on the Tortoise class and then click on each method to open the tab for that method)*.

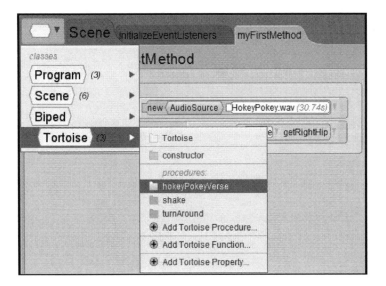

24. We already programmed the tortoise to do the hokey pokey with his right leg, but if we wanted to switch body parts, we shouldn't have to rewrite the same methods over and over again for every body part. Since the only thing that will be changing will be the body part, we can set up a parameter to pass the body part into the methods that we already created. Let's click on the **hokeyPokeyVerse** method tab to open up the code for this method.

25. We are going to add a parameter to this method. You can do this by clicking on the **Add Parameter...** button.

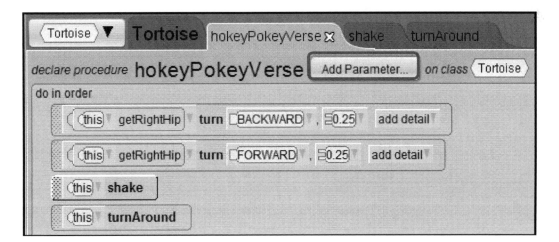

26. This parameter should have a type of **Other Types… SJoint**, name it **bodyPart**, and check the box that reads **I understand….**

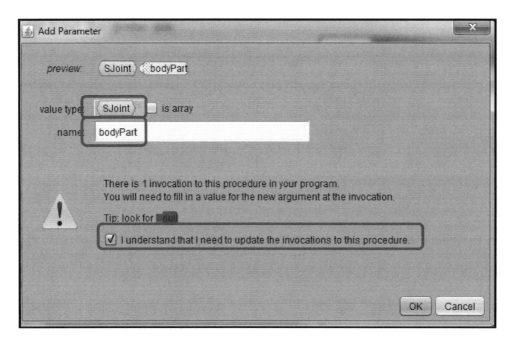

27. Now we are going to replace the right hip with the new bodyPart variable. Drag the bodyPart parameter onto the **this.getRightHip** as shown below. You can also click the drop down next to this.getRightHip to select the bodyPart variable.

28. Now we have to go back to **myFirstMethod**. We need to pass a bodyPart as an argument to the hokeyPokeyVerse method. Click the drop-down next to hokeyPokeyVerse and choose the getRightHip. If you do not change the bodyPart from unset to a body part, Alice will crash *(it cannot do the verse without a body part)*.

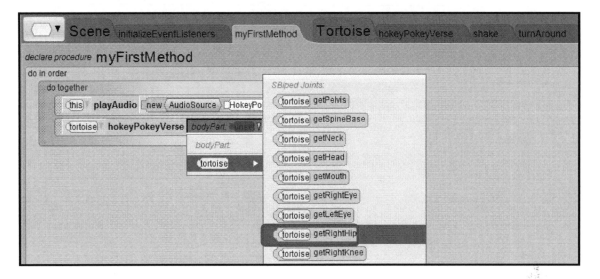

29. Play your animation. It should still look the same since we are using the right leg.

30. Now, we need to fix the shake method the same way. We should add a parameter and we can name it bodyPart. Go to the **shake** method tab. We are going to add a parameter to this method. You can do this by clicking on the **Add Parameter...** button. This parameter should be type of **OtherTypes.... SJoint,** name it **bodyPart**, and check the **I understand....** box.

31. We are going to replace the **this.getRightHip** with the bodyPart (parameter) as shown below.

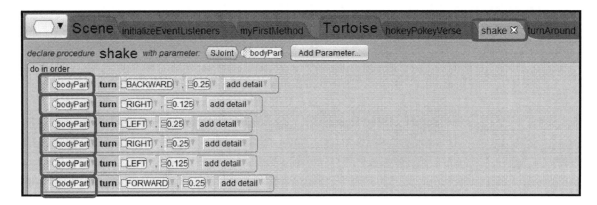

32. Now we need to go back to the place where we called this method. Click on the **hokeyPokeyVerse** method tab. Select bodyPart from the drop-down next to the shake method bodyPart parameter. We are actually using the **bodyPart** that was passed in to the hokeyPokeyVerse (the right leg in this case) and passing that into our shake method.

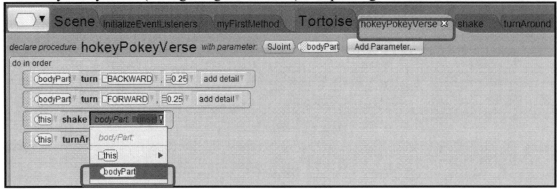

33. Now play your animation. It should still work for the right leg. We don't need to worry about adding a parameter for the turnAround method since the tortoise will be raising his arms and turning around exactly the same way each time.

34. Let's go back to the **myFirstMethod** and call the **hokeyPokeyVerse** method again this time with the **left leg**.

35. You will notice that the right hip and left hip move at the same time. You will need to add a DoInOrder to fix this issue as shown below:

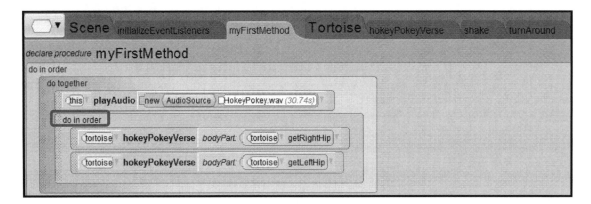

36. Everything works fine except the timing with the song may be off by 2 seconds. We need a delay at the end of the turnAround so that it doesn't start the next leg too soon. Click on the turnAround method and adjust it to have the delay of 2 seconds.

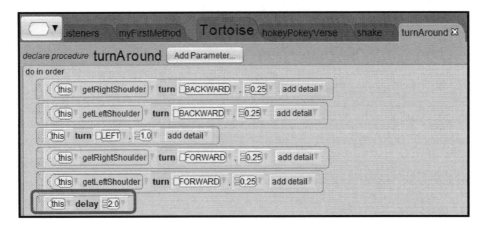

37. We need to have one method called hokeyPokey which calls the hokeyPokeyVerse which calls the shake and turnaround methods. Create the **hokeyPokey** method for the Tortoise.

38. Drag the DO IN ORDER block from myFirstMethod onto the clipboard *(if you hold down the ctrl key while you drag to the clip board it will copy and if you just drag to the clip board it will cut)*. Since we want to remove this code from myFirstMethod, we should use cut instead of copy.

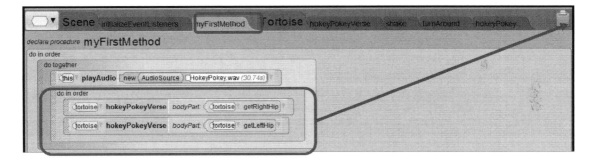

39. Click on the hokeyPokey method tab and drag the code from the clipboard to the hokeyPokey method *(the white piece of paper on the clipboard represents your code)*.

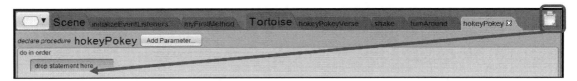

40. DO NOT run your program yet. You will notice some red in you the code that you pasted *(red indicates errors in code)*. You still have a reference to a particular tortoise and it should be referencing the current object (this) instead of a particular object. Change the reference to the tortoise object named "tortoise" to be the word **this** to represent any tortoise object. The concept of "this" will make more sense as we progress through the course.

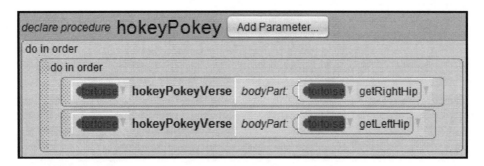

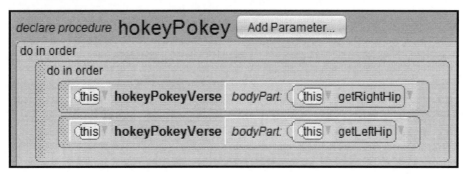

41. Invoke (call) the hokeyPokey method for the tortoise in myFirstMethod *(make sure that you select the tortoise object and click on the procedures tab)*.

42. You may need to add a delay before your DoTogether block to give the animation a chance to load the sound file. Make sure that you are in myFirstMethod and you have the scene selected "this". Drag the delay statement above the DoTogether block and choose 2 seconds as the argument.

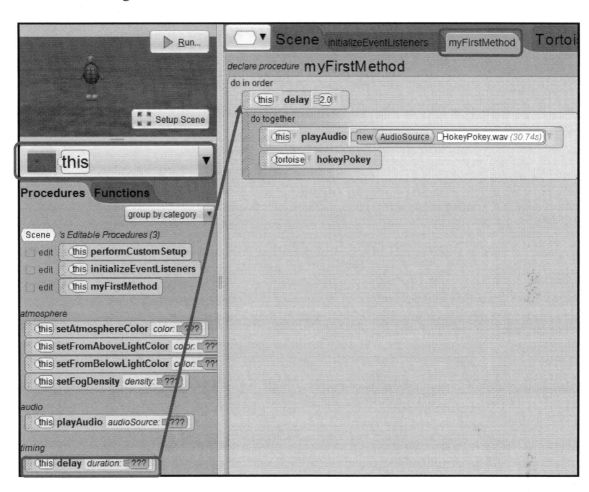

43. Add another tortoise called tortoise2 to the scene. Have that tortoise do the Hokey Pokey also.

44. Run your animation. Both tortoises should do the Hokey Pokey dance.

45. Let's add the right and left shoulder to the hokeyPokey method as shown below. This verse doesn't work for all of the body parts, since some body parts need to turn forward and some need to turn backward.

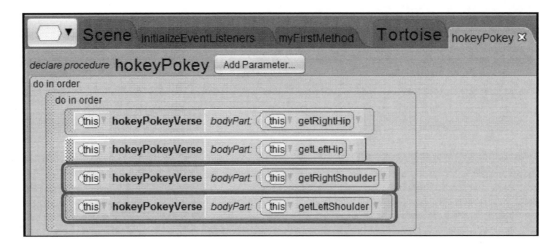

46. Run your animation. You should notice that the song stops after 2 body parts. We need the song to play twice. Copy the playAudio statement so it looks as follows:

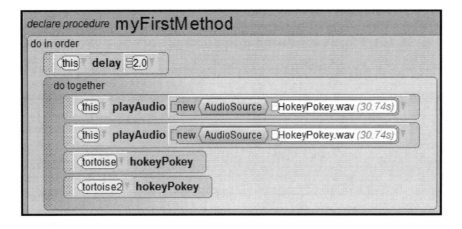

47. Run the animation. You should notice that the song isn't any longer than it was before. Even though we have the line of code twice, it is inside a DoTogether block and so it happens at the same time, therefore canceling the second playAudio line out. We need to put these 2 lines in a **do in order** to keep them from playing at the same time.

48. Run the animation. Looks pretty good. Now we are going to add some more characters to your environment.

49. Add an alien and a baby yeti to the environment to do the Hokey Pokey.

50. Why isn't there a hokeyPokey method for the alien? The hokeyPokey is a method that belongs to the Tortoise class and therefore the alien and baby yeti do not have access to this method. Do not worry about making the alien and baby yeti do the Hokey Pokey. We will cover this in a later chapter.

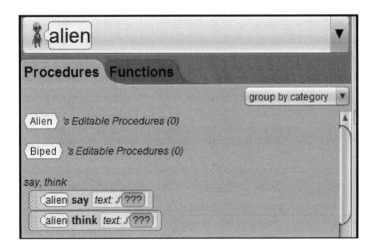

51. Save your Alice project and close the Alice environment.

52. Now, let's transfer our Alice project into NetBeans and see what the Java code looks like. Open NetBeans. Click **File**, **New Project**, and select **Java Project from Existing Alice Project**. Click the **Next** button.

53. Browse for the HokeyPokey Alice file and then be sure to change the location of where you are saving the new NetBeans project. Click **Finish**.

54. Open the **Tortoise.java** file. You should see the hokeyPokeyVerse, shake, turnAround, and newly added hokeyPokey methods. Notice how none of the methods that we created are static? Static methods are methods that are not called on an object and since most of the methods that we will write in Alice will be using objects, they will not be static.

```java
public void hokeyPokeyVerse(final SJoint bodyPart) {
    bodyPart.turn(TurnDirection.BACKWARD, 0.25);
    bodyPart.turn(TurnDirection.FORWARD, 0.25);
    this.shake(bodyPart);
    this.turnAround();
    this.delay(2.0);
}

public void shake(final SJoint bodyPart) {
    bodyPart.turn(TurnDirection.BACKWARD, 0.25);
    bodyPart.turn(TurnDirection.RIGHT, 0.125);
    bodyPart.turn(TurnDirection.LEFT, 0.25);
    bodyPart.turn(TurnDirection.RIGHT, 0.25);
    bodyPart.turn(TurnDirection.LEFT, 0.125);
    bodyPart.turn(TurnDirection.FORWARD, 0.25);
}

public void turnAround() {
    this.getRightShoulder().turn(TurnDirection.BACKWARD, 0.25);
    this.getLeftShoulder().turn(TurnDirection.BACKWARD, 0.25);
    this.turn(TurnDirection.LEFT, 1.0);
    this.getLeftShoulder().turn(TurnDirection.FORWARD, 0.25);
    this.getRightShoulder().turn(TurnDirection.FORWARD, 0.25);
}

public void hokeyPokey() {
    this.hokeyPokeyVerse(this.getRightHip());
    this.hokeyPokeyVerse(this.getLeftHip());
    this.hokeyPokeyVerse(this.getRightShoulder());
    this.hokeyPokeyVerse(this.getLeftShoulder());
}
```

55. Run your animation to ensure that it still works. Close your NetBeans project.

Exercise 4: Writing "Old MacDonald Had a Farm" Song

1. Get into **NetBeans** and close any previous projects by right clicking on them and selecting **Close**.

2. From the **File** menu, choose **New Project…**

3. Choose the **Java folder** on the left hand side of the window, then choose **Java Application.** Click **Next.**

4. In the New Java Applications dialog give your project the name **MacDonald**, select the **location** of where you would like to save your file. Click the **Finish** button.

5. Put your comments at the top of the program:

```
/*
 * Name
 * Date
 * This program is going to write the Old MacDonald song by using a method
 * JDK version
 */
```

6. In this program, we are going to print out the "Old MacDonald Had a Farm" song, but we do NOT want to write out the whole song. If you look closely at the song, you will notice that the song repeats over and over again with a new animal and a new animal sound for each verse of the song.

```
Old MacDonald had a farm, EE-I-EE-I-O.
And on that farm he had a [animal name], EE-I-EE-I-O,
With a [animal noise twice] here and a [animal noise twice] there
Here a [animal noise], there a [animal noise], everywhere a [animal noise twice]
Old MacDonald had a farm, EE-I-EE-I-O.
```

7. We are going to create a method called **animalVerse**. This method is going to have 2 parameters (the **animal** and the animal **sound**). Thus, we will need to set up 2 parameters for our new method. Both of these parameters are going to be Strings since we are just printing the text to the screen. We aren't actually using any sounds for this program, just text.

```java
/*
 * Name
 * Date
 * This program is going to write the Old MacDonald song by using a method
 * JDK version
 */

public class MacDonald {
    public static void main(String[] args) {

    }

    public static void animalVerse(String animal, String sound){

    }
}
```

8. Now we would like to add the generic verse into the animalVerse method using our animal name and our animal sound variables.

```java
public static void animalVerse(String animal, String sound) {
    System.out.println("Old MacDonald had a farm, EE-I-EE-I-O."
        + "\nAnd on this farm he had a " + animal + ", EE-I-EE-I-O,"
        + "\nWith a " + sound + " " + sound + " here and a "
        + sound + " " + sound + " there.  "
        + "\nHere a " + sound + " there a " + sound
        + " everywhere a " + sound + " " + sound
        + "\nOld MacDonald had a farm, EE-I-EE-I-O.\n");
}
```

9. Next, we need to call the animalVerse method that we created and pass in the 2 arguments that we need (the animal and the animal sound) for each verse. You will need to call the method 3 times to get 3 different verses. Each time, you will need to pass in the animal and sound to the parameters of the animalVerse method.

```java
public static void main(String[] args) {
    animalVerse("pig", "oink");
    animalVerse("cow", "moo");
    animalVerse("sheep", "baa");
}
```

10. Compile and run your program.

```java
/*
 * Name
 * Date
 * This program will write the Old MacDonald song using methods
 * JDK
 */

public class MacDonald {

    public static void main(String[] args) {
        animalVerse("pig", "oink");
        animalVerse("cow", "moo");
        animalVerse("sheep", "baa");
    }

    public static void animalVerse(String animal, String sound) {
        System.out.println("Old MacDonald had a farm, EE-I-EE-I-O."
                + "\nAnd on this farm he had a " + animal + ", EE-I-EE-I-O,"
                + "\nWith a " + sound + " " + sound + " here and a "
                + sound + " " + sound + " there.  "
                + "\nHere a " + sound + " there a " + sound
                + " everywhere a " + sound + " " + sound
                + "\nOld MacDonald had a farm, EE-I-EE-I-O.\n");
    }
}
```

```
Old MacDonald had a farm, EE-I-EE-I-O.
And on this farm he had a pig, EE-I-EE-I-O,
With a oink oink here and a oink oink there.
Here a oink there a oink everywhere a oink oink
Old MacDonald had a farm, EE-I-EE-I-O.

Old MacDonald had a farm, EE-I-EE-I-O.
And on this farm he had a cow, EE-I-EE-I-O,
With a moo moo here and a moo moo there.
Here a moo there a moo everywhere a moo moo
Old MacDonald had a farm, EE-I-EE-I-O.

Old MacDonald had a farm, EE-I-EE-I-O.
And on this farm he had a sheep, EE-I-EE-I-O,
With a baa baa here and a baa baa there.
Here a baa there a baa everywhere a baa baa
Old MacDonald had a farm, EE-I-EE-I-O.
```

11. For each new verse that you want to add to the song, you would just need to call the animalVerse method and pass in the animal and the sound. This is much more efficient than writing out the whole song without using a method. Imagine if you wanted to print out the song with 30 different animals…it would take forever to write out the whole song. Close your project.

Exercise 5: Alice Card Game with Methods (ongoing exercise)

1. Open up Alice 3. Open the file named **CardGame** from the Chapter1Exercises or **MyCardGame** from Chapter1 Assignments.

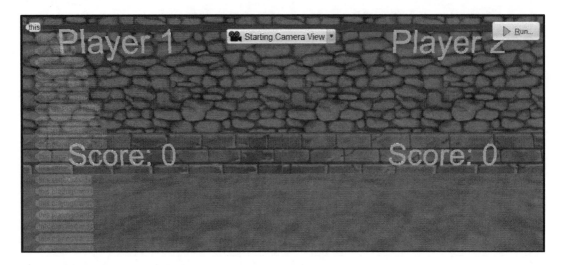

2. To remind you of what this program does, click on the RUN button and see the cards deal out, WIN flash, score change, and cards disappear. Then the program repeats with different cards.

3. The storyboard for this program was:

> - Scene opens with the CardGame
> - Player cards are dealt out onto screen
> - Display winner
> - Have these cards disappear
> - New Player cards are dealt out on screen
> - Determine and display winner
> - Have these cards disappear

4. In chapter 1, each of the above tasks were then broken down into more detailed tasks. For instance, "Player cards are dealt out onto screen" task was then broken down using stepdown refinement to the following:

> Player Cards are dealt out onto screen
> - Make an announcement that cards will now be dealt out
> - Playing card for player 1 moves from off screen to cone1 marker
> - Playing card for player 2 moves from off screen to cone2 marker

5. Grouping sections of program together will make the program more understandable. Complicated games can have over 100,000 lines of code, so good programmers break their programs into small sections and tackle each section. It also isn't unusual for an entire team of programmers to be working on one game with each team member being responsible for particular sections of code. We already have this program broken down into sections. In this chapter, you learned about methods. We will now convert each of these sections into a method.

6. The first section with code is the "deal out cards section". It appeared as follows:

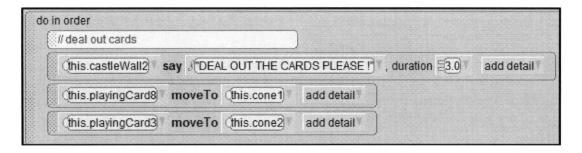

7. We will convert this section of code into a method. To create a new method for the scene that will be named **dealOutCards** you will need to go to the top of screen and click on the down arrow for the class selection (next to Scene tab), choose **Scene**, then choose **Add Scene Procedure**:

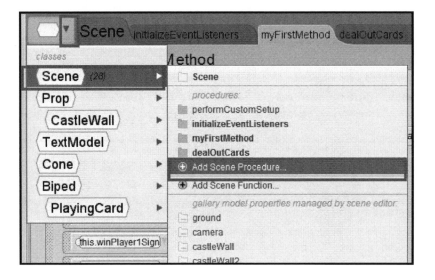

8. To name the new method, a box will pop up and you should fill it in with the name of **dealOutCards**. Click **OK.**

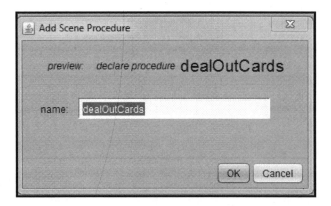

9. A new method called **dealOutCards** will open up to the right of myFirstMethod and it will be empty. You should place the statements that you want in this method inside of this tab.

10. The code that we want in this method is all of the code for the first "deal out cards" section in the myFirstMethod. To return to myFirstMethod, click on that tab at top of your screen.

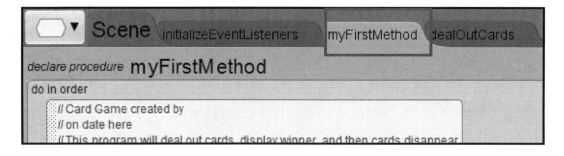

11. Hold down the **CTRL** key and drag the section of code (block for "deal out cards") to the **clipboard** until the clipboard turns green.

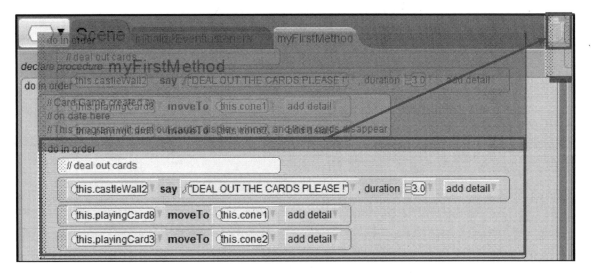

12. A copy of this code should now be on the clipboard. Make sure that there still is a copy of the "deal out cards" section in myFirstMethod in case the copy didn't work. *Click Edit > Undo if the copy did not work.* Click on dealOutCards method tab.

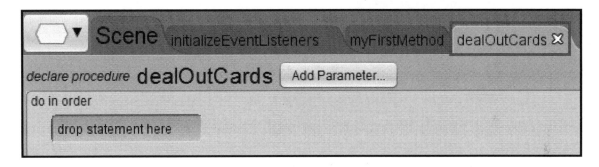

13. Now, drag the clipboard contents down into the dealOutCards method. Your screen will look as follows:

14. Click on **myFirstMethod** tab. Since your copy was successful, you no longer need the first section of code referring to "deal out cards" in this method. You can right click on this first section of code (click on the left side of the block of code with the dots) and choose **Delete**.

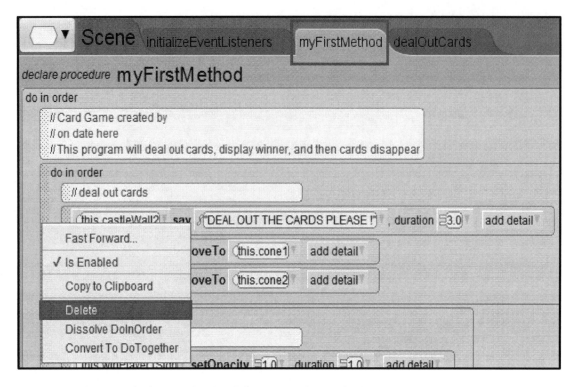

15. Since all of the code is now in the dealOutCards method, we will need to call (invoke) that method when we want the computer to perform those lines of code. Look at the left side of screen and make sure that your object is pointing to **this** (referring to scene) and that there is a **dealOutCards** method.

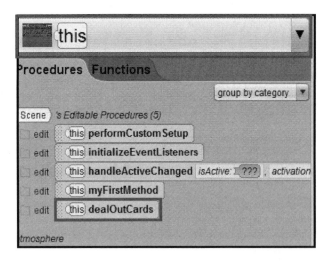

16. Drag the **dealOutCards** procedure from the Procedures tab on the lower left of your screen to the code editor and drop it under the comments in the **myFirstMethod** tab.

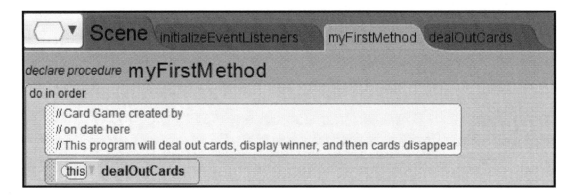

17. Run the program. It should look exactly as it did when we started. The only difference now is that we are doing it by calling a method instead of having all the code in myFirstMethod.

18. We will do the same thing for the next section which is "display winner". Hold down the **CTRL** key and drag the DO IN ORDER block for the "display winner" section to the clipboard. The clipboard will turn green. Make sure that the original lines of code are still in myFirstMethod. Now, create a new scene method by clicking on down arrow for the class selection (next to Scene tab), choose the **Scene** class, and then and choosing **Add Scene Procedure**. Name this method **displayWinner**

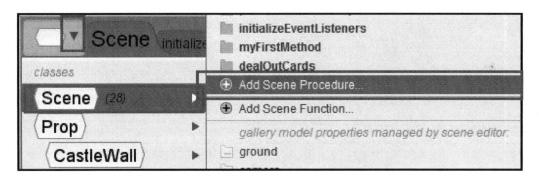

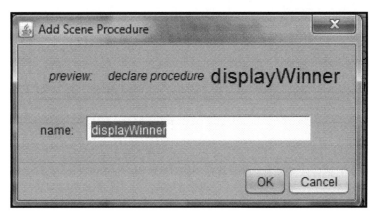

19. This method will open up to the right of the dealOutCards method. Drag the contents of the clipboard down into the coding area of this method. It should appear as follows:

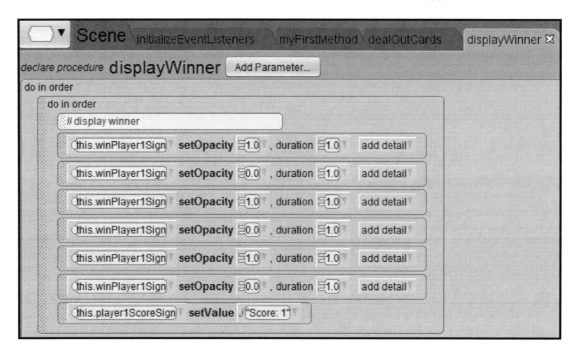

20. Return to myFirstMethod tab. Click on the **Procedures** tab for the **this** object and drag the **displayWinner** method to the code editor. This method should be placed under the call to the dealOutCards method as follows:

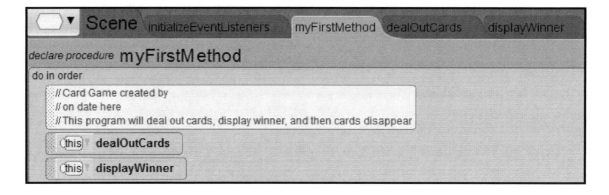

21. Right click on the section that says "displayWinner" in comments and delete this section from myFirstMethod. We have replaced these deleted lines with a call to the displayWinner method. Your program should look as follows:

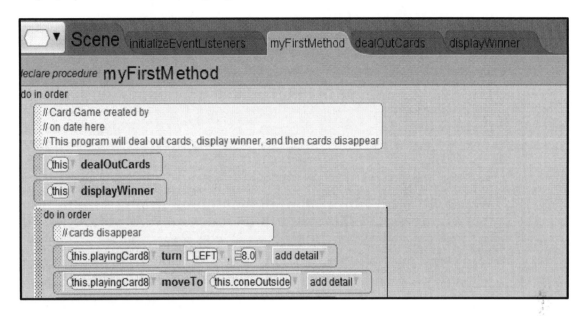

22. Run the program and it should run as it did before. The next section of code is for the cards disappearing. Copy this section of code to the clipboard. Create a new scene procedural method with the name **disappearCards**. Drag the contents of the clipboard to the disappearCards method. You should have the following:

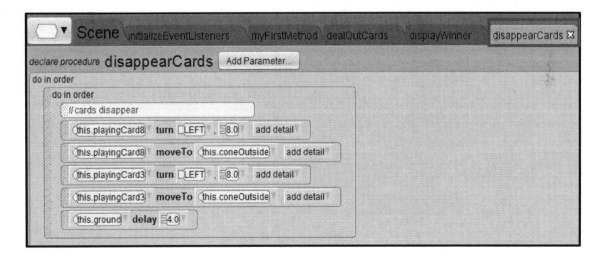

23. Return to the myFirstMethod. Drag the **disappearCards** method to the code editor below the call to displayWinner method. Delete the "disappear cards" block of code.

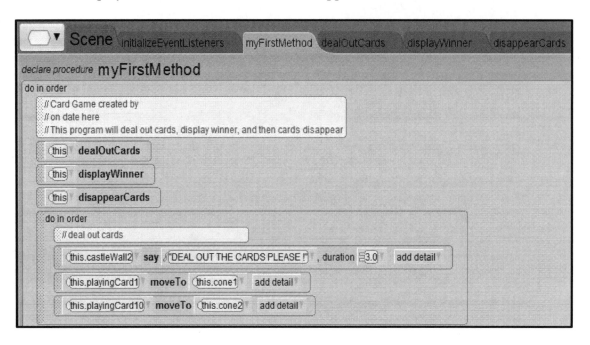

24. Run the program. It should still be running the same. The next section of code is again the dealing out of cards. Look carefully at the details of this section of code vs the code in the dealOutCards method, you will see that they are very similar but not exactly the same. What is different? In **myfirstMethod**, it appears as:

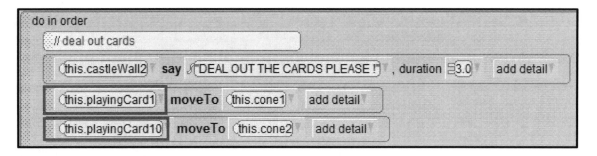

In the **dealOutCards** method, it appears as:

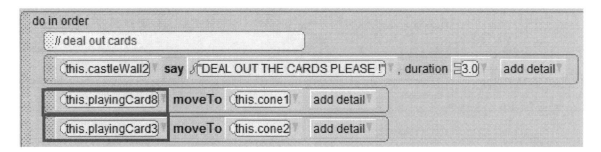

25. If we want to set up a method to work for both of these sections of code, what would be changing? The first statement is identical in both sections. In the second and third statements, different cards are being displayed. In the first game, it refers to playingCard8 and playingCard3. In the second game, it refers to playingCard1 and playingCard10. If we just call the dealOutCards method again, it will use playingCard8 and playingCard3 again and that is not what we want. Instead, we want to use the dealOutCards method for both sections, but we want to be able to change the 2 cards we are dealing each time. We will use 2 parameters to represent the data that is changing each time the method is executed.

26. Click on the **dealOutCards** tab at top of screen. Click on **Add Parameter**. A window will open. Name the parameter as **chosenPlayer1Card**. Check the **I understand that I need to update the invocation to this procedures** box. This means that you will go back and add an argument for your dealOutCards method wherever it was previously called. Do not click OK yet.

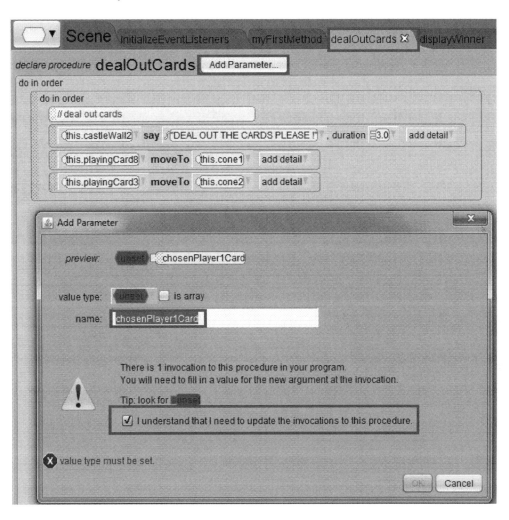

27. For the **value type**, click the down arrow, choose **Gallery** class, **Biped** class, then **PlayingCard**. Click **OK**.

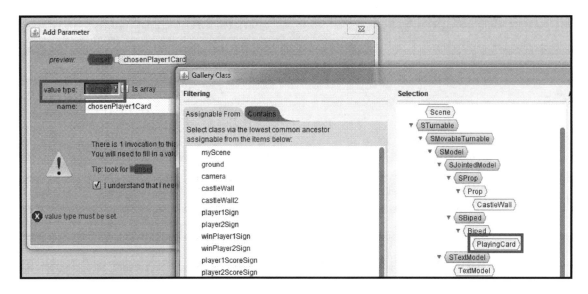

28. You will need another parameter. Click on **Add Parameter**, name it **chosenPlayer2Card**, check the **I undersand…** box, and choose the value type as **Gallery** class, **Biped**, **PlayingCard**. Then click **OK**.

29. Your dealOutCards method should now have 2 parameters which means it has two items that you can change each time you call this method.

30. You will notice that the dealOutCards method is referring specifically to playingCard8 in statement 2 and playingCard3 in statement 3. We want this method to be generic so that any cards could be chosen. We will drag the parameter of chosenPlayer1Card down to second statement and hover over and replace playingCard8. When you are dragging this parameter, many black boxes will show up on screen showing you where you could drag it. Make sure that you put it on top of playingCard8. Now, drag the second parameter called chosenPlayer2Card and hover it over playingCard3 so it replaces it.

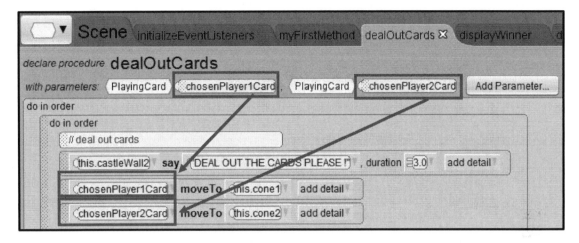

31. Click on the myFirstMethod. You will see that the call to dealOutCards now has red errors. It is saying that you now need to tell the computer what actual cards should be transferred to this method and be used (known as an argument). We want to use playingCard8 and playingCard3. Click on the down arrows next to the red errors and place playingCard8 in the first one and then playingCard3 in the second one.

32. Now, the method called dealOutCards, can be used for ANY 2 cards instead of specific cards. The new line of code should appear as:

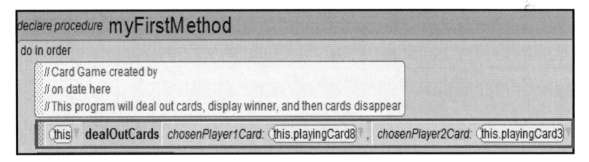

33. In myFirstMethod, we have another "deal out cards" section of code that could also use the **dealOutCards** method that we created. The call to the dealOutCards method could replace this section but we would be using playingCard1 and playingCard10. Drag the dealingOutCards method to the program. Since it has parameters, it will ask you which cards you want to use and you should respond with playingCard1 and playingCard10 as the arguments. This is how we set up generic methods. For instance, the person who wrote the TURN method in Alice, set up parameters for direction (LEFT, RIGHT, etc.) and amount of rotation so that we wouldn't need separate methods for turning right vs turning left, etc. We just set up a generic dealOutCards method that will work for any 2 cards to be dealt out. Make sure that you remove the "deal out cards" section and replaced it with the dealOutCards method.

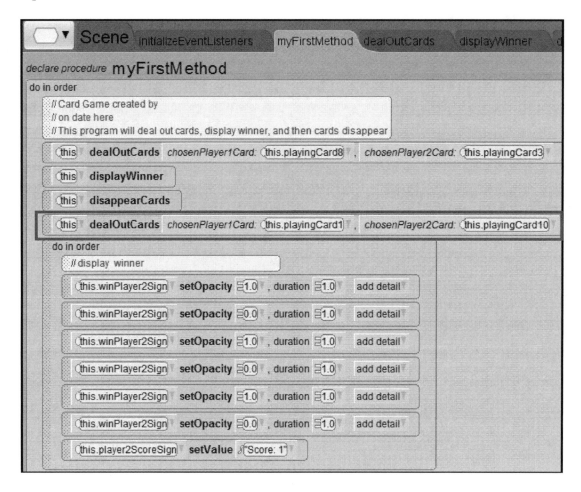

34. In the above step, look at the "display winner" section. Now, compare it to the displayWinner method as follows:

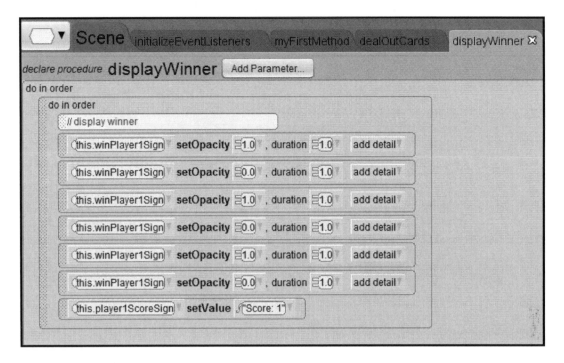

35. What is different? If we call this method as it is now, what would happen? The WIN on the player1 will flash and the score will be changed for player 1. Is this what we want? No. We will need parameters in the displayWinner method. The 2 things that are changing are the winPlayer1Sign and the player1ScoreSign. Thus, we will make these parameters in the displayWinner method.

36. Click on the **displayWinner** method tab. Choose **Add Parameter**. Choose the name as **winSign**, click on check mark for **I understand…**, and choose the **value type** as **Gallery Class**, **STextModel**, **TextModel**, click **OK**, and then **OK** again. For the second parameter, choose to **Add Parameter**. Choose the name as **scoreSign**, click on check mark for **I understand…**, and choose the **value type** as **Gallery Class**, **STextModel**, **TextModel**, then click **OK**, and then **OK** again.

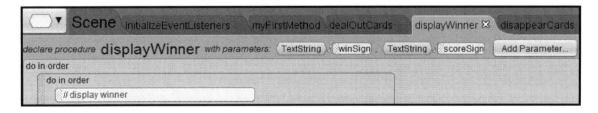

37. Drag the **winSign** parameter over top of the **winPlayer1Sign**. You will need to do this for all 6 lines. Drag the **scoreSign** parameter over top of the **player1ScoreSign** in last line of code. Your final version of displayWinner method is shown below:

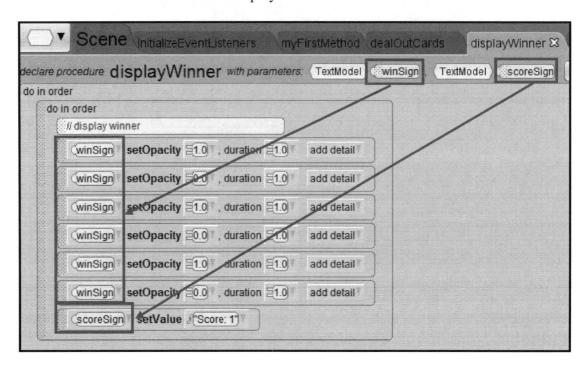

This program will now flash any TextModel sign you send to the method and change any TextModel with new score. This method is now generic instead of referring specifically to player 1's win sign and score.

38. Click on **myFirstMethod** and you will see that it now has errors. It wants you to tell it specifically which signs it should send to the **displayWinner** method. For the first call, the one with the red marks, you should change the first red error to be **winPlayer1Sign** and the second red error to be **player1ScoreSign**. This program will now flash any TextModel sign you send to the method and change any TextModel with new score. This method is now generic instead of referring specifically to player 1's win sign and score.

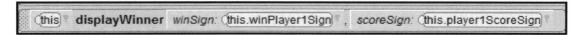

39. The section of code that has the comments of **displayWinner** can now be deleted and replaced with a call to the displayWinner method. When it asks for the arguments, you will choose winPlayer2Sign for the first argument and player2ScoreSign for the second.

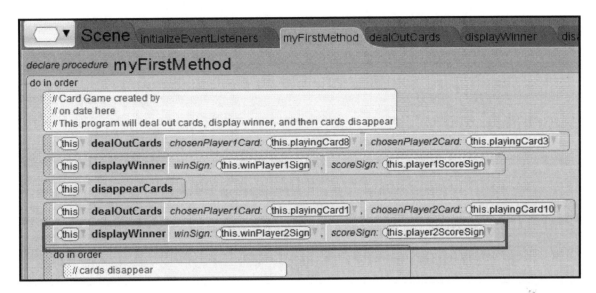

40. The last part is to adjust the **disappearCards** method to have parameters. What is changing? How many items will need to be parameters? You will need 2 parameters that you can name yourself. They will be of value type of Gallery Class, Biped, PlayingCard. You will also need to adjust the calls in myFirstMethod to this disappearCards so that it calls it first with playingCard8 and playingCard3. You will delete the block of code in myFirstMethod that has the details of disappearing cards. Replace it with another call to the disappearCards method with the appropriate arguments. Do this on your own.

41. The final version of **myFirstMethod** should look as follows:

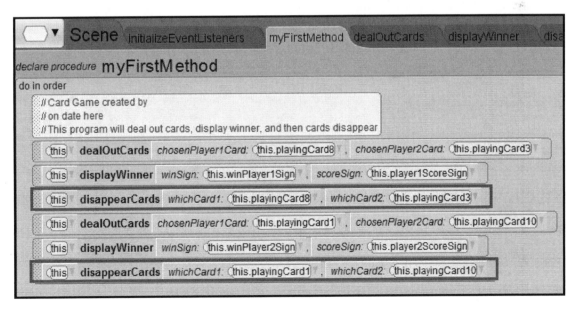

The final version of the dealOutCards method should look as follows:

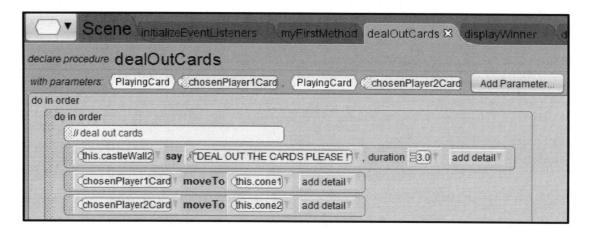

The final version of the displayWinner method should look as follow:

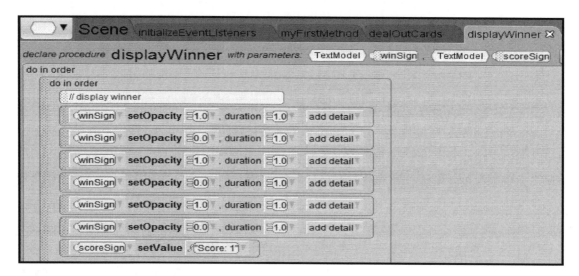

The final version of the disappearCards method should look as follows:

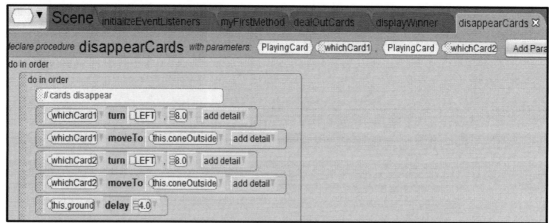

Note: Assuming that you called your two parameters in disappearCards as whichCard1 and whichCard2.

40. Look how short the myFirstMethod is now. It had so many lines originally that it could not be seen on one screen. Now, it is just a few statements that call other methods. It is now easy to adjust a section of the program without looking at the entire program. If you want to have the cards dance onto screen instead of just moving out, you would just adjust the dealOutCards method. Looking at smaller sections of code to make adjustments makes programming easier and less likely to have mistakes. Certain sections could be assigned to certain team members. For instance, you may be assigned to change the special effect of how the cards are removed from screen. You could edit your method without impacting the other methods. Methods and parameters are not easy for beginning programmers to understand but they are powerful and necessary. This program doesn't do anything different when running the program, but it is much more organized.

To see how much you understand, add statements to the myFirstMethod that would have an additional game played using cards 6 and 4. The score won't work correctly but that will be updated in a later chapter. Do not change the dealOutCards, displayWinner, and disappearCards methods.

Summary

- Methods are a series of statements that perform some task.
- Methods must include a declaration, an opening curly brace, a body of statements, and a closing curly brace.
- The syntax of a declaration of a method is:

    modifier   static   return-type   method-name   (list of parameters){
        .... statements in method
    }

- The modifier of a method can be public or private. Public methods can be used in other programs while private methods can only be used in the method that calls them. A modifier is optional.
- The method name follows same rules as the rules for variable names.
- The list of parameters in a declaration of a method should be the values a list of all of the data that you want to transfer TO the method when it is called. The parameters must be in parenthesis. You can have any number of parameters from zero to many. Each of the parameters should have a type such as int or double and a name such as y or fahrenheit. Each parameter in the list is separated by a comma.
- When a method is called, the computer transfers the arguments in the call one-by-one to the method. The arguments you send to the method must match both in number and in type as the parameters listed in the declaration of the method.
- A class defines a particular kind of object. Each class is a blueprint that tells Java exactly how to create and display an object. The name of a class begins with a capital letter.
- Objects are an instance of a class. Example: bob, joe, sue come from a Person class. The name of an object begins with a lowercase letter.
- A method is a coordinated sequence of instructions that will be carried out when requested. Procedure methods carry out actions: swim, dance, jump, etc.
- An object method belongs to a particular class and can be saved and used again in other worlds. Example: You can write a dance method for the Person class and then save and import that Person class into another world and use the newly created dance method.
- A parameter allows you to send information to a method when the method is called.

Review Questions

1. An object is an instance of a class.
    a. True
    b. False

2. A class can be thought of as an action.
    a. True
    b. False

3. Class names begin with a lowercase letter.
    a. True
    b. False

4. You can define multiple parameters for one method.
    a. True
    b. False

5. Parameters give users options when using methods.
    a. True
    b. False

6. Programs are broken up into small manageable pieces known as:
    a. pieces
    b. sections
    c. methods
    d. categories

Solutions: *1) a 2) b 3) b 4) a 5) a 6) c*

Assignments

4-1   **Creating a Dance in Alice**: Your goal is to create a dance method in Alice for a character. You should select a character of your choosing. Have this character dance to a song of your choosing. Insert your song into your project with the play audio method. Make sure that you play the song and the dance method at the same time. You should create a dance method for your character and this dance method should include 2 other methods of your choosing (example: split and jump). You must create at least 1 parameter for your dance method or in your other 2 methods.

4-2   **Writing "If You're Happy and You Know It" Song In Java Using a Method**: Your goal is to recreate the "If You're Happy and You Know It" song, but you are **NOT** going to write out the whole song line by line. You are going to write out one verse of the song in a method using 2 parameters as shown below to fill in the parts of the song that change. You will then invoke this method that you created from the main method passing in the arguments that are needed to complete each verse.

If you're happy and you know it, clap your hands (clap clap)
If you're happy and you know it, clap your hands (clap clap)
If you're happy and you know it, then your face will surely show it
If you're happy and you know it, clap your hands. (clap clap)

Invoke the name of your method **happyVerse** and the 2 parameters **action** and **sound**. You will not actually use sounds for this song, just the word that represents the sound in the verse. The full song is listed below. DO NOT WRITE OUT THE WHOLE SONG.

```
If you're happy and you know it, clap your hands(clap clap)
If you're happy and you know it, clap your hands(clap clap)
If you're happy and you know it, then your face will surely show it
If you're happy and you know it, clap your hands(clap clap)

If you're happy and you know it, stomp your feet(stomp stomp)
If you're happy and you know it, stomp your feet(stomp stomp)
If you're happy and you know it, then your face will surely show it
If you're happy and you know it, stomp your feet(stomp stomp)

If you're happy and you know it, shout "Hurray!"(hoo-ray! hoo-ray!)
If you're happy and you know it, shout "Hurray!"(hoo-ray! hoo-ray!)
If you're happy and you know it, then your face will surely show it
If you're happy and you know it, shout "Hurray!"(hoo-ray! hoo-ray!)
```

Chapter 5

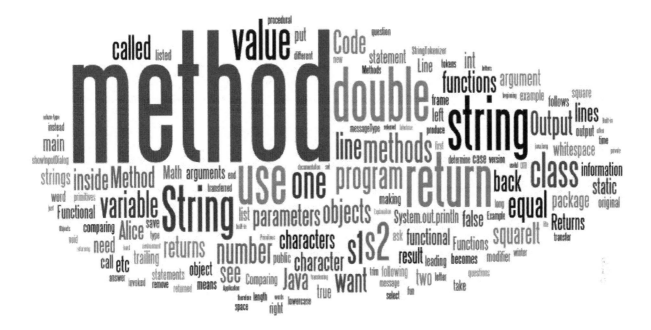

Functional Methods

Objectives

- ☑ Properly construct and use methods when programming.
- ☑ Describe the difference between a procedural method and a functional method.
- ☑ Use the Java Application Interface to code programs.
- ☑ Place methods into a separate file and call them from the main program.

Functional Methods Explained

Both procedural and functional methods need to be called (invoked) to be used, but a functional method returns a value when it is invoked. Procedures carry out an action and do not return a result. Procedures have a return type of void. Functions are useful for doing calculations and returning a result. Functions will have a return type of int, double, String, etc. You can think of a procedural method as a command and a functional method as a question. When you give a command, you don't expect an answer, but when you ask a question, you expect an answer. Functions ask questions about our environment. In Alice, functions ask questions about objects, for example: the **getDistanceTo** method calculates the distance from one object to another and returns the result.

Java Built-in Functional Methods

Java Application Programming Interface (API)

The Java API (libraries) has all the classes/methods that Oracle has provided to programmers. To see the Java 2 Platform Standard Edition 8.0 go to the following site:

http://docs.oracle.com/javase/8/docs/api/

On the left side of the screen in its own frame is an alphabetical list of all classes in the JDK. On the right side is a list of all the packages.

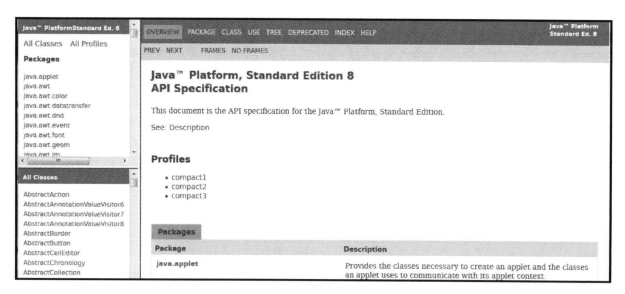

You can also select a package (folder) from the upper left frame, then select a class (file) from the bottom left frame. Once you select a specific class, you will see a list of methods that belong to that class in the right frame.

Let's look at the JOptionPane class that you have been using for input and output to your program. Click on the **javax.swing** package (listed alphabetically), then the **JOptionPane** class (listed alphabetically) as shown below:

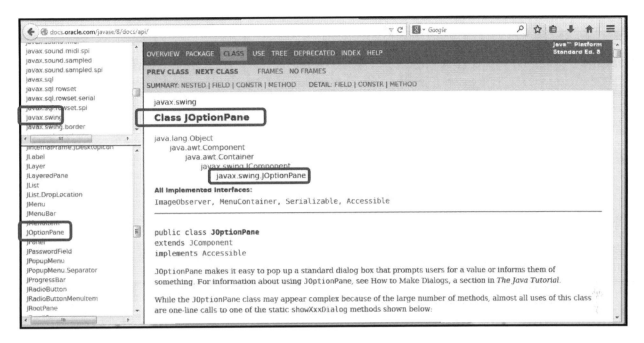

Scroll down to see the **Method Summary** for this class. There are different methods called showInputDialog. Each one has different parameters as follows:

static `String`	`showInputDialog(Component` parentComponent, `Object` message)` Shows a question-message dialog requesting input from the user parented to parentComponent.
static `String`	`showInputDialog(Component` parentComponent, `Object` message,` `Object` initialSelectionValue)` Shows a question-message dialog requesting input from the user and parented to parentComponent.
static `String`	`showInputDialog(Component` parentComponent, `Object` message, `String` title,` int messageType)` Shows a dialog requesting input from the user parented to parentComponent with the dialog having the title title and message type messageType.
static `Object`	`showInputDialog(Component` parentComponent, `Object` message, `String` title,` int messageType, `Icon` icon, `Object[]` selectionValues,` `Object` initialSelectionValue)` Prompts the user for input in a blocking dialog where the initial selection, possible selections, and all other options can be specified.
static `String`	`showInputDialog(Object` message)` Shows a question-message dialog requesting input from the user.
static `String`	`showInputDialog(Object` message, `Object` initialSelectionValue)` Shows a question-message dialog requesting input from the user, with the input value initialized to initialSelectionValue.

We have been using the one that has two parameters of parentComponent for which we put in null, and then the message where we put a String which usually is a question to the user. The method then returns a String. None of these versions returns a double and that is why we have to convert the returned String to a double or integer if we want to use it in a formula.

The third version of showInputDialog still has the parent component that we set to null, then the message, but has two more parameters. It has a String title and an int messageType. The String title is what message you want displayed at top of your window instead of it simply saying *Input*. The last parameter of messageType is an int that determines what kind of window you get.

Symbol	int messageType
X	0
i	1
!	2
?	3
Blank	-1

You can see more information about this version of the showInputDialog by scrolling down to the **Method Detail** section in the documentation. Each method is described with more detail at the end of the documentation for that class.

```
showInputDialog

public static String showInputDialog(Component parentComponent,
                                     Object message,
                                     String title,
                                     int messageType)
                              throws HeadlessException
```

Shows a dialog requesting input from the user parented to parentComponent with the dialog having the title title and message type messageType.

Parameters:

parentComponent - the parent Component for the dialog

message - the Object to display

title - the String to display in the dialog title bar

messageType - the type of message that is to be displayed: ERROR_MESSAGE, INFORMATION_MESSAGE, WARNING_MESSAGE, QUESTION_MESSAGE, or PLAIN_MESSAGE

Throws:

HeadlessException - if GraphicsEnvironment.isHeadless returns true

See Also:

GraphicsEnvironment.isHeadless()

Math Functions

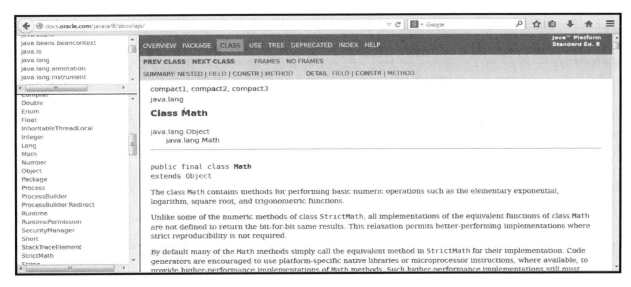

The **Math** class in the Java library performs a number of useful mathematical operations. The Math class is located in the java.lang package. The **java.lang** package is a default package that is automatically imported into every program, therefore there is no need to import this package to use the Math class.

Some functional methods in the Math class

Method Description	Method Call Example	Result	Argument	Returns
Returns the absolute value	Math.abs(-5.5);	5.5	double	double
Returns the value of the first argument raised to the power of the second argument	Math.pow(5, 2);	25	double, double	double
Returns a positive number that is greater than or equal to 0.0 and less than 1.0.	Math.random( );	Number between 0 and 1	none	double
Returns the closest whole number to the argument	Math.round(6.45);	6	double	double
Returns the rounded positive square root	Math.sqrt(7);	2.6457513	double	double

Example:

Code:	Output:
```double number = 5.49;``` ```System.out.println(Math.round(number));```	```run:``` ```5``` ```BUILD SUCCESSFUL```

String Functions

Let's take a look at some of the methods that can be performed on a String object. We will use String s1 and s2 as examples for the methods.

```
String s1 = "Now is the winter of our discontent";
String s2 = "Java can be fun and hard ";
```

Method or Class	Explanation
s1.length( ) s2.length( )	Gives the length of the string in number of characters In this case, the length of s1 is **35**. The length of s2 is **25. Make sure you counted the space at end**.
s1.toUpperCase() s2.toUpperCase()	Converts string to all uppercase characters s1 becomes, **NOW IS THE WINTER OF OUR DISCONTENT** s2 becomes **JAVA CAN BE FUN AND HARD**
s1.toLowerCase() s2.toLowerCase()	Converts string to all lowercase characters s1 becomes, **now is the winter of our discontent** s2 becomes, **java can be fun and hard**
s1.startsWith("st") s2.startsWith("Java")	Tests to see if string starts with characters inside (). For s1, would be **false.** For s2, it would be **true.**
s1.endsWith("tent") s2.endsWith("so")	Tests to see if string ends with characters inside (). For s1, it would be **true.** For s2, it would be **false.**
s1.replace('e' ,'L') s2.replace('a' , '*')	Replace all occurences of first character with second character. In s1, all 'e' will be replaced by 'L' in the string s1 making the string be **Now is thL wintLr of our discontLnt** In s2, all the 'a' will be replaced by '*" in the string s2 making the string be **J*v* c*n be fun *nd h*rd** You can only replace single characters with this method.
s1.trim( ) s2.trim( )	Removes leading and trailing white space. In s1, there is none. In s2, it would take the last space off the s2 string.
s1.equals(s2)	This would compare if the 2 Strings are equal. In this case, they are not equal. It would return true or false. This example would return **false.**
s1.equalsIgnoreCase(s2)	This is similar to .equals except the case (upper or lower) of each character is ignored.

s1.contains("winter") s2.contains("@")	Determines if a String contains a certain char or String. If it does, it will return **true** and if it doesn't it will return **false**. This method needs you to pass in a String and so you must use double quotes, even if you only want to check for one character. The String s1 will return **true**. The String s2 will return **false**.
StringTokenizer tokens = new StringTokenizer(s1); int x = tokens.countTokens();	StringTokenizer is a library class program that is in java.util. It breaks up strings into individual pieces called tokens. Tokens are separated typically by whitespace characters such as blanks, tabs, newlines, and carriage returns. The variable x would contain **7** as a count of number of tokens (words).

Comparing Objects vs Primitives

Comparing objects is different than comparing primitives. You use relational operators (==, !=, >, <, etc.) when comparing primitives, but you need to use functions to do those comparisons with objects. Since strings are objects, you should not use == to determine if they are equal.

Comparing Objects	**Comparing Primitives**

Code:
 	
``java
String message1 = "Hello";
String message2 = "hello";
boolean result = message1.equals(message2);
System.out.println(result);
``
 	
Output:
 	
``
run:
false
BUILD SUCCESSFUL
``
	Code:
	
	``java
	int a = 1;
	int b = 1;
	boolean result = a == b;
	System.out.println(result);
	``
	
	Output:
	
	``
	run:
	true
	BUILD SUCCESSFUL
	``

Code:
 	
``java
DecimalFormat format1=new DecimalFormat(".##");
DecimalFormat format2=new DecimalFormat(".##");
boolean result=format1.equals(format2);
System.out.println(result);
``
 	
Output:
 	
``
run:
true
BUILD SUCCESSFUL
``
	Code:
	
	``java
	char a = 'N';
	char b = 'Y';
	boolean result = a == b;
	System.out.println(result);
	``
	
	Output:
	
	``
	run:
	false
	BUILD SUCCESSFUL
	``

String Comparisons

Capitalization is important when you are comparing if 2 strings are equal. If one character in one of the strings is capital and it is not capitalized in the other string, then they are not equal. You can use the equalsIgnoreCase to determine if strings are equal regardless of case.

Code:

```
String message1 = "Hello";
String message2 = "hello";
boolean result = message1.equalsIgnoreCase(message2);
System.out.println(result);
```

Output:

```
run:
true
BUILD SUCCESSFUL
```

If one string has leading or trailing whitespace before or after it and the other doesn't, then they would not be equal. You may want to use the trim method to remove trailing and leading whitespace before comparing the strings. Notice that in the following example, message1 has a trailing whitespace that makes them not equal. Using the trim method will remove any leading and trailing whitespacing and return the result of this new string. If you code the program as follows, it will remove the whitespace, but since it is not being saved back into the original string, then it will use the old string when doing the comparison and therefore they will not be equal.

Code:

```
String message1 = "Hello ";
String message2 = "hello";
message1.trim();
message2.trim();
boolean result = message1.equalsIgnoreCase(message2);
System.out.println(result);
```

Output:

```
run:
false
BUILD SUCCESSFUL
```

To save the returned version of the string with the whitepace removed, you would need to save it back into a new variable or an original variable.

Code:

```
String message1 = "Hello ";
String message2 = "hello";
message1 = message1.trim();
message2 = message2.trim();
boolean result = message1.equalsIgnoreCase(message2);
System.out.println(result);
```

Output:

```
run:
true
BUILD SUCCESSFUL
```

You could also just use the trim function in the actual comparison itself instead of saving into variables.

Code:

```
String message1 = "Hello ";
String message2 = "hello";
boolean result = message1.trim().equalsIgnoreCase(message2.trim());
System.out.println(result);
```

Output:

```
run:
true
BUILD SUCCESSFUL
```

You should take some time to try and experiment with the other string functions. Remember that functions return a value. If you want to change the capitalization of a string or replace letters in the string, you need to save it back into the original string or use the result (example printing) so that you can see the changes.

Alice Built-in Functional Methods

Alice functions allow you to ask questions about objects in the environment. Alice provides built-in functions that return information about objects in your world. You can find the distance from one object to another, the width of an object, etc. Since functions return a value, we need to either use the value right away or save it in a variable for future use. Functional methods are great for making decisions. We will discuss decision making later in the course, but we will use the built-in Alice functions to get information about our Alice world.

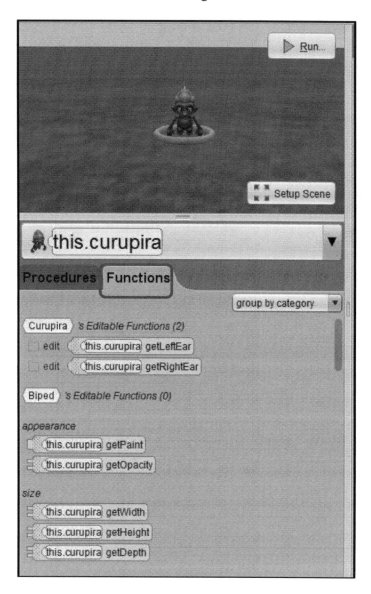

Method Declaration

The syntax for creating a method is:

         modifier static return-type   method-name (list of parameters){
           .... statements to do inside of method
         }

- The first thing in a method is the **modifier**. Modifiers determine the scope of a method. The two most common modifiers are public and private. The modifier **public** means that the method is available in this class (program) and other classes. The modifier **private** means that you intend to use the variable or method only in this program.

- The word "**static**" means that the method is not associated with an object. Most of the Alice methods that we create will not be static since they will be created for objects. If a method is not static, then leave the word static off of the declaration.

- The **return-type** can be any of the primitives that you have seen such as int, double, float, etc. If you don't plan on returning any value back from the method then you use the word "*void*". All functional methods return a value and should not use the word "void".

- A **method-name** uses the same guidelines as described for variables as follows:
  - Consists of letters, digits, underscores (_) or $ (no spaces allowed).
  - First character can't be a digit. (First character is generally lowercase letter.)
  - Cannot be keywords (see Keywords section).
  - Stylistic rule: all method names begin with a lowercase letter with all other words beginning with uppercase letter such as displayIt, sumNumbers, etc.
  - Method names should be meaningful.

- List of parameters is a list of all the data that you will be transferring into the method. You might want to transfer nothing to the method, or you might want to transfer several items. These parameters can be integers, doubles, Strings, other objects, etc. The information transferred to a method is often referred to as **arguments** while the actual placeholders for the information in the method are often called **parameters**.

- A set of left and right curly braces that surround the statements that you want to accomplish inside of the method.

Functional Method Example

We could write a method that took a number and multiplied it by itself and returned the answer to the main program. Let's assume that we want the name of the method to be *squareIt*; it is to be public; it is to accept a double argument into the method; and it is to return a double value back to the main method. We could declare the method as:

public static double squareIt (double x) {
    return x * x;
}

The keyword "return" means to return the value of the expression (calculation) back to the main program. Let's put it together with the main method as follows:

```
1   /*
2    * This program will square numbers using a squareIt method
3    */
4
5   public class SampleMethods5 {
6
7       public static void main(String[] args) {
8           double number = 5;
9           System.out.println(number + " has a square of "
10                  + squareIt(number));
11          double squareNum = squareIt(22.5);
12          System.out.println(22.5 + " has a square of "
13                  + squareNum);
14          System.out.println(8 + " has a square of "
15                  + squareIt(8));
16      }
17
18      public static double squareIt(double x) {
19          return x * x;
20      }
21  }
```

Explanation line by line:

Line 8: Declares a double variable called *number* and initializes it to 5.

Line 9 & 10: Takes the number variable of 5 and transfers it to the method of squareIt which can be seen beginning on line 10. This value of 5 is transferred into the argument of x and will be referred to as x inside the squareIt method. Line 19 says to take x times itself giving you 25.0 and returns that value back to where you left off in the main method. Thus, it returns to line 10 with the value of 25.0 and prints the result to the screen. These lines are really one *System.out.println* statement but it is too long for one line again. This statement shows how to put the call to the squareIt method inside of the *System.out.println*. These two lines produce the following output line:
   5 has a square of 25.0

Line 11: Tells the computer to call the method of squareIt again but with the number of 22.5 this time. It is transferring a numeric literal this time instead of a variable. The 22.5 will be placed into the x variable inside of the squareIt method on line 18. Line 19 tells it to return the value of 506.25 back to line 12 and into the variable called squareNum.

Lines 12 and 13: These lines are really one *System.out.println* statement but it is too long for one line. These two lines produce the following output line:
   22.5 has a square of 506.25

Lines 14 and 14: These lines are just one long *System.out.println* statement spanning over two lines. This statement shows how to put the call to the squareIt method inside of the *System.out.println*. These lines produce an output of:
   8 has a square of 64.0

When a method is called, argument values are automatically transferred into the method. (The exact number of arguments, type of arguments, and order of arguments must match the parameters listed in the declaration of method and the arguments listed in the call to the method.) This transfer process is a duplication process, in that the original values remain intact (*except for objects*). The program then executes the statements in the body of the called method. When the method reaches the end of all the statements in this called method, it returns to point in the program where the method was invoked (it may return a value).

Hands-on Exercises

Exercise 1: Using Alice Built-in Functional Methods

Our goal is to have a bird fly to the top of a tree using built in Alice functional methods. You can use the built in functions answer questions you have about your objects. For example, the **getDistanceTo** function will return the distance from one object to another.

1. Get into **Alice**.

2. Choose a land template of your choice.

3. Click on the Setup Scene button and add a bird (it doesn't matter which bird) and a tree (it doesn't matter what type of tree) to your world. You can leave the default names for the objects, or create your own names. Just be sure to follow the naming rules if you are going to name them yourself. Place the bird on the ground and be sure that you can see the top of your tree since the bird is going to fly to the top of it.

4. Save your project as **BirdToTree** to the appropriate exercise folder. Go back to the code editor. Add your comments to the top of the program.

5. Select the **bird** and then drag the **turnToFace** method onto the editor and select the **tree** object as the argument.

6. Next, drag the **moveToward** method onto the editor selecting the **tree** as the first argument and **10** meters as the second argument as shown below.

7. Click the **run** button to watch the animation. The bird bypasses the tree object. This tells us that 10 meters is too large of a number, but we still don't know how far the tree truly is. We would need to keep guessing and running the animation to see if we choose the right number. This trial and error process can be very frustrating and is unneccessary. Alice has a built in function called getDistanceTo that will measure the distance from one object to another and return the result.

8. Let's use the **getDistanceTo** function *(function tab)* to find the actual distance between the **bird** and the **tree** object. You will need to select the bird, click on the functions tab, and then drag the getDistanceTo function to replace the 10 meters argument. Select tree as the argument.

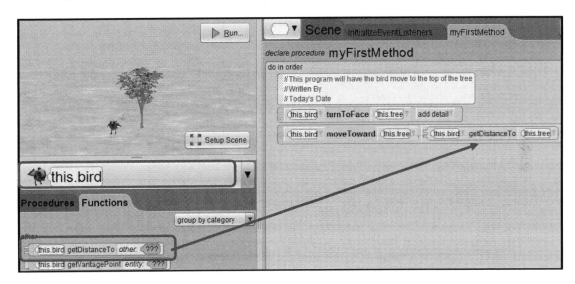

9. Click **run** to view the animation. The bird ends up inside the tree object. This is okay because we are going to add a move up method that fixes this to look like he is flying to the top of the tree object.

10. Go ahead and drag the **move** method onto the editor and select **up** as the first argument and **2** meters as the second argument. The 2 meters is just a guess.

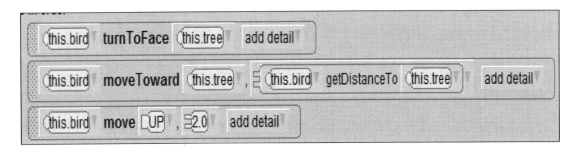

11. Click **run**. The 2 meters is too far. Again, we don't want to spend time playing this guessing game of trying to guess the height of the tree; there are built in Alice functions that will give you this information so that we don't have to guess. Click on the **tree** object, then click on the functions tab, and then drag the **getHeight** function *(function tab)* for the tree to replace the 2 meters for the distance on the move method.

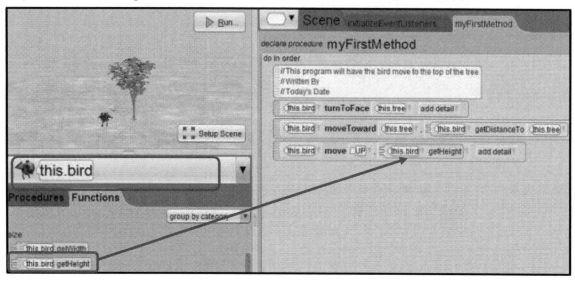

12. Click **run** to view the animation. The bird ends up on the top of the tree, but he goes to the middle of the tree and then up. This doesn't look very natural. If we change the moveToward and move method so that they happen at the same time, this will fix it so that he moves at a diagonal and doesn't end up inside the tree. Drag the **do together** block onto the editor and place the **moveToward** and **move** methods inside of this block.

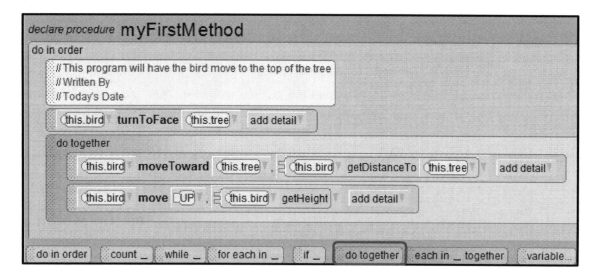

13. Click **run** to view the animation. The bird should now fly to the top of the tree. Save and close this project.

Exercise 2: Finding the Circumference of Alice UFOs

Our goal is to find the circumference of a UFO to help an alien clear space for its landing. We will write our own circumference function that will calculate and return the circumference.

1. Get into **Alice**.

2. Choose the **Desert Project** template.

3. Click the Setup Scene button and add an alien, a few boulders of your choosing, a plateau, and 3 UFOs (make sure that your objects have different names, it won't let you create another object with the same name). You can name these objects as you wish, just be sure to follow the naming rules.

4. Go back to the code editor. Save your project as **UFOCircumference** to the appropriate exercise folder. Your scene should look similar to the following.

5. Let's **transfer our program into NetBeans**. Leave the name UFOCircumference as the name of the new NetBeans project. Open up the **Scene.java** file and add your **comments** to the top of the file as shown below.

```
1  /* Your Name
2   * JDK Version
3   * Date
4   * This program will calculate the circumference of UFOs using a functional method
5   */
```

6. Now scroll down to the bottom of the file to **myFirstMethod**. We should create a story for this animation to make it more interesting. You can have the alien say something similar to the following.

```
public void myFirstMethod() {
    alien.say("I will need to clear space for the UFOs to land.");
    alien.say("Determining circumference will help me to figure "
            + "out how much space to clear.");
}
```

7. Next, we need to create the functional method to calculate the circumference. This method is going to be used on the UFO and so we will put this new functional method under the UFO class. Open up the **UFO.java** file. The functional method is going to have the name **calculateCircumference**, it is going to be **public** (it has to be public if we are going to use this method from within another method in a different class…we will be calling it from the myFirstMethod from within the Scene class), and it will be returning the calculated circumference which will be a **double**. Since this will be used on the UFO object, this method will NOT be static. Please don't forget the beginning and ending curly braces for this new functional method. NetBeans underlines the method in red because we haven't added the return statement yet. We will add this later and the red should disappear. Open up the **UFO.java** file and position your cursor before the very last curly brace of the program to type the following method declaration.

```
public double calculateCircumference() {

}
```

8. Now we need to calculate the circumference. The equation is $c = \pi d$ where d is the diameter. In order to find the radius, we will need to first find the diameter. We can do this by using the getWidth built in Alice function for the UFO and saving it in a variable called **diameter**. The type for this variable should be **double** and the value should be the result of the **getWidth** function from the UFO. This will be a little bit different from how we did it before. We normally would say ufo.getWidth() to return the width of the ufo, but now that we are inside the UFO class, we cannot specify an object, we have to use the object that we called the method on. For example, we have 3 UFOs in our world, we can choose to use the calculateCircumference on any of those UFOs. This is why Java won't allow us to specify a particular UFO. The object that you call the method on is the current object and is referred to as **this**.

```
public double calculateCircumference() {
    double diameter = this.getWidth();
}
```

9. Now we can calculate the circumference which is π * d. Let's create a variable for the **circumference**. It should be a double and we should multiply **PI * diameter**. You could use 3.14 to represent PI, but we are going to use Math.PI in place of 3.14 to get a more precise result. Math is a Java class and PI is a constant within that class that would represent the 16 digit decimal number for π.

```
public double calculateCircumference() {
    double diameter = this.getWidth();
    double circumference = Math.PI * diameter;
}
```

10. Every function MUST return a value. We are going to return the result stored in the circumference variable back to where we called the method by adding the **return** statement to our method.

```
public double calculateCircumference() {
    double diameter = this.getWidth();
    double circumference = Math.PI * diameter;
    return circumference;
}
```

11. Open the Scene.java and scroll down to myFirstMethod. We will need to call the calculateCircumference method for each UFO and use the say method to display the results as shown below. *Note: You may have named your UFOs differently instead of ufo, ufo2, and ufo3.*

```
public void myFirstMethod() {
    alien.say("I will need to clear space for the UFOs to land.");
    alien.say("Determining circumference will help me to figure "
            + "out how much space to clear.");
    alien.say("The circumference of the UFOs are as follows");
    alien.say("UFO 1: " + ufo.calculateCircumference());
    alien.say("UFO 2: " + ufo2.calculateCircumference());
    alien.say("UFO 3: " + ufo3.calculateCircumference());
}
```

12. Run the animation to see if the alien says the circumference for all 3 UFOs.

13. **Challenge:** format the circumference to have 2 decimal places.
    Answer:
    - Add the import for the DecimalFormat class
    - Create the DecimalFormat object with your 2 decimal pattern
    - Apply the decimal pattern to the circumference results

```
public void myFirstMethod() {
    alien.say("I will need to clear space for the UFOs to land.");
    alien.say("Determining circumference will help me to figure "
            + "out how much space to clear.");
    alien.say("The circumference of the UFOs are as follows");
    DecimalFormat twoDecimals = new DecimalFormat("0.00");
    alien.say("UFO 1: " + twoDecimals.format(ufo.calculateCircumference()));
    alien.say("UFO 2: " + twoDecimals.format(ufo2.calculateCircumference()));
    alien.say("UFO 3: " + twoDecimals.format(ufo3.calculateCircumference()));
}
```

14. **Challenge:** Use the JOptionPane input dialog to ask the user for a width of the UFO. Use this width to resize one of the UFOs. Run the program again. Did the circumference for that UFO change?

Answer:
- Add the import for the JOptionPane class
- Prompt the user for a width
- Convert the String from the user to a double
- Use the setWidth function to change the size of the UFO

```
public void myFirstMethod() {
    alien.say("I will need to clear space for the UFOs to land.");
    alien.say("Determining circumference will help me to figure "
            + "out how much space to clear.");
    String input=JOptionPane.showInputDialog(null,"Enter a width for UFO 1");
    double ufo1Width = Double.parseDouble(input);
    ufo.setWidth(ufo1Width);
    alien.say("The circumference of the UFOs are as follows");
    DecimalFormat twoDecimals = new DecimalFormat("0.00");
    alien.say("UFO 1: " + twoDecimals.format(ufo.calculateCircumference()));
    alien.say("UFO 2: " + twoDecimals.format(ufo2.calculateCircumference()));
    alien.say("UFO 3: " + twoDecimals.format(ufo3.calculateCircumference()));
}
```

Exercise 3: Calculating BMI Using a Functional Method

Our goal is to write an interactive program that will allow a user to enter their height and weight, calculate and return their BMI (Body Mass Index) by using a functional method, and display their BMI using a message box. The body mass index measures the relation of a person's weight to their height.

1. Get into NetBeans and start a new Java project. The name of the project should be: **BodyMassIndexCalc**. Be sure to save this project to the appropriate exercise folder and do not create a Package statement.

2. Add comments to the program as shown below:

```
/**
 * Your name
 * Date
 * JDK version
 * This program will calculate BMI with a functional method
 */

public class BodyMassIndexCalc {
    public static void main(String[] args) {


    }
}
```

3. We are now going prompt the user for their height in inches and their weight in pounds via the JOptionPane input dialog. You will need to import the package for the JOptionPane and add the JOptionPane input dialogs to the main method as shown below:

```
import javax.swing.JOptionPane;

public class BodyMassIndexCalc {
    public static void main(String[] args) {
        String response;
        response = JOptionPane.showInputDialog(null,
                "Enter your height in inches");
        double height = Double.parseDouble(response);
        response = JOptionPane.showInputDialog(null,
                "Enter your weight in pounds");
        double weight = Double.parseDouble(response);
    }
}
```

4. We are now going to add calculateBMI functional method to our program. This method is going to take in the height and weight argument when the method is called. The height and weight argument will be passed into the height and weight parameter of the method declaration shown below. The BMI will then be calculated using this height and weight variable. The BMI will be returned as a double from wherever the method was called.

public static double calculateBMI(double height, double weight) {
**   return (weight*703)/(height*height);**
}

Key:
.... Modifier – determines the scope of the method
.... Static – is not associated with an object
.... Return type – double means that we will be sending a double answer back from where the method was called
.... Method name
.... Parameters

The program should look as follows so far:

```
import javax.swing.JOptionPane;

public class BodyMassIndexCalc {
    public static void main(String[] args) {
        String response;
        response = JOptionPane.showInputDialog(null,
                "Enter your height in inches");
        double height = Double.parseDouble(response);
        response = JOptionPane.showInputDialog(null,
                "Enter your weight in pounds");
        double weight = Double.parseDouble(response);
    }

    public static double calculateBMI(double height, double weight){
        return (weight*703)/(height*height);
    }
}
```

5. We have created a functional method that calculates the BMI, but we have not used this method. We need to call this method in order to use it. When we call the method, we need to pass in the height and weight argument. It is important that you pass the height and weight arguments in the same order that the calculateBMI parameters are set up to accept the arguments. If you pass the weight first and then the height, it will plug the variables into the wrong part of the equation and return the incorrect result. Add the following method call after the input dialogs in the main method:

double bmi = calculateBMI(height, weight);

6. We now need to format and display the BMI result in a message box. The final program is shown below.

```
import java.text.DecimalFormat;
import javax.swing.JOptionPane;

public class BodyMassIndexCalc {
    public static void main(String[] args) {
        String response;
        response = JOptionPane.showInputDialog(null,
                "Enter your height in inches");
        double height = Double.parseDouble(response);
        response = JOptionPane.showInputDialog(null,
                "Enter your weight in pounds");
        double weight = Double.parseDouble(response);
        double bmi = calculateBMI(height, weight);
        DecimalFormat pattern = new DecimalFormat("###.00");
        JOptionPane.showMessageDialog(null, "Height: " + height +
                "\nWeight: " + weight +
                "\nBMI: " + pattern.format(bmi) +
                "\n\nBMI Categories: " +
                "\nUnderweight = <18.5" +
                "\nNormal weight = 18.5-24.9" +
                "\nOverweight = 25-29.9" +
                "\nObesity = 30 or greater");
    }

    public static double calculateBMI(double height, double weight){
        return (weight*703)/(height*height);
    }
}
```

7. Run your project to test it.

8. Close your project

Exercise 4: Writing and Calling Multiple Methods

Our goal is to write an interactive program that will allow a user to enter a Fahrenheit temperature into the program, and then, with a GUI message, be told what the corresponding Celsius temperature is. The calculation of the conversion of temperatures should be done with a method called *convertToCelsius*.

1. Get into NetBeans and create a new Java project called **MultipleMethods**. Be sure to save this project to the appropriate exercise folder. Do not create a Package statement.

2. Add comments to your program as follows:

```
/*
 * Practice with writing and calling methods in separate classes
 * Written by your name, date, and JDK version
 */

public class MultipleMethods {

    public static void main(String[] args) {

    }
}
```

3. If you compile this program, nothing will happen since we don't have any code yet.

4. Let's create a new file for this project that is going to contain all of our methods. We could write our methods in this file or we could separate them into a new class to make it more reusable. Choose **File**, **New File**, **Java Class**, and click **Next**.

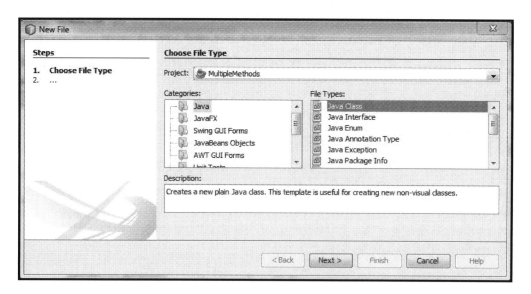

5. Name this class file **MyLibrary** and click **Finish**.

6. Add the following code to the MyLibrary class:

```java
/*
 * Practice with writing and calling methods in separate classes
 * Written by your name, date, and JDK version
 */

import javax.swing.JOptionPane;

public class MyLibrary {
    public static void printName() {
        System.out.println("My name is ...");
    }

    public static void printIt(String message) {
        System.out.println(message);
    }

    public static void convertToCelsius(double fah) {
        double cel = 5.0 / 9.0 * (fah - 32);
        JOptionPane.showMessageDialog(null,
                "The fahrenheit temperature is " + fah
                + "\nThe corresponding celsius temperature is " + cel);
    }

    public static double squareIt(double num) {
        return num * num;
    }
}
```

7. If you run the program nothing will happen, because even though we have created all these methods, we haven't called any of them.

8. We need to go back to the MultipleMethods class which contains our main method and call our methods from here.

9. Our first statement should call the printName method so that your name displays in the output. The line that will do that is:

   MyLibrary.printName( );

   Note: Since the printName method is not in current class, we must tell it what class it is in by saying MyLibrary. The printName methods has no arguments so the parenthesis are empty.

10. Our second statement should call the printIt method so that the words "I love Java" show on display. Type the line you think will do that.

11. Our third statement should take the number of 30.5 and square it and place it in a double variable called x. Type the line you think will do that.

12. Our fourth statement should take the x variable and use the method of convertToCelsius to convert this x temperature to Celsius. Type the line you think will do that.

13. Our last statement in the main program should nest several methods. This one is tricky. All in one statement, you want the computer to square the number of 12.0 and take that result and pass it to the convertToCelsius method. Type the line you think will do that.

14. Compile and test your program to see how close your answers were. Here is what you should have so far:

```
MultipleMethods.java    MyLibrary.java

1  /*
2   * Practice with writing and calling methods in separate classes
3   * Written by your name, date, and JDK version
4   */
5
6  public class MultipleMethods {
7
8      public static void main(String[] args) {
9          MyLibrary.printName();
10         MyLibrary.printIt("I love Java");
11         double x = MyLibrary.squareIt(30.5);
12         MyLibrary.convertToCelsius(x);
13         MyLibrary.convertToCelsius(MyLibrary.squareIt(12.0));
14     }
15  }
```

15. The above program utilizes all the methods discussed in this chapter. They were all placed into a class file called MyLibrary. First, your name shows up in the Output window followed by the String "I love Java". This occurred because you called the printName and printIt methods from the MyLibrary class.

16. Next, the computer squares the 30.5 using the squareIt method. It then uses that result in the call to the convertToCelsius method where the dialog box as follows shows up on screen:

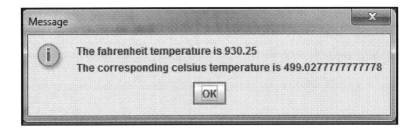

After clicking on OK, the second dialog box as follows shows up on screen:

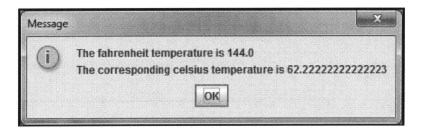

17. **Challenge:** Create a method to sum any two numbers. These numbers should both be integers. It should return an integer value. This new method should be added to your MyLibrary class. Call this method from your main method passing in 10 and 20 as your arguments. You will need to either save the result in a variable and then print that result or call the method from a printout statement.

18. Compile and test your program to see how close your answers were. Here is one possible solution:

```java
/*
 * Practice with writing and calling methods in separate classes
 * Written by your name, date, and JDK version
 */

import javax.swing.JOptionPane;

public class MyLibrary {
    public static void printName() {
        System.out.println("My name is ...");
    }

    public static void printIt(String message) {
        System.out.println(message);
    }

    public static void convertToCelsius(double fah) {
        double cel = 5.0 / 9.0 * (fah - 32);
        JOptionPane.showMessageDialog(null,
                "The fahrenheit temperature is " + fah
                + "\nThe corresponding celsius temperature is " + cel);
    }

    public static double squareIt(double num) {
        return num * num;
    }

    public static int sum (int num1, int num2) {
        return num1 + num2;
    }
}
```

```java
/*
 * Practice with writing and calling methods in separate classes
 * Written by your name, date, and JDK version
 */

public class MultipleMethods {

    public static void main(String[] args) {
        MyLibrary.printName();
        MyLibrary.printIt("I love Java");
        double x = MyLibrary.squareIt(30.5);
        MyLibrary.convertToCelsius(x);
        MyLibrary.convertToCelsius(MyLibrary.squareIt(12.0));
        System.out.println("The sum of 10 + 20 is " + MyLibrary.sum(10,20));
    }
}
```

19. Make the **sum** method **private**. Compile and run your program. You should have an error in your program. Since the sum method is private, it will not be able to be used in any other class. All the previous methods in the MyLibrary class were declared as public so they were able to be used in the MultipleMethods class or in any other class that you write *(Note: the MyLibrary class has to be in same directory on your disk as the program that calls them).* You cannot call the sum method from the MultipleMethods class if is it declared as private in the MyLibrary class *(Note: private access only allows the class that the method was written in to access it. Since it was written in the MyLibrary class, another method within this class has access to it).*

20. Change it back to being public.

21. Compile and run your program.

Exercise 5 – Counting Words

This hands-on exercise allows a user to type in a message and counts the number of words in that message.

1. Get into NetBeans and start a new Java program. The name of the project and main class file should be: **CountWords.** Type in the following portion of the Java program.

```
/* This program will count the number of words in a message
 * Your name
 * Date
 * JDK Version
 */

import javax.swing.JOptionPane;

public class CountWords {
    public static void main(String[] args) {


    }
}
```

2. Next we need to display a window on screen, requesting the user to type a message:

String input = JOptionPane.showInputDialog(null, "Enter a message");

3. To use the String Tokenizer, the computer must be told where it is. You should add your imports to the top of the program before your class declaration. *Note: you should put your imports in alphabetical order.* It is in the **util** directory of java and thus we need to add the following import:

import java.util.StringTokenizer;

4. Then, we should feed that message variable into the String Tokenizer to create a Tokenizer object called tokens. Put this line at the top of the main method.

StringTokenizer tokens = new StringTokenizer(input);

5. Take the tokens object and run a predefined method called countTokens (means count words) and puts the number of tokens (words) into a variable called *sum*.

int sum = tokens.countTokens();

6. Finally, print out the results. This output should repeat the message inside quotes. You must use \" to get a quote inside of a string in Java.

> **JOptionPane.showMessageDialog(null, "The message \"" + input +**
> **"\" has " + sum + " words");**

7. Your final program should look as follows:

```
/* This program will count the number of words in a message
 * Your name
 * Date
 * JDK Version
 */

import java.util.StringTokenizer;
import javax.swing.JOptionPane;

public class CountWords {
    public static void main(String[] args) {
        String input = JOptionPane.showInputDialog(null,"Enter a message");
        StringTokenizer tokens = new StringTokenizer(input);
        int sum = tokens.countTokens();
        JOptionPane.showMessageDialog(null, "The message \"" + input +
                "\" has " + sum + " words");
    }
}
```

8. Be sure your code is properly indented by selecting **Source** from the menu, then **Format**. Compile and execute. Close project.

Summary

- Methods are a series of statements that perform some task.
- Methods must include a declaration, an opening curly brace, a body of statements, and a closing curly brace.
- The syntax of a declaration of a method is:

  > **modifier   static   return-type   method-name   (list of parameters) {**
  >   .... statements in method
  > }

- The modifier of a method can be public or private. Public methods can be used in other programs while private methods can only be used in the method that calls them. A modifier is optional.
- The return-type of a method can be int, double, float, etc depending upon what value is to be returned from the method. If no value is to be returned the keyword of "void" is used as the return-type.
- The method name follows same rules as the rules for variable names.
- The list of parameters in a declaration of a method should be the values a list of all of the data that you want to transfer TO the method when it is called. The parameters must be in parenthesis. You can have any number of parameters from zero to many. Each of the parameters should have a type such as int or double and a name such as y or fahrenheit. Each parameter in the list is separated by a comma.
- When a method is called, the computer transfers the arguments in the call one-by-one to the method. The arguments you send to the method must match both in number and in type as the parameters listed in the declaration of the method.
- When executing a method, the statements in the method are executed. Then, the program returns to the place in the main method where the call was made and continues with the program.
- A parameter allows you to send information to a method when the method is called.
- Functional methods must return a value.
- If you place a method call within a class that does not contain the method, you must use the class name, followed by a dot, followed by the method name. For instance, MyLibrary.printName() means to call a method named printName which is in the class called MyLibrary.
- Private methods cannot be accessed by another class.

Review Questions

1. All methods must return a value.
    a. true
    b. false

2. If you don't have any arguments to transfer to a method, you can eliminate the parenthesis.
    a. true
    b. false

3. A call to the method called calculate is as follows:
    int x = 10;
    double y = 45.6;
    calculate (x, y);

    The beginning of the calculate method should look as follows:

    a. public static double calculate (double a, int b)
    b. public static double calculate(double b, int a)
    c. public static double calculate (int a, double b)
    d. public static double calculate (a, b)

4. If you have a programmer-defined method called calculate that has 2 integer parameters, the call to the method must have 2 integer arguments.
    a. true
    b. false

5. A private method named computeSum ( ) is located in ClassOne. To call the method from within ClassTwo, use the statement:
    a. computeSum(ClassOne);
    b. computeSum(ClassTwo);
    c. ClassTwo.computeSum( ):
    d. ClassOne.computeSum( );
    e. You can't call the method computeSum in ClassOne from ClassTwo.

6. Which of the following method declarations is correct for a method named **add**, if the method receives 2 double arguments and returns a double result?
    a. public static void double add (number1, number2)
    b. public void add (double number1; double number2)
    c. public static void add (double number1, double number2)
    d. public static double add (double number1, double number2)

7. If a method is declared as:
   public static int aMethod (int x)
   Which of the following would be a correct call to this method?
   a. aMethod (14.5);
   b. aMethod ( );
   c. int aMethod ( );
   d. aMethod (10);

8. A method is declared as:
   public static int showMe (double b, int a)
   Which of the following would be a correct call to this method?
   a. showMe(double d, int c);
   b. showMe(10, 54.5);
   c. showMe (54.5, 10);
   d. None of the above

9. What is the length of the following String?
   String s1 = "Java is fun!"

Solutions: 1)b 2)b 3)c 4)a 5)e 6)d 7)d 8)c 9)12

Assignments

5-1   Creating an Area and Perimeter Function in Java: Your goal is to ask the user for the length of one side of a square, invoke a functional method called **calculateArea** that returns the area of the square, invoke a functional method called **calculatePerimeter** that returns the perimeter of the square, and show the results in a message box.

Main method:
- Ask the user via a JOptionPane box for length of one side of a square and parse and save that response into a double variable.
- Call the area method and save the result in a variable
- Call the perimeter method and save the result in a variable
- Display the area and perimeter results in a JOptionPane message box.

calculateArea Functional Method:
- Take in the length of the side of the square that the user typed.
- Return the area of the square using the following equation:
  lengthOfSide * lengthOfSide

calculatePerimeter Functional Method:
- Take in the length of the side of the square that the user typed.
- Return the perimeter of the square using the following equation:
  lengthOfSide * 4

Chapter 6

Conditionals

Objectives

- ☑ List relational operators.
- ☑ List logical operators.
- ☑ Use the hierarchy of operators chart to properly construct if/else statements.
- ☑ Construct switch statements.
- ☑ Use nested if statements.

Conditional Execution

In life, sometimes we must make decisions. If the traffic light is red, we stop the car. If the dishwasher is full of dirty dishes, we run the dishwasher. Decisions are vital to computer programming, too, and exist in all computer languages.

When a decision is being made, a question is asked about a current condition in the world. For example, "Is the rabbit visible?" or "Is the color of the cone blue?" Clearly the answer is either true or false. True and false values are also known as *Boolean values*, named after the 19th century English mathematician George Boole.

Conditional execution is where some condition is checked for being true or false. If the condition is true, one block of code of the program will be executed. If the condition is false, a different block of code of the program will be executed.

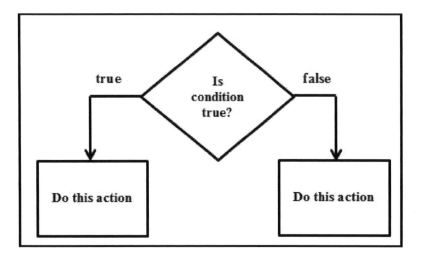

A Boolean condition compares primitives, constants, variables and/or objects using the following relational operators:

Alice	Java	Relational Operator
EQUALS	==	To test for two items to be equal *Note: In Java, the double equal sign means equality. The single equal sign is used to assign a value to a variable or object. Be careful to **never** use the single equal sign for comparison in conditional statements.*
≠	!=	To Test for two items not being equal
<	<	To test for one item to be LESS THAN another item
≤	<=	To test for one item to be LESS THAN OR EQUAL to another item
>	>	To test for one item to be GREATER THAN another item
≥	>=	To test for one item to be GREATER THAN OR EQUAL to another item.

Note: These relational operators must be typed exactly as above. You can't type a space between the two equal signs and you can't put =< to mean less than or equal.

Alice Functions

Alice provides built-in Alice functional methods that can be used for decision making. The following example shows 2 monkeys competing for a banana. The monkey that is closest to the banana will say "Yippee" since they will most likely be the one that gets to eat it. The **getDistanceTo** Alice function will return the distance from one object to another *(in this case the monkey to the banana)*. If the determined distance for the black monkey is less than the distance for the brown monkey, the black monkey will say "Yippee". Otherwise (else), the brown monkey will say "Yippee".

Java Functions

The most common Java functions are in the Math class of the Java API. Some common Math functions in the Java API are:

Math Functions (Methods) Partial List	
Return type	**Function**
double	**abs**(double a) Returns the absolute value of a double value.
int	**abs**(int a) Returns the absolute value of an int value.
double	**ceil**(double a) Returns the smallest (closest to negative infinity) double value that is greater than or equal to the argument and is equal to a mathematical integer.
double	**floor**(double a) Returns the largest (closest to positive infinity) double value that is less than or equal to the argument and is equal to a mathematical integer.
double	**max**(double a, double b) Returns the greater of two double values.
int	**max**(int a, int b) Returns the greater of two int values.
double	**min**(double a, double b) Returns the smaller of two double values.
int	**min**(int a, int b) Returns the smaller of two int values.
double	**random**() Returns a double value with a positive sign, greater than or equal to 0.0 and less than 1.0.
int	**round**(float a) Returns the closest int to the argument.
double	**sqrt**(double a) Returns the correctly rounded positive square root of a double value.

To see the entire list of math functions, go to the URL of
http://docs.oracle.com/javase/8/docs/api/

A common Math function used in games is called random which generates a random number between .0000000000 and .9999999999. When using this function, you should refer to the Math class where the function is found and then the call to the random method without any parameters as follows:

Math.random( )

This call to this static method (function) will return a double number between .0000000000 and .9999999999. This can then be adjusted to become an int by using the following:

(int)(Math.random( ))

For instance if you have a deck of playing cards that are numbered from 1 to 52 and you want to generate a random number so that a random card is shown on the screen, you would need the computer to generate integers between 1 and 52. This would be done by adjusting the formula to be something similar to the following:

int cardNumber = (int)(Math.random( ) * 52 + 1);

The lowest number this can generate is calculated by multiplying .000000000 by 52 which is still .0000000000 and then adding 1 to it. Thus, the lowest number generated is 1 which is exactly what we want. The highest number this can generate is calculated by multiplying .9999999999 by 52 which results in 51.9999999948, then we add 1 and get 52.99999999948. Taking the integer part of that result gives you 52 which is exactly the highest number that we want.

Java If Statements

The "if conditional statement" is used when you want to execute different statements based on a Boolean test. The syntax contains the keyword **if**, followed by a **condition (Boolean test) in parenthesis**, followed **a block of statements to execute if the test is true.** An **optional else** keyword provides the alternative statements to execute if the test is false. The syntax of an if statement is:

```
if ( condition )
    {   statements to do when conditional is true  }
else
    {   statements to do when conditional is false  }
```

Note: Statements to be done for true and false options should be indented to make the IF statement more understandable.

Samples:

The following is a sample of an IF block with one condition and one action to be taken if the one condition is true. In this case, if x is less than y, the computer will display the words "x is smaller than y". If x is NOT less than y, no action has been specified.

```
if ( x  <  y )
        {    System.out.println ( "x is smaller than y" );  }
```

The following is a sample of an if statement with one condition and one action to be taken if the condition is true and one action to be taken if the condition is false. In this case, if x is less than y, the computer will display the words "x is smaller than y". If x is NOT less than y, the computer will display "x is not smaller than y".

```
if  ( x  <  y )
        {  System.out.println ("x is smaller than y" );  }

else
        {  System.out.println ("x is not smaller than y" );  }
```

The following is a sample of an *if* statement with one condition and two actions to be taken if the condition is true and two actions to be taken if the condition is false. . In this case, if guess is exactly equal to correctAnswer, the computer will add 10 to the variable *score* and then display the words "You are right. You get 10 points." If guess is NOT exactly equal to correctAnswer, the computer will subtract 5 from the variable *score* and then display the words "Sorry,that is wrong. You lose 5 points."

```
if ( guess  = =  correctAnswer ) {
      score = score + 10;
      System.out.println ( "You are right. You get 10 points.");
} else {
      score  = score - 5;
      System.out.println ( "Sorry, that is wrong. You lose 5 points.");
}
```

The following is a sample of nesting if statements. The computer will first test to see if x is less than zero. If x is less than zero, it will perform one action and that is displaying the words ""X is negative." If x is not less than zero, the computer will go to the else portion of the first if statement and find a nested if statement. It will now test to see if x is equal to zero. If x is equal to zero, then it displays the words "X is equal to 0." and is done. If x is not equal to zero, the computer will perform the second *else* which will display the words "X is positive." The benefit of nesting the if statements is that the computer will not bother to test for x being equal to 0 if it already found that x was less than 0.

```
if ( x < 0 )
    { System.out.println ( "X is negative." );    }
else if (x = = 0)
    {  System.out.println ( "X is equal to 0." );  }
else
    { System.out.println ( "X is positive." );    }
```

Java Switch Statements

The "switch" statement does much the same job as if statements, but it is more appropriate for situations where you have many choices, rather than only a few. In the switch statement, the test (a variable or expression that evaluates to a **byte, char, short, int, or String**) is compared with each of the case values in turn. If a match is found, all the statements after the test are executed until the computer reaches the end of switch statement or encounters a break statement. **If no match is found, the optional default statement is executed.**

The arguments to case labels must be constants or constant expressions. You can't use a variable or expression involving variables since it won't have a value at compile time.

Execution falls thru and does each case after finding a matching case unless a break is encountered. If a break is encountered, it stops execution of the switch and program continues. *Therefore, in most instances, a programmer wants to place a break statement at the end of each case.*

Done with if statements:	Done with switch statements:

if (x == 1)
{ y = 5; }
else if (x == 2)
{   y = 8; }
else if (x == 3)
{ y = 13; }
	switch **(x)**
	{
	    case1:
	       y=5:
	       break;
	    case 2:
	       y=8;
	       break;
	    case 3:
	       y=13;
	       break;
	}

The sample below shows you a switch statement using char (one character). When nesting several if statements or switch statements, we generally don't indent or not as much because the program will become too lengthy.

Done with if statements:	Done with switch statements:

if (grade = = 'A')
　{ System.out.println ("Great!"); }
else if (grade = = 'B')
　{ System.out.println ("Good!"); }
else if (grade = = 'C')
　{ System.out.println ("Nice."); }
else
　{ System.out.println ("Not Good."); }
	switch (grade) {
	　case **'A':**
	　　System.out.println ("Great!");
	　　break;
	　case **'B':**
	　　System.out.println ("Good!");
	　　break;
	　case **'C':**
	　　System.out.println ("Nice.");
	　　break;
	　default:
	　　System.out.println ("Not Good.");
	}

Nested If Statements vs. Switch Statements

Nested If Statements:	Switch Statements:

if (month = = 2)
　{ noOfDays =28; }
else if　((month = = 4) || (month = = 6) ||
　(month = = 9) || (month = = 11))
　{ noOfDays=30; }
else
　{ noOfDays=31; }
	switch (month) {
	　case 2:
	　　noOfDays = 28;
	　　break;
	　case 4:　case 6:　case 9:　case 11:
	　　noOfDays = 30;
	　　break;
	　default:
	　　noOfDays = 31;
	}

Java Logical Operators

Sometimes, Boolean tests (conditions) may become more complex by combining ORs and ANDs. The most common logical operators are && for AND and the || for OR. The following is a complete list:

Logical Operator	Explanation
&&	**Short-circuiting AND** - Both conditions on both sides of the && must be true for the result to be TRUE. The first condition will be tested and if it is false, the computer will not bother to test the second condition since there is now no way for both conditions to be true.
||	**Short-circuiting OR** - If either condition is true on both sides of the || then the result is true. The first condition will be tested and if it is true, the computer will not bother to test the second condition since it only needs one condition to be true and it already found one to be true.
&	**AND** -Same as logical AND but it tests both sides of & no matter what.
|	**OR** - Same as logical OR but it tests both side of | no matter what.
!	**NOT** - Negates the condition (i.e. - if result was false, it will become true and vice versa).
^	**Exclusive OR** - Results in true value if and only if one of its operands is true and the other is false.

Using Logical Operators:

The following only prints if x is less than y and x is less than z. The && means if x is NOT less than y it won't even bother to test to see if x is less than z.

if ((x < y) && (x < z))
        { System.out.println ("x is less than both y and z"); }

The following calculates grossPay if either condition is true. The || means that if weeklyHours is less 40, it won't bother to test to see if employeeType is 'P'.

if ((weeklyHours< 40) || (employeeType = = 'P'))
        { grossPay = weeklyHours * hourlyRate; }

Java Hierarchy of Operators

The following is a list of various operators and their corresponding hierarchical ranking. You can use the list below to determine the hierarchy that Java will use to evaluate commands containing multiple operators. (Note: Operators on same level are executed from left to right.) My advice: **Use parentheses as much as possible to eliminate the confusion!!!**

Hierarchy Operator Chart:

Operator	Rule
( )	Parenthesis left to right
++ -- casts	Incrementing, decrementing and casting (left to right)
* / %	Multiplication, division, and modulus (left to right)
+ -	Addition and subtraction (left to right)
< <= > >=	Relational operators (left to right) -- used in conditionals
== !=	Equality operators (left to right) -- used in conditionals
&& || & |	Complex logical operators for and / or
= += -= *= /= %=	Shorthand Assignment operators (right to left)

Hands-on Exercises

Exercise 1: Shark Moves to Closest Fish in Alice

Our goal is to use conditionals to have a shark move to the fish that is closest to it and eat that fish.

1. Open Alice 3.

2. Scene setup: Begin with a Sea_Floor template. Add a shark and 2 fish. It does not matter which type of fish you choose. Give these objects a name (be sure to start your object names with a lowercase letter). Place one fish closer to the shark (this will be the fish that unfortunately gets eaten).

3. Name this program **SharkToClosestFish**

4. Go to edit code. Add your comments to the top of the program (name, date, description of the program.

5. Have the shark open its mouth. Select the shark object, then arrow over to the mouth subpart. Drag the turn procedure for the shark's mouth to the code editor as shown below.

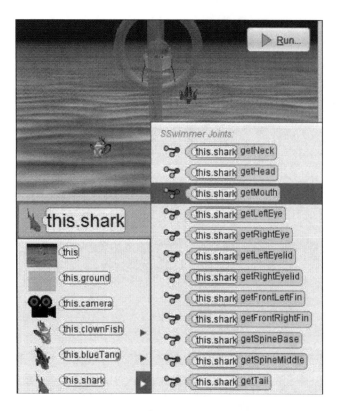

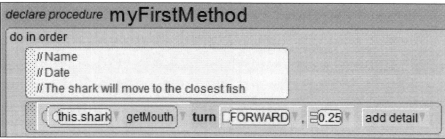

6. We want to program the shark to move to the closest fish. We will use a conditional to determine which fish is closer. Drag the **if** block to the editor and select **true** as the condition as shown below:

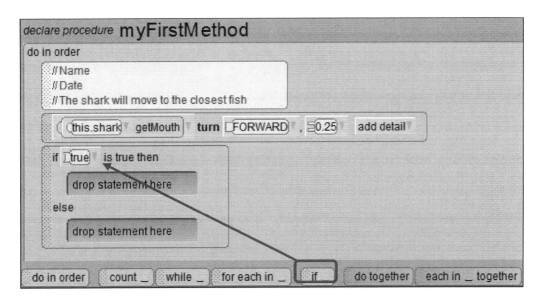

7. Now we need to figure out how far away each fish is from the shark. Click on the down arrow next to the first true and then choose **Relational Decimal number**, and then choose **??? < ???** then **0.25** and finally then choose **0.25**. Your conditional should look as follows:

8. It doesn't make sense for us to compare 0.25 to see if it is less than 0.25. This was just a placeholder, but now we need to use the distance from the shark to the fish. Click on the shark. Click on **functions** tab and you will see a **getDistanceTo** function and notice that it has a parameter of other. You should drag this function up to the conditional to replace the first **0.25**. Select your first fish as the argument.

9. Drag the **getDistanceTo** function for the shark to replace the second **0.25** in the conditional statement. Select the other fish as the argument.

10. Now, let's have the shark move to the closer fish. Click on the **shark** object, then click on the **procedures** tab, then drag the **moveTo** method to the editor under the **if** statement. Select the fish that match the fish before the less than sign (this would be the closer fish). Run your program. Does the shark move to the closer fish?

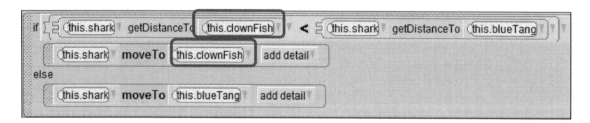

11. Final touch: Let's make the shark close his mouth after the conditional block. Your code should look as follows:

12. Run your program. Does the shark eat the closer fish? If so, then move the other fish so that it is closer to the shark and run it again. Does your program still work? The shark should move to the fish that is closer even after you adjust the scene setup. *Note: You should always test all possibilities of a program.* Save your file. Exit Alice.

Exercise 2: Determining the Tallest Object

Our goal is to use conditionals to determine the tallest object.

1. Open Alice 3.

2. Scene setup: Begin with a grass template. Add 3 female children from the Biped class (change the characteristics of each person to make them unique). Give them the names of becca, jess, and anne respectively. Move them away from each other. Adjust their heights to be different.

3. Name this project **TallestPerson** in the appropriate chapter folder.

4. Get into NetBeans and start a New Project from existing Alice project and use the TallestPerson.a3p file. Open up the **Scene.java** file and locate **myFirstMethod**:

```
public void myFirstMethod() {

}
```

5. We will need to determine the height for each person. To make it easier to do our comparisons, we will save the heights into variables. We can use the Alice **getHeight** function on each of the girl objects to determine their height.

```
public void myFirstMethod() {
    double beccaHeight = becca.getHeight();
    double jessHeight = jess.getHeight();
    double anneHeight = anne.getHeight();
}
```

6. Now that we have the heights for each of the girls saved into variables, we can use condtionals to compare their heights. Let's start with the first 2 girls.

```java
public void myFirstMethod() {
    double beccaHeight = becca.getHeight();
    double jessHeight = jess.getHeight();
    double anneHeight = anne.getHeight();
    if(beccaHeight>jessHeight){
        becca.say("I am the tallest");
    }
}
```

7. This doesn't quite work for Becca being the tallest yet. Just because she is taller than Jess doesn't necessarily mean that she is taller than Anne. We need to add another condition (compound condition) to ensure that Becca is taller than both Jess and Anne. We will use the short-curcuiting AND (&&) for this compound conditional. The short-curcuit AND will not bother testing Becca to Anne if Becca is not taller than Jess.

```java
public void myFirstMethod() {
    double beccaHeight = becca.getHeight();
    double jessHeight = jess.getHeight();
    double anneHeight = anne.getHeight();
    if(beccaHeight>jessHeight && beccaHeight>anneHeight){
        becca.say("I am the tallest");
    }
}
```

8. Next, we can compare Jess and Anne. We can factor Becca out of the comparison, since we already know that she is not the tallest if we make it past the first conditional.

```java
public void myFirstMethod() {
    double beccaHeight = becca.getHeight();
    double jessHeight = jess.getHeight();
    double anneHeight = anne.getHeight();
    if(beccaHeight>jessHeight && beccaHeight>anneHeight){
        becca.say("I am the tallest");
    } else if(jessHeight>anneHeight){
        jess.say("I am the tallest");
    }
}
```

9. Finally, if Becca is not the tallest and Jess is not the tallest, then Anne has to be the tallest. We are not accounting for them being the same size in this program.

```java
public void myFirstMethod() {
    double beccaHeight = becca.getHeight();
    double jessHeight = jess.getHeight();
    double anneHeight = anne.getHeight();
    if(beccaHeight>jessHeight && beccaHeight>anneHeight){
        becca.say("I am the tallest");
    } else if(jessHeight>anneHeight){
        jess.say("I am the tallest");
    } else {
        anne.say("I am the tallest");
    }
}
```

10. Run the program to test it. Does it work? Unfortunately, we no longer have the scene editor to resize the girls to ensure that the program is working properly. We can however, adjust their height by using the setHeight function for each of the girls. The following shows the adjustment for Jess's height, but you can do the same for the other 2 girls.

```java
public void myFirstMethod() {
    jess.setHeight(1.5);
    double beccaHeight = becca.getHeight();
    double jessHeight = jess.getHeight();
    double anneHeight = anne.getHeight();
    if(beccaHeight>jessHeight && beccaHeight>anneHeight){
        becca.say("I am the tallest");
    } else if(jessHeight>anneHeight){
        jess.say("I am the tallest");
    } else {
        anne.say("I am the tallest");
    }
}
```

11. Test your program by adjusting all of the girls' heights. Once you ensure that it works. Save your work and close your project.

Exercise 3 - Using Conditionals to Display a Greeting

The following is an application that uses the GregorianCalendar class. This class is located in the util package (UTILITIES) of java. This program instantiates a GregorianCalendar object called *calendar*. This object will contain the exact date and time from the user's computer internal clock. The constant HOUR_OF_DAY will be the hour in military time. (At 9 am, the hour will be 9. At 9 pm the hour will be 21.) The program tests the hour and prints an appropriate message.

1. Get into NetBeans and start a new Java **application** program. The name of the file project and the main class file should be: **Greeting**. Type in the beginning of the program as follows:

```
/* Name
 * Date
 * JDK version 1.7
 * This program will determine the time of day using a function.
 */

import java.util.GregorianCalendar;   //imports Calendar class for our time

public class Greeting {

    public static void main(String[] args) {
        GregorianCalendar calendar = new GregorianCalendar();
        int hour = calendar.get(calendar.HOUR_OF_DAY);
    }
```

2. The next to last line that you just typed says to instantiate the GregorianCalendar and name the object as calendar. The last line gets the HOUR_OF_DAY from your computer system puts it in the integer called hour. The GregorianCalendar class has all the properties and methods concerning dates and times. When you instantiate the default GregorianCalendar, the computer gets the time, date, etc. at that moment from the computer's internal clock. There are over 2000 lines of code in the GregorianCalendar class. For an explanation of GregorianCalendar, refer to the Java docs api.

Note: Variable names that are in all capital letters represent constants.

Some of the possible arguments to the get ( ) method are: DAY_OF_YEAR, DAY_OF_MONTH, DAY_OF_WEEK, YEAR, MONTH, MINUTE, SECOND, MILLISECOND.

3. Now, we are going to write function called **determineTimeOfDay**. This function is going to have a parameter to take in the hour and it is going to use conditional statements to determine whether it is morning or afternoon. This method will return a String of whether it is morning or afternoon. Your method should look as follows. You will have a red underline, since we didn't return a value yet.

```
public static String determineTimeOfDay(int hour) {

}
```

4. Let's create a string variable named **message** that will hold the message that will be displayed to the screen. We will initialize this variable at **null** since it does not have a value yet. The Boolean expression for morning should be **hour <12**, this would be before noon. After entering the Boolean expression, we need to type what we want the computer do when hour is less than 12. We need to set the message variable as **"Good morning"** inside our *if* conditional block. After the *if* conditional block, we will return the message variable back from our method.

```
public static String determineTimeOfDay(int hour) {
    String message = null;
    if (hour < 12) {
        message = "Good morning";
    }
    return message;
}
```

5. Now, let's add more conditions. We will add an **else if** to our conditions with the following criteria: **hour < 17**. Remember that we are using military time; 17 would be 5pm. The "Good afternoon" message will display if it is before 5pm. If it is not morning or afternoon, we are going to default to evening. To add a default option to your conditions, you would add an **else**. An *else* will NEVER have a Boolean condition since it is default if none of the other options matched. If the hour does not match the morning or afternoon conditions, then it will automatically match the *else*.

```
public static String determineTimeOfDay(int hour) {
    String message = null;
    if (hour < 12) {
        message = "Good morning";
    } else if (hour < 17) {
        message = "Good afternoon";
    } else {
        message = "Good evening";
    }
    return message;
}
```

6. Next, we need to call the determineTimeOfDay from the main method.

```
public static void main(String[] args) {
    GregorianCalendar calendar = new GregorianCalendar();
    int hour = calendar.get(calendar.HOUR_OF_DAY);
    System.out.println(determineTimeOfDay(hour));
}
```

7. Compile and execute this program. The output message will be based on the time of day that you execute the program. Adjust the time on your computer and test this Java program to see if it works for all 3 messages.

   Note: Every functional method (non-void) must return a value even if that value is null.

8. The final version of the program should look as follows:

```
/* Name
 * Date
 * JDK version 1.7
 * This program will determine the time of day using a function.
 */

import java.util.GregorianCalendar;   //imports Calendar class for our time

public class Greeting {

    public static void main(String[] args) {
        GregorianCalendar calendar = new GregorianCalendar();
        int hour = calendar.get(calendar.HOUR_OF_DAY);
        System.out.println(determineTimeOfDay(hour));
    }

    public static String determineTimeOfDay(int hour) {
        String message = null;
        if (hour < 12) {
            message = "Good morning";
        } else if (hour < 17) {
            message = "Good afternoon";
        } else {
            message = "Good evening";
        }
        return message;
    }
}
```

Exercise 4 - Using Conditionals for a Guessing Game

The following is a Java application that will be the beginning of a guessing game. The computer generates a random number between 1 and 100 and asks the user to guess the number. The computer will then respond with messages depending upon the user's answer.

1. Get into NetBeans and start a new Java program. The name of the project and main class file should be: **GuessingGame.** Type in the following portion of the Java program.

```
/*
 * This is a java program to allow a user
 * to guess the computer number 1 to 100
 * Name and Date
 * JDK version
 */

import javax.swing.JOptionPane;

public class GuessingGame {
    public static void main(String[] args) {

    }
}
```

2. The first task is for the computer to generate a random number between 1 and 100. There is a method called random in the Math class that generates a random double number approximately between .0000000000 and .9999999999. You can read about this method by going to the Java API documentation at the site of: http://docs.oracle.com/javase/8/docs/api/

3. If we simply have the statement of :

int computerNumber = Math.random( );

We will get a compiler error. Do you have any idea why? The problem is that Math.random() returns a double number and then you are trying to put it in an int variable of computerNumber. Java will require us to cast this double to an int. So now the line would be:

int computerNumber = (int) (Math.random( ));

This will make the random number generated an int by dropping off the decimal part of the number.

4. However, the game requires the number to be between 1 and 100. Our current statement is going to generate numbers between 0 and 0 because the lowest number of .0000000000000 will be converted to an int of 0 and the highest possible number of .9999999999 will be converted to an int of 0. Remember, that no rounding is done. So let's multiply by 100 as follows:

int computerNumber = (int) (Math.random( ) * 100);

5. The above statement will convert the smallest number of .000000 multiplied by 100 to an int of 0 and convert the largest number of .9999999999 multiplied by 100 to an int of 99. BUT, we wanted the numbers to be between 1 and 100 so we need to add 1 to the formula so that our final formula will be:

int computerNumber = (int) (Math.random( ) * 100 + 1);

6. The above line is the final formula to have the computer generate a number between 1 and 100 and put that random number in the integer variable called computerNumber.

7. Next we need to display a window on screen, requesting the user to guess a number between 1 and 100. On this same screen, the user should be able to type in her guess. The statement will be as follows:

String response = JOptionPane.showInputDialog(null,
        "Enter a guess between 1 and 100");

The above statement will display a screen as follows:

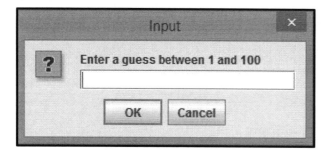

8. The user will type in a guess and that guess will be placed into the String variable called response. To use this string as an integer later in the program, it will need to be converted into an int by using the following statement:

int userAnswer = Integer.parseInt(response);

9. Now we are going to create a method called **determineGuess**. This method is going to take in the userAnswer (user's guess) and the computerNumber (randomly generated number). The method is going to return a message based on whether the guess is invalid, correct, or incorrect.

```java
public static String determineGuess(int userAnswer, int computerNumber) {
    String message = null;
    if (userAnswer <= 0 || userAnswer > 100) {
        message = "Invalid guess";
    } else if (userAnswer == computerNumber) {
        message = "Correct";
    } else {
        message = "Incorrect";
    }
    return message;
}
```

10. Next, we need to call the determineGuess method from the main method.

```java
public class GuessingGame {
    public static void main(String[] args) {
        // generate a random number from 1 to 100
        int computerNumber = (int) (Math.random() * 100 + 1);
        String response = JOptionPane.showInputDialog(null,
                "Enter a guess between 1 and 100");
        int userAnswer = Integer.parseInt(response);
        JOptionPane.showMessageDialog(null, determineGuess(userAnswer, computerNumber));
    }
    public static String determineGuess(int userAnswer, int computerNumber) {
        String message = null;
        if (userAnswer <= 0 || userAnswer > 100) {
            message = "Invalid guess";
        } else if (userAnswer == computerNumber) {
            message = "Correct";
        } else {
            message = "Incorrect";
        }
        return message;
    }
}
```

Chapter 6 – Conditionals

11. To truly test this program, you need to guess incorrectly once and you need to guess correctly at least once. This way you will see if your *if* statement is working. However, it will be near impossible for you to guess the random number that the computer generated. Thus, we will need some way of seeing the correctNumber before we guess so we can guess correctly (cheating really ☺). Put in the following line after the computer generates its random number:

System.out.println("The correct guess would be" + computerNumber);

12. You should place appropriate comments throughout the statements where you feel some explanation may be needed.

13. Now compile the program and execute it. You should be able to see the guess in the output window at the bottom of NetBeans. Test all the possibilities by guessing 0 (invalid), guessing 125 (invalid), guessing the exact number (correct), and guessing the wrong number (incorrect).

© Daly & Wrigley

Exercise 5 –Validating a Password Entry

The following is a Java application that will prompt the user for a password. This password must be between 8 and 12 characters long and contain a digit. It will then ask the user to repeat this password to determine if the 2 passwords are equal.

1. Get into NetBeans and start a new Java program. The name of the project and main class should be: **PasswordRules**. Please put your comments at the top of the program.

2. Since we are going to be using the JOptionPane class to take in input from the user, we will need the following import at the top of our program:

    import javax.swing.JOptionPane;

3. Let's prompt the user for a password. Also, we will add the password validation rules to this box. We will not need to convert the string to a double or integer since we need it to remain a string to use the string functions.

    ```java
    String pass1 = JOptionPane.showInputDialog(null, "Enter a password "
            + "\nMust be between 6-12 characters long"
            + "\nMust contain a number");
    ```

4. First we need to check the length of the password. We will use the pass1 string and test the length of that string to ensure that it is between 6 and 12.

    ```java
    if(pass1.length()>=6 && pass1.length()<=12){

    }
    ```

5. Now we will add an else for the if in case it does not match the criteria for the if.

    ```java
    if (pass1.length() >= 6 && pass1.length() <= 12) {

    } else {
        JOptionPane.showMessageDialog(null,
                "Your password needs to be between 6-12 characters");
    }
    ```

6. After we verify that the password is between 6 and 12 characters long, we need to ensure that it contains a digit. We can add an if statement inside the if statement that we already have. We will check the password string to see if it contains a digit by checking all the digits with the contains method. Unfortunately, you will need to check each digit 1 by 1. We will use the OR to compare each of the digits since it only needs to contain one of the digits, not all of them. If we use the short-circuit OR ||, then if the statement contains a "1", it will not bother to test the rest of the digits. After the password passes both of the conditions, we can prompt the user to repeat their password via a JOptionPane.

```java
if (pass1.length() >= 6 && pass1.length() <= 12) {
    if (pass1.contains("1") || pass1.contains("2")
            || pass1.contains("3") || pass1.contains("4")
            || pass1.contains("5") || pass1.contains("6")
            || pass1.contains("7") || pass1.contains("8")
            || pass1.contains("9") || pass1.contains("0")) {
                String pass2 = JOptionPane.showInputDialog(null,"Repeat password");
    }
} else {
    JOptionPane.showMessageDialog(null,
            "Your password needs to be between 6-12 characters");
}
```

7. If the password string does not contain a digit, then we should display a message that informs the user that it must include a digit.

```java
if (pass1.length() >= 6 && pass1.length() <= 12) {
    if (pass1.contains("1") || pass1.contains("2")
            || pass1.contains("3") || pass1.contains("4")
            || pass1.contains("5") || pass1.contains("6")
            || pass1.contains("7") || pass1.contains("8")
            || pass1.contains("9") || pass1.contains("0")) {
                String pass2 = JOptionPane.showInputDialog(null,"Repeat password");
    } else {
        JOptionPane.showMessageDialog(null, "Your password must contain a digit");
    }
} else {
    JOptionPane.showMessageDialog(null,
            "Your password needs to be between 6-12 characters");
}
```

8. Finally, we need to validate that the passwords are equal. We should add a condition that checks to see if the first password string that was entered (pass1) is equal to the second password string that was entered (pass2). If they are equal we will display "Successful", else we will display "The passwords are not equal".

```java
if (pass1.length() >= 6 && pass1.length() <= 12) {
    if (pass1.contains("1") || pass1.contains("2")
            || pass1.contains("3") || pass1.contains("4")
            || pass1.contains("5") || pass1.contains("6")
            || pass1.contains("7") || pass1.contains("8")
            || pass1.contains("9") || pass1.contains("0")) {
                String pass2 = JOptionPane.showInputDialog(null,"Repeat password");
                if(pass1.equals(pass2)){
                    JOptionPane.showMessageDialog(null,"Successful");
                } else {
                    JOptionPane.showMessageDialog(null,"The passwords are not equal");
                }
    } else {
        JOptionPane.showMessageDialog(null, "Your password must contain a digit");
    }
} else {
    JOptionPane.showMessageDialog(null,
            "Your password needs to be between 6-12 characters");
}
```

9. The final version of the program should look as follows:

```java
/* Your name and date
 * JDK version
 * This program will validate that a password is between 6-12 characters long,
 * contains a digit, and is equal to the retype password field */
import javax.swing.JOptionPane;
public class PasswordRules {
    public static void main(String[] args) {
        String pass1 = JOptionPane.showInputDialog(null, "Enter a password "
                + "\nMust be between 6-12 characters long"
                + "\nMust contain a number");
        if (pass1.length() >= 6 && pass1.length() <= 12) {
            if (pass1.contains("1") || pass1.contains("2")
                    || pass1.contains("3") || pass1.contains("4")
                    || pass1.contains("5") || pass1.contains("6")
                    || pass1.contains("7") || pass1.contains("8")
                    || pass1.contains("9") || pass1.contains("0")) {
                        String pass2 = JOptionPane.showInputDialog(null,"Repeat password");
                        if(pass1.equals(pass2)){
                            JOptionPane.showMessageDialog(null,"Successful");
                        } else {
                            JOptionPane.showMessageDialog(null,"The passwords are not equal");
                        }
            } else {
                JOptionPane.showMessageDialog(null, "Your password must contain a digit");
            }
        } else {
            JOptionPane.showMessageDialog(null,
                    "Your password needs to be between 6-12 characters");
        }
    }
}
```

Exercise 6 – Setting up a Simple Calculator

The following is a Java application that will take in two numbers from the user and add, subtract, multiply, or divide based on user selection.

1. Get into NetBeans and start a new Java program. The name of the project and main class should be: **SimpleCalculator**. Please put your comments at the top of the program.

2. We are going to be using the Scanner class to take in input from the user and we are going to be formatting our output to have 2 decimal places. We must have the following imports at the top of our program.

   import java.util.Scanner;
   import java.text.DecimalFormat;

3. Next we should create our scanner object so that we can take in input from the user:

   Scanner scan = new Scanner(System.in);

4. We will create a DecimalFormat object that will format our result to have commas and 2 decimal places:

   DecimalFormat formatter = new DecimalFormat("#,###,###.##");

5. Now, we need to ask the user for 2 numbers and an operator. We will use our scan object to take in the data from the user. You can add a bit more text to make it look nicer. Be sure to give the user choices for the operator. We will use integers as our selection choices because we haven't discussed how to break apart Strings yet. Please see the code below:

```
System.out.println("Simple Calculator");
System.out.print("Enter a number:");
double number1 = scan.nextDouble();
System.out.print("Enter another number:");
double number2 = scan.nextDouble();
System.out.println("Mathmatical Operators: \n1 - Addition "
        + "\n2 - Subtraction \n3 - Multiplication \n4 - Division");
System.out.print("Please enter your choice:");
int operator = scan.nextInt();
```

6. Your program should look as follows so far:

```java
import java.util.Scanner;
import java.text.DecimalFormat;

public class SimpleCalculator {
    public static void main(String[] args) {
        Scanner scan = new Scanner(System.in);
        DecimalFormat formatter = new DecimalFormat("#,###,###.##");
        System.out.println("Simple Calculator");
        System.out.print("Enter a number:");
        double number1 = scan.nextDouble();
        System.out.print("Enter another number:");
        double number2 = scan.nextDouble();
        System.out.println("Mathmatical Operators: \n1 - Addition "
                + "\n2 - Subtraction \n3 - Multiplication \n4 - Division");
        System.out.print("Please enter your choice:");
        int operator = scan.nextInt();
    }
}
```

7. Now we will write a function to add, subtract, multiply, or divide the 2 numbers. We will call this method **calculate**. It will return a **double** as an answer. It will need 3 variables in order to do the calculation: number1, number2, and the operator. You will need to pass these variables into the method as arguments. If the operator is 1, then you will add…if it is 2, then you will subtract…and so on. Please add the following code:

```java
public static double calculate(double number1, double number2, int operator) {
    double result = 0;
    if (operator == 1) {
        result = number1 + number2;
    } else if (operator == 2) {
        result = number1 - number2;
    } else if (operator == 3) {
        result = number1 * number2;
    } else if (operator == 3) {
        result = number1 / number2;
    } else {
        System.out.println("Invalid");
    }
    return result;
}
```

Note: Every function must return a value.

8. Now we need to call this new method that we created from the main method. The call to the method would be as follows: **calculate (number1, number2, operator);** If we just type the method call without saving the result that is returned or without printing off the result we will lose it.

   You can call the method and save the result in a variable and then print it:
   double result = calculate (number1, number2, operator);
   System.out.println("Result: " + result);

   or you call the method from the print out statement:
   System.out.println("Result: " + calculate(number1, number2, operator));

9. You should format your result to have 2 decimals places. You should use the formatter object that we set up.

   The first way would look as follows:
   double result = calculate (number1, number2, operator);
   System.out.println("Result: " + formatter.format(result));

   The second way would look as follows:
   System.out.println("Result: " +
   formatter.format(calculate(number1, number2, operator)));

10. Finally, we should be aware of the fact that we can't divide by 0. To add this functionality to your code, you would add an **if** condition that checked to see if number2 was 0 and if the operator was 4. If number2 was 0 and the operator was 4, then you would display a message stating that you can't divide by 0. It wouldn't even bother to call the **calculate** method, since the result would be mathematically impossible. If number2 wasn't 0 and the operator 4, then it would match the **else** and state the result of the calculation.

```
if (number2 == 0 && operator == 4) {
    System.out.println("You can not divide by zero.");
} else {
    System.out.println("Result: "+
            formatter.format(calculate(number1, number2, operator)));
}
```

11. The final program should look as follows:

```java
/* This program will take in two numbers from the user and add, subtract, multiply
 * or divide based on user selection
 * written by name and date
 * JDK version
 */

import java.util.Scanner;
import java.text.DecimalFormat;

public class SimpleCalculator {

    public static void main(String[] args) {
        Scanner scan = new Scanner(System.in);
        DecimalFormat formatter = new DecimalFormat("#,###,###.##");
        System.out.println("SimpleCalculator");
        System.out.print("Enter a number:");
        double number1 = scan.nextDouble();
        System.out.print("Enter another number:");
        double number2 = scan.nextDouble();
        System.out.println("Mathematical Operators:  \n1  Addition"
                + "\n2  Subtraction" + "\n3  Multiplication"
                + "\n4  Division");
        System.out.print("Please enter your choice:");
        int operator = scan.nextInt();
        if (number2 == 0 && operator == 4) {
            System.out.println("You can not divide by zero.");
        } else {
            System.out.println("Result: "+
                    formatter.format(calculate(number1, number2, operator)));
        }
    }

    public static double calculate(double number1, double number2, int operator) {
        double result = 0;
        if (operator == 1) {
            result = number1 + number2;
        } else if (operator == 2) {
            result = number1 - number2;
        } else if (operator == 3) {
            result = number1 * number2;
        } else if (operator == 3) {
            result = number1 / number2;
        } else {
            System.out.println("Invalid");
        }
        return result;
    }
}
```

12. Run and test the program.

Note: In NetBeans when using a Scanner class to receive input, you need to place the cursor in the output window in order to type in input.

Exercise 7 – Card Game with Conditionals (ongoing exercise)

1. In Chapter 4, you set up a Card Game with the following scene:

2. This program has the cards deal out, WIN sign flash, score change, and cards disappear. Then the program repeats with different cards. This program was adjusted earlier to use methods to perform the different tasks.

3. The storyboard for this program was:

> - Scene opens with the CardGame
> - Player cards are dealt out onto screen.
> - Display winner
> - Have these cards disappear.
> - New Player cards are dealt out on screen.
> - Determine and display winner
> - Have these cards disappear.

4. We will continue to work on this Card Game by converting it from Alice to Java. Get into NetBeans. Click on File menu, New Project, choose Java From Existing Project, and then browse to find the Alice **CardGame** file you completed in Chapter 4. *You may alternately use **MyCardGame** file if you completed the assignment in Chapter 4.* Adjust the location to put this file in the **Chapter6Exercises** folder.

5. Get into the Scene.java file. This program should have a myFirstMethod that looks as follows:

```
    public void myFirstMethod() {//Card Game created by
//on date here
//This program will deal out cards, display winner, and then cards disappear
        this.dealOutCards(this.playingCard8, this.playingCard3);
        this.displayWinner(this.winPlayer1Sign, this.player1ScoreSign);
        this.disappearCards(this.playingCard8, this.playingCard3);
        this.dealOutCards(this.playingCard1, this.playingCard10);
        this.displayWinner(this.winPlayer2Sign, this.player2ScoreSign);
        this.disappearCards(this.playingCard1, this.playingCard10);
    }
```

Note: If you are using a JDK earlier than 1.8, the Alice comments will not transfer into NetBeans.

6. Click on the RUN button in NetBeans. You should get to see the program play a game with cards 8 and 3. Then, it will play a second game with cards 1 and 10. This program will always play with those cards and only those cards.

7. The program needs to be adjusted so that it gets 2 random cards each time instead of the same 2 cards. There is a random number generator function (Math.random) which generates a double number approximately from .0000000 to .999999. To adjust it to generate numbers between 0.00 and 9.9999, we multiply it by 10. To adjust that to generate numbers between 1.000 and 10.9999, you add 1 to the earlier result. Finally, to get it to be an integer number between 1 and 10, we will cast it with (int). The following formula will generate a random number between 1 and 10 and place the result in a variable called randomNumber1:

int randomNumber1 = (int) (Math.random( )*10 +1);

8. Since we need 2 random cards, we will need 2 random numbers so you will need another line for randomNumber2 so that myFirstMethod looks as follows:

```
    public void myFirstMethod() {//Card Game created by
//on date here
//This program will deal out cards, display winner, and then cards disappear
        int randomNumber1 = (int) (Math.random() * 10 + 1);
        int randomNubmer2 = (int) (Math.random() * 10 + 1);
        this.dealOutCards(this.playingCard8, this.playingCard3);
        this.displayWinner(this.winPlayer1Sign, this.player1ScoreSign);
        this.disappearCards(this.playingCard8, this.playingCard3);
        this.dealOutCards(this.playingCard1, this.playingCard10);
        this.displayWinner(this.winPlayer2Sign, this.player2ScoreSign);
        this.disappearCards(this.playingCard1, this.playingCard10);
    }
```

9. Since it is possible that these random numbers will be identical, we will put in a decision to compare the 2 numbers and if they are equal, it will generate another randomNumber1 with the hope that it will be different. We could continue to put in more decisions to make sure they are not identical but this process will never be certain because it could generate the random number of 5 a hundred times in a row (unlikely, but possible). We will solve this issue with loops in a later chapter, so this is the best that can be done at this time. The code for myFirstMethod should now look as follows:

```java
    public void myFirstMethod() {//Card Game created by
//on date here
//This program will deal out cards, display winner, and then cards disappear
        int randomNumber1 = (int) (Math.random() * 10 + 1);
        int randomNumber2 = (int) (Math.random() * 10 + 1);
        if (randomNumber1 == randomNumber2) {
            randomNumber1 = (int) (Math.random() *10 +1);
        }
```

10. Now, there are 2 random numbers. These numbers will be used to select which playing cards will appear. If the number is 1, then playingCard1 should appear. If the number is 2, then playingCard2 should appear, etc. We will write a function named determineRandomCard which will take in the randomNumber that we generated and return the corresponding player card. Because it is returning something, it is a function. This function will be placed immediately after the myFirstMethod. Create a function called **determinePlayingCard**. Make this method **public** with the return type of the PlayingCard object which we will name **determinePlayingCard**. It should have a parameter of an integer which will be referred to as **num** in this function. Place this new functional method after the myFirstMethod.

```java
public PlayingCard determinePlayingCard (int num){

}
```

11. So now we have to think out how to associate the number 1 with playingCard1 and 2 with playingCard2, etc. We could do it with 10 nested if statements but this would be a good case for using a switch statement. When num is 1, we want to return playingCard1 back to the calling method. The function should look as follows:

```java
public PlayingCard determinePlayingCard ( int num){
    switch (num) {
        case 1:  return playingCard1;
        case 2:  return playingCard2;
        case 3:  return playingCard3;
        case 4:  return playingCard4;
        case 5:  return playingCard5;
        case 6:  return playingCard6;
        case 7:  return playingCard7;
        case 8:  return playingCard8;
        case 9:  return playingCard9;
        case 10: return playingCard10;
        default: return playingCard1;
    }
}
```

Note: the default line is added just in case some number comes into the function that is not 1 to 10. In that case, it will return playingCard1.

12. In myFirstMethod, this new function will be called as follows:

```java
    public void myFirstMethod() {//Card Game created by
//on date here
//This program will deal out cards, display winner, and then cards disappear
        int randomNumber1 = (int) (Math.random() * 10 + 1);
        int randomNumber2 = (int) (Math.random() * 10 + 1);
        if (randomNumber1 == randomNumber2) {
            randomNumber1 = (int) (Math.random() *10 +1);
        }
        PlayingCard firstCard = determinePlayingCard (randomNumber1);
        PlayingCard secondCard = determinePlayingCard (randomNumber2);
        this.dealOutCards(this.playingCard8, this.playingCard3);
        this.displayWinner(this.winPlayer1Sign, this.player1ScoreSign);
        this.disappearCards(this.playingCard8, this.playingCard3);
        this.dealOutCards(this.playingCard1, this.playingCard10);
        this.displayWinner(this.winPlayer2Sign, this.player2ScoreSign);
        this.disappearCards(this.playingCard1, this.playingCard10);
    }
```

13. The randomNumber1 is pased to the function called determinePlayingCard and referred to as num in that function. It finds the case that matches the num and returns the corresponding playing card back to myFirstMethod and places that card in firstCard. The same process is done for randomNumber2 and places the corresponding playing card into secondCard.

14. Now that you have the 2 random cards determined and placed into the PlayingCard called firstCard and the PlayingCard called secondCard, you can adjust the program so that it doesn't refer all the time to cards 8 and 3. Replace the first call to dealOutCards and disappearCards as follows:

```
    public void myFirstMethod() {//Card Game created by
//on date here
//This program will deal out cards, display winner, and then cards disappear
        int randomNumber1 = (int) (Math.random() * 10 + 1);
        int randomNumber2 = (int) (Math.random() * 10 + 1);
        if (randomNumber1 == randomNumber2) {
            randomNumber1 = (int) (Math.random() *10 +1);
        }
        PlayingCard firstCard = determinePlayingCard (randomNumber1);
        PlayingCard secondCard = determinePlayingCard (randomNumber2);
        this.dealOutCards(firstCard, secondCard);
        this.displayWinner(this.winPlayer1Sign, this.player1ScoreSign);
        this.disappearCards(firstCard, secondCard);
        this.dealOutCards(this.playingCard1, this.playingCard10);
        this.displayWinner(this.winPlayer2Sign, this.player2ScoreSign);
        this.disappearCards(this.playingCard1, this.playingCard10);
    }
```

15. Run the program to see how it works. Did it generate a random first and second card? It may or may not display correctly the win and score. Run this program several times and see if the first game played generates different playing cards each time. The second game will always be cards 1 and 10 because we didn't change that part of the program yet.

16. What is our problem with the WIN sign and the score? When the program was using cards 8 and 3, we knew that player1 had won and set the win sign and score appropriately. However, now the computer will need to make a decision about who won. We have no idea which cards it will generate each time. How does a player win? If they have the bigger card. How do we know if they have a bigger card? If the number associated with the first card is greater than the number associated with the second card, then player 1 wins. Thus, we need to compare the randomNumbers that were generated. This can be done as follows in the myFirstMethod:

```
    public void myFirstMethod() {//Card Game created by
//on date here
//This program will deal out cards, display winner, and then cards disappear
        int randomNumber1 = (int) (Math.random() * 10 + 1);
        int randomNumber2 = (int) (Math.random() * 10 + 1);
        if (randomNumber1 == randomNumber2) {
            randomNumber1 = (int) (Math.random() *10 +1);
        }
        PlayingCard firstCard = determinePlayingCard (randomNumber1);
        PlayingCard secondCard = determinePlayingCard (randomNumber2);
        this.dealOutCards(firstCard, secondCard);
        if (randomNumber1 > randomNumber2) {
            displayWinner(winPlayer1Sign, player1ScoreSign);
        } else {
            displayWinner(winPlayer2Sign, player2ScoreSign);
        }
```

17. If the first random number is greater than the second random number then the WIN sign will show up for player1 and the score will be adjusted for player 1. If that is not the case, then the WIN sign will show up for player2 and the score will be adjusted for player 2.

18. You will then delete out the line as follows since it is being done inside the if statement:

this.displayWinner(this.winPlayer1Sign, this.player1ScoreSign);

19. Run the program several times to see if it works for just the first game set. We will not pay attention to the second game yet. Is it always working for the first game? It should be working properly.

20. To adjust the second game so that it no longer refers always to cards 1 and 10, we will use random numbers again. Actually, we will repeat all the statements for first game to do the second game. Get rid of the last 3 lines of the myFirstMethod which refer cards 1 and 10. Copy all the statements in myFirstMethod and paste them at the bottom of this same method so you have the following:

```
23    public void myFirstMethod() {//Card Game created by
24    //on date here
25    //This program will deal out cards, display winner, and then cards disappear
26        int randomNumber1 = (int) (Math.random() * 10 + 1);
27        int randomNumber2 = (int) (Math.random() * 10 + 1);
28        if (randomNumber1 == randomNumber2) {
29            randomNumber1 = (int) (Math.random() *10 +1);
30        }
31        PlayingCard firstCard = determinePlayingCard (randomNumber1);
32        PlayingCard secondCard = determinePlayingCard (randomNumber2);
33        this.dealOutCards(firstCard, secondCard);
34        if (randomNumber1 > randomNumber2) {
35            displayWinner(winPlayer1Sign, player1ScoreSign);
36        } else {
37            displayWinner(winPlayer2Sign, player2ScoreSign);
38        }
39        this.disappearCards(firstCard, secondCard);
          int randomNumber1 = (int) (Math.random() * 10 + 1);
          int randomNumber2 = (int) (Math.random() * 10 + 1);
42        if (randomNumber1 == randomNumber2) {
43            randomNumber1 = (int) (Math.random() *10 +1);
44        }
          PlayingCard firstCard = determinePlayingCard (randomNumber1);
          PlayingCard secondCard = determinePlayingCard (randomNumber2);
47        this.dealOutCards(firstCard, secondCard);
48        if (randomNumber1 > randomNumber2) {
49            displayWinner(winPlayer1Sign, player1ScoreSign);
50        } else {
51            displayWinner(winPlayer2Sign, player2ScoreSign);
52        }
53        this.disappearCards(firstCard, secondCard);
54    }
```

21. You will get some errors. It doesn't like that in this second set of statements, you have declared a new variable called randomNumber1. It already has a variable called randomNumber1 declared in myFirstMethod. You can only declare this variable once, but you can reuse it over and over again. Thus, we will move the declaration for randomNumber1 to the beginning of myFirstMethod. You will notice that it is having the same problem with randomNumber2, firstCard and secondCard. These are all being declared more than once and it is not allowed. Thus, we will move the declarations for rancomNumber2, firstCard, and secondCard to the beginning of myFirstMethod.

```
public void myFirstMethod() {//Card Game created by
//on date here
//This program will deal out cards, display winner, and then cards disappear
        int randomNumber1, randomNumber2;
        PlayingCard firstCard, secondCard;
```

22. You will still see errors because you need to remove the declarations off the other statements that declare randomNumber1, randomNumber2, firstCard, and secondCard:

```
public void myFirstMethod() {//Card Game created by
//on date here
//This program will deal out cards, display winner, and then cards disappear
        int randomNumber1, randomNumber2;
        PlayingCard firstCard, secondCard;
        randomNumber1 = (int) (Math.random() * 10 + 1);
        randomNumber2 = (int) (Math.random() * 10 + 1);
        if (randomNumber1 == randomNumber2) {
            randomNumber1 = (int) (Math.random() *10 +1);
        }
        firstCard = determinePlayingCard (randomNumber1);
        secondCard = determinePlayingCard (randomNumber2);
        this.dealOutCards(firstCard, secondCard);
        if (randomNumber1 > randomNumber2) {
            displayWinner(winPlayer1Sign, player1ScoreSign);
        } else {
            displayWinner(winPlayer2Sign, player2ScoreSign);
        }
        this.disappearCards(firstCard, secondCard);
        randomNumber1 = (int) (Math.random() * 10 + 1);
        randomNumber2 = (int) (Math.random() * 10 + 1);
        if (randomNumber1 == randomNumber2) {
            randomNumber1 = (int) (Math.random() *10 +1);
        }
        firstCard = determinePlayingCard (randomNumber1);
        secondCard = determinePlayingCard (randomNumber2);
        this.dealOutCards(firstCard, secondCard);
        if (randomNumber1 > randomNumber2) {
            displayWinner(winPlayer1Sign, player1ScoreSign);
        } else {
            displayWinner(winPlayer2Sign, player2ScoreSign);
        }
        this.disappearCards(firstCard, secondCard);
    }
```

23. Run the program several times and see if it works for both the first game and second game. Are the cards randomized? Are the WIN signs working correctly? Are the scores showing correctly? Everything should be working except the score when player1 or player 2 win both times.

24. Ultimately, we need to have this program work for a score of zero, one, or two. Instead of just displaying a number, we will need to tally two separate scores – one for player1 and one for player2. We will name these two integer tallies as **scorePlayer1** and **scorePlayer2**. In myFirstMethod, declare scorePlayer1 as an int and initialize it to 0. Do the same thing for scorePlayer 2 as follows:

```
    public void myFirstMethod() {//Card Game created by
//on date here
//This program will deal out cards, display winner, and then cards disappear
        int scorePlayer1 = 0;
        int scorePlayer2 = 0;
```

25. When the player wins, it should add 1 to their appropriate score. Where do we work with determining who won? It is done in the *if* statement that compares the random numbers inside of the myFirstMethod. To adjust the *if* statement to add to the appropriate score, we will adjust the code as follows:

```
if (randomNumber1 > randomNumber2) {
    scorePlayer1 ++;
    displayWinner(winPlayer1Sign, player1ScoreSign);
} else {
    scorePlayer2 ++;
    displayWinner(winPlayer2Sign, player2ScoreSign);
}
```

26. The above if statement says that if randomNumber1 is higher, add 1 to scorePlayer1 and then display the WIN for player 1, etc. If randomeNumber1 is not higher, it will add 1 to scorePlayer2 and display the WIN for player 2, etc. If scorePlayer2 was zero, it will become 1. If scorePlayer2 was 1, it will become 2.

27. Do the same thing for the corresponding *if* statement in game 2.

28. Run the program several times until the same player wins both games. Did it change the score to be 2? NO. Why not? We never adjusted the **displayWinner** method. The last statement of this method says to always show the score as "Score: 1". We want it to be possibly 0, 1, or 2. We want to use the tally which we just created and increased when they won. To do that, we will need another parameter in the displayWinner method. We will name it **transferredScore** and it is an **int**. Since this line will be too long, we will put the comma at end of line and put the third parameter on the next line. The displayWinner method should be changed to:

```
public void displayWinner(final TextModel winSign, final TextModel scoreSign,
        int transferredScore) {
```

29. Inside the displayWinner method, we need to adjust the displaying of the score to use our tally. We will concatenate the word "Score: " with the tally which will be transferred into transferredScore, so that are displayWinner method appears as follows:

```
public void displayWinner(TextModel winSign, TextModel scoreSign,
    int transferredScore) {
    /*do in order*/ {//display winner
        winSign.setOpacity(1.0, SetOpacity.duration(1.0));
        winSign.setOpacity(0.0, SetOpacity.duration(1.0));
        winSign.setOpacity(1.0, SetOpacity.duration(1.0));
        winSign.setOpacity(0.0, SetOpacity.duration(1.0));
        winSign.setOpacity(1.0, SetOpacity.duration(1.0));
        winSign.setOpacity(0.0, SetOpacity.duration(1.0));
        scoreSign.setValue("Score: " + transferredScore);
    }
}
```

30. You will notice that some of your lines in myFirstMethod have errors on them now. This is because we adjusted the displayWinner method to have 3 parameters but we didn't adjust the calls to that method inside of myFirstMethod. Adjust myFirstMethod as follows:

```java
    public void myFirstMethod() {//Card Game created by
//on date here
//This program will deal out cards, display winner, and then cards disappear
        int scorePlayer1 = 0;
        int scorePlayer2 = 0;
        int randomNumber1, randomNumber2;
        PlayingCard firstCard, secondCard;
        randomNumber1 = (int) (Math.random() * 10 + 1);
        randomNumber2 = (int) (Math.random() * 10 + 1);
        if (randomNumber1 == randomNumber2) {
            randomNumber1 = (int) (Math.random() *10 +1);
        }
        firstCard = determinePlayingCard (randomNumber1);
        secondCard = determinePlayingCard (randomNumber2);
        this.dealOutCards(firstCard, secondCard);
        if (randomNumber1 > randomNumber2) {
            scorePlayer1 ++;
            displayWinner(winPlayer1Sign, player1ScoreSign, scorePlayer1);
        } else {
            scorePlayer2 ++;
            displayWinner(winPlayer2Sign, player2ScoreSign, scorePlayer2);
        }
        this.disappearCards(firstCard, secondCard);
        randomNumber1 = (int) (Math.random() * 10 + 1);
        randomNumber2 = (int) (Math.random() * 10 + 1);
        if (randomNumber1 == randomNumber2) {
            randomNumber1 = (int) (Math.random() *10 +1);
        }
        firstCard = determinePlayingCard (randomNumber1);
        secondCard = determinePlayingCard (randomNumber2);
        this.dealOutCards(firstCard, secondCard);
        if (randomNumber1 > randomNumber2) {
            scorePlayer1 ++;
            displayWinner(winPlayer1Sign, player1ScoreSign, scorePlayer1);
        } else {
            scorePlayer2 ++;
            displayWinner(winPlayer2Sign, player2ScoreSign, scorePlayer2);
        }
        this.disappearCards(firstCard, secondCard);
    }
```

31. Run the program several times and see if it works when the same player wins both games. Did the score update to 2 when the player won twice? Are the cards randomizing? Is it deciding correctly which player wins? It should be working fine.

32. You can see the entire myFirstMethod above and the rest of the methods shown below.

```
public PlayingCard determinePlayingCard ( int num){
    switch (num) {
        case 1:  return playingCard1;
        case 2:  return playingCard2;
        case 3:  return playingCard3;
        case 4:  return playingCard4;
        case 5:  return playingCard5;
        case 6:  return playingCard6;
        case 7:  return playingCard7;
        case 8:  return playingCard8;
        case 9:  return playingCard9;
        case 10: return playingCard10;
        default: return playingCard1;
    }
}
```

```
public void dealOutCards(PlayingCard chosenPlayer1Card, PlayingCard chosenPlayer2Card) {
    /*do in order*/ {//deal out cards
        this.castleWall2.say("DEAL OUT THE CARDS PLEASE !", Say.duration(3.0));
        chosenPlayer1Card.moveTo(this.cone1);
        chosenPlayer2Card.moveTo(this.cone2);
    }
}
```

```
public void displayWinner(TextModel winSign, TextModel scoreSign,
    int transferredScore) {
    /*do in order*/ {//display winner
        winSign.setOpacity(1.0, SetOpacity.duration(1.0));
        winSign.setOpacity(0.0, SetOpacity.duration(1.0));
        winSign.setOpacity(1.0, SetOpacity.duration(1.0));
        winSign.setOpacity(0.0, SetOpacity.duration(1.0));
        winSign.setOpacity(1.0, SetOpacity.duration(1.0));
        winSign.setOpacity(0.0, SetOpacity.duration(1.0));
        scoreSign.setValue("Score: " + transferredScore);
    }
}
```

```
public void disappearCards(PlayingCard whichCard1, PlayingCard whichCard2) {
    /*do in order*/ {//cards disappear
        whichCard1.turn(TurnDirection.LEFT, 8.0);
        whichCard1.moveTo(this.coneOutside);
        whichCard2.turn(TurnDirection.LEFT, 8.0);
        whichCard2.moveTo(this.coneOutside);
        this.ground.delay(4.0);
    }
}
```

33. A good programming practice is to put in comments to describe methods and key points in the program. Please place comments in each of the methods stating what the methods do. Also, place comments on key statement lines that you feel need described further. This will document your program and help you to understand all of the methods, statements, and variables used in the program.

Summary

- The Java relational operators are: <   >   ==   <=   >=   !=
- The Java Boolean test or condition of an if statement should be in parenthesis and test to be either true or false.
- The Java *if* statement syntax

if (condition) {
    statements to do when conditional is true
} **else** {
    statements to do when conditional is false
}

- The else part of a Java *if* statement is optional but is required in this text.
- If multiple actions are to be taken on the true or false parts of a Java *if* statement, they must be enclosed in curly braces.
- In the Java switch statement, the test (a variable or expression that evaluates to a **byte, char, short, int, or Strings**) is compared with each of the case values in turn. If a match is found, the statement(s) after the test is executed until the computer reaches the end of switch statement or encounters a break statement. **If no match is found, the optional default statement is executed.**
- The most common Java logical operators are **&&** for AND and the || for OR.
- Use parentheses as much as possible to eliminate the confusion of the hierarchy of arithmetic, relational, and logic operators.

Review Questions

1. After these statements execute, what is y equal to?

    ```
    int x = 15;
    int y = 45;
    if ( ( x < 25 ) && (y > 35 ) )
        {    y=50;    }
    ```

    a. 15
    b. 40
    c. 50
    d. 45

2. After these statements execute, what is y equal to?

    ```
    int x = 15;
    int y = 45;
    if ( ( x < 25 )  &&   (y > 50 ) )
        {    y=50;    }
    ```

    a. 15
    b. 40
    c. 50
    d. 45

3. After these statements execute, what is y equal to?

    ```
    int x = 25;
    int y = 45;
    if ( ( x < 25 ) || (y > 35 ) )
        {    y=50;    }
    ```

    a. 15
    b. 40
    c. 50
    d. 45

4. If code is set to 3 prior to entering this switch statement, what would display on print line?

```
switch (code) {
  case 1:
     System.out.println("Full time");
     break;
  case 2:
     System.out.println("Part time");
     break;
  default:
     System.out.println("Unknown");
}
```

   a. Full time
   b. Part time
   c. Unknown

5. What would the following program display?

```
1: public class SwitchSample1
2: {
3:   public static void main (String args [ ] )
4:   {
5:     int month = 2;
6:     int noOfDays = 0;
7:     switch (month)
8:     {
9:     case 4:  case 6:  case 9:  case 11:
10:      noOfDays = 30;
11:       break;
12:     case 2:
13:      noOfDays = 28;
14:       break;
15:     default:
16:      noOfDays = 31;
17:     }
18:     System.out.println ("This is answer " + noOfDays);
19:   }// ends main
20: }// ends program
```

   a. This is answer 28
   b. This is answer 30
   c. This is answer 31
   d. Error

6. What would be displayed when these if statements are executed?

```
1: public class NestedIfs
2: {
3:   public static void main (String args [ ] )
4:   {  int x=7, y=8, z=18;
5:     if ( x >5 )
6:     {
7:       if (y > 5)
8:       {   System.out.println("message one");   }
9:       else
10:      {   System.out.println("message two");   }
11:    }
12:    else
13:      if (z >5 )
14:      {   System.out.println("message three"); }
15:      else
16:      {   System.out.println("message four");   }
17:
18:   } //ends main
19: } //ends program
```

    a. message one
    b. message two
    c. message three
    d. message four

7. What is in the variable called **number1** at the end of the main method?

```
1: public class IfsSample1
2: {
3:   public static void main (String args [ ] )
4:   {
5:     int number1 = 3;
6:     int number2 = 7;
7:     if (number1 <= number2 )
8:     {
9:       number1 = number1 - 2;
10:      number2 = number2 + 5;
11:      System.out.println("The number 1 is now " + number1);
12:      System.out.println("The number 2 is now " + number2);
13:    }
14:    else
15:    {
16:      number1 = number1 + 3;
17:      number2 = number2 - 1;
18:      System.out.println("The number 1 is now " + number1);
19:      System.out.println("The number 2 is now " + number2);
20:    }// ends if
21:   } //ends main
22: } //ends program
```

    a. 1
    b. 3
    c. 7
    d. 12

8. How can the following computer program be changed to fix the error?

```
import javax.swing.JOptionPane;

public class GuessingGame {
    public static void main (String [ ] args) {
        int computerNumber = (int) (Math.random()*100 +1);
        System.out.println("The correct guess would be " +
                computerNumber);
        String response = JOptionPane.showInputDialog (null,
                "Enter a guess between 1 and 100", "Guessing Game", 3);
        int userAnswer = Integer.parseInt(response);
        JOptionPane.showMessageDialog (null, "Your guess is " +
                determineGuess(userAnswer, computerNumber));

    }

    public static String determineGuess(int userAnswer, int computerNumber){
        if (userAnswer <=0 || userAnswer>=100) {
            return "invalid";
        }
        else if (userAnswer = computerNumber) {
            return "correct";
        }
        else {
            return "incorrect";
        }
    }
}
```

Solutions: 1)c   2)d   3)c   4)c   5)a   6)a   7)a   8) You need to use == to compare

Assignments

6-1 Determining the Season in Java: You should adjust the following code to output a "probable" season (winter, spring, summer, or fall) depending on a temperature inputted from the user. This program prompts the user for a temperature, parses that response to an integer, and displays a message box that reads "Based on the temperature of (whatever temperature they entered) it is most likely ". This program will not compile at this time since you do not have a *determineSeason* method yet. Your job is to create a new functional method called *determineSeason* that returns the season based on the temperature. You will need to use conditionals to make this program determine the probable season that matches what the user entered for their temperature.

```java
/* This is a simple Java program that guesses the season
 * depending on the temperature entered.*/

import javax.swing.*;

public class Seasons {

    public static void main(String[] args) {
        int inputTemp;
        String response = JOptionPane.showInputDialog(null,
                "Enter the temperature", "Probable season", 1);
        inputTemp = Integer.parseInt(response);
        String message = "Based on the temperature of "
                + inputTemp + " it is most likely "
                + determineSeason(inputTemp);
        JOptionPane.showMessageDialog(null, message);
    }
}
```

Criteria:
- **Invalid:** Temperature is greater than 130 or less than -20
- **Summer:** Temperature is greater than or equal to 90
- **Spring:** Temperature is greater than or equal to 70 and less than 90
- **Fall:** Temperature is greater than or equal to 50 and less than 70
- **Winter:** Temperature is less than 50

Chapter 7

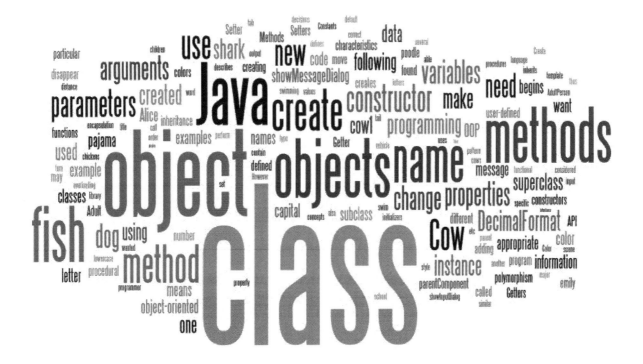

Classes and Objects

Objectives

- ☑ Explain encapsulation.
- ☑ Explain the purpose of inheritance.
- ☑ Explain the purpose of overriding and overloading.
- ☑ Create and explain the use of constructors.
- ☑ Use setter and getter methods.
- ☑ Create a basic UML diagram.
- ☑ Create a program that inherits properties from another program.

Object-Oriented Concepts

Object-oriented programming enables you to think of program elements as objects. To learn about object-oriented programming (OOP), you need to understand three main concepts that are the backbone of OOP. These concepts are encapsulation, inheritance, and polymorphism.

One major difference between structured programming and object-oriented programming is **encapsulation**. Encapsulation lets you create a class template for creating objects. It is the process of hiding the attributes of a class and making them accessible via the object's methods.

Inheritance enables you to create a class that is similar to a previously defined class, but one that still has some of its own properties. If you create a new class by inheritance, the new class inherits all the data and methods from the tested *superclass*. The newly created class is called the *subclass*. The designers of OOP languages picked the word "inheritance" very carefully. Think of how human children inherit many of their characteristics from their parents. But the children also have characteristics that are uniquely their own. In object-oriented programming you can think of a *superclass* as a parent and a *subclass* as a child. However, Java can only have single-inheritance (one parent).

The last major feature of object-oriented programming is **polymorphism**. By using polymorphism, you can create new objects that perform the same methods as the base object but which perform one or more of these functions in a different way. Reusing the same method name in the same class with different parameters is called **overloading**. In a subclass, using the same method name with the same parameters as the superclass means that the subclass method **overrides** the superclass method.

Inheritance Example:

Let's say that we have a superclass, also known as a parent class, named *Vehicle*. Examples of subclasses for this superclass, also known as child classes, would be: *Car*, *Truck*, and *Motorcycle*. The *Car*, *Truck*, and *Motorcyle* classes inherit (extend) from the *Vehicle* class which means that all attributes and methods of the *Vehicle* class will be passed on to the subclasses. All of the common attributes (example: number of seats, color, speed) and methods (example: vehicle movements: right, left, etc.) should be written for the superclass *Vehicle*. Attributes and methods that are specific to an individual class should be written in that particular class (example: the bed size attribute for the *Truck* class).

Overriding Example:

When a subclass has an attribute or a method that behaves differently than the attribute or method listed in the superclass class, then the subclass method can override the superclass. For example, if the *Vehicle* class had a method named lockDoors, but motocycles don't have doors, then the *Motorcycle* class would have a method named lockDoors that would override the *Vehicle* lockDoors method. This method wouldn't do anything since the motorcycle doesn't have doors to lock.

Overloading Example:

The showInputDialog and showMessageDialog methods from the JOptionPane class have various examples of overloading. The input and output dialogs that we have been using thus far have a parentComponent and a message parameter, but there are more options available than just these 2 parameters. The showMessageDialog and showInputDialog are overloaded which means that the same method has been written several times with different parameters. Java uses the name of the method and the paramters to find the correct method.

The Java API defines the syntax and semantics of the Java language and can be found at the following location: https://docs.oracle.com/javase/8/docs/api/

Java API for showMessageDialog with 2 parameters (parentComponent, message):

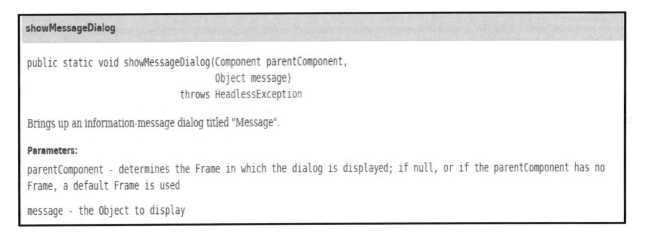

JOptionPane.*showMessageDialog*(null, "Your name is " + name);

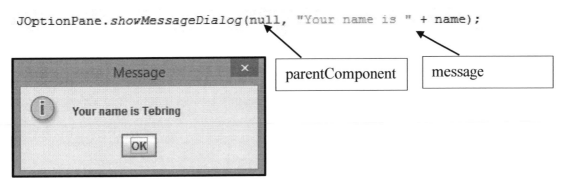

parentComponent   message

There is an option to change the title bar and icon for the input and output message boxes. You can do this by adding more arguments. The number and type of parameters for the method declaration has to match the number and type of arguments for the method call.

Java API for showMessageDialog with 4 parameters (parentComponent, message, title, messageType):

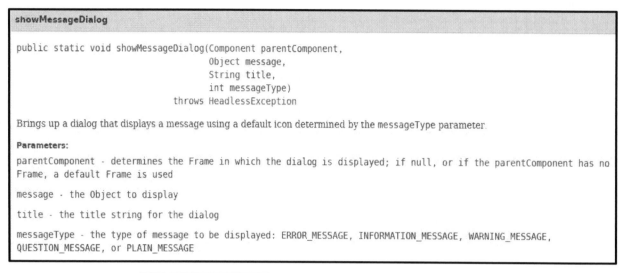

```
showMessageDialog

public static void showMessageDialog(Component parentComponent,
                                     Object message,
                                     String title,
                                     int messageType)
                    throws HeadlessException

Brings up a dialog that displays a message using a default icon determined by the messageType parameter.

Parameters:
parentComponent - determines the Frame in which the dialog is displayed; if null, or if the parentComponent has no
Frame, a default Frame is used

message - the Object to display

title - the title string for the dialog

messageType - the type of message to be displayed: ERROR_MESSAGE, INFORMATION_MESSAGE, WARNING_MESSAGE,
QUESTION_MESSAGE, or PLAIN_MESSAGE
```

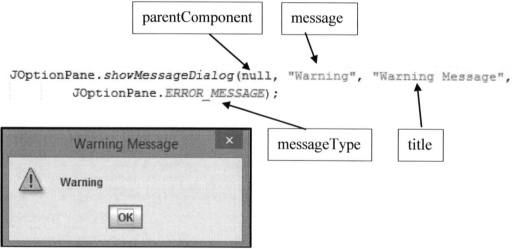

```
JOptionPane.showMessageDialog(null, "Warning", "Warning Message",
        JOptionPane.ERROR_MESSAGE);
```

```
JOptionPane.showMessageDialog(null, "Error", "Error Message",
        JOptionPane.ERROR_MESSAGE);
```

Java Classes

A *class* defines a particular kind of object. **The name of a class begins with a capital letter.** Each class is a blueprint that tells Java exactly how to create an object and what its properties and methods are.

When an object is created and displayed, we call this instantiating the class because an object is an instance of that class. Objects cow1 and cow2 are instances of the Cow class while emily is an instance of the Adult class. **Notice that the name of an object begins with a lowercase letter.** This naming style helps us to easily distinguish the name of a class which begins with a capital letter versus the name of an object which begins with a lowercase letter. All objects of the same class share some common properties and methods. All Adult objects have properties such as hair color, eye color, body style, etc.

Alice allows us to create and use objects such as cows and chickens that we have in our everyday lives and thus makes understanding classes and objects more understandable. By adding Alice classes to the library of classes (via plugins to NetBeans), we will be able to use cows, chickens and adults in Java. However, in Java, we don't ordinarily create cow and chicken objects but instead have DecimalFormat objects or Scanner objects.

Declaring an object in Java will contain the class name (always capitalized) such as Cow, Chicken, or DecimalFormat followed by the name given to that particular object by the programmer. An object is then created by using the word "new" and then a constructor that has the name of the class with optional parameters. Examples of declaring and creating objects are:

```
Cow  cow1  =  new Cow ( ........);
AdultPerson  emily =   new  AdultPerson( .....);
DecimalFormat pattern = new DecimalFormat("0.00");
```

In the above examples, Cow, Adult, and DecimalFormat are the names of classes that have been defined with methods and data. The names of cow1, emily, and pattern are names that a programmer created (according to the rules for variable names) to give a name to this particular object (instance of that class).

Constructors are methods that are used when an object is first being created. The purpose of a constructor is to set up any variables and other things that need to be established. When Java creates objects, it goes to the appropriate class and looks for the appropriate constructor with the correct number of parameters.

A constructor is a method with the same name as the class (including case sensitivity). A class can contain several constructors to provide a variety of means for initializing objects of that class. When an object of a class is created, initializers can be provided in parentheses to the right of the class name. These initializers are passed as arguments to the class's constructor. If no constructors are defined for a class, the compiler creates a default constructor that takes no arguments.

For example:
>   **Cow cow1 = new Cow ( );**

The above line declares and creates an object (at same time) called *cow1*. It will create this object using the class Cow and with the constructor with no arguments. The constructor for this would be:
>   **public Cow ( ) {}**

Setter and Getter Methods

Alice Setter and Getter Methods

Setters are procedural methods that are used to change properties of an object. Getters are functional methods that are used to get information about an object. Let's use the following Alice scene as an example:

In our scene, we have 2 pajama fish swimming and there is a shark lurking in the background. Let's imagine that we wanted the shark to eat one of the fish.

Getters
We may have the shark move towards the fish, but we wouldn't know the exact distance to the fish so we would use the following code segment: **shark.getDistanceTo(pajamaFish)**. If we wanted the shark to swim to the fish and turn his tail while swimming we would need to use the **shark.getTail()**. The getDistanceTo and the getTail are examples of functional methods and can be found under the functions tab for the appropriate object. Getters are functions that return information about an object. This information can be used in combination with a procedural method (make the shark move the distance to the pajama fish and make the shark's tail turn as he swims) or to make decisions.

Setters

We may want the pajama fish to disappear so that it appears as if the shark ate the fish. To make the fish disappear, we need to use the following code: **pajamaFish.setOpacity(0.0);** This would make the fish disappear. We could change the color of the fish by adding the following code: **pajamaFish.setPaint(Color.CYAN);** To change the color of an object, you need to use the Java Color class. There are predefined colors in the Color class and these colors are considered properties. The colors are in all capital letters because they are considered constants. Constants are represented in Java in all capital letters. Constants do not change values. We decide that we want to have a school of fish that swim together. To do this, we could set the vehicle property of the one pajama fish to another. When the head fish moves, then the school of fish would move with it by default. Setting the vehicle would look similar to the follow code: **pajamaFish.setVehicle(pajamaFish2);** We could also change the size of the fish by setting its width, height, or depth. The setOpacity, setPaint, and setVehicle are all examples of procedural methods and can be found under the procedures tab for the appropriate object. Setters are procedures that change the property of an object.

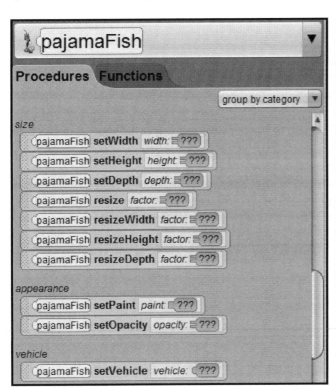 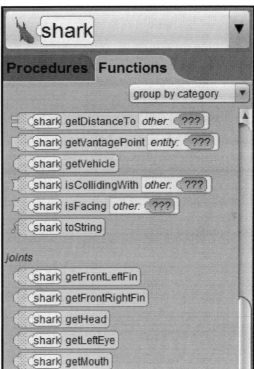

Java Setter and Getter Methods

If you want to represent objects, you can do so by defining a class template which combines class fields (attributes) with class methods. This class template can be used over and over again. Class fields, also known as instance variables, are used to store the information for each object. Remember that an instance is a representation of a class. It is often considered good programming practice to mark instance variables as private so that they cannot be accessed directly from another class. If you want to allow other classes to be able to modify and retrieve private instance variables you can do so by using a public **setter** and **getter** (sometimes referred to as mutator and accessor) method. One of the biggest benefits to this approach is to have the capability to add validation logic in a single place. For example if we were representing a person, we could have a setAge method that would ensure that the age instance variable would be set to 0 if an invocation attempts to set the age to a negative number.

You will need an application to test out your class template. This application is sometimes referred to as the client class. The class template does not have main method since it is only a template, but the client class (application) does have a main method. The code for instantiating an object is placed in the client class.

Visualizing Your Application with UML

Unified Modeling Language (UML) is sometimes used to graphically represent the fields and methods of a class. The following is an example of a very basic UML diagram.

UML Example:
Let's say that we wanted to set up a class template for a college student. We could create a CollegeStudent class. This class may include fields such as: name, gpa, and creditHours. Methods might include a getter and setter for each field and a constructor to set the fields when the object is first created. The diagram is split into 3 sections: top the section represents the class name, the middle section represents the class fields, and the bottom section represents the class methods. The fields and methods are denoted with a plus or minus sign in front of the name: the minus sign indicates that it is private and the plus sign indicates that it is public. Private methods and fields are only accessible from within the class that they were defined. Each method lists the method parameters inside parenthesis and the method return type after the colon.

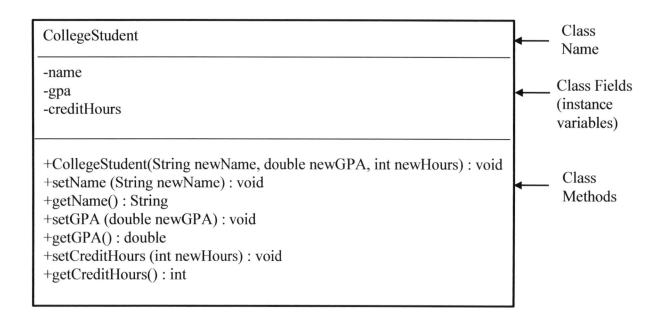

CollegeStudent ← Class Name

-name
-gpa
-creditHours ← Class Fields (instance variables)

+CollegeStudent(String newName, double newGPA, int newHours) : void
+setName (String newName) : void
+getName() : String
+setGPA (double newGPA) : void
+getGPA() : double
+setCreditHours (int newHours) : void
+getCreditHours() : int ← Class Methods

The following code describes the attributes and methods for the CollegeStudent class template.

```java
public class CollegeStudent {
    //define instance variables
    private String name;
    private double gpa;
    private int creditHours;

    //constructor to set instance variables when object is created
    public CollegeStudent(String newName, double newGPA, int newHours) {
        setName(newName);
        setGPA(newGPA);
        setCreditHours(newHours);
    }

    //setter for the name
    public void setName(String newName){
        name = newName;
    }

    //getter to retrieve the name
    public String getName(){
        return name;
    }

    //setter for the GPA
    public void setGPA(double newGPA){
        gpa = newGPA;
    }

    //getter to retrieve the gpa
    public double getGPA(){
        return gpa;
    }

    //setter for the number of credit hours
    public void setCreditHours(int newHours){
        creditHours = newHours;
    }

    //getter to retrieve the number of credit hours
    public int getCreditHours(){
        return creditHours;
    }

}
```

You will need a client class (application) to test out your class template. The following client will create a student object named student1 and will set the name to Bill, the GPA to 3.7, and the number of credit hours to 55 when the student is created. This is handled through the constructor in the CollegeStudent class. The constructor in the CollegeStudent class, then calls the setter for each attribute. Each of the getter methods are used on student1 to retrieve the information about this student.

```java
public class CollegeStudentCreator {
    public static void main(String[] args) {
        CollegeStudent student1 = new CollegeStudent("Bill",3.7,55);
        System.out.println("Name: " + student1.getName() +
                "\nGPA: " + student1.getGPA() +
                "\nCredit Hours: " + student1.getCreditHours());
    }
}
```

The following output is a result running the CollegeStudentCreator application with the CollegeStudent template class.

```
Name: Bill
GPA: 3.7
Credit Hours: 55
```

Hands-on Exercises

Exercise 1 - Using Setters and Getters

The following program is a user-defined Dog class that uses setter methods to set the name and weight instance variables, getter methods to get the name and weight instance variables, and a method to compare the weight of 2 animals.

1. Get into NetBeans and start a new Java **application** program. The name of the project should be **DogCreator**. Take a look at the main class and notice that NetBeans automatically names it **dogcreator.DogCreator**. The name before the period is the package name which in this case is dogcreator and the name after the period is the main class name (filename) which in this case is DogCreator. Leave the generated main class name and click Finish.

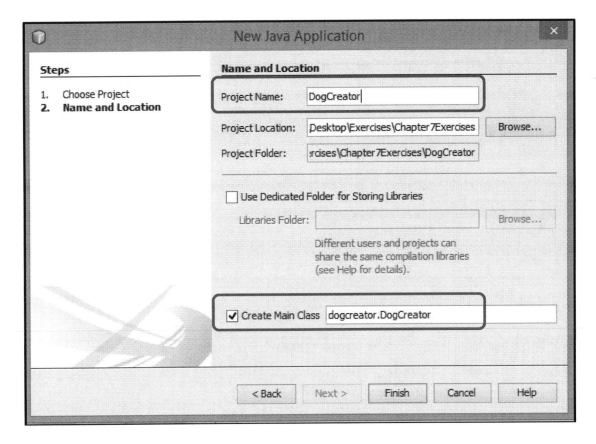

2. There is a new line of code that is added on line 6. This line of code tells Java that the DogCreator file belongs to the dogcreator package (folder). Up until this point, we have been erasing the package statement by deleting the name before the period for our main class when we create our projects. When we erase the package name, NetBeans places our files into a default package. This made the code less confusing because default packages do not have the package line of code. If the files are placed into a named package, then you will need to have the package statement at the top of your code. We cannot erase this package line or the code will not compile. Go ahead and erase the comments throughout, add your own comments, but be careful not to erase the package statement. It is up to you from this point on if you want to create package names for your projects.

```
DogCreator.java ×
Source  History

1   /*
2    * To change this license header, choose License Headers in Project Properties.
3    * To change this template file, choose Tools | Templates
4    * and open the template in the editor.
5    */
6   package dogcreator;
7
8   /**
9    *
10   * @author Tebring
11   */
12  public class DogCreator {
13
14      /**
15       * @param args the command line arguments
16       */
17      public static void main(String[] args) {
18          // TODO code application logic here
19      }
20
21  }
```

```
DogCreator.java ×
Source  History

1   /*
2    * Name and date
3    * JDK version
4    * Practice with Setters and Getters
5    */
6   package dogcreator;
7
8   public class DogCreator {
9       public static void main(String[] args) {
10
11      }
12  }
```

3. Click on **New File...** from the **File** drop down menu in NetBeans. Click **Next**.

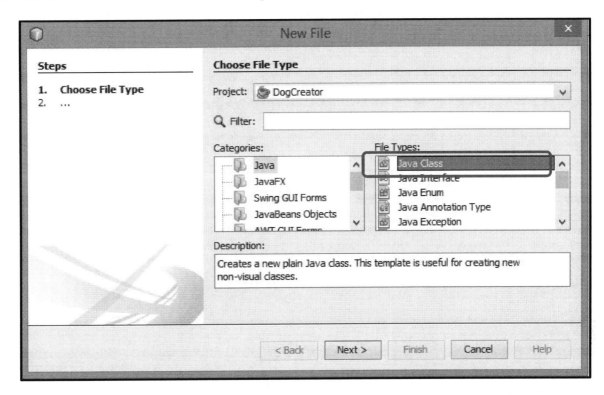

4. Name the class **Dog** and click **Finish**.

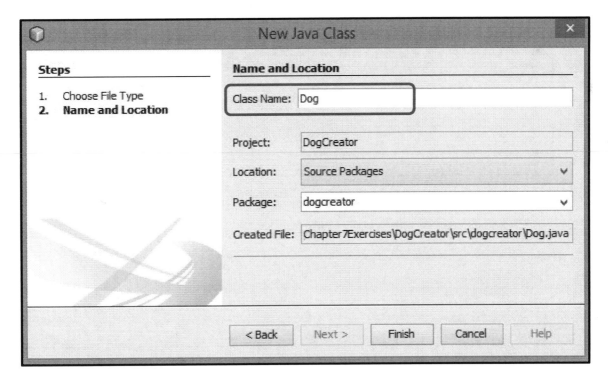

5. You should notice that this Dog class file has the dogcreator package statement same as the DogCreator class file. This statement tells Java that the Dog class belongs to the dogcreator package (folder). You must leave the line of code in the file.

```
1  /*
2   * To change this license header, choose License Headers in Project Properties.
3   * To change this template file, choose Tools | Templates
4   * and open the template in the editor.
5   */
6  package dogcreator;
7
8  /**
9   *
10   * @author Tebring
11   */
12  public class Dog {
13
14  }
```

6. Please adjust the comments to be your own.

```
1  /*
2   * Name and date
3   * JDK version
4   * Practice with Setters and Getters
5   */
6  package dogcreator;
7
8  public class Dog {
9
10  }
```

7. In the **Dog** class file, we are going to add instance variables (properties) for the dog (object). Remember that instance is just another word for object. For this example, we will use **name** and **weight** as our properties. There are many more properties for the dog such as birthdate, type, etc., but we will stick with just 2 to make the program easier to understand. Since we do not have a name and weight before we create the dog object, we will initialize (set) the name to null and the weight to 0. Make these instance variables private. Making a variable private, means that it cannot be accessed directly from another class. This will force the use of setters and getters to access the variables.

```
/*
 * Name and date
 * JDK version
 * Practice with Setters and Getters
 */
package dogcreator;

public class Dog {
    //define instance variables
    private String name = null;
    private double weight = 0;

}
```

8. Next, we are going to create a setter for the name of the dog called **setName**. Make sure that you are in the Dog class. This method is going to be *public* so that the DogCreator class can access this method. We do not add the word *static* to our method since this method is going to be used on an object. We are going to make this method *void* because it is not going to return any data. The method should have a parameter to take in the name; we will name this variable **newName** and it will be a string since the name will be text. The purpose of this method is to set the name of the dog (this.name) to the name that is passed into the method (newName). The word **this** refers to the current object that the method was called on and is optional. Type in the following code for the setName method.

```
/*
 * Name and date
 * JDK version
 * Practice with Setters and Getters
 */
package dogcreator;

public class Dog {
    //define instance variables
    private String name = null;
    private double weight = 0;

    //Setter method to set the animal name
    public void setName(String newName) {
        this.name = newName;
    }
}
```

9. Now we are going to create a setter for the weight of the dog called **setWeight**. You should be in the Dog class. This method is going to be *public* so that the DogCreator class can access this method. We do not add the word *static* to our method since this method is going to be used on an object. We are going to make this method *void* because it is not going to return any data. The method should have a parameter to take in the weight; we will name this variable **newWeight** and it will be a double since the weight can be a decimal amount. The purpose of this method is to set the weight of the dog (this.weight) to the weight that is passed into the method (newWeight), but only if the weight that is passed in is greater than 0. The word **this** refers to the current object that the method was called on and is optional. Type in the following code for the setName method:

```java
/*
 * Name and date
 * JDK version
 * Practice with Setters and Getters
 */
package dogcreator;

public class Dog {
    //define instance variables
    private String name = null;
    private double weight = 0;

    //Setter method to set the animal name
    public void setName(String newName) {
        this.name = newName;
    }

    //Setter method to check validity of data and set dog weight
    public void setWeight(double newWeight) {
        if (newWeight > 0) {
            this.weight = newWeight;
        } else {
            System.out.println("Weight cannot be negative or zero.");
        }
    }
}
```

10. Let's add a dog constructor to the Dog class. Constructors are methods that have the same name and capitalization as the class. When an instance (object) of a class is created, the constructor is automatically called. The name of this constructor should be **Dog** and it should have 2 parameters to take in the name and weight (newName and newWeight) when the object is created. This constructor will call the setName and setWeight methods to set the name and weight of the dog object. Add the following constructor to the program.

```java
/*
 * Name and date
 * JDK version
 * Practice with Setters and Getters
 */
package dogcreator;

public class Dog {
    //define instance variables
    private String name = null;
    private double weight = 0;

    //Dog Constructor
    public Dog(String newName, double newWeight) {
        setName(newName);
        setWeight(newWeight);
    }

    //Setter method to set the animal name
    public void setName(String newName) {
        this.name = newName;
    }

    //Setter method to check validity of data and set dog weight
    public void setWeight(double newWeight) {
        if (newWeight > 0) {
            this.weight = newWeight;
        } else {
            System.out.println("Weight cannot be negative or zero.");
        }
    }
}
```

Note: you will notice that there are warnings (yellow light bulb) on the setName and setWeight method calls (line 15 and 16). We will fix this in the next step.

11. You may notice warnings on the setName and setWeight method calls in the constructor. The warning may be worded as follows: *Overridable method call in constructor*. These are just warnings, not errors and so you can ignore them, but we will fix the code so that the setters are not overridable. If you had a class that extended the Dog class (known as a subclass), it could have a setName and setWeight method. Subclass methods override the superclass (Dog) and this could create an issue for our constructor in the Dog class which uses these methods to set the instance variables. Right now, we do not have a subclass that is going to have setName and setWeight methods and so it will not make a difference with our functionality. It is not imperative that we heed to these warnings, but let's change it so that you know how. Since it is not good practice to use methods in a constructor that can be overridden, let's change our setter methods (setName and setWeight) to be **final** as shown below. Setting a method to final tells Java that it cannot be overridden by a subclass.

```java
/*
 * Name and date
 * JDK version
 * Practice with Setters and Getters
 */
package dogcreator;

public class Dog {
    //define instance variables
    private String name = null;
    private double weight = 0;

    //Dog Constructor
    public Dog(String newName, double newWeight) {
        setName(newName);
        setWeight(newWeight);
    }

    //Setter method to set the animal name
    public final void setName(String newName) {
        this.name = newName;
    }

    //Setter method to check validity of data and set dog weight
    public final void setWeight(double newWeight) {
        if (newWeight > 0) {
            this.weight = newWeight;
        } else {
            System.out.println("Weight cannot be negative or zero.");
        }
    }
}
```

12. Now that we have the basic code for creating a dog object object with a name and weight, let's go ahead and create some dogs. We are going to create 3 dogs: Texie, Juicy, and Penny. Each of these dogs will have a different starting weight. The name and weight of the dog will get passed in as arguments to the Dog constructor in the Dog class. Click on the DogCreator file and add the following code.

```java
/*
 * Name and date
 * JDK version
 * Practice with Setters and Getters
 */
package dogcreator;

public class DogCreator {
    public static void main(String[] args) {
        //Create dog objects
        Dog dog1 = new Dog("Texie", 25);
        Dog dog2 = new Dog("Juicy", 15);
        Dog dog3 = new Dog("Penny", 28);
    }
}
```

13. If you run this program, you will notice that nothing happens. It creates the 3 dogs, but you won't see this happening. If you want to find out the dog's name and weight, you would need to access the name and weight variables. If the name and weight variables weren't private, then you could access them directly (example: dog1.name or dog1.weight). Because our instance variables are private (defined in the Dog class), we will need to access them through getters. To create or getters, let's go back to the Dog class. Our getters are going to be *public* so that we can access them from the DogCreator file, they will not have the word *static* since they will be used on a dog object. The getName method will return the name of the dog (this.name) which is a string and the getWeight method will return the weight of the dog (this.weight) which is a double. The word **this** refers to the current object that the method was called on and is optional. Add the following getters under the setters in the Dog class.

```java
//Getter method to get the animal name
public String getName() {
    return this.name;
}

//Getter method to get dog weight
public double getWeight() {
    return this.weight;
}
```

Note: you could make these methods final if you didn't want them to be overridden by a subclass.

14. Now that we have the getters in place for the Dog class, let's test them out by going to the DogCreator class and adding the following code:

```java
/*
 * Name and date
 * JDK version
 * Practice with Setters and Getters
 */
package dogcreator;

public class DogCreator {
    public static void main(String[] args) {
        //Create dog objects
        Dog dog1 = new Dog("Texie", 25);
        Dog dog2 = new Dog("Juicy", 15);
        Dog dog3 = new Dog("Penny", 28);

        //Print out dog name and weight
        System.out.println("Name: " + dog1.getName());
        System.out.println("Weight: " + dog1.getWeight()+"lbs.");
        System.out.println("Name: " + dog2.getName());
        System.out.println("Weight: " + dog2.getWeight()+"lbs.");
        System.out.println("Name: " + dog3.getName());
        System.out.println("Weight: " + dog3.getWeight()+"lbs.");
        System.out.print("\n");
    }
}
```

15. Run the program. You should get the following output:

```
Name: Texie
Weight: 25.0lbs.
Name: Juicy
Weight: 15.0lbs.
Name: Penny
Weight: 28.0lbs.
```

16. Let's make it more interesting by comparing the dog weights. In the Dog class, we will add a **compare** method. This method will be *public* so that it can be accessed by the DogCreator file, it will return a string stating which dog weighs more, and it will take in another dog object as a parameter to do the comparison. We will create a variable named **message** and initialize it to *null*. This variable will be used to hold the message that we want to return. We will need to use conditionals to do the comparison to determine which dog is heavier between 2 dogs. When the method is called from the DogCreator method it will be called on a dog object (dog object will be referred to as *this*) and it will pass in another dog object to compare it to (dog object will be referred to as *dogCompare*).

```java
//method to compare weight of 2 dogs
public String compare(Dog dogCompare) {
    String message = null;
    if(dogCompare.weight > this.weight) {
        message = dogCompare.name + " weighs more than " + this.name;
    } else if(dogCompare.weight < this.weight){
        message = this.name + " weighs more than " + dogCompare.name;
    } else {
        message = this.name + " weighs equal to " + dogCompare.name;
    }
    return message;
}
```

17. The finished Dog class should looks as follows:

```java
/*
 * Name and date
 * JDK version
 * Practice with Setters and Getters
 */
package dogcreator;

public class Dog {
    //define instance variables
    private String name = null;
    private double weight = 0;

    //Dog Constructor
    public Dog(String newName, double newWeight) {
        setName(newName);
        setWeight(newWeight);
    }

    //Setter method to set the animal name
    public final void setName(String newName) {
        this.name = newName;
    }

    //Setter method to check validity of data and set dog weight
    public final void setWeight(double newWeight) {
        if (newWeight > 0) {
            this.weight = newWeight;
        } else {
            System.out.println("Weight cannot be negative or zero.");
        }
    }

    //Getter method to get the animal name
    public String getName() {
        return this.name;
    }

    //Getter method to get dog weight
    public double getWeight() {
        return this.weight;
    }

    //method to compare weight of 2 dogs
    public String compare(Dog dogCompare) {
        String message = null;
        if(dogCompare.weight > this.weight) {
            message = dogCompare.name + " weighs more than " + this.name;
        } else if(dogCompare.weight < this.weight){
            message = this.name + " weighs more than " + dogCompare.name;
        } else {
            message = this.name + " weighs equal to " + dogCompare.name;
        }
        return message;
    }
}
```

18. Let's test the compare method that we just created by going back to the DogCreator class and calling the compare method using our 3 dogs as shown below:

```java
public static void main(String[] args) {
    //Create dog objects
    Dog dog1 = new Dog("Texie", 25);
    Dog dog2 = new Dog("Juicy", 15);
    Dog dog3 = new Dog("Penny", 28);

    //Print out dog name and weight
    System.out.println("Name: " + dog1.getName());
    System.out.println("Weight: " + dog1.getWeight()+"lbs.");
    System.out.println("Name: " + dog2.getName());
    System.out.println("Weight: " + dog2.getWeight()+"lbs.");
    System.out.println("Name: " + dog3.getName());
    System.out.println("Weight: " + dog3.getWeight()+"lbs.");
    System.out.print("\n");

    //Comparisons
    System.out.println(dog1.compare(dog2));
    System.out.println(dog1.compare(dog3));
    System.out.println(dog2.compare(dog3));
    System.out.print("\n");
}
```

19. You should now have the following output:

```
Name: Texie
Weight: 25.0lbs.
Name: Juicy
Weight: 15.0lbs.
Name: Penny
Weight: 28.0lbs.

Texie weighs more than Juicy
Penny weighs more than Texie
Penny weighs more than Juicy
```

20. Now let's say that Texie gains weight. We can adjust her weight using the setWeight method and then we can do the comparisons again using the compare method to see if anything has changed. Add the following code to the DogCreator class:

```java
public static void main(String[] args) {
    //Create dog objects
    Dog dog1 = new Dog("Texie", 25);
    Dog dog2 = new Dog("Juicy", 15);
    Dog dog3 = new Dog("Penny", 28);

    //Print out dog name and weight
    System.out.println("Name: " + dog1.getName());
    System.out.println("Weight: " + dog1.getWeight()+"lbs.");
    System.out.println("Name: " + dog2.getName());
    System.out.println("Weight: " + dog2.getWeight()+"lbs.");
    System.out.println("Name: " + dog3.getName());
    System.out.println("Weight: " + dog3.getWeight()+"lbs.");
    System.out.print("\n");

    //Comparisons
    System.out.println(dog1.compare(dog2));
    System.out.println(dog1.compare(dog3));
    System.out.println(dog2.compare(dog3));
    System.out.print("\n");

    //dog1 gains weight
    dog1.setWeight(28);
    System.out.println("Name: " + dog1.getName());
    System.out.println("Weight: " + dog1.getWeight()+"lbs.");
    System.out.println(dog1.compare(dog3));
}
```

21. Run the program again to see that Texie gained weight and now her weight is equal to Penny's weight.

```
Name: Texie
Weight: 25.0lbs.
Name: Juicy
Weight: 15.0lbs.
Name: Penny
Weight: 28.0lbs.

Texie weighs more than Juicy
Penny weighs more than Texie
Penny weighs more than Juicy

Name: Texie
Weight: 28.0lbs.
Texie weighs equal to Penny
```

Exercise 2: Adjusting Hokey Pokey for all Bipeds (ongoing Exercise)

1. In Chapter 4, you created a HokeyPokey program which had 2 tortoises, an alien, and a baby yeti. The tortoises were programmed via methods to do the hokeypokey dance. Get into NetBeans and start a new project created from this existing Alice project from the HokeyPokey Alice file. Name this new NetBeans project HokeyPokeyInheritance and save it in the Chapter7Exercises folder.

2. Run the program to make sure that the tortoises still dance.

3. Look at the **Tortoise.java** file. The hokeyPokey, hokeyPokeyVerse, shake, and turnAround methods are in this file. These methods were defined specifically for the tortoise so currently the alien and babyYeti can't do that dance. At the top of the Tortoise.java file you will see that the Tortoise class extends the Biped which means that it is subclass of Biped class.

```
import ...

public class Tortoise extends Biped {

    public Tortoise() {
        super(TortoiseResource.DEFAULT);
    }

    public void hokeyPokeyVerse(final SJoint bodyPart) {
        bodyPart.turn(TurnDirection.BACKWARD, 0.25);
        bodyPart.turn(TurnDirection.FORWARD, 0.25);
        this.shake(bodyPart);
        this.turnAround();
        this.delay(2.0);
    }
}
```

4. The alien and baby yeti are unable to do the Hokey Pokey because the Hokey Pokey methods are in the Tortoise class and the alien and baby yeti are not tortoises. Sometimes we want methods to belong to a specific class (for example: we may create a moo method for a Cow class), but other times we want all classes of a certain category (upper level class) to have access to our methods. If we want the alien and the baby yeti to be able to do the Hokey Pokey, then we need to move all of our Hokey Pokey methods to the super class (Biped).

5. If we put all the Hokey Pokey methods in the **Biped** class, then all Bipeds should be able to do the Hokey Pokey. Let's try it. Cut/paste all 4 methods so that your Biped class looks as follows:

```java
public class Biped extends SBiped {
    public Biped(final BipedResource resource) {
        super(resource);
    }
    public void hokeyPokeyVerse(final SJoint bodyPart) {
        bodyPart.turn(TurnDirection.BACKWARD, 0.25);
        bodyPart.turn(TurnDirection.FORWARD, 0.25);
        this.shake(bodyPart);
        this.turnAround();
        this.delay(2.0);
    }
    public void shake(final SJoint bodyPart) {
        bodyPart.turn(TurnDirection.BACKWARD, 0.25);
        bodyPart.turn(TurnDirection.RIGHT, 0.125);
        bodyPart.turn(TurnDirection.LEFT, 0.25);
        bodyPart.turn(TurnDirection.RIGHT, 0.25);
        bodyPart.turn(TurnDirection.LEFT, 0.125);
        bodyPart.turn(TurnDirection.FORWARD, 0.25);
    }
    public void turnAround() {
        this.getRightShoulder().turn(TurnDirection.BACKWARD, 0.25);
        this.getLeftShoulder().turn(TurnDirection.BACKWARD, 0.25);
        this.turn(TurnDirection.LEFT, 1.0);
        this.getLeftShoulder().turn(TurnDirection.FORWARD, 0.25);
        this.getRightShoulder().turn(TurnDirection.FORWARD, 0.25);
    }
    public void hokeyPokey() {
        this.hokeyPokeyVerse(this.getRightHip());
        this.hokeyPokeyVerse(this.getLeftHip());
        this.hokeyPokeyVerse(this.getRightShoulder());
        this.hokeyPokeyVerse(this.getLeftShoulder());
    }
}
```

Note: Be sure that all of the Hokey Pokey methods were removed from the Tortoise class.

6. Run the program and see what happens. You still have the tortoises dancing. We need to adjust the **Scene.java** file's **myFirstMethod** so that it has the babyYeti and alien dancing also. You can copy/paste to get all the punctuation right. Be careful. Use Source from the menu, then Format to indent your code correctly.

Note: If you are using a JDK prior to 1.8, your doTogether statements will look different.

```
public void myFirstMethod() {
    this.delay(2.0);
    doTogether(() -> {
        this.playAudio(new AudioSourc
        this.playAudio(new AudioSourc
    }, () -> {
        this.tortoise.hokeyPokey();
    }, () -> {
        this.tortoise2.hokeyPokey();
    }, () -> {
        this.babyYeti.hokeyPokey();
    }, () -> {
        this.alien.hokeyPokey();
    });
}
```

7. Run your animation. Now, all of them are dancing. However, the babyYeti has a tough time getting his arms up and turning so he likes to just spin around a 3 times. We will override the Biped's turnAround method by putting a specific turnAround method in the BabyYeti class.

8. Go to the BabyYeti class and declare a turnAround method with 5 spins around:

```
public class BabyYeti extends Biped {

    public BabyYeti(final BabyYetiResource resource) {
        super(resource);
    }

    public void setBabyYetiResource(final BabyYetiResource babyYetiResource) {
        this.setJointedModelResource(babyYetiResource);
    }

    public void turnAround() {
        this.turn(TurnDirection.LEFT,1.0);
        this.turn(TurnDirection.LEFT,1.0);
        this.turn(TurnDirection.LEFT,1.0);
        this.turn(TurnDirection.LEFT,1.0);
        this.turn(TurnDirection.LEFT,1.0);
    }
}
```

9. In the future, you will be learning how to do loops so that you won't have to type or copy the turn statement 5 times. Run your program and see if all of them now dance due to placing the methods in the Biped superclass and babyYeti does everything the same as the rest except his turnAround is just him spinning 5 times because his turnAround method overrode the superclass method. You can add or delete turns if the timing is off.

10. You should notice a yellow light bulb next to the turnAround declaration. If you click on the light bulb, you will notice that NetBeans prompts you to add the override annotation.

```
          public void turnAround() {
19        Add @Override Annotation    ▶   tion.LEFT,1.0);
20                          this.turn(TurnDirection.LEFT,1.0);
```

11. This annotation is not necessary, but let's go ahead and add it. This not only shows others looking at your code that this turnAround method overrides a method in a super class, but it shows that you did it on purpose.

```
          @Override
19        public void turnAround() {
20            this.turn(TurnDirection.LEFT,1.0);
21            this.turn(TurnDirection.LEFT,1.0);
22            this.turn(TurnDirection.LEFT,1.0);
23            this.turn(TurnDirection.LEFT,1.0);
24            this.turn(TurnDirection.LEFT,1.0);
25        }
```

12. Try to change the name of the method to **turnsAround**. The annotation prevents you from changing the name of this method since the goal was to override a higher level class.

```
          @Override
19        public void turnsAround() {
20            this.turn(TurnDirection.LEFT,1.0);
21            this.turn(TurnDirection.LEFT,1.0);
22            this.turn(TurnDirection.LEFT,1.0);
23            this.turn(TurnDirection.LEFT,1.0);
24            this.turn(TurnDirection.LEFT,1.0);
25        }
```

13. Inheritance is a powerful concept. It allows you to set up a template of "common methods" in a superclass and then use the subclass to show the specific differences. In this case, by putting the Hokey Pokey methods in the superclass of Biped, we now have shown all bipeds how to dance and now anyone of them could do this dance. However, we also have the ability to make baby yeti's turnAround different. We could make the alien's shake a little different, etc.

Exercise 3: Practicing with Object Oriented Concepts

This exercise will present many OOPs concepts.

- We are going to describe a superclass called **Quadruped**. In this superclass, we will assume that all quadrupeds rollover and snore when sleeping. We will also assume that all quadrupeds eat the same by moving their mouth left and right. Since all quadrupeds speak differently, we will **not** describe the speak method in the superclass.
- We will then describe three subclasses – Cow, ScottyDog, and AbyssianCat. Each of these subclasses will have its own speak method. The first subclass of Quadruped is ScottyDog. The speak method for dog will be Arf! Arf! The second subclass of Quadruped is Cow. The speak method for cow will be "Moooooo". The third subclass of the Quadruped is AbyssianCat. The speak method for the cat will be "Meow".
- We will then have a main part program that creates objects and use the methods.

Let's begin the exercise.

1. We will begin by setting up a scene of Quadrupeds in Alice 3. We want to place a ScottyDog named dog, AbyssinianCat named cat, and Cow named cow onto a scene as follows: (Leave lots of empty space in middle of scene.)

2. Next, we will set up some statements for the cow to do so we can adjust these statements later in Java. First, have the cow say "ZZZZzzzzZZZZ", then have the cow's mouth turn left 0.25, then have the cow's mouth turn right 0.25 and finally have the cow roll right 0.25. The statements should look as follows:

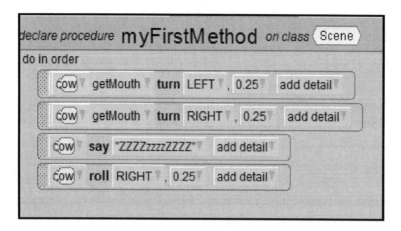

3. Save the program in the appropriate chapter folder and call it **Inheritance**.

4. Get into NetBeans and start a New Project from existing Alice project and use the Inheritance.a3p file. If you look at the Scene.java file, you will see that the myFirstMethod looks as follows:

```
public void myFirstMethod() {
    this.cow.getMouth().turn(TurnDirection.LEFT, 0.25);
    this.cow.getMouth().turn(TurnDirection.RIGHT, 0.25);
    this.cow.say("ZZZZzzzzZZZZ");
    this.cow.roll(RollDirection.RIGHT, 0.25);
}
```

5. If you RUN the program as is, you will see the cow's mouth turn left and right, the cow say ZZZZzzzzZZZZ and the roll left.

6. We believe that all quadrupeds will roll over to sleep and snore by saying *ZZZZzzzzZZZZ*. Therefore, we will put a method into the Quadruped file called sleep and cut/paste the say and roll statements into it from the myFirstMethod. The Quadruped file should look as follows:

```
imports

class Quadruped extends SQuadruped {

    public Quadruped(QuadrupedResource resource) {
        super(resource);
    }

    public void sleep() {
        this.roll(RollDirection.RIGHT, 0.25);
        this.say("ZZZZzzzzZZZZ");
    }
}
```

The sleep method is placed in the Quadruped so that all 4-legged animals can sleep in this way. There are no parameters to the method and it is made public so we can access it from other classes. Notice, you must remove that the object is the cow because this will work for any and all quadrupeds.

7. We want another method for eating that will be the same for all Quadrupeds. They all turn their mouth to left and right to chew food. We will cut/paste the statements from the myFirstMethod into a new method called eat (no parameters and public) as follows:

```
imports

class Quadruped extends SQuadruped {

    public Quadruped(QuadrupedResource resource) {
        super(resource);
    }

    public void sleep() {
        this.roll(RollDirection.RIGHT, 0.25);
        this.say("ZZZZzzzzZZZZ");
    }

    public void eat() {
        this.getMouth().turn(TurnDirection.LEFT, 0.25);
        this.getMouth().turn(TurnDirection.RIGHT, 0.25);
    }
}
```

8. Now, in the ScottyDog class, we want the dog to speak by saying ARF! ARF! Change the ScottyDog class to look as follows:

```
imports

class ScottyDog extends Quadruped {

    public ScottyDog() {
        super(ScottyDogResource.DEFAULT);
    }

    public void speak() {
        this.say("ARF! ARF!");
    }
}
```

9. Now, create a speak method in the Cow class which say "MoooOOOO" and a speak method in the AbyssinianCat class which says "MEOW". Each of these classes will have its own speak method since all quadrupeds speak differently.

10. In the Scene.java file, you will see the declaration and creation of the objects for this program as:

```
private final SGround ground = new SGround();
private final SCamera camera = new SCamera();
private final Cow cow = new Cow();
private final AbyssinianCat cat = new AbyssinianCat();
private final ScottyDog dog = new ScottyDog();
```

11. In the Scene.java file, find the empty myFirstMethod. In the body of this method write the code to have the objects actually speak, sleep and eat:

```
public void myFirstMethod() {
    cow.eat();
    cow.speak();
    cow.sleep();
    dog.eat();
    dog.speak();
    dog.sleep();
    cat.eat();
    cat.speak();
    cat.sleep();
}
```

12. Run the program and each of the objects (cow, dog, and cat) should eat, speak, and then sleep. What is the program doing so far? The first statement in myFirstMethod, says to execute the eat method for the cow object. The program goes to the Cow class and looks for the eat method. Because the Cow class is a subclass of the Quadruped, it will then move up the chain to the superclass Quadruped class and look for the eat method and it finds it there. The next statement has the cow speak. The program goes to the Cow class for the speak method and finds it there so it doesn't move up to the superclass at all. For the sleep method, it again doesn't find it in the Cow class so it finds it in the superclass of Quadruped. By placing the eat and sleep methods in the superclass Quadruped you don't have to tell every animal how to eat and sleep. You only need to describe what is unique to each animal in its specific class.

13. Now, let's take a quick glance at access modifiers. The two most common modifiers are private and public. In the Quadruped class, we have a sleep method with a public modifier. Change the modifier to be private as follows:

```
private void sleep() {
    this.roll(RollDirection.RIGHT, 0.25);
    this.say("ZZZZzzzzZZZZ");
}
```

14. What do you think this will do? Run the program and see what it does. You should get error messages. Why? The program looks for a sleep method in the Cow class but doesn't find it. It then goes up the inheritance to the Quadruped class (since Cow extends Quadruped) and finds a sleep method but that method is private to Quadruped so it can't use it. Thus, you get a compilation error. Change the "private" back to "public" so it will work again and run the program to make sure that everything is working fine.

15. Now, let's assume that cows are one of the few animals that don't lay down to sleep. We want the sleep method for most quadrupeds to remain as the turn right (to fallover) and then say ZZZZzzzzZZZZ. However, specifically for the cow, we want the cow to remain standing. We will write a sleep method in the Cow class that will override the sleep method in the Quadruped class. The Cow class will be changed to:

```
class Cow extends Quadruped {

    public Cow() {
        super(CowResource.DEFAULT);
    }

    public void speak() {
        this.say("MoooOOOO");
    }

    @Override
    public void sleep(){
        this.say("ZZZZzzzzZZZZ");
    }
}
```

16. Run the program and see if the cow stays standing up while sleeping.

17. Now, look at the ScottyDog file. The current constructor has no parameters. We want to add a String in the class which will represent the gender of the ScottyDog. Make a second constructor which has a parameter of gender. The ScottyDog will refer to its gender when speaking:

```java
imports

class ScottyDog extends Quadruped {

    String gender;

    public ScottyDog() {
        super(ScottyDogResource.DEFAULT);
        gender = "unknown";
    }

    public ScottyDog(String x) {
        super(ScottyDogResource.DEFAULT);
        gender = x;
    }

    public void speak() {
        this.say("ARF! ARF! My sex is " + gender);
    }
}
```

18. Now, we need to create a ScottyDog object in the Scene file. Locate the section of your program where all the other objects are declared and created. We will create a ScottyDog object called rover. We will use the constructor that takes the gender parameter and make the dog a female as follows:

```java
private final SGround ground = new SGround();
private final SCamera camera = new SCamera();
private final Cow cow = new Cow();
private final AbyssinianCat cat = new AbyssinianCat();
private final ScottyDog dog = new ScottyDog();
private final ScottyDog rover = new ScottyDog("female");
```

19. For most Java objects, this would be sufficient, but because this is really an Alice object, we need to use some setters to setup the object on the scene properly. In the Scene.java file, you will see a ***performGeneratedSetUp*** method, but it needs to be expanded to see the code.

```
⊞        boiler plate code: performGeneratedSetUp
```

20. Copy all of the setter statements for the dog and paste them to the end of the method. Change all references to "dog" to be "rover". We want rover to be in middle of scene, so change the location to **0,0,0** and leave everything else the same as follows:

```
this.dog.setPaint(Color.WHITE);
this.dog.setOpacity(1.0);
this.dog.setName("dog");
this.dog.setVehicle(this);
this.dog.setOrientationRelativeToVehicle(new Orientation(0.0, 0.0, 0.0, 1.0));
this.dog.setPositionRelativeToVehicle(new Position(-2.53, 0.0, 0.959));
this.dog.setSize(new Size(0.324, 0.616, 0.826));
this.rover.setPaint(Color.WHITE);
this.rover.setOpacity(1.0);
this.rover.setName("rover");
this.rover.setVehicle(this);
this.rover.setOrientationRelativeToVehicle(new Orientation(0.0, 0.0, 0.0, 1.0));
this.rover.setPositionRelativeToVehicle(new Position(0, 0, 0));
this.rover.setSize(new Size(0.324, 0.616, 0.826));
```

21. Now, adjust the myFirstMethod so that rover does speak. Rover should say that she is a female. You can also make him eat and sleep (optional):

```
public void myFirstMethod() {
    cow.eat();
    cow.speak();
    cow.sleep();
    dog.eat();
    dog.speak();
    dog.sleep();
    cat.eat();
    cat.speak();
    cat.sleep();
    rover.speak();
}
```

Review of Exercise 3:

- We created a Quadruped class with 2 methods -- eat and sleep. This Quadruped class is a template for all quadrupeds and we described in this class what was common to most quadrupeds. The Quadruped class was a **superclass.**

- We described a Cow class which was a **subclass** of Quadruped. It inherited its eat method from the Quadruped class. It **overrode** the sleep method because cows sleep standing up. It also had its own speak method which was different than other quadrupeds.

- We described a ScottyDog class which was a **subclass** of Quadruped. It had two constructors. One with no arguments. One with a string argument of the dog's gender. The ScottyDog class inherited its' eat and sleep methods from the Quadruped class and saved us time in coding. It had its own speak method which was different than other quadrupeds.

- We described a Cat class which was a **subclass** of Quadruped. It inherited its eat and sleep method from the Quadruped class. It also had its own speak method which was different than other quadrupeds.

- We created multiple ScottyDogs called dog and rover. Actually **we could create as many objects of each** of these classes as we wanted. Because these are Alice objects, we needed to use setters to associate a name, color, opacity, vehicle property and location to the object.

- We adjusted the Quadruped sleep method modifier to be private. This meant that the ScottyDog and other classes were not able to use this sleep method.

Summary

- The three main concepts that are the backbone of OOP are encapsulation, inheritance, and polymorphism.
- One major difference between structured programming and object-oriented programming is encapsulation.
- **Encapsulation** lets you create a class template for creating objects. It is the process of hiding the attributes of a class and making them accessible via the object's methods.
- **Inheritance** enables you to create a class that is similar to a previously defined class, but one that still has some of its own properties. If you create a new class by inheritance, the new class (subclass) inherits all the data and methods from the tested superclass.
- Java can only have single-inheritance.
- When a subclass has an attribute or a method that behaves differently than the attribute or method listed in the superclass class, then the subclass method can **override** the superclass.
- Reusing the same method name in the same class with different parameters is called **overloading**.
- The keyword "new" is used to create an object.
- A constructor is a method with the same name as the class (including case sensitivity).
- **Setters** are procedural methods that are used to change properties of an object.
- **Getters** are functional methods that are used to get information about an object.
- If you want to represent objects, you can do so by defining a class template which combines class fields (attributes) with class methods.
- It is often considered good programming practice to mark instance variables as private so that they cannot be accessed directly from another class. If you want to allow other classes to be able to modify and retrieve private instance variables you can do so by using a public setter and getter method.
- **Unified Modeling Language** (UML) is sometimes used to graphically represent the fields and methods of a class.

Review Questions

1. An object is created by using what keyword?
   a. create
   b. make
   c. new
   d. init

2. If we create a class X that extends another class Y, the class called X is a _____ of Y?

3. If we create a new program called Dog that uses all the characteristics of an old program called Mammal we would write
   a. public class Dog extends Mammal
   b. public class Mammal extends Dog
   c. public class Dog extends JFrame
   d. public class Dog implements Mammal

4. _____ is sometimes used to graphically represent the fields and methods of a class.
   a. JLR
   b. FML
   c. UML
   d. CMR

5. True or false. A constructor is a method with the same name as the class.

6. True or false. Java allows for multiple inheritance.

7. True or false. Reusing the same method name in the same class with different arguments is called overriding.

8. True or false. The three main concepts of OOPS is encapsulation, inheritance, and polymorphism.

9. True or False. Getter methods are void.

10. True or False. The code for instantiating an object should be placed in the object constructor.

Solutions: *1)c 2)subclass 3)a 4)c 5)true 6)false 7)false 8)true 9)false 10)false*

Assignments

7-1   Working with Setters and Getters: Two java files have been added to this project: StudentCreator.java and Student.java. Use the StudentCreator project located in your Data_Files to get started. The Student class should encapsulate the concept of a student, assuming that a student has the following attributes: a name and age. Include a constructor and setter and getter methods for name, age, and type of student. Add the code to the Student class that already exists. Use the StudentCreator class to test all the methods in your class. Do NOT make changes to the StudentCreator class.

- Include the proper instance variables (name, age, and type). Initialize the *name* variable to *null*, the *age* variable to *0*, and the *type* variable to *null*. These variables should be *private*. The *type* variable will be used to store the schooling level of the student based on age.
- Include a constructor to set the name and age of the student when the object is created. The constructor should take in two parameters (*newName* and *newAge*) and should call setter methods for name and age.
- Create a *setName* method that sets the value of the student's name
- Create a *getName* method that returns the name of the student.
- Create a *setAge* method.
    - If the age is greater than 0, this method should:
        - Set the age
        - Call the setType method
- Create a *getAge* method that returns the age of the student.
- Create a *setType* method that sets the type of the student based on age. This type will be the level of schooling of the student. It is just an approximation based on age.
    - Preschool (age 0 – 4)
    - Kindergarten (age 5)
    - Elementary School (age 6-10)
    - Middle School (age 11-13)
    - High School (age 14-17)
    - College (age 18 & up)
- Create a *getType* method that returns the type of the student.

When you are finished, your results should look as follows:

```
Name: Bob
Age: 17
Type of Student: High School


Name: Jan
Age: 13
Type of Student: Middle School


Name: Bob
Age: 18
Type of Student: College
```

StudentCreator Class *(it will have errors since the Student code has not yet been written)*

```
/* This program will use setters and getters to compile a user-defined class
 * Name and Date
 * JDK version
 */

package studentcreator;

public class StudentCreator {
    public static void main(String[] args) {
        //Create student objects
        Student student1 = new Student("Bob", 17);
        Student student2 = new Student("Jan", 13);

        //Print out student name, age, and schooling type
        System.out.println("Name: " + student1.getName());
        System.out.println("Age: " + student1.getAge());
        System.out.println("Type of Student: " + student1.getType());
        System.out.println("\nName: " + student2.getName());
        System.out.println("Age: " + student2.getAge());
        System.out.println("Type of Student: " + student2.getType());

        //Change student1 age
        student1.setAge(18);
        System.out.println("\nName: " + student1.getName());
        System.out.println("Age: " + student1.getAge());
        System.out.println("Type of Student: " + student1.getType());
    }
}
```

Student Class *(You need to add the code to this class to make the program work)*

```
/* This program will use setters and getters to compile a user-defined class
 * Name and Date
 * JDK version
 */

package studentcreator;

public class Student {
    //Define instance variables

    //Student Constructor

    //Setter method to set the student name

    //Getter method to get the student name

    //Setter method to check validity of data, set age, and call setType method

    //Getter method to get the student age

    //Setter method to set the student's type based on age

    //Getter method to get the student type

}
```

Chapter 8

GUI and Graphics

Objectives

- ☑ Creating windows with GUI
- ☑ Use graphic components:
  - o Strings
  - o Lines
  - o Rectangles
  - o Ovals
  - o Arcs
- ☑ Change the color and font of elements.

Introduction to Graphical User Interfaces

GUI Packages – AWT and Swing

GUIs (Graphical User Interfaces) have become very popular. In Java, you can create windowing programs using a group of classes called the Swing Set and Abstract Windowing Toolkit (AWT). The older GUI classes that belong to the AWT catered to the Microsoft Windows-style of windowing. The newer GUI classes (preceded by a "J") that belong to the Swing Set are flexible cross-platform GUIs that allow windows to appear in a similar format on different operating systems. Since the Swing Set has become very popular, this text will emphasize that approach.

Even though we will be using the updated swing components in this text, you will still need to use some of the classes in the awt package. To include the container, change colors, or change fonts you must include the following awt import statements:

import java.awt.Color;
import java.awt.Container;
import java.awt.Font;

Since we are using more than one class from the awt package, we can use the wildcard symbol * in place of the class name to allow any classes listed in the awt folder to be used in the program. If you don't use the * in place of the class, you need to list each individual class. You can use the awt import with the wildcard symbol as follows:

import java.awt.*;

To use Swing JComponent and JFrame we will need to import those classes:

import javax.swing.JComponent;
import javax.swing.JFrame;

Since we are using more than one class from the swing package, we can use the wildcard symbol * in place of the class name to allow any classes listed in the swing folder to be used in the program. If you don't use the * in place of the class, you need to list each individual class. You can use the swing import with the wildcard symbol as follows:

import javax.swing.*;

Creating a Window

There are many GUIs available in Java, but before any of these GUI components can be placed onto the screen, a window must first be created to hold these components. This window is called a JFrame. This JFrame is simply a window that has a title, size, etc. The following statement will create a JFrame called frame and set the title bar of the frame as "Title of window here".

JFrame frame = new JFrame("Title of window here ");

Some of the methods used with JFrames are:

frame.setSize(200, 100);   // sets the width and height of the frame (200 is the width & 100 is the height)
frame.setLocationRelativeTo (null);   // sets the window to appear in center of the screen
frame.setDefaultCloseOperation(JFrame.EXIT_ON_CLOSE); //closes window
frame.setVisible(true);   // makes the frame visible on screen.

The default location of the window will appear in the upperleftmost corner 0,0. If you want to center the frame on the screen, be sure to set the size of the frame before using the setLocationRelativeTo method.

The above statements would create a JFrame as follows:

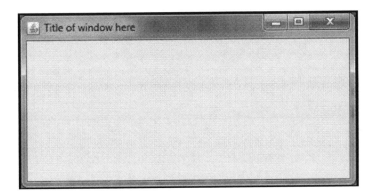

Place GUI Components in the Window

Every JFrame has a container called a content pane. The purpose of this container is to provide a visual area in which to place GUI components. The content pane has a background property, which we can use to control the color that will appear in the background of the window.

Container content = frame.getContentPane();   // creates the content pane in the JFrame
content.setBackground(Color.YELLOW);   // sets the background color of the frame to yellow

If your programs extend the JComponent class and you create an object of this class, you can add this JComponent to your content pane called content.

content.add(this);

Graphics

Drawing

Java's **AWT** (Abstract Windowing Toolkit) includes methods for drawing many different types of shapes, everything from lines to polygons; using colors; using fonts; and drawing images.

Painting: The paintComponent method allows us to draw graphics on the screen, be it text, a line, a colored graphic, or an image. Painting can occur many thousands of times during a session. The paintComponent takes an argument of a Graphics object which in the sample below is called **g**. The JComponent has a paintComponent method associated with it. For example, when we write *g.drawLine,* we are telling the computer to do the method called drawLine on the Graphics object called *g.* The paintComponent method is already defined in the Java API under the JComponent class in the java.swing package. We are going to override the paintComponent method that Java created. This method will automatically be called when our JComponent object is created.

```
public void paintComponent (Graphics g) {
    ....
}
```

Layout

You specify the location for drawing lines, rectangles, ovals, etc. by using x and y coordinates. This coordinate system has its origin of (0,0) in the upper leftmost corner, with the X axis increasing to the right, and the Y axis increasing downward. All pixel values are positive integers. The coordinates are represented as the x coordinate (horizontal) first and then the y coordinate (vertical) second.

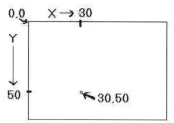

Changing the Font

The default font is Times New Roman 12 point. If you want a different font, you must use the Font class to create your new font. When you are displaying Strings, you may want to use different fonts. If you don't specify a font, the system will use the default font for your computer. There are three things you need to know about a font to display it:

1. **Typeface** (font name): Helvetica, Courier, Dialog, DialogInput, and TimesRoman (these are platform independent)
2. **Style:** Font.PLAIN, Font.BOLD, Font.ITALIC, Font.BOLD+Font.ITALIC
3. **Size:** Point size such as 24 point. (Note: These are points -- not pixels) The standard typewriter size font is 12 point. There are 72 points in 1 inch.

To use a font without saving it in a variable for later use, do the following:

g.setFont(new Font ("TimesRoman", Font.ITALIC, 72));

You can save the font object in a variable when you are going to be switching back and forth through many fonts and you wish to use the font over and over again. You create a font object by doing the following:

Font f = new Font("TimesRoman", Font.BOLD, 36);

Later in your program you would set the font by referring to this font object called *f*.

g.setFont(f) ;   // g is the graphics object & f is font object

Once a font has been set then everything you write with g.drawString will be written with this font until you change the font to something else.

g.drawString("something", 10, 100); // writes *something* at x=10 and y=100 using the current font

The following shows you the most common fonts. You may decide to use a different font that is better, but remember if you are writing for the web, other people may not have your fonts. It is best to use the ones listed below.

TimesRoman 14 pt	Helvetica 14 pt	Courier 14 pt
plain text	plain text	plain text
italic text	*italic text*	*italic text*
bold text	**bold text**	**bold text**

Changing the Color

The default color for drawing is black. If you want to use a different color, you must specify by using the Color class. Color constants and color methods are defined in the Color class. Java provides methods for setting the current foreground and background colors so that you can draw with the colors you created. Java's abstract color model uses 24-bit color, where a color is represented as a combination of red, green, and blue values. Each component of the color can have a number between 0 and 255 which gives you approximately 16 million colors.

The 13 predefined colors are **white, black, lightGray, gray, darkGray, red, green, blue, yellow, magenta, cyan, pink and orange.** When using each of these colors in a program, you must refer to the Color program such as *Color.BLUE* which tells the computer that blue is defined in a library class of Java called Color.

You can define your own colors by saying ***new Color (50, 75, 100)*** in place of where you might put a predefined color such as ***Color.PINK***. This says that you want a color that is 50 Red, 75 Green, and 100 Blue. How do you know how much red, green and blue compose the color you want? **One way to know the numbers to use for creating your own colors is to retrieve this information from the software package called Microsoft Paint in Accessories of Windows.** In Microsoft Paint, go to Edit colors and select a color. Go to the far right skinny color bar and click on a color and below the skinny color bar you will see 3 numbers for red, green, and blue. These are the numbers you need to use that color in Java.

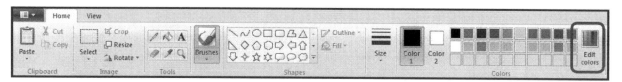

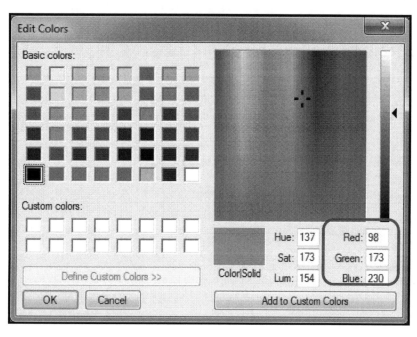

Using the Java Color class: To set the color of text or an object before you draw it, you must set the color before drawing. You can pick one of the predefined colors in the Color class.

g.setColor(Color.GREEN);   // where g is your graphics object

Creating your own color: You can use the red, green, and blue values to create your own color.

g.setColor(new Color(100,50,25));

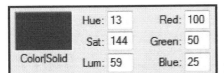 *This creates a brown color.*

Creating your own color and saving it for later use: If you want to create a new color that will be used over and over again, you could create declare and create a color object:

Color myTeal = new Color (0,128,128);

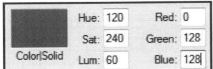 *This creates a teal color.*

Right before you want to draw with that color, set the color as your new color object.

g.setColor(myTeal);

Be sure not to put Color.myTeal because myTeal is not in Color class.

Printing Strings

Strings are a series of characters. A string may include letters, digits and various special characters. Java string literals are written as a sequence of characters in double quotes.

Drawing of strings is done with the drawString method as:

g.drawString("This is great", 20,50);
// The string displayed would be: This is great
// It is displayed at x position of 20 and y position of 50
// right 20 and down 50 from upper left corner
// It is displayed with current font and current color set
// The x,y parameters specify left edge of the baseline of the string.
// Characters with descenders (g, j, p, q and y) extend below the baseline.

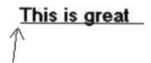

This following code statement places the words and the actual total beginning at pixel position 15, 50

g.drawString("The total is " + total, 15, 50);

Drawing Lines

You can draw straight lines from one point to another point by using the drawLine method from the Graphics class.

When you use a drawLine, you must specify a graphics object to draw the line onto then a period and then drawLine. Inside paretheses are the 4 arguments you need for drawing the line. There should be exactly 4 integers. **The first 2 integers represent the x and y pixels where the line should begin. The last 2 integers represent the x and y pixels of where the line should end.** The syntax of a drawLine is as follows:

g.drawLine(x1, y1, x2, y2);   draws from point x1,y1 to x2, y2

Let's take a look at an example of a drawLine:

g.drawLine(10,20,50,75);

In the above example, a line is drawn on a graphics object called g. The line begins at pixel position 10,20 which means from the upper left corner of applet, go across 10 pixels and down 20 pixels. That is your starting point. Draw a line to position 50,75 which means from the upper left corner, go to right 50 pixels and down 75 pixels and that is ending point of line. All points are relative to the 0,0 upper-leftmost position of the frame. The line can be drawn from right to left by saying: **g.drawLine(50,75,10,20);**

Samples:

```
g.drawLine(x1, y1, x2, y2);  // syntax of drawLine;
g.drawLine(0,0,50,50);       // draws diagonal line below   0,0  to point 50, 50
g.drawLine(50,0,50,75);      // draws vertical line below    50,0  to point 50,75
```

Above commands drawn:

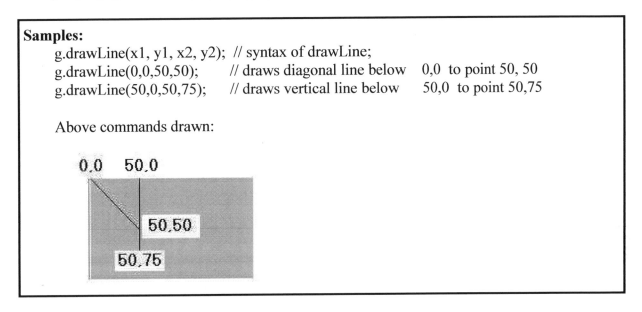

Drawing Rectangles

There are several Graphics methods for various kinds of rectangles such as outlined rectangles (drawRect), filled rectangles (fillRect), rounded corner rectangles (drawRoundRect and fillRoundRect), and more advanced rectangles (clearRect, draw3DRect, and fill3DRect).

Type of Rectangle	Syntax
Empty rectangle with border	g.drawRect(x1, y1, width, height);
Filled rectangle with current color	g.fillRect(x1, y1, width, height);
Empty rectangle with round corners	g.drawRoundRect(x1, y1, width, height, arcwidth, archeight); *Note: arcwidth and archeight are the number of pixels of the curve.*
Filled rectangle with round corners	g.fillRoundRect(x1, y1, width, height, arcwidth, archeight); *Note: arcwidth and archeight are the number of pixels of the curve.*
Rectangle which shows background through it	g.clearRect(x1, y1, width, height);
3D rectangle (raised or not)	g.draw3DRect(x1, y1, width, height, Boolean raise); *Note: If last argument is true, you get a raised rectangle.*
Filled 3D rectangle (raised or not)	g.fill3DRect(x1, y1, width, height, Boolean raise); *Note: If last argument is true, you get a raised rectangle.*

Examples of each of these are as follows:

1. g.drawRect(0, 0, 50, 25);
   g.setColor(Color.green);
2. g.fillRect(100,0,50,40);
   g.setColor(Color.red);
3. g.drawRoundRect(175,0,50,50,20,20);   (20 pixel curve)
4. g.fillRoundRect(0,75,50,50,35,35);   (35 pixel curve)
5. g.fillRect(100,100,50,50);
   g.clearRect(120,120,10,10);
6. g.draw3DRect(175,100,50,30,true);   (true means raised)
7. g.draw3DRect(250,100,50,20,false);   (false means indented)
8. g.fill3DRect(250,175,50,20,false);   (false means indented)

The coordinates for the rounded corners are given as the width and height of the rectangle that encloses the rounded corner.

For raised (true) 3D rectangles, the top and left edges are drawn lighter and the bottom and right edges are drawn darker. For indented (false), the opposite lighting is done. The lighting effects make the rectangles look raised and indented.

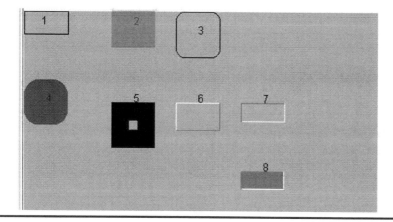

Drawing Ovals

There are two Graphics methods for ovals which are *drawOval* and *fillOval*. An oval has 4 integer arguments which are the x and y coordinates, width, and height. You might be wondering where the x and y coordinates are since an oval has no corners. Actually, to draw an oval, you must imagine a rectangle surrounding the oval. The x, y coordinates are the upperleft corner of that rectangle. **Thus, the x,y coordinates of an oval are not even contained within the oval as can be seen below:**

The following are the syntax for each of these:

g.drawOval (x1, y1, width, height);
g.fillOval (x1, y1, width, height);

Examples:

```
g.drawOval(0,0,30,60);
// draws an oval starting at point 0,0 width=30, height =60
// see the first circle below

g.fillOval(50,0,100,40);
// draws oval starting pt is 50,0 width =100, height = 40
// see the second filled in oval below
```

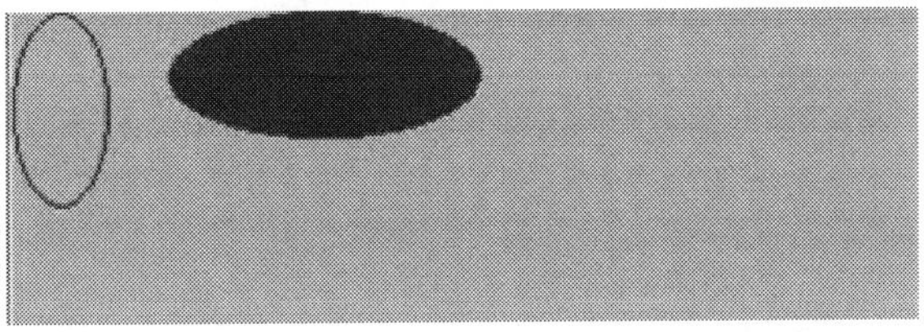

Drawing Arcs

Of all the drawing methods, the arcs (drawArc and fillArc) are the most complex. Before you can start an arc, you must visualize the arc as a complete oval. Then the 6 arguments for the arc are the x coordinate of the upperleftmost corner of the oval; the y coordinate of the upperleftmost corner of the oval; the oval's width; the oval's height; the starting angle; and the degrees. The first four arguments are the same as those for an oval. The *arc's starting angle* ranges from 0 to 359 degrees in a counterclockwise direction. **For the starting angle, use the diagram below. The numbers on the diagram are just reference points. The number of degrees traveled by an arc ranges from 0 to 359 degrees in a counterclockwise direction and 0 to -359 degrees in a clockwise direction.**

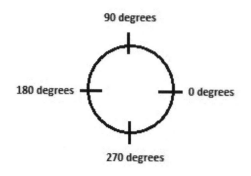

The syntax is:
g.drawArc (x, y, width, height, startangle, degrees);
g.fillArc (x, y, width, height, startangle, degrees);

Examples:

g.setColor(Color.black);
g.drawArc(0, 40, 50, 50, 0, 75);   // the first arc shown below
// Picture an oval with upperleft corner of its rectangle at 0,40 and its 50 wide and 50 high
// starting angle is 0 which is 3 o'clock
// degrees is 75 which means to go counterclockwise 75 degrees.

g.fillArc(100, 75, 50, 50, 90, 180); // the filled in black arc below
// Picture an oval with upperleft corner of its rectangle at 100,75 and its 50 wide and 50 high
// starting angle is 90 which is 12 o'clock
// degrees is 180 which means to go counterclockwise 180 degrees
// the same arc could be drawn clockwise with g.fillArc(100, 75, 50, 50, 270, -180);

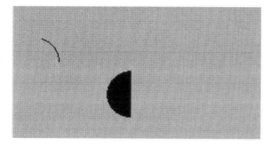

Using Paint to Determine Pixel Locations

You can resize the painting area in Microsoft Paint to determine a good size for your drawing. You can drag the handles on the right or bottom of the white canvas to resize. You should notice the size of the canvas at the bottom center. The following canvas is 450 (width) x 300px (height).

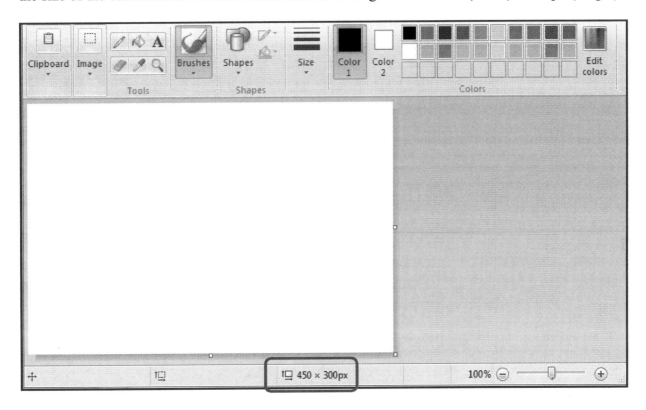

Instead of having to guess pixel locations for your drawing, you can use the Paint program to guide you. You may want to draw your picture in Paint before trying to code it in Java. This is part of the planning process. Creating a sketch of the drawing could save you time when programming it. Select the **View** tab, then check the **Rulers** box to make it easier to figure out pixel locations for your drawing.

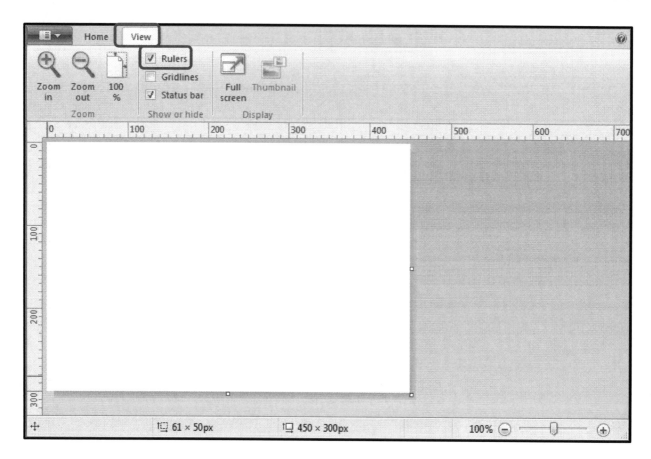

Click back on the **Home** tab to switch colors, shapes etc.

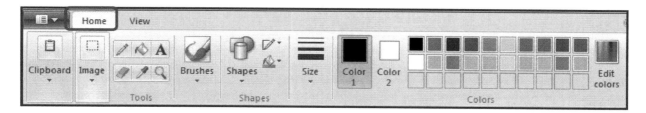

For example, let's say that you wanted to draw a stick figure using the Java drawing methods. You would not want to keep guessing coordinates when coding. Drawing your stick figure in Paint and writing down pixel locations could help you easily write the code for your drawing.

Let's take a look at the start of a stick figure, the head. If you draw a circle in Paint, you will see a dotted bounding box around the circle. This is very helpful to us, because it allows us to get a starting x and y coordinate for drawing our circle. When you draw a circle using the Java drawing methods, you use the drawOval method on the graphics object g. You would need 4 arguments for this method (x, y, width, height). The x and y are the starting point of where you want to draw the circle, but remember that it is actually using the bounding box for the circle. The width and height would be the same number if you wanted a circle.

If we have a 450 x 300 frame size, then 450 would be the width of the frame and 225 would be the horizontal center. To draw the head for the stick figure, we would need to decide on a width for our circle and divide that with by 2 to determine how much to subtract from the frame center to get the circle horizontally aligned in the center of the frame. If we want a 50 (width) x 50 (height) circle, we would need to subtact half of the circle from the 225. This would give us 200 as a starting point *x* point (horizontal) for drawing our 50 x 50 circle. The *y* point would be based on the vertical point of where you wanted your drawing to start. If you were drawing a stick figure, you probably wouldn't want it in the vertical center since you would not have enough room to finisht the body for the stick figure. The Java command for drawing this circle would be: **g.drawOval(200, 50, 50, 50);**

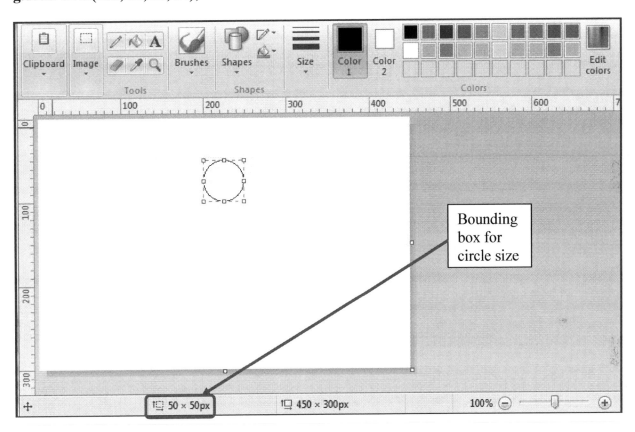

Bounding box for circle size

Hands-on Exercises

Exercise 1: Drawing a Happy Face

We are going to create a program that displays a smiley face.

1. Create a new project in NetBeans called **HappyFace**. The class file should also be HappyFace.

2. Add your comments to the top of the program.

3. Add the imports needed for drawing. You can use the wildcard notation so that you don't have to import the Container class, Font class, Color class, JComponent class, and JFrame class.

    import java.awt.*;   //needed for the Container, Font, Color class
    import javax.swing.*;   //needed for the JComponent, JFrame

4. Add **extends JComponent** to the class

    ```
    public class HappyFace extends JComponent {
    ```

5. Declare and create a JFrame object named **frame**.

    ```
    public class HappyFace extends JComponent {
        JFrame frame = new JFrame("Happy Face");
    ```

6. Get the container for the frame and name it content.

    ```
    public class HappyFace extends JComponent {
        JFrame frame = new JFrame("Happy Face");
        Container content = frame.getContentPane();
    ```

7. Now let's create an object named **drawing** of our HappyFace class and a new method named **setUp** that will be invoked on our new drawing object. The setUp method will be void since we aren't going to return a value, it is going to be used to set up our container and frame.

```java
import java.awt.*;
import javax.swing.*;

public class HappyFace extends JComponent {
    JFrame frame = new JFrame("Happy Face");
    Container content = frame.getContentPane();

    public static void main(String[] args) {
        HappyFace drawing = new HappyFace();
        drawing.setUp();
    }

    public void setUp() {

    }
}
```

8. Next, we need to add the code to our **setUp** method.

   Container: We need to add the color for the container and add the JComponent object to the container.

   Frame: We need to set the width and height of the frame, stop the program from running in the background when the frame is closed, and make the frame visible. You could also add the following line **frame.setLocationRelativeTo(null);** to center the frame on the screen. If you do not add this line of code, it will default to the upper left corner of the screen.

```java
public void setUp() {
    content.setBackground(Color.YELLOW);
    content.add(this);

    frame.setSize(200, 300);
    frame.setDefaultCloseOperation(JFrame.EXIT_ON_CLOSE);
    frame.setVisible(true);
}
```

9. If you run the program, you will see a yellow window, but you will not see a drawing since we didn't draw anything yet. We need to add our paintComponent method and drawing methods to create our drawing.

10. Add the **paintComponent** method to your code. This method needs to be placed within the class opening and closing curly braces and outside of your other methods. You should notice a yellow light bulb to the left of your code. A yellow light bulb indicates a NetBeans warning. Our paintComponent method is overriding the paint method that comes with the JComponent and NetBeans wants to know if we want to add the override annotation. Go ahead and add the annotation.

```
public void paintComponent(Graphics g) {


}
```

11. Add the following code to the paintComponent method to create the drawing:

```
@Override
public void paintComponent(Graphics g) {
    g.drawOval(50, 75, 100, 100); //face
    g.drawLine(100, 110, 100, 130); //nose
    g.drawOval(70, 100, 12, 5); //left eye
    g.drawOval(110, 100, 12, 5); //right eye
    g.drawArc(70, 95, 60, 60, 225, 90); //smile
}
```

12. Run the program. You should have created the following drawing:

13. If you want to adjust the colors of this drawing, you can easily do so. For example, we could add some color to the face. You can use a color in the Java Color class or you can create your own. Let's create our own. Use Microsoft Paint find the red, green, and blue numbers for a color. You do not have to pick the same color.

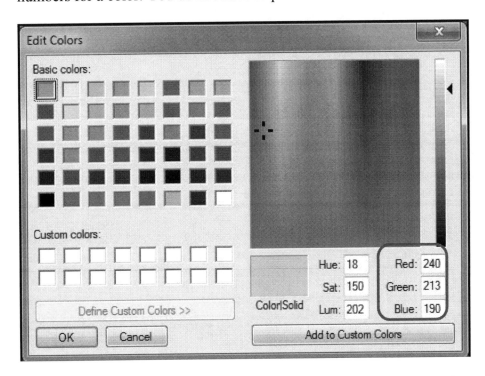

14. Add the setColor method to your code before you code for which you want to change the color. This is not a color in the Java Color class, and so we will need to create this new color using the red, green, and blue numbers that represent the color. We also want to fill the face color in instead of outlining the face with this color, so we will need to adjust the drawOval statement to be a fillOval.

```java
@Override
public void paintComponent(Graphics g) {
    g.setColor(new Color(240, 213, 190)); //face color
    g.fillOval(50, 75, 100, 100); //face
    g.drawLine(100, 110, 100, 130); //nose
    g.drawOval(70, 100, 12, 5); //left eye
    g.drawOval(110, 100, 12, 5); //right eye
    g.drawArc(70, 95, 60, 60, 225, 90); //smile
}
```

15. Notice that now the whole face is that color, but we can't see the nose, eyes, or mouth. These parts are no longer visible because they are all drawn with that face color instead of black. We will need to change the color back to black before drawing the nose. Since black is a color in the Java Color class, we do not need to create a new color.

```java
@Override
public void paintComponent(Graphics g) {
    g.setColor(new Color(240, 213, 190)); //face color
    g.fillOval(50, 75, 100, 100); //face
    g.setColor(Color.BLACK); //nose color
    g.drawLine(100, 110, 100, 130); //nose
    g.drawOval(70, 100, 12, 5); //left eye
    g.drawOval(110, 100, 12, 5); //right eye
    g.drawArc(70, 95, 60, 60, 225, 90); //smile
}
```

16. Now, using this same logic, let's change the color of the eyes and the mouth. Pick your own colors. You can use the colors from the Java Color class or create your own. You will need to change the eyes to fillOval if you want them to be colored in. The following is an example of how your code might look:

```java
@Override
public void paintComponent(Graphics g) {
    g.setColor(new Color(240, 213, 190)); //face color
    g.fillOval(50, 75, 100, 100); //face
    g.setColor(Color.BLACK); //nose color
    g.drawLine(100, 110, 100, 130); //nose
    g.setColor(Color.BLUE); //eye color
    g.fillOval(70, 100, 12, 5); //left eye
    g.fillOval(110, 100, 12, 5); //right eye
    g.setColor(Color.RED); //mouth color
    g.drawArc(70, 95, 60, 60, 225, 90); //smile
}
```

17. Now, let's add text above the drawing. We will need to specify the message for the text and the coordinates of where the text will be located. To do this, we will need to use the **drawString** method.

```
@Override
public void paintComponent(Graphics g) {
    g.drawString("Happy Face", 20, 20);
    g.setColor(new Color(240, 213, 190)); //face color
    g.fillOval(50, 75, 100, 100); //face
    g.setColor(Color.BLACK); //nose color
    g.drawLine(100, 110, 100, 130); //nose
    g.setColor(Color.BLUE); //eye color
    g.fillOval(70, 100, 12, 5); //left eye
    g.fillOval(110, 100, 12, 5); //right eye
    g.setColor(Color.RED); //mouth color
    g.drawArc(70, 95, 60, 60, 225, 90); //smile
}
```

18. If you want to change the font of the text, you can do this before you use the drawString method. Also, you may want to adjust your coordinates of your drawString method depending upon your font size.

```
@Override
public void paintComponent(Graphics g) {
    g.setFont(new Font("Arial", Font.BOLD, 20));
    g.drawString("Happy Face", 20, 40);
    g.setColor(new Color(240, 213, 190)); //face color
    g.fillOval(50, 75, 100, 100); //face
    g.setColor(Color.BLACK); //nose color
    g.drawLine(100, 110, 100, 130); //nose
    g.setColor(Color.BLUE); //eye color
    g.fillOval(70, 100, 12, 5); //left eye
    g.fillOval(110, 100, 12, 5); //right eye
    g.setColor(Color.RED); //mouth color
    g.drawArc(70, 95, 60, 60, 225, 90); //smile
}
```

19. Run your program to see if you are happy with your happy face. Feel free to make changes to it. Close this project.

Exercise 2: Drawing a Car

We are going to create a program that displays a car. This car was drawn by Robert Lochner, a previous student in this course.

1. Create a new project in NetBeans called **Car**. The class file should also be Car.

2. Add your comments to the top of the program.

3. Add the imports needed for drawing. You can use the wildcard notation so that you don't have to import the Container class, Font class, Color class, JComponent class, and JFrame class.

   import java.awt.*;   //needed for the Container, Font, Color class
   import javax.swing.*;   //needed for the JComponent, JFrame

4. Add **extends JComponent** to the class

   ```
   public class Car extends JComponent  {
   ```

5. Declare and create a JFrame object named **frame**.

   ```
   public class Car extends JComponent  {
        JFrame frame = new JFrame("Car");
   ```

6. Get the container for the frame and name it content.

   ```
   public class Car extends JComponent  {
        JFrame frame = new JFrame("Car");
        Container content = frame.getContentPane();
   ```

7. Now let's create an object named **drawing** of our Car class and a new method named **setUp** that will be invoked on our new drawing object. The setUp method will be void since we aren't going to return a value, it is going to be used to set up our container and frame.

```java
import java.awt.*;
import javax.swing.*;

public class Car extends JComponent {

    JFrame frame = new JFrame("Car");
    Container content = frame.getContentPane();

    public static void main(String[] args) {
        Car drawing = new Car();
        drawing.setUp();
    }

    public void setUp() {

    }
}
```

8. Next, we need to add the code to our **setUp** method.

   Container: We need to add the color for the container and add the JComponent object to the container.

   Frame: We need to set the width and height of the frame, center the frame on the screen, stop the program from running in the background when the frame is closed, and make the frame visible.

```java
public void setUp() {
    content.setBackground(Color.CYAN);
    content.add(this);

    frame.setSize(475, 325);
    frame.setLocationRelativeTo(null);
    frame.setDefaultCloseOperation(JFrame.EXIT_ON_CLOSE);
    frame.setVisible(true);
}
```

9. If you run the program, you will see a cyan window, but you will not see a drawing since we didn't draw anything yet. We need to add our paint method and drawing methods to create our drawing.

10. Add the paintComponent method to your code. This method must be within the class opening and closing curly braces and outside of your other methods. You should notice a yellow light bulb to the left of your code. A yellow light bulb indicates a NetBeans warning. Our paintComponent method is overriding the paint method that comes with the JComponent and NetBeans wants to know if we want to add the override annotation. Go ahead and add the annotation.

```
public void paintComponent(Graphics g) {


}
```

11. Add the following code to the paint method to create the drawing:

```
@Override
public void paintComponent(Graphics g) {
    g.setColor(Color.RED); //draw a red car
    g.drawLine(7, 206, 7, 141); //car
    g.drawLine(7, 141, 64, 88); //car
    g.drawLine(64, 88, 181, 88); //car
    g.drawLine(181, 88, 214, 7); //car
    g.drawLine(214, 7, 335, 7); //car
    g.drawLine(335, 7, 364, 89); //car
    g.drawLine(364, 89, 427, 89); //top of car
    g.drawLine(427, 89, 427, 159); //car
    g.drawLine(427, 159, 377, 206); //car
    g.drawLine(377, 206, 7, 206); //front
    g.drawOval(60, 155, 100, 100); //front tire
    g.drawOval(300, 155, 100, 100); //back tire
}
```

12. Run the program. You should have created the following drawing:

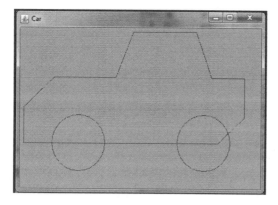

13. Close this project.

Summary

- There are two sets of GUI classes provided in the Java library. They are the older AWT (Abstract Windowing Toolkit) and the Swing Set classes. The Swing set classes are the more recent set of GUI classes and generally are preceded by a "J" before the class name.

- The window onto which you place components in a Java application is called a JFrame.

- There are many methods for drawing:
    - drawString – print text on the drawing canvas
    - drawLine – draw a line on the drawing canvas
    - drawRect – draw a rectangle or a square on the drawing canvas
    - drawOval – draw an oval or a circle on the drawing canvas
    - drawArc – draw an arc on the drawing canvas
    - setColor – change the color of a component of the drawing
    - setFont – change the font of text printed to the drawing canvas

- To use a GUI in your Java program, you must include the following imports:

  import javax.swing.*;   // import for JComponent and JFrame classes
  import java.awt.*;   // import for Container, Font, and Color classes

Review Questions

1. A JFrame with a setSize(600,100) means
   a. The JFrame will be 600 pixels tall and 100 pixels wide
   b. The JFrame will be 600 pixels wide and 100 pixels tall
   c. The JFrame will be 600 cm tall and 100 cm wide
   d. The JFrame will be 600 cm wide and 100 cm tall

2. Which of the following commands draws this arc:

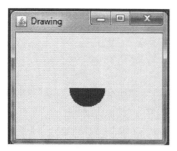

   a. g.fillArc(75, 50, 50, 50, 180, 180);
   b. g.fillArc(75, 50, 50, 50, 0, 180);
   c. g.fillArc(75, 50, 50, 50, 180, 90);
   d. g.fillArc(75, 50, 50, 50, 0, 90);

3. Which of the following commands draws this line:

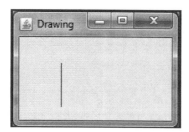

   a. g.drawLine(30,50,50,80);
   b. g.drawLine(30,80,50,50);
   c. g.drawLine(80,80,30,50);
   d. g.drawLine(50,30,50,80);

4. Which of the following commands draws this oval:

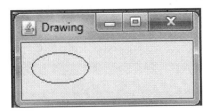

   a. g.drawOval(10,10,30,60);
   b. g.drawOval(10,10,60,30);
   c. g.drawOval(10,10,60,60);
   d. g.drawOval(10,10,30,30);

5. In the following code **setColor** is known as a(n):
   Color myTeal = new Color (0,128,128);
   g.setColor(myTeal);

   a. Method
   b. Class
   c. Object

6. In the following code **myTeal** is known as a(n):
   Color myTeal = new Color (0,128,128);
   g.setColor(myTeal);

   a. Method
   b. Class
   c. Object

7. **True or False.** The setFont method is known as a functional method.

8. **True or False.** The drawRect method is known as a procedural method.

Solutions: 1)b   2)a   3)d   4)b   5)a   6)c   7)False   8)True

© **Daly & Wrigley**

Assignments

8-1 **Creative Drawing**: You get a chance to be creative with this assignment. Create a GUI that draws a design or a recognizable drawing. It should include the following:

- Give the project and file a meaningful name. Use correct capitalization throughout your program (class, variables, methods, etc.).
- You should create a drawing. Use at least **3 *different*** graphics statements (drawing a line, rectangle, oval, arc, String, and/or changing color) in your drawing. This should be recognizable drawing. Do not draw random shapes. Do NOT use examples that were given to you in the text or that you found on the Internet.
- Proper indentation should be used throughout program.
- Comments should be included throughout program to explain your statements. You don't have to explain every statement, but explain the statements that you think are important. You should have at least 3 comments in your program not including the comments for your name, date, and description of the program at the top of the program. These comments must be meaningful.

Examples of previous student work:

 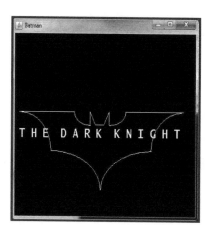 

By: John Bemenderfer   *By: Jonathan Romo*   *By: Brett Holman*

Chapter 9

Repetition

Objectives

- ☑ Code programs using the following looping techniques:
  - While Loop
  - Do While Loop
  - For Loop
- ☑ Explain when the Break and Continue statements would be used when coding loops.
- ☑ Walk through While, Do While, and For loops documenting variables as they change.

Loops

Often, we would like to repeat steps in programs. This repetition is referred to as looping and loop statements are often referred to as control structures. There are 3 ways in which programmers can instruct the computer to perform repetition:

- while
- do while
- for

Although, you can use any of the above statements to create a loop, there are extreme differences between these statements.

Alice Loops

While

The **while loop** repeats the steps inside the block as long as the condition on the while statement is true. Generally, a while loop is used when you don't know exactly how many times to execute a loop but instead execute as long as some condition exists. Below is a sample of an Alice while loop that has a shark move forward as long as it is facing the camera. This will give you a close up of the shark as he moves toward the camera (audience).

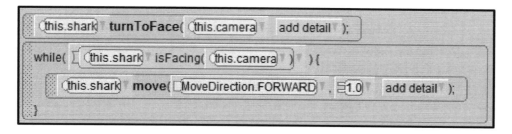

```
this.shark  turnToFace( this.camera    add detail );
while( I  this.shark  isFacing( this.camera )  ){
    this.shark  move( MoveDirection.FORWARD , 1.0   add detail );
}
```

For

The for and while loops are used for repetition. Alice refers to the **for loop** as a **count loop**. When you know how many times you would like to perform a block of statements, you typically use the for loop (count loop in Alice). For example, if we want a penguin to turn around 5 times, we would write the following code:

Alice View:

```
count up to 5
    this.penguin  turn RIGHT , 1.0  add detail
loop
```

Java View:

```
final Integer N = 5 ;
for( Integer i = 0; i < N; i++ ){
    this.penguin turn( TurnDirection.RIGHT , 1.0  add detail );
}
```

Java Loops

While

The initialization for a while loop is done before the WHILE. The Boolean test is done in the WHILE statement. The actual statements to be repeated are in curly braces. When a program reaches the while statement for the first time, it tests the condition inside parentheses after the word *while*. If the tested condition is false, the statements inside the loop (curly braces) will be ignored. If the while condition is true, the loop goes through the statements inside the loop once and then tests the while condition again.

Note: If the tested condition never changes inside the loop, the loop will keep looping indefinitely.

While Loop Syntax:	Flowchart:

while (Boolean condition) {
    repeated statements
}
	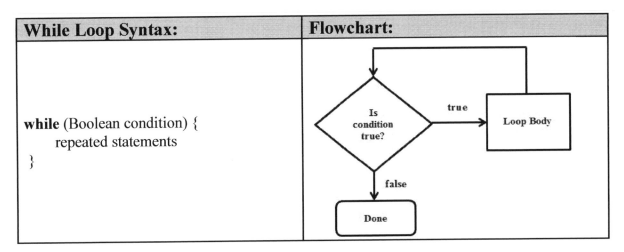

The following is an example of a Java while loop:

While Loop:	Output:

// Prints Hello and the current value of counter on 5 lines
 	
int counter = 1;
while (counter <=5) {
   System.out.println ("Hello " + counter);
   counter ++;
}
	Hello 1
	Hello 2
	Hello 3
	Hello 4
	Hello 5

Do/While

The do-while loop is similar in function to the while loop, but the conditional test goes in a different place. When the do loop is reached for the first time as a program runs, the statements between the do and the while are handled automatically. Then the while condition is tested to determine whether the loop should be repeated. If the while condition is true, the loop is repeated. If the condition is false, the loop ends. Something must happen inside the do and while statements that changes the condition tested with while, or the loop will continue indefinitely. **The statements inside a do-while will always be handled at least once.**

Do While Loop Syntax:	Flowchart:
do { repeated statements } **while** (Boolean condition);	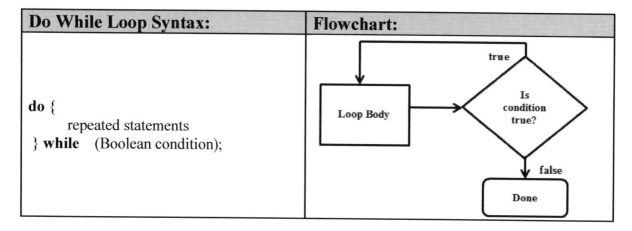

The following is an example of a Java do-while loop:

Do While Loop:	Output:

// Prints Hello and the current value of counter on 5 lines
int counter = 1;
do {
    System.out.println("Hello " + counter);
    counter++;
} **while** (counter <=5);
	Hello 1
	Hello 2
	Hello 3
	Hello 4
	Hello 5

For Loop

The FOR loop repeats a statement or block of statements while a condition is matched. The FOR loop looks as follows:

```
for (initialization;   test;   increment) {
     statements;
}
```

Initialization is an expression that initializes the start of the loop for example *int i =0*   The initialization can be more than one variable such as int x=0, y=5   BUT all variables in initialization must be of same type such as int.

Test is the Boolean test that occurs before each pass of the loop for example *i < 10.* If the test is true, the loop executes. Once the test is false, the loop stops executing.

Increment is any expression which is updated at the end of each trip through the loop for example *i ++   Note: You can also use a for loop to count backwards, for example: x-=5 is called decrementing. You can use more than one increment (decrement) but they must of same type. An example is   i ++, j+=3*

Statements are the statements that are executed each time the loop is executed.

Note: Be careful not to put semicolon after the first line of the for loop or else it won't execute.

The flowchart for the logic of a FOR loops is as follows:

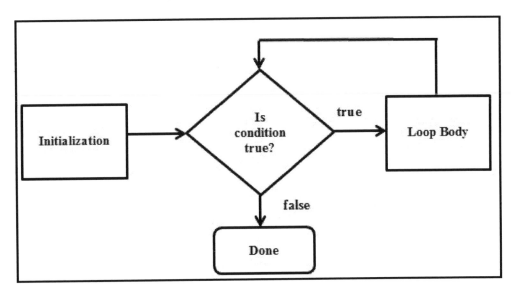

How a For loop works   for (x = 1; x< 4 ; x++)

1. When the computer firsts enters a *for* loop, it sets all the **initialization** variables to whatever values are listed. In the above example it sets x to be equal to 1.
2. Next, it tests the **TEST** which means it checks to see if x is less than 4. In this case it is true so it begins doing the statements inside the for loop.
3. When the computer gets done executing the statements inside the *for* loop it comes back and does the **INCREMENT** stage. In this case that is x++ which means to add 1 to x. Thus, x is now 2.
4. The computer will now do the **test** again which is to see if x is less than 4. It is true, so it repeats the statements inside of *for* loop.
5. When the computer gets done executing the statements inside the *for* loop it comes back and does the **INCREMENT** stage. In this case that is x++ which means to add 1 to x. Thus, x is now 3.
6. The computer will now do the **test** again which is to see if x is less than 4. It is true, so it repeats the statements inside of *for* loop.
7. When the computer gets done executing the statements inside the *for* loop it comes back and does the **INCREMENT** stage. In this case that is x++ which means to add 1 to x. Thus, x is now 4.
8. The computer will now do the test again which is to see if x is less than 4. IT IS NOT TRUE. The computer will now skip over the statements in the *for* loop and do the next statement after the end of the *for* loop body (after the curly brace for the *for* loop).

For loop	Results

// Prints the current value of counter on 5 lines
// counter is a local int
 	
for (int counter =1; counter <=5; counter++){
    System.out.println ("Hello " + counter);
}
	Hello 1
	Hello 2
	Hello 3
	Hello 4
	Hello 5

For loop with Modulus	Results

// Example to display every number from 0 to 999
// that is evenly divisible by 12.
// modulus tests for remainder of 0 which is evenly divisible
// number is local for loop
 	
for (int number = 0; number <1000; number++) {
    if number % 12 == 0) {
        System.out.println("Number is " + number);
    }
}
	Number is 0
	Number is 12
	Number is 24
	Number is 36
	Number is 48
	Number is 60
	Number is 72
	Number is 84
	Number is 96
	Number is 108
	Number is 120
	Number is 132
	Number is 144
	
	...... etc.
	Number is 996

For loop to print even numbers from 1 to 20	Results

//This will begin i at 2, increment i by 2 each time through the
//loop and go to and including i being 20.
// number is local for loop
 	
for (int number = 2;   number <=20;   number+=2) {
        System.out.println("Number is " + number);
}
	The number is 2
	The number is 4
	The number is 6
	The number is 8
	The number is 10
	The number is 12
	The number is 14
	The number is 16
	The number is 18
	The number is 20

For loop with Multiple Initialization & Increments	Results

/* A for loop can have **more than one variable set up**
   during the initialization and more than one statement
   in the change section, as in the following:
   This for loop starts i and j at 0.
   It increments i by 1 each time through
   and j by 2 each time through loop.
   It goes until the product of i and j is not less than 1000.
   First time through it prints "The answer is 0 * 0 = 0"
   .... next time it prints "The answer is 1 * 2 = 2 ... etc.
*/
 	
// i is a local integer for loop
 	
for (int i=0, j=0 ;   i*j < 1000;   i++, j+=2) {
     System.out.println("The answer is " + i +
         " * " + j + " = " + i*j);
}
	The answer is 0 * 0 = 0
	The answer is 1 * 2 = 2
	The answer is 2 * 4 = 8
	The answer is 3 * 6 = 18
	The answer is 4 * 8 = 32
	The answer is 5 * 10 = 50
	The answer is 6 * 12 = 72
	The answer is 7 * 14 = 98
	The answer is 8 * 16 = 128
	The answer is 9 * 18 = 162
	The answer is 10 * 20 = 200
	The answer is 11 * 22 = 242
	The answer is 12 * 24 = 288
	The answer is 13 * 26 = 338
	The answer is 14 * 28 = 392
	The answer is 15 * 30 = 450
	The answer is 16 * 32 = 512
	The answer is 17 * 34 = 578
	The answer is 18 * 36 = 648
	The answer is 19 * 38 = 722
	The answer is 20 * 40 = 800
	The answer is 21 * 42 = 882
	The answer is 22 * 44 = 968

Branching Statements

Break Statement

The **break** keyword, when used with a loop, halts execution of the current loop. If you've nested loops within loops, execution picks up in the next outer loop; otherwise, the program merely continues executing the next statement after the loop.

```
/*This FOR loop says to do looping until the value of the index variable is greater than
1000. However, when index equals 400 exactly, the loop ends immediately. */

// index variable is local to for loop

for (int   index =1;   index<= 1000;   index ++)  {
        if (index   ==   400) {
            break;
        }
        System.out.println("The index is " + index);
}
```

Continue Statement

The **continue** keyword is similar to break except that instead of halting execution of the loop entirely, the loop starts over at the next iteration.

```
/* This FOR loop says to do looping until the value of the index variable is greater than 1000.
However, if index equals 400, the continue statement causes the loop to go back to the "for
statement" instead of the System.out.println statement. (continues with next iteration of loop
and skips the printing for index =400.)  */

// index variable is local to for loop

for (int index =1, index <=1000; index ++) {
        if (index == 400) {
            continue;
        }
        System.out.println("The index is " + index);
}
```

Hands-on Exercises

Exercise 1: Hokey Pokey with a For Loop (ongoing exercise)

1. Open the **HokeyPokeyInheritance** project from chapter 6 in NetBeans. Copy this file to the appropriate chapter folder with the name **HokeyPokeyInheritanceLoop**.

2. Open up the BabyYeti.java file. Scroll down to the turnAround method. This turnAround method for the baby yeti overrides the turnAround method for the biped. Instead of having the baby yeti put his arms in the air and spin around, we just had him spin 5 times. Writing the code as follows is very inefficient.

```java
public void turnAround() {
    this.turn(TurnDirection.LEFT, 1.0);
    this.turn(TurnDirection.LEFT, 1.0);
    this.turn(TurnDirection.LEFT, 1.0);
    this.turn(TurnDirection.LEFT, 1.0);
    this.turn(TurnDirection.LEFT, 1.0);
}
```

3. Whenever code repeats, we use a loop instead of typing the same code over and over again. Since we know that we want the baby yeti to turn 5 times, we could use a **for loop** to rewrite this code. Let's add the *for* loop before the first turn method. The *for* loop should start with an initial variable with a value, we can use i (i stands for index that moves through the loop) and start it at 1, **int i=1**. The next, part of the for loop will be the test, this should be as long as **i<=5** since we want him to spin 5 times. The last part will be the incrementation. This tells Java what number you are increasing by. We will increase by 1 more each time and therefore we will use **i++**. We only want the turn method once inside our loop since our loop is going to repeat 5 times, this method will happen 5 times even though the line is only written one time. Your code should look as follows:

```java
public void turnAround() {
    for (int i = 1; i <= 5; i++) {
        this.turn(TurnDirection.LEFT, 1.0);
    }
}
```

You could also rewrite this for loop as follows and it would have the same result:

```
public void turnAround() {
    for (int i = 5; i > 0; i--) {
        this.turn(TurnDirection.LEFT, 1.0);
    }
}
```

4. Run the animation. It should look that same as it did before.

5. Close the project.

Exercise 2: While Loop Tree Growing

1. Open Alice 3. Set the scene with a tree and a water hole. You can create a water hole by using the disc shape, naming it "water", and setting the color to blue. If your water looks a bit grainy, move the disc up because this means it is down below ground level. Name this program **TreeGrows**.

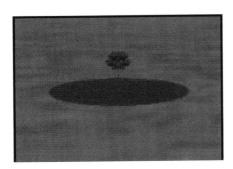

2. We do not know in this situation how many times the tree is going to grow since it will be based on the size of the water supply. Because the number of executions for the loop is unknown, we will need to use the while loop instead of the *for* loop. Drag the **while** loop onto the editor and choose **true**.

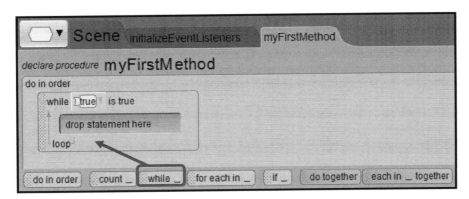

3. We want the while loop to be executed as long as there is still water left (based on width of disc shape). We need to select the drop down arrow next to true for the while loop and select **Relational (Decimal Number)**, then **??? > ???**, then **0.1**, and **0.1** as shown below:

4. Now, select the function for the water, drag the getWidth function for the water onto the first 0.1 for the while loop as shown below. We used 0.1 so that it will stop when the water supply is very close to 0. We didn't use 0, because the object won't shrink down to exactly 0 or less than 0, but it will get very close. If you were to use 0, then the animation would never stop since it will never become exactly 0 and the width of an object won't become negative.

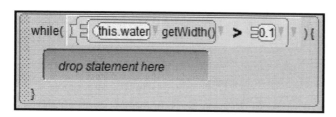

5. Then, inside the while loop, let's set the width of the water so that it shrinks. We can do this by setting the width as the width minus 0.1. Drag the **setWidth** procedure for the water onto the editor inside of your loop. You will need to select a number first as a placeholder, then drag the **getWidth** function from the water onto the placeholder number. After you have this, you can drop down next to the getWidth function, select **Math**, then select **water.getWidth() - ???**, and then choose **Custom DecimalNumber** and type in **0.1**.

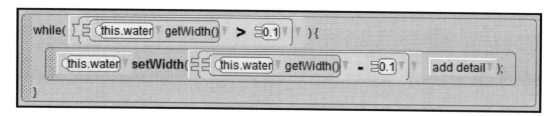

6. Run your code to see what happens. The water shrinks, but the tree doesn't grow. We need to add the code to make the tree grow as the water supply shrinks. Select the tree and drag the **setHeight** procedure for the tree under the water setWidth procedure inside the loop. Select a default placeholder for the size. We will need to change this placeholder so that we can get the current size of the tree and add to that current size. To do this we will need to select the **getHeight** function for the tree and drag this onto the placeholder. Then, we will click on the drop down next to the getHeight function and select **Math**, then **tree.getHeight + ???**, and finally choose **Custom DecimalNumber** and type in **0.1**.

7. Now, the ending code should look as follows:

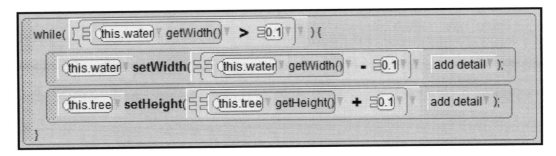

8. Run the animation. The water supply should shrink and the tree should grow, then the water supply should shrink, and the tree should grow, this will continue to happen as long as there is water.

9. Adjust the size of the water supply, does the tree grow taller? Shrink the water supply, does the tree stay short? Adjust the tree size to see if the animation still works.

10. Transfer this program into NetBeans. Open the Scene.java and scroll down to the bottom. Your code in myFirstMethod should look as follows:

```java
public void myFirstMethod() {
    while (water.getWidth() > 0.1) {
        water.setWidth(water.getWidth() - 0.1);
        tree.setHeight(tree.getHeight() + 0.1);
    }
}
```

Exercise 3: While Loop to Sum and Average Numbers

1. Open NetBeans and begin a new project called **Average**

2. This is a simple program with a **while** loop inside of the main method. Type the following Java program into NetBeans.

```java
import javax.swing.JOptionPane;

public class Average {
    public static void main(String[] args) {
        double number=0;
        double sum = 0;
        String input;
        while(number != 0){
            input = JOptionPane.showInputDialog(null,
                    "Enter a number to sum (enter 0 to stop):");
            number = Double.parseDouble(input);
            sum += number;
            System.out.println("The sum is " + sum );
        }
    }
}
```

3. Why doesn't this work? The while loop won't execute if the number variable is 0. Since we start the number variable at 0, this causes the while loop to never execute.

4. Set the **number** variable at **-1** to get it to execute. The loop will continue as long as the number variable is not 0. The user enters a number into the input message box and this String is then converted to a double. If the user enters 0 (number variable) then the loop will stop. The number that the user entered is then added to the sum and then the result is displayed in the output window. The number, sum, and input variables are declared before the while loop so that they are not reinitialized every time through the loop. If you define variables inside a set of curly braces, they are local to (can only be used inside) that set of curly braces. The variable number is set at -1 to start the program because it will be tested to see if it is 0 to determine whether the loop should run. If number was set at 0 to start, the loop would never execute.

5. If you wanted you could change your while loop to a do/while loop and then you could set your number variable at 0 without having to worry about the loop executing the first time.

```java
import javax.swing.JOptionPane;

public class Average {
    public static void main(String[] args) {
        double number=0;
        double sum = 0;
        String input;
        do {
            input = JOptionPane.showInputDialog(null,
                    "Enter a number to sum (enter 0 to stop):");
            number = Double.parseDouble(input);
            sum += number;
            System.out.println("The sum is " + sum );
        } while (number != 0);
    }
}
```

6. The program was printing the sum each time through the loop (each time a new number was entered). We can move the println method after the loop so that it just prints the final sum after all the numbers were totaled.

```java
import javax.swing.JOptionPane;

public class Average {
    public static void main(String[] args) {
        double number=0;
        double sum = 0;
        String input;
        do {
            input = JOptionPane.showInputDialog(null,
                    "Enter a number to sum (enter 0 to stop):");
            number = Double.parseDouble(input);
            sum += number;
        } while (number != 0);
        System.out.println("The sum is " + sum );
    }
}
```

7. Now, how could we find the average? We don't know how many times the loop is going to execute when the program is run. We must keep track of how many times the loop executes so that we can divide the sum by the total number of times that the loop executes. We will create a variable called **times**. This variable will be declared with the other variables before the loop and will be incremented inside the loop by stating **times++**. We will need to test that the number that the user entered was not 0 (number that stops loop) before we add one to the **times** variable. The user has to enter a 0 to stop the loop and you don't want to include this 0 as a number that you are tallying. Your program should look as follows:

```java
import javax.swing.JOptionPane;

public class Average {
    public static void main(String[] args) {
        double number=0;
        double sum = 0;
        String input;
        int times=0;
        do {
            input = JOptionPane.showInputDialog(null,
                    "Enter a number to sum (enter 0 to stop):");
            number = Double.parseDouble(input);
            sum += number;
            if (number != 0){
                times++;
            }
        } while (number != 0);
        System.out.println("The sum is " + sum);
    }
}
```

8. Now, we must add the average to our println method.

```java
import javax.swing.JOptionPane;

public class Average {
    public static void main(String[] args) {
        double number = 0;
        double sum = 0;
        String input;
        int times = 0;
        do {
            input = JOptionPane.showInputDialog(null,
                    "Enter a number to sum (enter 0 to stop):");
            number = Double.parseDouble(input);
            sum += number;
            if (number != 0) {
                times++;
            }
        } while (number != 0);
        System.out.println("The sum is " + sum
                + "\nThe average is " + sum / times);
    }
}
```

9. Run your program to test that it works.

10. Close your project.

Exercise 4: For Loop to Print 99 Bottles of Soda Song

1. Open NetBeans and begin a new project called **BottlesOfSoda**.

2. This program is modeled after the "99 Bottles of Beer" song. We are going to use soda instead of beer. Add your comments to the top of the program.

```
/* This program will write the "99 Bottles of Soda" song
 * using a method and for loop
 * Name and Date
 * JDK Version
 */
```

3. This song repeats the following verse over and over again until you get to 0 bottles of soda.

   99 bottles of soda on the wall, 99 of bottles of soda.
   Take one down and pass it around, 98 of bottles of soda on the wall.

4. Since this song repeats this verse over and over again, we can write the verse in a method so that it can be reused.

```
public static void printBottlesVerse(int numberOfBottles) {
    System.out.println(numberOfBottles
            + " bottles of soda on the wall, "
            + numberOfBottles + " of bottles of soda."
            + "\nTake one down and pass it around, "
            + (numberOfBottles - 1)
            + " of bottles of soda on the wall.\n");
}
```

5. We need to call this printBottlesVerse from the main method. You need to pass a whole number into the printBottleVerse. Pass **99** for now as shown below:

```
public static void main(String[] args) {
    printBottlesVerse(99);
}
```

This will give you the following output:

```
99 bottles of soda on the wall, 99 of bottles of soda.
Take one down and pass it around, 98 of bottles of soda on the wall.
```

6. We do not want to call this method with 98, 97, 96, 95, 94…. This would be very inefficient. We could use a **for** loop to repeat this verse. We would start the for loop at 99 (int x=99) since that is what number the song starts with and we would subtract 1 from our number each time through the loop (x--). We would continue the loop (Boolean condition/test) until the number got to 0 (x > 0). Add the following code:

```
public static void main(String[] args) {
    for (int x = 99; x > 0; x--) {
        printBottlesVerse(x);
    }
}
```

7. Run your program. It should print the song from 99 bottles to 0 bottles of soda.

8. The song should end with the following verse:

```
Go to the store and buy some more,
99 bottles of soda on the wall.
```

Add a println statement in the main method after the for loop. You don't want to put it in the for loop or else it will print this statement after each verse of your song.

```
System.out.println("Go to the store and buy some more, " +
        "\n99 bottles of soda on the wall.\n");
```

9. Your finished program should look as follows:

```
/* This program will write the "99 Bottles of Soda" song
 * using a method and for loop
 * Name and Date
 * JDK Version
 */

public class BottlesOfSoda {

    public static void main(String[] args) {
        for (int x = 99; x > 0; x--) {
            printBottlesVerse(x);
        }
        System.out.println("Go to the store and buy some more, "
                + "\n99 bottles of soda on the wall.\n");
    }

    public static void printBottlesVerse(int numberOfBottles) {
        System.out.println(numberOfBottles
                + " bottles of soda on the wall, "
                + numberOfBottles + " of bottles of soda."
                + "\nTake one down and pass it around, "
                + (numberOfBottles - 1)
                + " of bottles of soda on the wall.\n");
    }
}
```

Exercise 5: For Loop to Print Checkerboard

1. Open NetBeans and begin a new project called **Checkerboard**.

2. We will create the basic frame for our checkerboard. We will need to add our GUI imports for drawing and a container. We will then create our frame and container and set the properties for the frame (size, location, etc.). You will need to type in the following code:

```java
import java.awt.*;
import javax.swing.*;

public class Checkerboard extends JComponent {
    JFrame frame = new JFrame("Checkerboard");
    Container content = frame.getContentPane();


    public static void main(String[] args) {
        Checkerboard drawing = new Checkerboard();
        drawing.setUp();
    }

    public void setUp() {
        content.setBackground(Color.WHITE);
        content.add(this);

        frame.setSize(220, 240);
        frame.setLocationRelativeTo(null);
        frame.setDefaultCloseOperation(JFrame.EXIT_ON_CLOSE);
        frame.setVisible(true);
    }
}
```

3. Now, we need to create a paintComponent method (as follows) so that we can draw our squares for the checkerboard.

```java
public void paintComponent(Graphics g){

}
```

4. Next, we need to add a *for* loop inside the paintComponent method that will print 1 column of 5 rows. The **x** variable won't change since we are adding rows, not columns. The **y** variable will adjust by 40 pixels to allow for the previous squares above it since each square has a height of 40 pixels.

```
@Override
public void paintComponent(Graphics g) {
    for (int r = 0; r < 5; r++) {
        int x = 0;
        int y = r * 40;
        g.drawRect(x, y, 40, 40);
    }
}
```

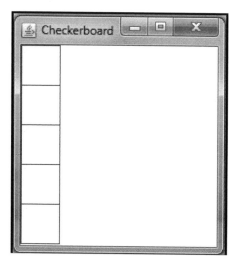

5. Then, we will add our columns to our checkerboard. We will need to create an inner loop for this, also known as a nested loop. The inner loop will handle the columns and will adjust the **x** variable by 40 pixels to allow for the previous squares to the left of it since each square has a width of 40 pixels.

```
@Override
public void paintComponent(Graphics g) {
    for (int r = 0; r < 5; r++) {
        for(int c = 0; c < 5; c++){
            int x = c * 40;
            int y = r * 40;
            g.drawRect(x, y, 40, 40);
        }
    }
}
```

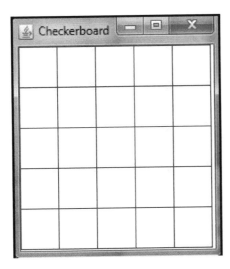

6. Now, we need to change the drawRect method to a **fillRect** to make it look more like a checkerboard. If we use fillRect for every square, then the whole checkboard will be filled it. We need to determine whether to draw a black square based on the row and column. If the row and column added together is not divisible by 2, then we fill a black square on the checkerboard.

```java
@Override
public void paintComponent(Graphics g) {
    for (int r = 0; r < 5; r++) {
        for(int c = 0; c < 5; c++){
            int x = c * 40;
            int y = r * 40;
            if((r+c) % 2 != 0){
                g.fillRect(x, y, 40, 40);
            }
        }
    }
}
```

Logic behind filling in the black squares:

Row	Column	Row + Column	Draw Filled Rectangle (Row + Column) is not divisible by 2
0	0	0	No
0	1	1	Yes
0	2	2	No
0	3	3	Yes
0	4	4	No
0	5	5	Yes
1	0	1	Yes
1	1	2	No
1	2	3	Yes
1	3	4	No
1	4	5	Yes
1	5	6	No
2	0	2	No
2	1	3	Yes
2	2	4	No
2	3	5	Yes
2	4	6	No
2	5	7	Yes
Etc.			

7. If you wanted to adjust the colors of the board you could add the following code:

```java
@Override
public void paintComponent(Graphics g) {
    for (int r = 0; r < 5; r++) {
        for(int c = 0; c < 5; c++){
            int x = c * 40;
            int y = r * 40;
            if((r+c) % 2 != 0){
                g.setColor(Color.BLUE);
                g.fillRect(x, y, 40, 40);
            } else {
                g.setColor(Color.CYAN);
                g.fillRect(x, y, 40, 40);
            }
        }
    }
}
```

8. The finished program should look as follows:

```java
import java.awt.*;
import javax.swing.*;
public class Checkerboard extends JComponent {
    JFrame frame = new JFrame("Checkerboard");
    Container content = frame.getContentPane();
    public static void main(String[] args) {
        Checkerboard drawing = new Checkerboard();
        drawing.setUp();
    }
    public void setUp() {
        content.setBackground(Color.WHITE);
        content.add(this);
        frame.setSize(220, 240);
        frame.setLocationRelativeTo(null);
        frame.setDefaultCloseOperation(JFrame.EXIT_ON_CLOSE);
        frame.setVisible(true);
    }
    public void paintComponent(Graphics g) {
        for (int r = 0; r < 5; r++) {
            for(int c = 0; c < 5; c++){
                int x = c * 40;
                int y = r * 40;
                if((r+c) % 2 != 0){
                    g.setColor(Color.BLUE);
                    g.fillRect(x, y, 40, 40);
                } else {
                    g.setColor(Color.CYAN);
                    g.fillRect(x, y, 40, 40);
                }
            }
        }
    }
}
```

Exercise 6: For Loop to Print Piano

1. Open NetBeans and begin a new project called **PianoKeys**.

2. We will create the basic frame for our piano. We will need to add our GUI imports for drawing and a container. We will then create our frame and container and set the properties for the frame (size, location, etc.). You will need to type in the following code:

```java
import java.awt.*;
import javax.swing.*;

public class PianoKeys extends JComponent {

    JFrame frame = new JFrame("Piano");
    Container content = frame.getContentPane();

    public static void main(String[] args) {
        PianoKeys drawing = new PianoKeys();
        drawing.setUp();
    }

    public void setUp() {
        content.setBackground(Color.WHITE);
        content.add(this);

        frame.setSize(300, 110);
        frame.setDefaultCloseOperation(JFrame.EXIT_ON_CLOSE);
        frame.setVisible(true);
    }
}
```

3. Now, we need to create a paintComponent method (as follows) so that we can draw our rectangles for the piano keys. You can add the override annotation to make the NetBeans hint disappear (yellow line and light bulb).

```java
public void paintComponent(Graphics g){

}
```

4. Next, we need to add a **for** loop to the paintComponent method that will print 14 piano keys of the same size. The first argument of the drawRect method is the x coordinate. You should multiply the **i** variable by 20 to get the x coordinate to change each time through the loop. The first time through the loop x will be 0, next it will be 20, then 40, etc. The y coordinate will not change since all of the piano keys are at the same level across the y plane. The size of the keys will be a width of 20 and a height of 60.

```
@Override
public void paintComponent(Graphics g){
    for (int i = 0; i < 14; i++) {
        g.drawRect(i * 20, 0, 20, 60);
    }
}
```

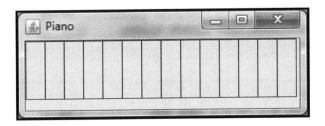

5. Next, we are going to add an **if** statement inside the **for** loop that checks to see if we need to add a black key. Inside the **if** statement we need to draw a rectangle and fill it in with the default color of black. The filled rectangle is only drawn when the variable **i** is not 0, 3, 7, and 10.

```
@Override
public void paintComponent(Graphics g){
    for (int i = 0; i < 14; i++) {
        g.drawRect(i * 20, 0, 20, 60);
        if (i!=0 && i!=3 && i!=7 && i!=10) {
            g.fillRect(i * 20 - 5, 0, 10, 30);
        }
    }
}
```

You could have listed all of the keys that should be drawn instead of those that should not be drawn for your conditional statement, but this would take more code. If you listed every black key, you would need to list 10 instead of 4. It would look as follows:

if (i==1 || i==2 || i==4 || i==5 || i==6 || i==8 || i==9 || i==11 || i==12 || i==13)

The && switches to an || because it is impossible for the variable **i** to be equal to all of the criteria at the same time.

6. The finished program should look as follows:

```java
import java.awt.*;
import javax.swing.*;

public class PianoKeys extends JComponent {

    JFrame frame = new JFrame("Piano");
    Container content = frame.getContentPane();

    public static void main(String[] args) {
        PianoKeys drawing = new PianoKeys();
        drawing.setUp();
    }

    public void setUp() {
        content.setBackground(Color.WHITE);
        content.add(this);

        frame.setSize(300, 110);
        frame.setDefaultCloseOperation(JFrame.EXIT_ON_CLOSE);
        frame.setVisible(true);
    }

    @Override
    public void paintComponent(Graphics g){
        for (int i = 0; i < 14; i++) {
            g.drawRect(i * 20, 0, 20, 60);
            if (i!=0 && i!=3 && i!=7 && i!=10) {
                g.fillRect(i * 20 - 5, 0, 10, 30);
            }
        }
    }
}
```

Exercise 7: For Loop to Animate Text

1. Open NetBeans and begin a new project called **TextAnimation**.

2. We will create the basic frame for our checkerboard. We will need to add our GUI imports for drawing and a container. We will then create our frame and container and set the properties for the frame (size, location, etc.). You will need to type in the following code:

```java
import java.awt.*;
import javax.swing.*;

public class TextAnimation extends JComponent {
    JFrame frame = new JFrame("Text Animation");
    Container content = frame.getContentPane();

    public static void main(String[] args) {
        TextAnimation drawing = new TextAnimation();
        drawing.setUp();
    }

    public void setUp() {
        content.setBackground(Color.WHITE);
        content.add(this);

        frame.setSize(500, 300);
        frame.setLocationRelativeTo(null);
        frame.setDefaultCloseOperation(JFrame.EXIT_ON_CLOSE);
        frame.setVisible(true);
    }
}
```

3. Next, we need to add the paintComponent method that will display text on the GUI. This paint method is going to set the font, color, and words that will display on the GUI. We are going to use a variable for the size of the font, the color of the font (red, green, and blue that make up the color), and the location (x and y) of the text. These variables will be declared at the top of the class so that all the methods in this class will have access to the variables (global).

```java
import java.awt.*;
import javax.swing.*;

public class TextAnimation extends JComponent {
    JFrame frame = new JFrame("Text Animation");
    Container content = frame.getContentPane();
    int x = 112;
    int y = 50;
    int red = 0;
    int green = 255;
    int blue = 255;
    int size = 8;
    int index = 1;
    public static void main(String[] args) {
        TextAnimation drawing = new TextAnimation();
        drawing.setUp();
    }
    public void setUp() {
        content.setBackground(Color.WHITE);
        content.add(this);

        frame.setSize(500, 300);
        frame.setLocationRelativeTo(null);
        frame.setDefaultCloseOperation(JFrame.EXIT_ON_CLOSE);
    }
    @Override
    public void paintComponent(Graphics g) {
        g.setFont(new Font("TimesRoman", Font.BOLD, size));
        g.setColor(new Color(red, green, blue));
        g.drawString("Java is fun!", x, y);
    }
}
```

4. The text is going to start off small and then we are going to animate it and have it grow in size, change color, and change location. To do this, we will add an animate method to our program as follows. Place this animate method after your paint method (it really doesn't matter where you place it as long as it is within the class and outside of your other methods). This method is going to print "Java is fun!" 37 times. The *for* loop will execute 37 times. Each time it will pause (Thread.sleep), call the paint method again using a method called repaint, change the location of the text (move it over to the left and down), change the color of the text, and change the size of the text. The following line pauses the animation for 100 milliseconds.

```java
public void animate(){
    for (index=1; index<=37; index++) {
        try { Thread.sleep(100); } catch (InterruptedException e) {}
        repaint();
        x -= 3;
        y += 2;
        red += 5;
        green -= 5;
        size += 2;
    }
}
```

5. Call (invoke) the animate method from within the SetUp method as shown below:

```java
public void setUp() {
    content.setBackground(Color.WHITE);
    content.add(this);

    frame.setSize(500, 300);
    frame.setLocationRelativeTo(null);
    frame.setDefaultCloseOperation(JFrame.EXIT_ON_CLOSE);
    frame.setVisible(true);
    animate();
}
```

6. Run the program to save and test it.

7. Close your project.

Exercise 8: Card Game with Loops (ongoing exercise)

1. Open NetBeans with the **CardGame** from the hands on exercise in Chapter 6. Copy this file to the appropriate chapter folder with the name CardGame.

2. Run the program several times to see that it works. Are the cards randomized? Are the WIN signs displaying appropriately. Do the scores add correctly?

3. There are several pieces of this program that would be improved by using loops. The first piece that we will adjust will be in myFirstMethod. Open the **Scene.java** file and scroll down to **myFirstMethod**.

4. The section of code that creates two random numbers needs adjusted. Currently, it creates 2 random numbers and then with an *if* statement it determines if the first two numbers were identical. However, it is possible that even after creating another random number that they are still identical. It could possibly create the random number of 5 over and over again but are existing code wouldn't solve the problem of ALWAYS having two different numbers. We want to keep creating 2 random numbers UNTIL our 2 random numbers are not equal. OR… another way of saying the same thing is that we want to keep creating 2 random numbers as long as the 2 numbers we created are identical. This lends itself to a *do while* loop. Our original code was:

```
randomNumber1 = (int) (Math.random() * 10 + 1);
randomNumber2 = (int) (Math.random() * 10 + 1);
if (randomNumber1 == randomNumber2) {
    randomNumber1 = (int) (Math.random() *10 +1);
}
```

5. This code can be changed to a DO WHILE loop as follows:

```
do {
    randomNumber1 = (int) (Math.random() * 10 + 1);
    randomNumber2 = (int) (Math.random() * 10 + 1);
} while (randomNumber1 == randomNumber2);
```

6. The previous step says to repeat generating randomNumber1 and randomNumber2 as long as they are both equal. As soon as 2 different random numbers are generated, the do while loop will be terminated and go to the next statement in the program. You will also need to change the second game done in myFirstMethod to have this same *do while* loop:

```java
    public void myFirstMethod() {//Card Game created by
//on date here
//This program will deal out cards, display winner, and then cards disappear
        int scorePlayer1 = 0;
        int scorePlayer2 = 0;
        int randomNumber1, randomNumber2;
        PlayingCard firstCard, secondCard;
        do {
            randomNumber1 = (int) (Math.random() * 10 + 1);
            randomNumber2 = (int) (Math.random() * 10 + 1);
        } while (randomNumber1 == randomNumber2);

        firstCard = determinePlayingCard (randomNumber1);
        secondCard = determinePlayingCard (randomNumber2);
        this.dealOutCards(firstCard, secondCard);
        if (randomNumber1 > randomNumber2) {
            scorePlayer1 ++;
            displayWinner(winPlayer1Sign, player1ScoreSign, scorePlayer1);
        } else {
            scorePlayer2 ++;
            displayWinner(winPlayer2Sign, player2ScoreSign, scorePlayer2);
        }
        this.disappearCards(firstCard, secondCard);

        do {
            randomNumber1 = (int) (Math.random() * 10 + 1);
            randomNumber2 = (int) (Math.random() * 10 + 1);
        } while (randomNumber1 == randomNumber2);
        firstCard = determinePlayingCard (randomNumber1);
        secondCard = determinePlayingCard (randomNumber2);
        this.dealOutCards(firstCard, secondCard);
        if (randomNumber1 > randomNumber2) {
            scorePlayer1 ++;
            displayWinner(winPlayer1Sign, player1ScoreSign, scorePlayer1);
        } else {
            scorePlayer2 ++;
            displayWinner(winPlayer2Sign, player2ScoreSign, scorePlayer2);
        }
        this.disappearCards(firstCard, secondCard);
    }
```

7. Another section of the program that would be improved by a loop would be the method called displayWinner as follows:

```
public void displayWinner(TextModel winSign, TextModel scoreSign,
    int transferredScore) {
    /*do in order*/ {//display winner
        winSign.setOpacity(1.0, SetOpacity.duration(1.0));
        winSign.setOpacity(0.0, SetOpacity.duration(1.0));
        winSign.setOpacity(1.0, SetOpacity.duration(1.0));
        winSign.setOpacity(0.0, SetOpacity.duration(1.0));
        winSign.setOpacity(1.0, SetOpacity.duration(1.0));
        winSign.setOpacity(0.0, SetOpacity.duration(1.0));
        scoreSign.setValue("Score: " + transferredScore);
    }
}
```

8. You will notice that the setting of the opacity of the WIN! flashing repeats itself 3 times. A *for* loop would work well for this section. For loops are great looping mechanisms when you know the exact number of times you want to complete the loop. The *for* loop in this method would begin x at 1, add 1 to x each time it executes the loop, and end when x is no longer less than or equal to 3. This means the following *for* loop will execute exactly 3 times:

```
public void displayWinner(TextModel winSign, TextModel scoreSign,
    int transferredScore) {
    /*do in order*/ {//display winner
        for (int x =1 ; x <=3 ; x++)
        {
            winSign.setOpacity(1.0, SetOpacity.duration(1.0));
            winSign.setOpacity(0.0, SetOpacity.duration(1.0));
        }
        scoreSign.setValue("Score: " + transferredScore);
    }
}
```

9. Adjust this *for* loop to repeat the flashing exactly 5 times but faster by also changing the duration to be .5 instead of 1.0. Make any further adjustments that you feel improve this loop.

10. The last section of the program that would be improved with a loop would be the entire myFirstMethod. Currently, it is repeating the exact same code for the first game and the second game as follows:

```java
    public void myFirstMethod() {//Card Game created by
//on date here
//This program will deal out cards, display winner, and then cards disappear
       int scorePlayer1 = 0;
       int scorePlayer2 = 0;
       int randomNumber1, randomNumber2;
       PlayingCard firstCard, secondCard;
       do {
           randomNumber1 = (int) (Math.random() * 10 + 1);
           randomNumber2 = (int) (Math.random() * 10 + 1);
       } while (randomNumber1 == randomNumber2);

       firstCard = determinePlayingCard (randomNumber1);
       secondCard = determinePlayingCard (randomNumber2);
       this.dealOutCards(firstCard, secondCard);
       if (randomNumber1 > randomNumber2) {
           scorePlayer1 ++;
           displayWinner(winPlayer1Sign, player1ScoreSign, scorePlayer1);
       } else {
           scorePlayer2 ++;
           displayWinner(winPlayer2Sign, player2ScoreSign, scorePlayer2);
       }
       this.disappearCards(firstCard, secondCard);

       do {
           randomNumber1 = (int) (Math.random() * 10 + 1);
           randomNumber2 = (int) (Math.random() * 10 + 1);
       } while (randomNumber1 == randomNumber2);
       firstCard = determinePlayingCard (randomNumber1);
       secondCard = determinePlayingCard (randomNumber2);
       this.dealOutCards(firstCard, secondCard);
       if (randomNumber1 > randomNumber2) {
           scorePlayer1 ++;
           displayWinner(winPlayer1Sign, player1ScoreSign, scorePlayer1);
       } else {
           scorePlayer2 ++;
           displayWinner(winPlayer2Sign, player2ScoreSign, scorePlayer2);
       }
       this.disappearCards(firstCard, secondCard);
    }
```

11. The card game is played twice because we repeated the code twice. However, we would like the cardGame to be played 5 times. Do we really want to repeat the code 5 times? What if we wanted to play the game 100 times? We definitely don't want to repeat the code 100 times. If you know the exact number of times you want to repeat statements, the *for* loop works well. You just set the *for* statement to work for the number of times you want to the loop so if we want it to play 5 times, we would have:

   for (int a = 1 ; a<=5; a++)   {

12. Look at what code is repeating and that is the code that goes inside of the *for* loop. You will need an ending curly brace } to end the for loop. You will also need to get rid of the repeated code that is now unnecessary. You may want to clean up your indents by using SOURCE menu and then FORMAT. Your entire myFirstMethod should look as follows:

```java
    public void myFirstMethod() {//Card Game created by
//on date here
//This program will deal out cards, display winner, and then cards disappear
        int scorePlayer1 = 0;
        int scorePlayer2 = 0;
        int randomNumber1, randomNumber2;
        PlayingCard firstCard, secondCard;
        for (int a = 1; a <= 5; a++) {
            do {
                randomNumber1 = (int) (Math.random() * 10 + 1);
                randomNumber2 = (int) (Math.random() * 10 + 1);
            } while (randomNumber1 == randomNumber2);
            firstCard = determinePlayingCard(randomNumber1);
            secondCard = determinePlayingCard(randomNumber2);
            this.dealOutCards(firstCard, secondCard);
            if (randomNumber1 > randomNumber2) {
                scorePlayer1++;
                displayWinner(winPlayer1Sign, player1ScoreSign, scorePlayer1);
            } else {
                scorePlayer2++;
                displayWinner(winPlayer2Sign, player2ScoreSign, scorePlayer2);
            }
            this.disappearCards(firstCard, secondCard);
        }

    }
```

13. Run the program to see if it works. Are the cards randomized? Do the WIN signs flash rapidly 5 times? Are the scores working properly? Did it play exactly 5 games? Everything should be working fine. Make sure you save this program properly.

Summary

- The syntax for a **while loop** is:

      while (Boolean condition) {
          repeated statements
      }

- The syntax for a **do-while loop** is:

      do {
          repeated statements
      } while   (Boolean condition)

- The syntax for a **for loop** is:

      for (initialization; Boolean condition;   increment) {
          statements;
      }

Review Questions

1. Which of the following *for* statements could be used to print all the numbers from 1 to 19 inclusive?

   a. for (int i =0; i<=19; i++)
   b. for (int i =1; i<=19; i++)
   c. for (int i =1; i<=19; i+=2)
   d. for (int i =1; i<19; i+=2)

2. Which of the following *for* statements could be used to print all even numbers from 2 to 20 inclusive?

   a. for (int i = 0; i<=20 ; i++)
   b. for (int i = 2; i<=20 ; i++)
   c. for (int i = 2; i<20 ; i+=2)
   d. for (int i = 2; i<=20 ; i+=2)

3. In the following program, what values for k will be displayed during print?

```
 1: public class ForSample1
 2: {
 3:   public static void main (String args [] )
 4:   {
 5:     int sum = 0;
 6:     for ( int k = 1;   k < 10;  k++ )
 7:     {
 8:       sum = sum + k;
 9:       System.out.println ("sum is " + sum + " and k is " + k );
10:     }// ends for loop
11:   }// ends main method
12: }// ends program
```

   a. 0, 1, 2, 3, 4, 5, 6, 7, 8, 9, 10
   b. 1, 2, 3, 4, 5, 6, 7, 8, 9, 10
   c. 1, 2, 3, 4, 5, 6, 7, 8, 9
   d. program does not compile

4. In the following program, what values for sum will be displayed during print?

```
1: public class ForSample1
2: {
3:    public static void main (String args [] )
4:    {
5:      int sum = 0;
6:      for ( int k = 1;   k < 10;   k++ )
7:      {
8:        sum = sum + k;
9:        System.out.println ("sum is " + sum + " and k is " + k );
10:     }// ends for loop
11:   }// ends main method
12: }// ends program
```

    a. 0, 1, 3, 6, 10, 15, 21, 28, 36, 45

    b. 1, 3, 6, 10, 15, 21, 28, 36, 45

    c. 1, 3, 6, 10, 15, 21, 28, 36, 45, 55

    d. program does not compile

5. In the following program, what values for number will be displayed during print?

```
1: public class WhileSample1
2: {
3:    public static void main (String args [] )
4:    {
5:      int number =1;
6:      while ( number <=10)
7:      {
8:          System.out.println ("The number is " + number);
9:          number = number + 2;
10:     }// ends while loop
11:   }// ends main method
12: }// ends program
```

    a. 1, 2, 3, 4, 5, 6, 7, 8, 9, 10

    b. 1, 3, 5, 7, 9, 11

    c. 0, 2, 4, 6, 8, 10

    d. 1, 3, 5, 7, 9

Solutions: 1)b   2)d   3)c   4)b   5)d

Assignments

9-1   **Guessing Game with a Loop**: The previous guessing game program allowed the user to guess the computer's randomly generated number between 1 and 100 and then displays to the user if they guessed correctly, incorrectly, or didn't follow the directions. This would be a better game if the user was allowed to continue to guess until they guessed the correct number.

```java
import javax.swing.JOptionPane;

public class GuessingGame {
    public static void main(String[] args) {
        // generate a random number from 1 to 100
        int computerNumber = (int) (Math.random() * 100 + 1);
        //display the correct guess for testing purposes
        System.out.println("The correct guess would be " + computerNumber);
        String response = JOptionPane.showInputDialog(null,
                "Enter a guess between 1 and 100");
        int userAnswer = Integer.parseInt(response);
        JOptionPane.showMessageDialog(null, determineGuess(userAnswer, computerNumber));
    }
    public static String determineGuess(int userAnswer, int computerNumber) {
        String message = null;
        if (userAnswer <= 0 || userAnswer > 100) {
            message = "Invalid guess";
        } else if (userAnswer == computerNumber) {
            message = "Correct";
        } else {
            message = "Incorrect";
        }
        return message;
    }
}
```

Adjustments to be made to guessing game program:
- Adjust the program so that it uses a loop to allow the user to repeat guessing until they get the answer right. You can use a **for** loop, a **while** loop, or a **do/while** loop…it's your choice as long as it works. In this guessing game, the user should be prompted to type in a number as long as long as the user's answer doesn't match the number generated by the computer. This can be done in the main method.
- To adjust this program further, adjust and add lines to "count" the number of guesses that a user has taken. Create an integer variable called **count** to keep track of how many guesses a user has taken. Each time a user guesses, we will need to add 1 to the count variable. Display the number of guesses each time you tell the user whether their guess is correct, incorrect, or invalid. This should be added to the JOptionPane message box that is displayed in the main method.
- Instead of just testing for an incorrect number, you should determine if the guess is too high or low. If the user's guess is too low, you should display a message box that lets the user know that their guess is too low. If the user's guess is too high, you should display a message box that lets the user know that their guess is too high.

9-2   Adjust the CardGame completed in the hands on project in this chapter, to have the user input the number of times they would like to play the game via a JOptionPane. The *for* loop should then be adjusted appropriately.

Chapter 10

Arrays

Objectives

- ☑ Declare and use arrays in programs.
- ☑ Access array elements within an array.
- ☑ Calculate the sum, largest number, smallest number, and average of a group of numbers by using an array.
- ☑ Setup a program to store the arguments from command line into an array.

Declaring and Creating Arrays

A Java **array** is a group of contiguous memory locations that all have the <u>same name</u> and the <u>same type</u>. You can have arrays of any type of information that can be stored as a variable. Unlike in other languages, however, Java arrays are actual objects that can be passed around and treated just like other objects.

Declaring an array

```
int [] temps;      // an integer array called temps
Boolean[] hostilePeople;   // an array of Booleans called hostilePeople
String difficultWords [];      //  an array of Strings called difficultWords
double examScores[];   // an array of doubles called examScores
```

Note: Java is flexible about where the square brackets are placed when an array is being created. You can put them after the variable name instead of after the variable type.

Creating Array Objects

The previous examples declare arrays and their types, but they do not store any values in them initially or mention their size. To do this, you must use the **new** statement along with the variable or object type. You also must specify how many different items will be stored in the array. Each item in an array is called an **element.** The following statement creates an array of integers named temps and sets aside space for 250 values that it will hold:

```
int [ ] temps =  new int [ 250 ] ;
```

Each element of the array is given an initial value when it is set up; the value depends on the type of the array. All numeric arrays have the value 0, char arrays have the value '\0', and Boolean arrays have the value false. A String array and all other objects are created with the value of null.

We can also create an array by listing the initial values within { } marks. In the following example, the number of elements in the array is not specified in the statement because it is set to the number of elements in the comma-separated list in curly braces. Each element of the array in the list must be the same type.

String [ ] reindeerNames = { "Dasher", "Dancer", "Prancer", "Vixen", "Comet", "Cupid", "Donner", "Blitzen" } ;

The above line creates a String array called reindeerNames with 8 initial values. By default the computer knows that this array will only have 8 values. This is a shortcut method which bypasses the *new* operator.

Accessing and Using Created Arrays

Accessing Array Elements

Once you have an array with initial values, you can test and change the values in each element of that array. The position number in square brackets is more formally called a <u>subscript</u>. Tricky part: The first element of an array is referred to with the subscript 0 so be careful. To get a value stored within an array, use the array subscript expression [ ]

myArray [31] = 42; // refers to the 32nd element of the array called myArray
arr [5] = 129;   // refers to the sixth element of the array called arr

Length of Array

Every Java array knows its own length. The programmer can get and use this length by specifying the name of the array and then a period and then the word length such as follows:

String c [ ] = { "Mary", "John", "Susan", "Robert" };
int x = c.length;   // where c is the name of the array

The above statements create an array called c. The [ ] tells you it is an array. It is an array containing Strings. The actual Strings to be placed into the array are Mary, John, Susan, and Robert. The compiler will review this and realize there will be exactly 4 elements in this array. Therefore, the length of this array will be 4. So, c.length will give you 4 which will be placed into the int x. However, the tricky part is knowing which subscript goes with which String. Array subscripts start at 0 so:

c [0] = "Mary";
c [1] = "John";
c [2] = "Susan";
c [3] = "Robert";

Summary: The length of the array called c is 4. c[2] is "Susan" instead of "John" as you might expect.

Here is a sample program using an int array:

```
// sample of program to put the numbers 5, 10, 15 etc. into 10 elements of array
public class SampleArray {

    public static void main(String args[]) {
        int number = 5;
        int myArray[] = new int[10]; // declares integer array of 10 elements
        for (int i = 0; i < 10; i++) {
            myArray[i] = number; // puts 5, 10, 15 into elements of myArray
            System.out.println("The " + i + " element of the array is "
                    + myArray[ i]);
            number += 5;
        }
    }
}
```

The following are the results of the program:

```
The 0 element of the array is 5
The 1 element of the array is 10
The 2 element of the array is 15
The 3 element of the array is 20
The 4 element of the array is 25
The 5 element of the array is 30
The 6 element of the array is 35
The 7 element of the array is 40
The 8 element of the array is 45
The 9 element of the array is 50
```

How could you change the FOR loop in the above program so that variable *number* is a part of the FOR loop instead of a separate statement inside the FOR loop?

```
// sample of program to put the numbers 5, 10, 15 etc. into 10 elements of array
public class SampleArray {

    public static void main(String args[]) {
        int myArray[] = new int[10]; // declares integer array of 10 elements
        for (int i = 0, number = 5; i < 10; i++, number += 5) {
            myArray[i] = number; // puts 5, 10, 15 into elements of myArray
            System.out.println("The " + i + " element of the array is "
                    + myArray[ i]);
        }
    }
}
```

In the above adjusted program, the line for *int number=5;* was moved down as part of the initialization in the *for* statement. The statement of *number +=5;* was moved to the increment part of the *for* statement instead of being a separate statement inside the loop.

We generally use arrays so that we can use a FOR loop to repeat some kind of processing of several variables/objects. For instance, say we have 5 variables called a, b, c, d and e. If we want a total of the values in these variables to be placed in a variable called sum, we could do the following:

```
sum = sum + a;
sum= sum + b;
sum = sum + c;
sum = sum + d;
sum = sum + e;
```

or we could also say

```
sum = sum + a + b + c + d + e;
```

If the values were in an int array called x, we could do the same thing as follows:

```
for ( i = 0;  i < 5 ; i++) {
        sum = sum + x [ i ];
}
```

My guess is that you are saying the first one looks easier, so the heck with arrays. How about if I say we have 1000 values and we want to total them. How complicated would it be without arrays vs. with arrays? Without arrays, you would need 1000 lines adding to sum or a very long arithmetic statement that is bound to have typos. With an array, you just change the i<5 to be i<1000 and you are done.

Note: Java does support multi dimensional arrays. To declare an array of multi dimensions, you use two brackets such as int temps[ ] [ ]; It works as if it were an array of arrays.

Hands-on Exercises

Exercise 1: Entering Scores into an Array

1. To gain practice with arrays, we are going to start a brand new program from scratch and add lines to it as we proceed. The name of this project and class should be **ArrayProgram1**. The simplest version of the program we are going to work with is as follows:

```
/* Calculate sum, average, min, and max from an array of scores
 * Written by
 * Written on
 * JDK Version */
import javax.swing.JOptionPane;
public class ArrayProgram1 {
    public static void main(String[] args) {
        // define array, sum, largest, and smallest variables
        int scores[] = {81, 92, 34, 89, 56};
        int sum = 0;
        //for loop to find sum, largest and smallest
        for (int i = 0; i < 5; i++) {
            sum = sum + scores[i];
        }
        //output
        JOptionPane.showMessageDialog(null, "The sum is " + sum);
    }
}
```

2. Get into NetBeans and start a new Java program. The name of the project and class should be: **ArrayProgram1**.

3. Type in the above program. Compile your program. Correct any typos that you made.

4. Execute this program. What did the program do? Did you get a sum of 352?

5. Now change the program to use different numbers in the array but keep with 5 values. What line will you change to do that? Compile it again and execute it again.

6. Think about how you would calculate the average of these numbers. You are already adding up the values and placing the total in a variable called sum. Now have the computer calculate the average (hint: there are 5 values) and display that average on the message box below the sum. What lines need adjusted? One possible answer is to adjust the message box as follows:

JOptionPane.showMessageDialog(null, "The sum is " + sum
        + "\nThe average is " + sum/5);

7. Adjust the program, compile it, and run it.

   Let's find the largest number in the array. We can do this by declaring an integer variable named **largest** after the declaration of the sum variable. We will initialize this *largest* variable using the smallest possible integer value possible (-2147483648). Using the smallest possible integer value possible ensures that any number that is found will be equal or greater than this number. If you arbitrarily choose a number to initialize the *largest* variable, it may turn out that your number is greater than the numbers in your array.

   int largest = Integer.MIN_VALUE;

   Note: MIN_VALUE is a constant property of the Integer class represented by -2147483648.

8. Inside the FOR loop, we will test each element to see if it is larger than the largest value we have seen so far and if it is larger we put the value of this element in largest:

   if (scores[i] > largest){
   **   largest = scores[i];**
   }

   Explanation of how the largest is found. Since *largest* variable is set to *MIN_VALUE* at beginning of main method, *largest* is really set to -2147483648. The above *if* statement is embedded in a for loop so the variable *i* will begin at 0 then become 1, then 2, etc. all the way to 5 but not including 5.

   1st loop with *i* variable being 0: The if statement will compare scores[0] which is 81 to largest which is also -2147483648. The condition is true and largest will be set to 81.
   2nd loop with *i* variable being 1: The if statement will compare scores[1] which is 92 to largest which is 81. The condition is true and largest will be set to 92.
   3rd loop with *i* variable being 2: The if statement will compare scores[2] which is 34 to largest which is 92. The condition is false and largest will stay 92
   4th loop with *i* variable being 3: The if statement will compare scores[3] which is 89 to largest which is 92. The condition is false and largest will stay 92.
   5th loop with *i* variable being 4: The if statement will compare scores[4] which is 56 to largest which is 92. The condition is false and largest will stay 92.

9. You will now need to add the largest to the message box. Try to figure this out yourself. Compile and run program. Did it work? Are you getting a total, average and correct largest score?

10. Next, we want to find the smallest number in array. You will need to declare a variable named **smallest**. Initialize the *smallest* variable to **Integer.MAX_VALUE** *(this value is 2147483647)*. Add conditional inside of the *for* loop (similar to the one for largest) that will test each element to see if it is smaller than the smallest so far. Last of all, you will need to add the smallest to the message box to display the smallest value in the array. Try to do this. Compile and run it. It should look as follows:

```java
/* Calculate sum, average, min, and max from an array of scores
 * Written by
 * Written on
 * JDK Version */
import javax.swing.JOptionPane;
public class ArrayProgram1 {
    public static void main(String[] args) {
        // define array, sum, largest, and smallest variables
        int scores[] = {81, 92, 34, 89, 56};
        int sum = 0;
        int largest = Integer.MIN_VALUE;
        int smallest = Integer.MAX_VALUE;
        //for loop to find sum, largest and smallest
        for (int i = 0; i < 5; i++) {
            sum = sum + scores[i];
            if (scores[i] > largest) {
                largest = scores[i];
            }
            if (scores[i] < smallest) {
                smallest = scores[i];
            }
        }
        //output
        JOptionPane.showMessageDialog(null, "The sum is " + sum
                + "\nThe average is " + sum/5
                + "\nThe largest number is " + largest
                + "\nThe smallest score is " + smallest);
    }
}
```

11. Now, how can we adjust the program so it will work no matter how many elements we enter? Currently, this program only works for specifically 5 elements in an array. This program can be made more generic by using the length of scores as scores.length. You will need to adjust the for loop statement to:

for (int i = 0; i <scores.length; i++)

Adjust the message box to:

JOptionPane.showMessageDialog(null, "The sum is " + sum
**   + "\nThe average is " + sum/scores.length**
**   + "\nThe largest score is " + largest**
**   + "\nThe smallest score is " + smallest);**

The correct answer for the above data is:

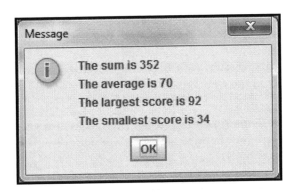

12. Now, adjust the following line to have your own 5 numbers:
    int scores[ ] = {81, 92, 34, 89, 56};

13. Test your program to see if it works. Try adding another number to your array. Does it still work? Adding the *scores.length* code to our program allowed for more flexibility. We can have as many numbers as we want in our array from this point on.

Exercise 2: Using Command Line Args Box to Enter Scores

In ArrayProgram1, the numbers you are using in your scores array are typed straight into the program. In ArrayProgram2, the scores are going to be entered via the arg box (command line).

1. Open the file you created in the previous exercise called ***ArrayProgram1.java*** in NetBeans.

2. Copy ArrayProgram1 and save the new copy as ***ArrayProgram2***.

3. When declaring the main method in all of your programs, you had to include an argument of (String args [ ]). You have been told in past to just do it. Now that you have learned about arrays, this is the time to now see what this means. The String args[ ] means that you have an array called args which will contain Strings. This data will come in on the command line if you are compiling programs using DOS and will come in as a special entry if using NetBeans. In the program (so far), the numbers you are using in your scores array are typed straight into the program. Then, the program must be compiled to get a proper class file. Then this class file is executed to get the results. Now, we will create the program generically so that the program will not need to be recompiled if you want to have a different set of numbers.

4. Replace the following line in program:
       int scores[] = {81, 92, 34, 89, 56};
   with:
       int scores[] = new int[args.length];

5. The above line means that you will have an integer array called scores and it will set the number of elements in this array to be whatever the length is of args.

   Note: args is the String array where we will be typing our numbers.

6. The values for the scores array are going to come into the program via the String array called args. However, we will need to convert each of these Strings to an integer and then place them into the integer array called scores. This is done with the following for loop:

   ```
   // for loop to convert String args array to integer scores array
     for (inta=0; a<scores.length; a++)  {
         scores[a] = Integer.parseInt(args[a]);
     }
   ```

7. The above for loop uses the integer variable called "**a**" to loop through each of the args elements and convert it to int and place it into the integer array called scores. Place this for loop immediately after the declaration of the scores array.

8. Your program should now look as follows:

```java
/* Calculate sum, average, min, and max from an array of scores
 * Written by
 * Written on
 * JDK Version */
import javax.swing.JOptionPane;
public class ArrayProgram2 {
    public static void main(String[] args) {
        // create array based on the number of args entered by user
        int scores[] = new int[args.length];
        // for loop to convert String args array to integer myArray
        for (int a = 0; a < args.length; a++) {
            scores[a] = Integer.parseInt(args[a]);
        }
        int sum = 0;
        int largest = Integer.MIN_VALUE;
        int smallest = Integer.MAX_VALUE;
        //for loop to find sum, largest and smallest
        for (int i = 0; i < scores.length; i++) {
            sum = sum + scores[i];
            if (scores[i] > largest) {
                largest = scores[i];
            }
            if (scores[i] < smallest) {
                smallest = scores[i];
            }
        }
        //output
        JOptionPane.showMessageDialog(null, "The sum is " + sum
                + "\nThe average is " + sum / scores.length
                + "\nThe largest number is " + largest
                + "\nThe smallest score is " + smallest);
    }
}
```

9. This program will be executed differently than you have done in past. You will need to tell NetBeans what arguments are coming in on the command line when you click on RUN. Click on the **Run** menu, select **Set Project Configuration**, then select **Customize**. Run should be selected on the left side of popup window and you should see a line called ARGUMENTS. Type your test scores separated by spaces into this line as follows:

    100 90 95 80 75 60 65 79 50 40

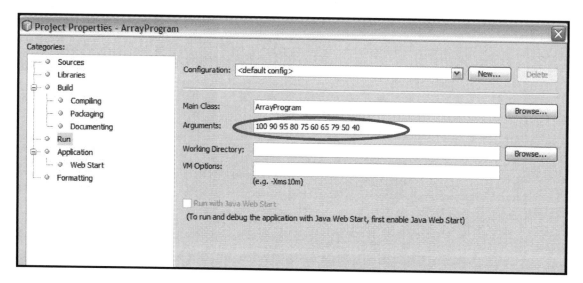

10. Click on **OK**.

11. Now, click on the **Run** button ▷ and you should get the following output:

    The sum is 734
    The average is 73
    The largest number is 100
    The smallest number is 40

12. Now, execute the program with just 6 numbers of: **9 46 11 15 21 50**. The computer takes the 6 numbers entered as Strings, converts them to integers and then proceeds to find the sum, average, largest, and smallest.

13. The advantage of this program is that we can change the numbers we want to use without touching the program. We can just execute it again and type in different numbers in the bottom box.

Exercise 3: Using JOptionPane to Enter Scores

In ArrayProgram1, the numbers you are using in your scores array are typed straight into the program. In ArrayProgram2, the scores are entered via the arg box (command line). In this program, we will enter the scores into the array through JOptionPane message boxes.

1. Open the file you created in the previous exercise called ***ArrayProgram2.java*** in NetBeans.

2. Copy ArrayProgram2 and save the new copy as ***ArrayProgram3***. Replace the following line in program:

   int scores[] = new int[args.length];

   With:

   String response = JOptionPane.showInputDialog(null, "Number of scores:");
   int number = Integer.parseInt(response);
   int scores[] = new int[number];

3. Replace the following loops:

   for (int a = 0; a <args.length; a++) {
       scores[a] = Integer.parseInt(args[a]);
   }

   With:
   for (int a = 0; a < number; a++) {
       response = JOptionPane.showInputDialog(null, "Enter score " + (a + 1));
       scores[a] = Integer.parseInt(response);
   }

4. The program should look as follows:

```
/* Calculate sum, average, min, and max from an array of scores
 * Name & Date
 * JDK Version */
import javax.swing.JOptionPane;
public class ArrayProgram3 {
    public static void main(String args[]) {
        String response = JOptionPane.showInputDialog(null, "Number of scores:");
        int number = Integer.parseInt(response);
        int scores[] = new int[number];
        // for loop to get the scores from the user and save them into the scores array
        for (int a = 0; a < number; a++) {
            response=JOptionPane.showInputDialog(null, "Enter score " + (a + 1));
            scores[a] = Integer.parseInt(response);
        }
        int sum = 0;
        int largest = Integer.MIN_VALUE;
        int smallest = Integer.MAX_VALUE;
        //for loop to find sum, largest and smallest
        for (int i = 0; i < scores.length; i++) {
            sum = sum + scores[i];
            if (scores[i] > largest) {
                largest = scores[i];
            }
            if (scores[i] < smallest) {
                smallest = scores[i];
            }
        }
        //output
        JOptionPane.showMessageDialog(null, "The sum is " + sum
                + "\nThe average is " + sum / scores.length
                + "\nThe largest number is " + largest
                + "\nThe smallest score is " + smallest);
    }
}
```

5. Compile the program. If you get errors, correct your typos.

6. Enter the following data into the dialog boxes:

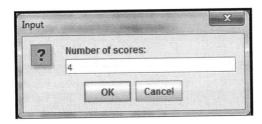

 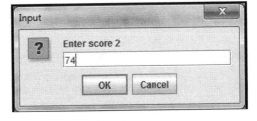

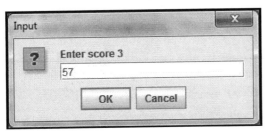 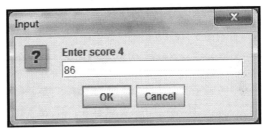

7. You should get the following output:

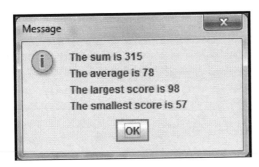

Exercise 4: Drawing Polygons

Polygons (odd shapes) can be drawn with the drawPolygon and fillPolygon methods of the Graphics class. To draw a polygon, you need x,y coordinates for each point on the polygon. Polygons can be thought of as a series of lines that are connected to each other -- one line is drawn from starting point to end point, that end point is used to start a new line, and so on. Once you have all the points you want to draw, you put all the x points into one array and then put all the y points into another array.

The syntax of the Graphics class methods are:

g.drawPolygon(*x array*, *y array*, number of points);   //draws the border of polygon
g.fillPolygon(*x array*, *y array*, number of points);   //fills the polygon

```
//Example to draw a triangle of 3 points  (0,50)  (100,100)  (0,100):

    public void paint(Graphics g) {
       g.setColor(Color.red);
       int x [ ] = {0, 100, 0};        // all x points above in the array called x
       int y [ ] = {50, 100, 100};  // all y points above in the array called y
       g.fillPolygon(x , y, 3);        // 3 points in polygon
    }
```

1. Open NetBeans and begin a new project called **TexasFlag**.

2. We are going to create a drawing of the Texas flag using the fillPolygon command to draw the star. This flag was drawn by Mark San Miguel, a previous student in this course.

3. We will create the basic frame for our drawing. We will need to add our graphic imports. Then we need to create our frame and container and set the properties for the frame (size, location, etc.). Type in the following code:

```java
import java.awt.*;
import javax.swing.*;

public class TexasFlag extends JComponent {

    JFrame frame = new JFrame("Texas Flag");
    Container content = frame.getContentPane();

    public static void main(String[] args) {
        TexasFlag drawing = new TexasFlag();
        drawing.setUp();
    }

    public void setUp() {
        content.setBackground(Color.WHITE);
        content.add(this);

        frame.setSize(615, 435);
        frame.setDefaultCloseOperation(JFrame.EXIT_ON_CLOSE);
        frame.setVisible(true);
    }

    @Override
    public void paintComponent(Graphics g) {

    }
}
```

4. Next, we will add the code to our paintComponent method that will create our blue and red stripes. The white strip will be added by default because the background color is white.

```java
@Override
public void paintComponent(Graphics g) {
    g.setColor(Color.BLUE); // Blue stripe
    g.fillRect(0, 0, 200, 400);

    g.setColor(Color.RED); // Red stripe
    g.fillRect(200, 200, 600, 400);
}
```

5. Run your program. You should have the stripes set up.

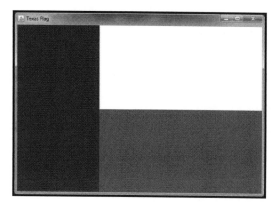

6. Finally, let's add our star.

```
@Override
public void paintComponent(Graphics g) {
    g.setColor(Color.BLUE); // Blue stripe
    g.fillRect(0, 0, 200, 400);

    g.setColor(Color.RED); // Red stripe
    g.fillRect(200, 200, 600, 400);

    g.setColor(Color.WHITE);  // Lone star
    int xpoints[] = {100, 114, 165, 125, 140, 100, 60, 75, 35, 86, 100};
    int ypoints[] = {124, 175, 175, 202, 250, 216, 250, 202, 175, 175, 124};
    g.fillPolygon(xpoints, ypoints, 11);
}
```

7. Run the program.

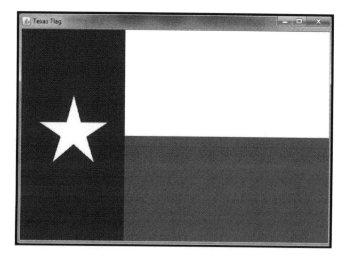

8. Close the program.

Exercise 5 (Challenge): Bubble Sort

The bubble sort is the simplest sorting algorithm. We are going to sort a list of numbers in an array and print out the sorted array.

1. The name of this project and class should be **BubbleSort**.

```java
/* Bubble sort is the simplest sorting algorithm
 * Written by
 * Date
 * JDK Version
 */

public class BubbleSort {

    public static void main(String[] args) {

        int number[] = {8, 5, 3, 2, 9};
        boolean swap = true;
        int temp;

        while (swap == true) {
            swap = false;
            for (int i = 0; i < number.length - 1; i++) {
                if (number[i] > number[i + 1]) {
                    temp = number[i + 1];
                    number[i + 1] = number[i];
                    number[i] = temp;
                    swap = true;
                }
            }
        }
        for (int i = 0; i < number.length; i++) {
            System.out.println(number[i]);
        }
    }
}
```

2. Type in the above program. Compile your program. Correct any typos that you made.

3. Execute this program. What did the program do? The numbers in the array (8, 5, 3, 2, 9) should have been sorted and printed as follows:

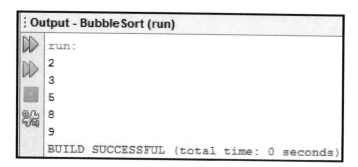

Explanation:

First Pass:
(**8 5** 3 2 9) ⟶ (**5 8** 2 3 9) Algorithm compares the first two elements and swaps them since 8>5
(5 **8 2** 3 9) ⟶ (5 **2 8** 3 9) Swap since 8 > 2
(5 2 **8 3** 9) ⟶ (5 2 **3 8** 9) Swap since 8>3
(5 2 3 **8 9**) ⟶ (5 2 3 **8 9**) No swap since 8 is not > 9

Second Pass:
(**5 2** 3 8 9) ⟶ (**2 5** 3 8 9) Swap since 5>2
(2 **5 3** 8 9) ⟶ (2 **3 5** 8 9) Swap since 5>3
(2 3 **5 8** 9) ⟶ (2 3 **5 8** 9) No swap since 5 is not > 8
(2 3 5 **8 9**) ⟶ (2 3 5 **8 9**) No swap since 8 is not > 9

Now, the array is already sorted, but our algorithm does not know if it is completed. The algorithm needs one **whole** pass without **any** swap to know it is sorted.

Third Pass:
(**2 3** 5 8 9) ⟶ (**2 3** 5 8 9)
(2 **3 5** 8 9) ⟶ (2 **3 5** 8 9)
(2 3 **5 8** 9) ⟶ (2 3 **5 8** 9)
(2 3 5 **8 9**) ⟶ (2 3 5 **8 9**)

Exercise 6: Card Game with Arrays (ongoing exercise)

1. Open the **CardGame** project completed in chapter 9 in NetBeans.

2. This CardGame works fine without arrays, but would be more efficient if it used an array. Currently, the game uses 2 random numbers to determine which cards should be displayed. There are currently 10 cards. However, in a normal card deck there would be 52 cards. This means that the determinePlayingCard method would need 52 cases to figure out the card, etc. An alternative solution would be to put the cards into an array and then use the random number to determine which element of the array to display.

3. We need to declare the array. It will be an array of type PlayingCard. It has as its elements playingCard1 through playingCard10. Thus, the declaration is as follows:

   PlayingCard cardArray [ ] = {playingCard1, playingCard2, playingCard3, playingCard4, playingCard5, playingCard6, playingCard1, playingCard7, playingCard8, playingCard9, playingCard10 };

4. The above line declares an array with the name of cardArray. Its type is PlayingCard which makes it an array of objects. It then fills the array with 10 PlayingCards starting with playingCard1 which is put into element 0. Then, playingCard2 is put into element1. The last card, playingCard10 is put into element 9.

5. Instead of referencing our cards with numbers 1 to 10, we will now reference them in an array. Elements of arrays always begin with 0. Thus, the numbers we will use in this version of the CardGame are 0 to 9 instead of 1 to 10. Therefore, the lines generating random numbers need adjusted to generate random numbers between 0 and 9 inclusive. This can be done by eliminating the +1 at end of formula as follows:

   randomNumber1 = (int) (Math.random() * 10);
   randomNumber2 = (int) (Math.random() * 10);

6. Instead of using the determinePlayingCard method to place the right cards into firstCard and secondCard, the program will now just reference the element of the array with this randomNumber as follows:

   firstCard =cardArray[randomNumber1];
   secondCard = cardArray[randomNumber2];

7. As an example, the computer generates the randomNumber1 to be 3. This means that cardArray[3] will be placed into firstCard. Since playingCard1 is in element 0 of cardArray; playingCard2 is in element 1 of cardArray; playingCard3 is in element 2 of cardArray, and playingCard4 is in element 3 of cardArray. This means the guy with 4 spades on his chest will appear on the screen as the first card for player 1.

8. The entire new version of the **myFirstMethod** should look as follows:

```java
    public void myFirstMethod() {//Card Game created by
//on date here
//This program will deal out cards, display winner, and then cards disappear
        int scorePlayer1 = 0;
        int scorePlayer2 = 0;
        int randomNumber1, randomNumber2;
        PlayingCard firstCard, secondCard;
        PlayingCard cardArray [] = {playingCard1, playingCard2,playingCard3,
            playingCard4, playingCard5,playingCard6, playingCard7,
            playingCard8,playingCard9, playingCard10 };

        for (int a = 1; a <= 5; a++) {
            do {
                randomNumber1 = (int) (Math.random() * 10 );
                randomNumber2 = (int) (Math.random() * 10 );
            } while (randomNumber1 == randomNumber2);
            firstCard = cardArray[randomNumber1];
            secondCard = cardArray[randomNumber2];
            this.dealOutCards(firstCard, secondCard);
            if (randomNumber1 > randomNumber2) {
                scorePlayer1++;
                displayWinner(winPlayer1Sign, player1ScoreSign, scorePlayer1);
            } else {
                scorePlayer2++;
                displayWinner(winPlayer2Sign, player2ScoreSign, scorePlayer2);
            }
            this.disappearCards(firstCard, secondCard);
        }

    }
```

9. The determinePlayingCard method is no longer needed so that entire method should be deleted. The rest of the methods remain the same and work the same way as they did without arrays.

10. This game plays a simple game of "War" where the higher card wins. Many of the same concepts would be used to produce a BlackJack or Poker game. You would need the concept of EVENTS to further develop this game. EVENTS are not discussed in this text and usually are taught in a second semester programming course.

Exercise 7: Using a For Each Loop for a Penguin Array

1. Open Alice 3. Set the scene with 3 penguins and a hole in the ice. You can create the hole in the ice by using the disc shape, naming it "hole", and setting the color to black. If your hole looks a bit grainy, move the disc up because this means it is down below ground level. Name this program **PenguinArray**. Give your penguins the following names: **tux**, **waddles**, and **icy**. The name of the hole should be **hole**.

2. Put comments at the top of the program:

3. Insert a **variable** by dragging the variable block under the comments. Select **Gallery List...** from the **value type** drop down.

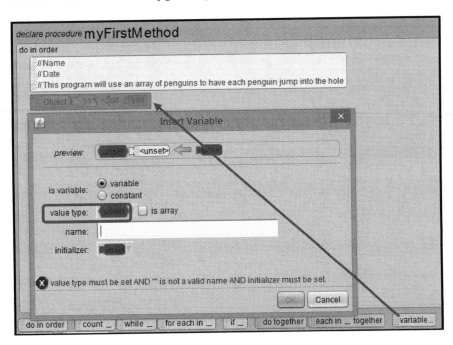

4. Click on the **Penguin** class since the all of our items in our array are penguins. Click **OK**.

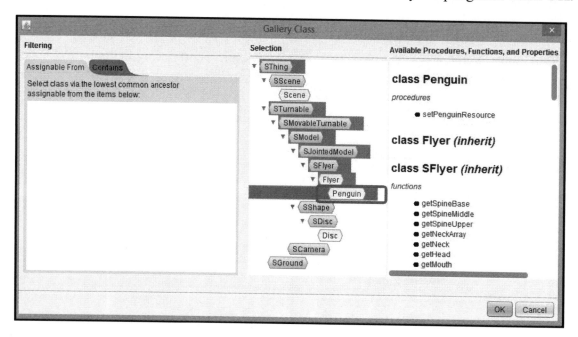

5. Name the array **penguinArray** and check the **is array** box as shown below:

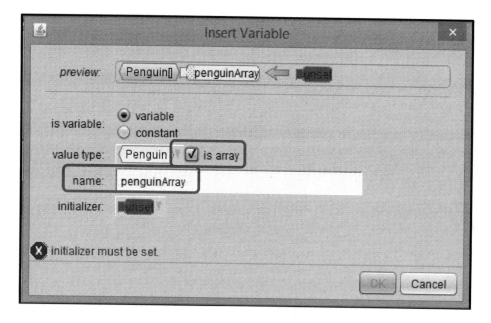

6. Click the drop down for the **initializer** and choose **Custom Array…**. Click the **add** drop down. Add **tux**, **waddles**, and **icey**. Click **OK**.

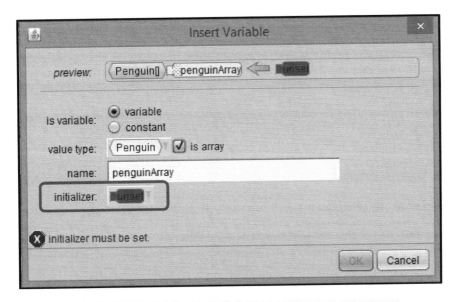

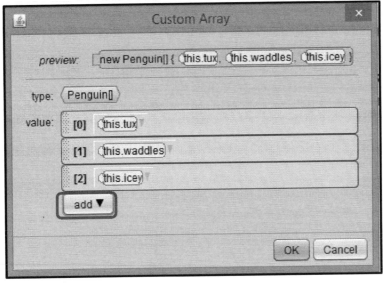

7. Drop the **for each in_** block of code under the Penguin array.

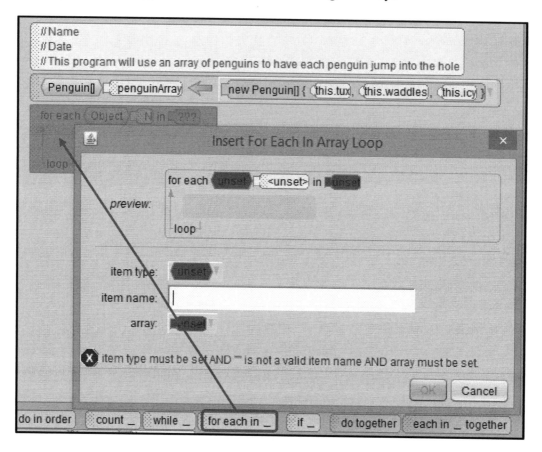

8. Select **Gallery List...** from the **item type** drop down. Select the **Penguin** class since the all of our items in our array are penguins. Click **OK**.

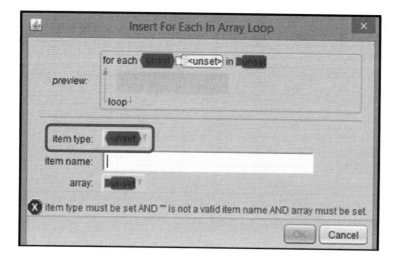

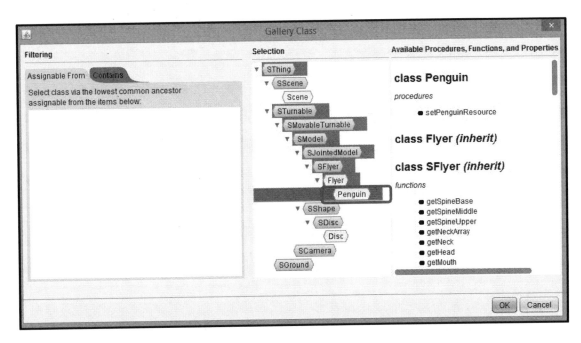

9. The item type should be named **item**. Select **penguinArray** in the drop down for the array since we will be using the penguin array for this loop.

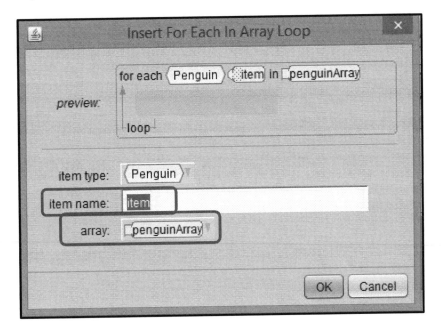

We have created a *for* loop that is going to loop through every item in our penguin array. This type of for loop is very useful for looping through arrays and is referred to as a **for each** loop.

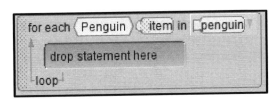

10. Select **item** for the object drop down as shown below. The *item* object refers to each item in the penguin array.

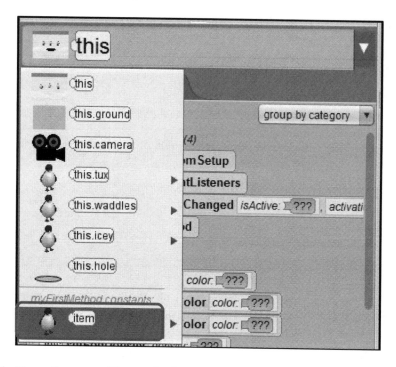

11. Drag the **moveTo** method to the **for each** loop. Choose **hole** as the argument.

12. Run the program. You should notice that each penguin moves to the hold one by one. The move in the order that they were entered into the array.

13. Click the object drop down and select the arrow next to the **item** object. This should bring up a list of subparts for the item object (penguin in this case). Select **item.getNeck** from the list.

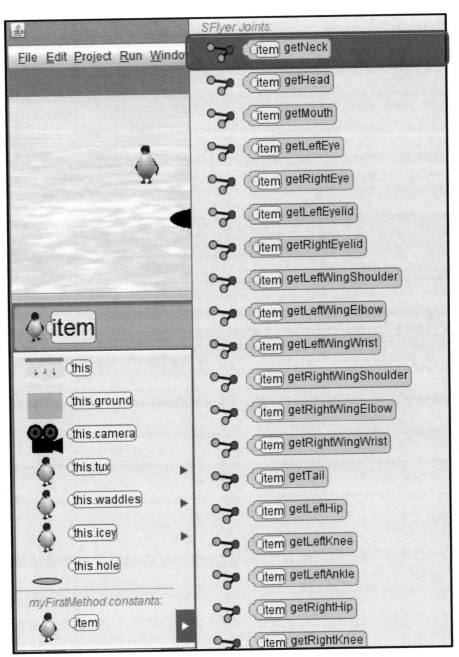

14. Add the **turn** method for the item's neck. The neck should turn **forward** an amount of **0.125** meters as shown below. Run the program and watch each penguin move to the hole and then turn their neck to look at the hole.

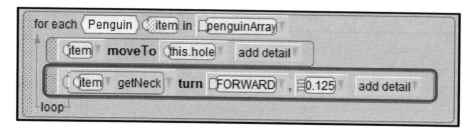

15. Select the whole item object from the object drop down. Add the **move** method with **down** and **2** meters as arguments. Run the program and watch each penguin move to the hole, turn their neck to look at the hole, and then jump in the hole.

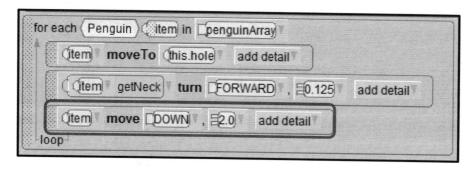

16. Transfer this project into NetBeans by creating a new project in NetBeans. Notice the object array of penguins and the *for each* loop that walks through every penguin object in the penguin array.

```java
public void myFirstMethod() {
//Name
//Date
//This program will use an array of penguins to have each penguin jump into the hole
    Penguin[] penguinArray = new Penguin[]{this.tux, this.waddles, this.icy};
    for (Penguin item : penguinArray) {
        item.moveTo(this.hole);
        item.getNeck().turn(TurnDirection.FORWARD, 0.125);
        item.move(MoveDirection.DOWN, 2.0);
    }
}
```

Summary

- A Java **array** is a group of contiguous memory locations that all have the <u>same name</u> and the <u>same type</u>. You can have arrays of any type of information that can be stored as a variable.

- To **declare an array** you must give the type (int, double, String, etc.) and the name of the array. You must also have square brackets but Java is flexible about where the [ ] can be place. An example of declaring an array is:

    int [ ] temps;   // an integer array called temps
    int temps [ ] ;   // an integer array called temps

- You can **create an array** in one of two ways. The first way is with the word new and stating a definite number of elements such as:

    int [ ] temps = new   int [250] ;

- The second way is by listing the values of the elements in curly braces and allowing the computer to count the elements such as:

    String c [ ] = { "Mary", "John", "Susan", "Robert" };

- **The first element of an array is referred to with the subscript 0 so be careful.** To get a value stored within an array, use the array subscript expression [ ]

    myArray [31] = 42;   // refers to the 32nd element of the myArray

- Every Java array knows its own length. The programmer can get and use this length by specifying the name of the array and then a period and then the word length. For example: **myArray.length**

- The main method always allows for an array of Strings to be entered directly into the main method. This array is generally called **args** but can actually be given any valid variable name. The elements of this array come in through the command line instead of being inside the program. If you want to use the data as anything other than Strings, you will need to convert the data to ints, doubles, etc.

Review Questions

1. Given the following:
   int   scores [ ] = { 14, 5, 16, 2, 23, 1 }
   How many elements are there in the scores array or what is the length of the scores array?
   a. 5
   b. 6
   c. 7
   d. 8

2. Given the following:
   int   scores [ ] = { 14, 5, 16, 2, 23, 1 }
   What is scores [2] ?
   a. 14
   b. 5
   c. 16
   d. 2

3. Given the following:
   String names [ ] = { "Bill", "Susan", "Robert", "Ralph");
   What is names [1] ?
   a. Bill
   b. Susan
   c. Robert
   d. Ralph

4. In the following program, what value would be placed into myArray[2] ?

```
1:  // Sample Array
2:
3:  public class TestArray
4:  {
5:    public static void main (String args [ ] )
6:    {
7:      int myArray [ ] = new int [ 6 ];
8:
9:      for (int a = 0;  a < 5;  a++)
10:     {
11:        myArray [a ] = a;
12:     }
13:
14:   }  // ends main
15: }   // end program
```

5. In the following code, what value is in myArray[3]?

```
int myArray [ ]  =  {3,15,8,27,6};
int sum = 0;
int largest = myArray[0];
int smallest = myArray[0];
for (int i = 0;  i<myArray.length;  i++ )
{
  sum =  sum + myArray [i];
  if (  myArray [ i ]  > largest    )
    largest = myArray [ i ];
  if (  myArray [ i ]  < smallest    )
    smallest = myArray [ i ];
}
System.out.println("The sum is " + sum);
System.out.println("The average is " + sum/myArray.length);
System.out.println("The largest number is " + largest);
System.out.println("The smallest number is " + smallest);
```

6. In the following code, what is the value in the variable called largest after completing the second loop?

```
int myArray [ ]  =  {3,15,8,27,6};
int sum = 0;
int largest = myArray[0];
int smallest = myArray[0];
for (int i = 0;  i<myArray.length;  i++ )
{
  sum =  sum + myArray [i];
  if (  myArray [ i ]  > largest    )
    largest = myArray [ i ];
  if (  myArray [ i ]  < smallest    )
    smallest = myArray [ i ];
}
System.out.println("The sum is " + sum);
System.out.println("The average is " + sum/myArray.length);
System.out.println("The largest number is " + largest);
System.out.println("The smallest number is " + smallest);
```

7. Challenge: In the following program, what value would be placed into myArray[5]? (be careful)

```
1: // Sample Array
2:
3: public class TestArray
4: {
5:   public static void main (String args [ ] )
6:   {
7:     int myArray [ ] = new int [ 6 ];
8:
9:     for (int a = 0;  a < 5;  a++)
10:    {
11:         myArray [a ] = a;
12:    }
13:
14:  }  // ends main
15: }  // end program
```

Solutions: 1)b 2)c 3)b 4)2 5) 27 6) 15 7) It will be initialized to 0 and remain 0 since the loop does not include 5

Assignments

10-1   **Using an Array to Determine Grades**: Complete hands-on exercises 1 to 3 in this chapter. There are 3 versions of the *ArrayProgram*. All 3 versions of this program, calculate the sum, average, largest, and smallest elements of an array. Pick the one that you like best. Add logic inside the *for* loop to test if the number is between 90 and 100. If the number is in this range, then it should add 1 to the tally of gradeA. You should have another test to see if the number is between 80 and 89 and if it is it should add 1 to the tally of gradeB. You should continue to have tests for 70 to79 being gradeC; 60-69 being graded; and below 60 as being gradeF. After the *for* loop is done, you should display a list of how many students had A's, B's, etc. in the output message box.

If the data is:
    90 100 80 85 63 73 80 92 90

The display should be something like this:

> **The sum is 753**
> **The average is 83**
> **The largest test score is 100**
> **The lowest test score is 63**
> **The number of students with scores of 90-100 (A) is 4**
> **The number of students with scores of 80-89 (B) is 3**
> **The number of students with scores of 70-79 (C) is 1**
> **The number of students with scores of 60-69 (D) is 1**
> **The number of students with scores below 60 (F) is 0**

- Initialize the variables of gradeA, gradeB, gradeC, gradeD, and gradeF to zero at beginning of program.
- Set up the 5 if statements appropriately to count the gradeA, gradeB, gradeC, gradeD, and gradeF variables.
- Print the counts for each grade in a message box.

Appendix

☑ Exception Handling

Exception Handling

The user doesn't always enter the data that they are supposed to enter. For example, you may ask the user to enter a number from 1 to 100 and they may enter "five". You were hoping to parse their number into an integer value so that you could use it in your program, but when you try to parse "five" an exception is thrown and the program crashes. We want our programs to be stable so that user error such as invalid data does not crash the program. A **try/catch** block handles thrown exceptions so that runtime errors are eliminated. If an exception occurs in the *try* block, the code in the *catch* block is executed. You may want to make the user aware of their error in the *catch* block. If no exceptions occur in the *try* block, the *catch* block is never executed. The following is the basic structure of a try/catch:

```
try {
    // code that may cause an exception
} catch(ExceptionClass exceptionName) {
    // code to execute if exception is found
}
```

There are various types of exceptions that can be thrown during runtime. The following are a few of the common exceptions:

- NumberFormatException
- ArithmeticException
- ArrayIndexOutOfBoundsException

The following is an example of how the **NumberFormatException** can be used:

```
String response = JOptionPane.showInputDialog(null, "Enter a whole number");
String response2 = JOptionPane.showInputDialog(null, "Enter another whole number");
try {
    int number1 = Integer.parseInt(response);
    int number2 = Integer.parseInt(response2);
    int answer = number1 + number2;
    JOptionPane.showMessageDialog(null, number1 + " + " + number2 + " = " + answer);
} catch (NumberFormatException nfe) {
    JOptionPane.showMessageDialog(null, "You must enter integers.");
}
```

It is possible to catch more than one exception in the *try* block by including several *catch* blocks. The following is an example of how the **NumberFormatException** and **ArithmeticException** can be used for one *try* block:

```
String response = JOptionPane.showInputDialog(null, "Enter a whole number");
String response2 = JOptionPane.showInputDialog(null, "Enter another whole number");
try {
    int number1 = Integer.parseInt(response);
    int number2 = Integer.parseInt(response2);
    int answer = number1 / number2;
    JOptionPane.showMessageDialog(null, number1 + " / " + number2 + " = " + answer);
} catch (NumberFormatException nfe) {
    JOptionPane.showMessageDialog(null, "You must enter integers.");
} catch (ArithmeticException ae) {
    JOptionPane.showMessageDialog(null, "Zero cannot be your divisor.");
}
```

Instead of having multiple *catch* blocks you can use **Exception** to catch all exceptions. Using the generic *Exception catch*, does not allow you to cater functionality to different types of errors.

```
String response = JOptionPane.showInputDialog(null, "Enter a whole number");
String response2 = JOptionPane.showInputDialog(null, "Enter another whole number");
try {
    int number1 = Integer.parseInt(response);
    int number2 = Integer.parseInt(response2);
    int answer = number1 / number2;
    JOptionPane.showMessageDialog(null, number1 + " / " + number2 + " = " + answer);
} catch (Exception e) {
    JOptionPane.showMessageDialog(null, "Error");
}
```

Made in the USA
Middletown, DE
21 April 2016